Y0-EBT-756

The New Islamic Presence in Western Europe

The New Islamic Presence in Western Europe

Edited by *Tomas Gerholm*
and *Yngve Georg Lithman*

Mansell Publishing Limited
London and New York

First published 1988 by Mansell Publishing Limited
6 All Saints Street, London N1 9RL, England

© Mansell Publishing Limited and the Contributors 1988

All rights reserved. No part of this publication may be reproduced or transmitted in any form or by any means, electronic or mechanical, including photocopy, recording or any information storage or retrieval system, without permission in writing from the publishers or their appointed agents.

British Library Cataloguing in Publication Data

The New Islamic presence in Western Europe.
  1. Islam——Europe
  I. Gerholm, Tomas II. Lithman, Yngve Georg
  297′.094   BP65

  ISBN 0-7201-1886-7

Library of Congress Cataloging in Publication Data

The New Islamic presence in Western Europe / edited by Tomas Gerholm and Yngve Georg Lithman.
    p.   cm.
  Papers from a conference held in Stockholm in June 1986 and organized by the Centre for Research in International Migration and Ethnicity at the University of Stockholm and the Royal Swedish Academy of Letters, History, and Antiquities.
  Includes index.
  ISBN 0-7201-1886-7
  1. Muslims——Europe——Congresses. 2. Civilization, Occidental——Islamic influences——Congresses. 3. Islam——Europe——History——20th century——Congresses. 4. Immigrants——Europe——History——20th century——Congresses. I. Gerholm, Tomas, 1942- . II. Lithman, Yngve Georg. III. Stockholms universitet. Centrum för invandringsforskning. IV. Kungl. Vitterhets, historie och antikvitets akademien.
D1056.2.M87N48   1988
940——dc 1987-31259.

This book has been printed and bound in Great Britain:
typeset in Times Roman by Colset Private Limited, Singapore,
printed on Redwood Bookwove paper by Redwood Burn Limited
and bound by Western Book Company

Contents

Preface — vii

Introduction — 1

Part I: The Institutionalization of Islam in Various Countries

1. The Institutionalization of Islam in the Netherlands, 1961–86 — 8
   Jacques Waardenburg, Department of Science of Religion, Rijksuniversiteit Utrecht
2. Making a Place for Islam in British Society: Muslims in Birmingham — 32
   Daniele Joly, Centre for Research in Ethnic Relations, University of Warwick, Coventry
3. Muslims in Britain and Local Authority Responses — 53
   Jørgen S. Nielsen, Centre for the Study of Islam and Christian–Muslim Relations, Selly Oak Colleges, Birmingham
4. The Religious Life of Muslims in Berlin — 78
   Hanns Thomä-Venske, Konsistorium der Evangelischen Kirche in Berlin-Brandenburg
5. Religion and Ethnicity: Orientations, Perceptions and Strategies among Turkish Alevi and Sunni Migrants in Berlin — 88
   Czarina Wilpert, Institut für Soziologie, Technische Universität Berlin
6. The Islamic Presence in France — 107
   Rémy Leveau, Institut d'Etudes Politiques, Paris

7. The Second Generation: the Children of Muslim Immigrants in France 123
   Annie Krieger-Krynicki, Paris
8. Islam in Belgium: Contradictions and Perspectives 133
   Albert Bastenier, Groupe d'Etude des Migrations et des Relations Interéthniques, Université Catholique de Louvain

Part II: Migration and Changes in the Religious Experience

9. Migration and Religiousness 146
   Werner Schiffauer, Institut für Soziologie, Wolfgang-Goethe-Universität
10. The Tabligh Organization in Belgium 159
    Felice Dassetto, Groupe d'Etude des Migrations et des Relations Interéthniques, Université Catholique de Louvain
11. Being an Alevi Muslim in South-western Anatolia and in Norway: The Impact of Migration on a Heterodox Turkish Community 174
    Ragnar Naess, Work Research Institutes, Oslo
12. Migrant Muslim Women in France 196
    Sossie Andezian, Institut d'Etudes et de Recherches Interéthniques et Interculturelles, Nice

Part III: Additional Themes for Future Research

13. The Urban Sociology of Religion and Islam in Birmingham 206
    John Rex, Centre for Research in Ethnic Relations, University of Warwick, Coventry
14. Ethnic Residential Patterns in Dutch Cities: Class, Race or Culture? 219
    Hans van Amersfoort, Subfaculteit der Sociale Geografie, Universiteit van Amsterdam
15. Social Relations and Cultural Continuities: Muslim Immigrants and their Social Networks 239
    Yngve Georg Lithman, Centre for Research in International Migration and Ethnicity, University of Stockholm
16. Three European Intellectuals as Converts to Islam: Cultural Mediators or Social Critics? 263
    Tomas Gerholm, Department of Social Anthropology, University of Stockholm

Glossary 278
Subject Index 281
Name Index 289
Index of Muslim Organizations 292

Preface

This volume stems from a conference that took place in Stockholm in June 1986. It was organized by the Centre for Research in International Migration and Ethnicity (CEIFO) at the University of Stockholm and the Royal Swedish Academy of Letters, History and Antiquities. On this occasion, some forty researchers spent five days discussing various aspects of the theme for the conference.

These discussions were made fruitful not only by the people represented in this volume but also by especially invited discussants: Mohamed Arkoun from Institut d'Etudes Islamiques in Paris, Jan Bergman from University of Uppsala, Jan Hjärpe from the University of Lund and Saad Eddin Ibrahim from Arab Thought Forum in Amman. Altan Gökalp, Christer Hedin, Jan Hjarnoe, Marianne Laanatza, and Parvez Manzoor also made valuable contributions, although their papers, for various reasons, could not be included in this volume.

The conference was financed primarily through contributions from the Royal Swedish Academy of Letters, History and Antiquities, made available through the energetic assistance of its president, Stig Strömholm, who also gave the opening address, and its secretary, Bertil Molde. The Ministries of Labour and of Education provided additional funding. The Minister of Immigration, Mrs. Anita Gradin, greeted the participants and attended part of the programme during the first day of the conference. Tomas Hammar, CEIFO's director, has been a constant support in all matters, organizational as well as scholarly. As many of the topics discussed in this book are undergoing rapid change and our purpose has been not only to document and analyse the present but also to stimulate further research, we are very pleased with the efforts of the publishers, especially through their editor Penny Beck, to facilitate early publication.

The contributions by Albert Bastenier (his was commissioned after the conference), Felice Dassetto, Annie Krieger-Krynicki and Rémy Leveau have been translated by the editors with the kind assistance of Eva Lundberg-Lithman.

A simplified system has been used in transcribing Arabic words. It is based on the system of the *Encyclopaedia of Islam*, with some of the common changes and simplifications; no diacritical marks, q for ķ, and j for dj. There is a special glossary for Arabic, Turkish and other terms.

As convenors of the conference and now as editors of the book based on it, our intentions were to bring together scholars both from the humanities, social sciences and from Islamic studies, as well as those in the field of minority and migration research. We are convinced that these specialities need to work in conjunction for the understanding of the new Islamic presence in western Europe.

Introduction

There is a growing interest in the new Islamic presence in western Europe among many researchers, and there is also a growing demand for knowledge that can be put to good use from many private persons, associations and state agencies involved in one way or another with Muslims. This interest derives from many sources.

One reason is that during the post-war period, and especially during the late 1950s and 1960s, there was a large-scale immigration of labourers from Muslim countries to western Europe. Today this is no longer the case. Labour migrations have been reduced to a trickle, compared with the situation before the oil crisis and the decline in the economy of most western European countries during the 1970s. Although the earlier labour immigration has led to continuing immigration for reasons of family reunification, it is the immigration of political refugees (not all of them Muslims) from Middle Eastern countries that has dominated the picture during recent years. These different types of immigration have resulted in the establishment of considerable Muslim minorities in several countries. Everything indicates that these minorities are here to stay, in one form or another. Will they be assimilated into the majority society and thus lose their distinctive traits? Will they be integrated into the host society, that is, allowed to retain some of their characteristics while in other respects becoming full participants in the social and political processes of their new country? And what will happen to these societies if the Muslims are assimilated? What will happen if they are integrated? These are obviously questions of great interest to anyone concerned with understanding his own society. The immigrant country *par excellence*, the United States, has a large literature — spanning the social sciences, the humanities and fiction — dealing with the American experience of immigration. The western European experience is different, but it will likewise generate intensive self-reflection. A general theoretical interest in society is now being turned to what appears to be a new significant aspect of western European society.

Another and more specific reason for this interest is the sentiment, in many countries, that Muslim immigrants often find themselves in very trying social conditions. Whether discussing Turks in Sweden or West Germany, Maghrebi immigrants in France, Southeast Asian Muslims in the Netherlands or Pakistani immigrants in Great Britain, one can often argue that they face greater problems than other immigrants. This is variously explained by reference to greater cultural differences *per se* or the discrimination and the outright rejection these immigrants often encounter in their new environment. There is an ameliorative, social-reform aspect to this interest.

The interest in Muslim immigrants is also spawned by a general increase in attention to the Muslim world due to major geo-political factors. The emerging political significance of several Muslim countries, in many instances related to their share of the world oil reserves, is one of the background factors. Another one is the armed conflicts in what are deemed to be highly important strategic areas. Last but not least among these factors is the major upheaval going on all through the Muslim world. It is not easily summarized in one concept, for it is a multifarious thing. Renaissance, resurgence, reaction, revolution, revitalization: all these labels are applicable to one side or the other of the Islamic landslide. The spectacular features of this phenomenon have received much coverage in western countries. To some extent, this attention has revived deeply-rooted sentiments to the effect that the Muslim world is incomprehensible, violent and frightening. There is thus a substantial component of fear in this new interest in Muslims wherever they are — and especially if they are here.

Theoretical understanding, social reform, the management of fear: if these are the general reasons for the growing interest in Islam in Europe, then this book is also meant to make a threefold contribution. We hope that it will increase theoretical understanding, facilitate social reform and alleviate fear.

Regardless of its degree of success on these three frontiers, it should be seen as a first attempt at comprehending a multi-faceted phenomenon: the New Islamic Presence in Western Europe. What is meant by this expression? There are four key concepts here that all need to be commented upon in order to have light thrown on the totality.

New. Muslims have been massively present in Europe before today. In fact, throughout the centuries Muslims have been engaged in the creation of Europe and European civilization, sometimes more actively, sometimes more passively. One could make a case for speaking of European civilization as the Jewish–Christian–Muslim civilization. But the new factor is, firstly, that within a very short span of time Europe has received Islam as an immigrant culture carried mainly by labour migrants; secondly, that it is now being realized that the Muslims and Islam are here to stay. More than ever before Europe will be the Jewish–Christian–Muslim continent, a place where these religions and the secular ideologies derived from them come together to fight, support and fertilize each other.

Islamic. Contrary to the wise counsel of Jacques Waardenburg we have not been able to use consistently the Islamic/Muslim distinction he suggests. "Islamic" would then refer to those things pertaining to the religion in a narrow sense and "Muslim" refer to the broader culture of a people whose religion is Islam. What this book is mainly concerned with is Islam in Europe as both religion and culture. Some contributions delve deeply into the purely religious aspects, others are more concerned with the wider culture brought by the immigrants, but none deals with Muslim immigrants merely as immigrants.

Presence. By this word we want to emphasize the fact that the culture of Islam is constituted not only by individual beliefs carried by migrant labourers and limited to their quarters. It is a whole ambience, stretching from ordinary apartments transformed into prayer-halls to glossy magazines published in London. There are many layers of Islam now being laid over Europe, and the near future will probably witness ever more layers as a new Muslim intellectual elite go to work on their heritage. The efforts of Mohamed Arkoun, for example, to examine critically the sacred texts of Islam, doing for Islam what Christian theologians and historians of Christianity have done for Christianity during the last hundred years, is also part of the phenomenon we are investigating. In the end, it has proved to be the least studied aspect in this book. We have no analysis of contemporary Muslim intellectuals in Europe and their work. We have no survey of the impressive Muslim publishing efforts centred largely in London. We have no study of the image of Islam propagated in the media.

Western Europe. By this term, somewhat too inclusive, we refer mainly to such core countries of Muslim immigration as West Germany, France, the Netherlands, Belgium and Great Britain. There are also contributions dealing with, in this respect, such marginal countries as Norway and Sweden; whereas there are none on either Spain or Italy, for example. This may be a reflection of the actual state of research on these matters in the various countries, but it may also be an accidental product of the personal networks of the editors.

A feature of the book that definitely reflects the state of research in the countries included is the fact that the various contributions are so different in focus, scope and ambition. Some are evidently based on years of research in well-established research teams, others are single, pioneering forays into the unknown. It is our hope that this juxtaposition of contributions on different levels will add up to a composite picture and also serve as a stimulus for further research.

The volume is divided into three sections. Under the first heading, 'The Institutionalization of Islam in Various Countries', we have collected papers reflecting the process through which, very gradually, a place is made for Islam in the new countries. Such a process entails a long series of measures, some of them of a very concrete nature, like the legal possibilities of building mosques, slaughtering in the ritually prescribed way, having schoolgirls exempted from co-educational classes, and others of a more diffuse kind, such as the right to expect a neutral image in the media, the right to be regarded as a neighbour, a workmate, a colleague first, and then a Muslim. The focus is on the process of settling into a new society and making room for the expression of one's identity.

Under the second heading, 'Migration and Changes in the Religious Experience', the focus shifts to the nature of the religious system itself. Several contributions attempt to delineate how a local version of Islam changes when it is uprooted from its original soil and transplanted to a radically different setting. It should not necessarily be thought that this must be a disastrous event leading to an impoverished religion. As the chapters show, the converse may result, especially if we are dealing with immigrant groups who, although Muslims, have been religious minorities in their home countries. Immigration may also provide women with new opportunities for religious action. It is true that in some cases they seem to be losers even in this respect, but there are also instances where they assume religious responsibilities that would not have been theirs in the home country. In terms of religious experience as a special domain of reality, it may also be the case that life in urban western Europe offers new opportunities not readily found in the rural village back home. In line with the general differentiation of life into separate compartments and exclusive specializations, Muslims with special religious interest may be brought together and insulated from their lukewarm co-religionists. A secular society based on the idea that religion belongs to the private domain and that the role of state intervention is only to make it possible for a hundred flowers to bloom, may provide new opportunities for an internationalization of Islam through its growing network of multinational organizations. On the one hand there is already a solid basis for such a development in the various brotherhoods that have existed throughout Islamic history. On the other hand, however, these brotherhoods now appear more and more like interest groups contending for the resources provided by the surrounding secular society.

A final section, under the somewhat cumbersome heading 'Some Additional Themes for Future Research', gathers together four papers pursuing as many different lines of thought. There is an effort to pull contemporary studies of immigrant Islam into the framework of the general tradition of the sociology of religion. There is a wholesome warning not to exaggerate the role of culture and religion. There is an experiment with a new research technique, and there is finally a reflection on the fate of Muslim converts. The cautious heading is intended to underline the fact that these are only a few of the avenues open for future research. No doubt, most of what is to come will develop within the two main fields contained in the first two sections of the book.

Rather than summarize and comment on the individual articles which, we hope, speak for themselves, we would like to devote some space to presenting a number of issues raised by these papers as a totality. In understanding the forms taken by Islam in its new countries and the activities engaged in by the Muslims, there are certain factors one should keep in mind.

1. There is the obvious influence of linguistic, national and social background. These factors are just as important as in Christianity. Islam is as highly differentiated and the product of as complex a history as Christianity. To say that one is a Muslim, therefore, is not saying much until these other gaps — and many more — have been filled.
2. The differences are well reflected in the diversity of Islamic organizations. But there is a further complexity. These organizations are not always and exclusively the outcome of the situation in the home countries of the immigrants. Often they are a spontaneous response to the conditions obtaining in the new country, almost as if they were prompted by the surrounding non-Muslim society. They should therefore be seen as attempts to articulate and negotiate the relation between the Muslim communities and the encompassing society.
3. The "larger society", and similar expressions already used several times, should be understood as a convenient shorthand to encompass a number of factors that must often be distinguished. On the one hand, there are governmental agencies, running from decision-making bodies on the national level to local authority councils and school boards. On the other hand there are all the informal structures and networks and, in the end, the individuals who make up civil society. The larger society is also the neighbour, the employer, the other parents in the Parent-Teacher Association, and so on. These are far from making up a homogeneous larger society. Their diverse and sometimes contradictory influences will contribute to shaping the forms taken by Islam in its new settings.
4. Another factor operating in the larger society and meriting an entry of its own is the role of the mass media. They are important for several reasons. They articulate common sentiments, they influence politicians and other decision-makers, they provide dramatizations — in the form of news coverage and talk shows, for example — of conflicts commonly experienced, and they play an educational role disseminating information. The role of mass media when it comes to promoting racism and fighting it has been hotly debated in several countries. This is as good a demonstration as any of the fact that mass media and other media are powerful when it comes to defining the situation, that is, telling people what things are like. As we know, such abstract definitions may have very concrete effects.
5. The countries of origin, as political entities, play an important role for many migrants, and a role of increasing significance, by providing teachers of Arabic and religious instruction and by acting as external guardians of their interests in the new countries. The view that their interest in the migrants is governed solely by self-interest — remittances from the migrants often play a decisive role in the balance of payments of these countries — is probably too narrow. These countries are part of a world system ruled not only by economic forces but also by the intangible consideration of prestige. The support given their nationals in other countries is part of a larger struggle for recognition and respect in the

world of nations. The big mosques in European cities that some Muslim states have financed may be significant places of worship, but they are also significant symbols.

6. The countries of origin are important to migrants not only because of state action but primarily as an environment left behind. To some migrants, even after many years, 'home' is still in the natal country, and a very considerable part of their activities is geared to family and relatives in the old country. Obligations of various kinds — economic, marital, religious — are honoured. To others, the migratory project is a means of escape from these obligations or, more often, from oppression by the state or the neighbours. One should not forget that there are immigrants who have come to Europe precisely because they themselves fear the consequences of the Islamic resurgence. There are others who come not because of the religious development in their home country, but because of the raging warfare. The home country is not one thing to all migrants. They are individuals and have individual relations to their countries of origin.

7. Although time in itself may change nothing — time is a way of measuring change — it is tempting to regard time as an important factor both for the adjustment of the immigrants and for the specific shape taken by Islam. Many things seem to come 'automatically' with the passing of time. Knowledge of language and society will increase, making the immigrants more competent actors on the new scene. Economic resources may be accumulated and the demographic structure of the immigrant community will become more balanced, more natural, more like home, as single migrants bring their family members. The most radical change 'automatically' brought by time is the new generation, the second generation, born in the country to which the parents immigrated. What will become of these young people? It is for this crucial stage in the development of the community that all parties mobilize their resources. It is now the infrastructure of an Islamic community will be most needed, for the competition from the larger society is formidable.

With these seven observations the editors leave the floor to the authors.

Part I
The Institutionalization of Islam in Various Countries

1
The Institutionalization of Islam in the Netherlands, 1961–86

Jacques Waardenburg

In the course of history religions have expanded mainly through conversions or through migrations which were closely linked to conquests. The history of the past twenty-five years has shown, however, that in Western Europe, one of the most industrialized areas in the world, a new and widely misunderstood religion, Islam, has grown to occupy second place after Christianity, simply because economic factors brought about an extensive migration of workers, which in turn was followed closely by a migration of workers' families.

Thus in the Netherlands the increase in the number of Muslims over the last twenty-five years, from a few hundred to more than 300,000 at present, has taken place almost entirely through immigration. Consequently Islam in the Netherlands is in practice an immigrant religion, a fact which heightens the 'foreign' character which it has in the eyes of most people in the country. It is probably due to this 'foreign' character of Islam that social scientists trained in research on western societies with the associated problems of housing, employment, health and practical aspects of life have little experience of Islam itself. Broadly speaking, little is known about the forms and contents of Islam which exist in Western Europe, and the Netherlands is no exception.

This first part of this paper concentrates on the question of which Islamic and Muslim institutions have arisen in the Netherlands due to the arrival of large numbers of Turkish, Morrocan and Surinamese Muslims in the period under discussion. Table 1 indicates the size of these groups as of 1 January 1984.

The arrival of other Muslim groups, for instance Indonesians, Pakistanis, Iranians and non-Moroccan Arabs, has also played a part in developing the

Table 1. Size of the main Muslim groups in the Netherlands on 1 January 1984

Nationality	Muslim population
Turkish	155,000
Moroccan	106,400
Surinamese (ca.185,000 of whom 174,000 have Dutch citizenship): estimated number of Muslims	23,600
TOTAL	ca. 285,000

presence of Islam, but as far as institutionalization is concerned their presence is much less important than that of the first three groups.

A distinction has to be drawn between Islamic and Muslim institutions. The former are those institutions which are strictly needed for the practice of Islam as a religion, their absence would imply that Muslims could not fulfil the essential prescriptions of their religious law. Prayer-halls (*musalla*), the means for slaughtering animals according to Islamic law (*halal*), and for performing the *hajj*, the possibility of burial according to Islamic ritual, as well as facilities for Quranic and other Islamic religious rites, and the presence of religious leaders (*imams, khojas, moulvis, mawlanas*) are cases in point. Muslim institutions are of a broader kind. They are important for the life of Muslim communities but they are not derived from the obligations of religious law. These institutions spring from the culture of the region or the country from which the relevant groups come. Examples include specifically Muslim forms of cultural organization, customs surrounding birth, circumcision, marriage and death, and specific pedagogical forms of transmission of the Muslim faith, religion, way of life and culture from one generation to the next, or to newcomers.

Research in the Netherlands until now

The Islam of the Muslim immigrants has been the subject of at least four different kinds of research up till now.

1. Islam has appeared indirectly in research about integration and assimilation of immigrants into Dutch society. In studies of this kind, often carried out at the request of public authorities, the focus is on the Dutch host society, and investigations are made on the basis of which government policies can be formulated and implemented. In this kind of research practical points of view prevail.
2. Islam also appears in practical research concerning welfare; the best ways to receive and support Muslims socially. It is not government policy but the desire to help the newcomers which is the prime motivation here. Research carried out on a limited scale under the auspices of the *Nederlands Centrum Buitenlanders* (Netherlands Centre for Foreigners) in Utrecht, the regional welfare foundations

(*welzijnsstichtingen*), various churches or councils of churches, and other more or less private initiatives including those of some trade unions are applicable to this category. All these examples are based on a desire to help the immigrants as human beings; the attitudes taken towards their religion vary widely.

3. Islam appears in a very different light in research carried out into the political trends among Muslim immigrants and the influence of varying political forces on them. The question here is to discover how Islam is used for political purposes, especially by groups and individuals in the countries of origin; these studies often explicitly warn against a 'reactionary' use of Islam. Other, non-political aspects and uses of Islam tend to be neglected in this kind of research, however, so that Islam is perceived in a rather one-sided way.

4. Sociological and anthropological research on specific Muslim groups in the Netherlands has produced few tangible results so far. There are few serious studies of the religious behaviour of Muslim Surinamese, Turkish and Moroccan groups, or the popular beliefs and practices current among them, or typically Muslim or Islamic institutions in the Netherlands. Islam is generally dealt with merely as one of the many factors — specifically as a particular tradition — in family life, education, or work situations. No research has been carried out up till now into the Muslim literature currently available in the Netherlands.

There are several reasons for this paucity of research. A general lack of familiarity with Islam as a faith, religion and way of life must be recognized as an important reason. Arabists, Turcologists and Islamicists for their part have not initiated such research until now either, being inhibited by the lack of familiarity with the necessary social and cultural modes of approach. In addition, most researchers find a switch in the focus of their attention, even under the pressure of circumstance, difficult, not only for purely scholarly reasons but also for more down to earth psychological ones. First of all, religion is not an intellectual issue in the present Dutch cultural climate. Some specific features of Dutch society, in which for a long time social distinctions were made according to religious, particularly confessional allegiances also account for scholarly neglect towards Islam. Thus any new religion tends to be perceived negatively both from the ideological and from the social point of view. There are few intellectuals among the Muslims in the Netherlands: most of the newcomers constitute a proletariat which presents problems of contact for researchers. Because of other processes taking place among Muslims in the country, Islam will probably play an increasing part in Dutch society especially for purposes of identification. Much will depend then, for any future integration, on the way in which Islam is accepted as a religion and identity without being denigrated.

Consequently there is reason to stress the need for Dutch social scientists, particularly cultural anthropologists, to carry out research into Islam in the Netherlands. The study of the emerging Islamic and Muslim institutions, in the sense indicated above, is a useful starting-point. I shall focus on two kinds of institution, Islamic prayer-halls and Muslim organisations.

The increase in Islamic prayer-halls

Mosques in general

The mosque which Muhammad erected in Medina on his arrival in 622 is generally regarded as the oldest mosque in Islam, even if the report that Muhammad established a prayer-place at Quba on his way from Mecca to Medina during the *hijra* is taken into consideration. The mosque in Medina was in practice an open court and it served both as a meeting place for the faithful and as the place where the *salat* was performed in common. It was in the mosque that Muhammad addressed the community and from there that he directed not only the religious but also the social and political activities of the community. The mosque of Medina was to serve as a model for all later mosques; whether emphasized as a social centre or as a place of prayer depended largely on circumstances. In contrast to nearly all other sacred buildings the mosque contains few specifically ritual objects, and it is unique in always possessing a niche in one wall to indicate the direction of Mecca (*qibla*), towards which prayer (*salat*) must be performed.

It is noteworthy that in all the conquered territories the Muslim generals immediately founded mosques; the new cities they established were built round a central mosque. To start with, these mosques were mostly a simple quadrangular open space, with some kind of protection on one side against the heat of the sun. Besides these main mosques (*jami*) which were intended for the whole community and were full on Fridays, different tribes and Muslim groups established their own local mosques (*masjid*) in parts of the town. Later, Christian churches and Zoroastrian fire temples were taken over and altered to serve as mosques. In the course of time more small mosques were built, often near the graves of Muslim saints or prophets recognized by Islam. Whereas in the earliest period the building of mosques was one of the duties of the local governor, increasingly it became a pious action which prominent Muslims performed. Founding a mosque ceased to be primarily a response to existing needs but was a religious action which bestowed merit; it took place through the legal instrument of an inalienable pious foundation (*waqf, habous*).

To Muslims a mosque means more than a place of worship. It is at the same time a place where people can meet and where a sense of community exists. It is also a place where instruction in the Quran is given and religious literature can be obtained. To the outside world, especially non-Muslims, the mosque functions as a symbol of the presence of Islam, which perhaps explains the irritation of some Europeans at the existence of mosques in their countries. Larger mosques have a religious staff of which the *imam* is the most important because of his social prestige and responsibilities; for long he was also distinguished by his religious knowledge. Originally, however, the *imam* was just the man leading the *salat* and any believer, in principle, could take this role when invited to do so.

Mosques in the Netherlands

One of the first mosques in the Netherlands was a small one built in Balk (Gaasterland, Frisland) in 1956 with a government subsidy for Muslim Moluccans from Ambon. The Ahmadiyya Mission to the Netherlands opened its Mobarak Mosque, the centre of the Rabwah Ahmadiyya community in the Netherlands, in the Hague in 1955.

Among the main immigrant groups, it was the Muslim Surinamese who first strove to establish mosques in the late sixties. They set up several Muslim associations and foundations which in principle were open to Muslims of any nationality for this purpose. Among Turkish and Moroccan immigrants the need for mosques began to be expressed at the beginning of the 1970s. This delay is probably connected to the fact that the initial residence of foreign workers from the Mediterranean region (Spaniards, Italians, Yugoslavs, Greeks, Moroccans, Turks) was regarded by everyone, including themselves, as temporary. In addition, only in the 1970s could the women and children of these workers obtain residence permits within the framework of the policy of family reunification. This not only implied a longer stay in the country but also a transfer of new forms of cultural and religious practice. Moreover it took these workers a considerable time to learn Dutch and familiarize themselves with the Dutch social system which was very different from that which the uneducated and often illiterate Turkish and Moroccan workers were accustomed to. Founding prayer-halls in a country presupposes a minimum of operational knowledge.

The first prayer-halls were usually ordinary rooms, the so-called 'front-room mosques'. The progress to specific prayer-halls was slow, dependent as it was on the availability of financial resources and space. These prayer-halls were mostly converted garages, sheds or abandoned buildings originally intended for quite different purposes and often not conforming to safety regulations. A utopian plan was floated in the sixties to build a larger mosque complex in Utrecht through the cooperation of Dutch business interests and Saudi generosity. This, however, came to nothing, as did a similar project in the Biljmer, south-east of Amsterdam, for which it was also hoped that money would be forthcoming from the Arabian peninsula. The Surinamese were particularly keen to see a complex like this with rooms for social and cultural activities adjoining the mosque.

Legally the foundation of a mosque takes place in Muslim countries through a *waqf* or *habous*, as explained above. In the Netherlands this legal construction does not exist, and either an association or a foundation must be the legal basis of a mosque or prayer-hall. It is noteworthy that Muslims in the Netherlands have not registered as a 'church', as the Jews did when the possibility became open to them in the mid-nineteenth century. Muslims do not want to have only a 'spiritual' organization; indeed one of their problems is the lack of any umbrella organization at all to defend their common religious interests.

As a result of the need for prayer-halls, Muslim groups have established many autonomous religious and cultural organizations which are distinguished from other immigrant organizations by their explicit ambition to realize Islamic religious aims, as is clear not only from their statutes but also from their names. These autonomous religious–cultural organizations are nearly always established on the basis of ethnicity or nationality; in the course of time splits have occurred, reflecting the existence of different currents among Turks, Moroccans and Surinamese. A single organization for all Muslims in one town, with a common mosque, is not a practical possibility given the differences in language, cultural background, ethnicity, sense of nationality and also ideas about Islam (for instance in its relation to politics) which the immigrants have brought with them from their countries of origin. Prayer-halls in the Netherlands thus have a certain ethnic character beside their religious and socio-cultural one.

Although the Dutch prayer-halls are mostly referred to as 'mosques' in Muslim usage, in fact they do not comply with the demands formulated in religious law for a proper mosque. The term mosque should be reserved for buildings which have either been built specifically as mosques or originally had a religious function (for instance churches or synagogues); their size also differentiates them from prayer-halls. A mosque in this sense exists in each of the four largest cities in the Netherlands.

These prayer-halls have functions and meanings for their users which can be distinguished as general or specific. Among the general functions and meanings are the following:

a. place of worship, in particular at the Friday *salat*;
b. meeting place for members of an ethnic group who feel united by their common religion;
c. centre in which the cultural and social values which people have brought with them from their country of origin and which they want to transmit to subsequent generations are adhered to;
d. place where children receive Quranic teaching and adults may be given religious instructions (e.g. in Ramadan);
e. an indirect mark of identity and of the difference between the identity of the ethnic group and that of Dutch society;
f. a symbol of the presence of Islam.

Specific functions and meanings include:

a. differentiation of one religious group from another within the same ethnic community;
b. differentiation of certain socio-political loyalties which vary within the same ethnic community;
c. differentiation on the basis of criteria which are neither religious nor political, for instance varying preferences for local leadership.

It is important, particularly with regard to such specific functions and meanings, to see how the executive (*bestuur*) of a particular organization is made up and who the *imam* is whom the executive has appointed.

The exact number of prayer-halls used by Muslims in the Netherlands cannot be known; there are 'unofficial' places of gathering which are not registered, and a certain number of prayer-halls are of such poor quality that they cannot be considered but as provisional. But roughly speaking there are about 200 prayer-halls for around 300,000 Muslims in the country.

A fact relevant here is that, even when a Muslim community has collected relatively large sums of money, most of these prayer-halls have been established with outside help or support too, including help from non-Muslims. The following list includes the kinds of groups and official bodies which have been involved in the establishment of the prayer-halls; it has been drawn up without regard for their relative importance:

1. Dutch volunteers who have helped with advice, information about which official bodies should be approached, or have sometimes collected money;
2. Dutch foundations or associations, sometimes of a religious character, which have given support either financially or in kind, for instance by providing rooms;
3. local church councils and parishes who, often by means of special committees of support, have provided help, sometimes in the form of a room or building; in a number of cases these committees have also supplied their parishes with constructive information about Islam and the Muslim immigrants;
4. local authorities, who in the second half of the 1970s started to feel a certain responsibility to look for prayer-halls or make room for them available. They have sometimes provided direct or indirect subsidies for them;
5. the Dutch government, who, from 1976 to 1983, provided an 'investment subsidy' through its Ministry of Welfare, Health and Culture to cover part of the expenses of renting or purchasing prayer-halls in a number of cases where Moroccan, Turkish and also Moluccan Muslim organizations had approached it for help. The same Ministry has also provided subsidies for social and cultural activities organized by the immigrant communities.
6. Dutch employers have in some cases provided support by making prayer-halls available at work, and in exceptional cases by contributing to the cost of a local prayer-hall;
7. foreign governments such as Saudi Arabia, Kuwait and Libya have given grants for the purchase or even building of prayer-halls, sometimes through an international Islamic organization (see below). A special form of support comes from the Turkish Directorate of Religious Affairs which since 1979 has been sending *imams* to serve among Turkish immigrants in Europe. Foreign governments have also supported some Muslim umbrella organizations.
8. International Muslim organizations such as the *Rabitat al-Alam al-Islami*

have also in some cases subsidized the purchase or construction of prayer-halls or supported umbrella organizations.

Muslim organizations in the Netherlands

As mentioned earlier, foundations and associations are the only legal basis for the founding of prayer-halls in the Netherlands. Of course Turkish, Moroccan and Surinamese Muslims have always had their own forms of social organization where strictly defined aims, tasks and management are perceived as alien and of western provenance, but in the Netherlands strict organization became a *sine qua non* for any permanent institutions. According to Dutch law the executive of a foundation appoints itself and members can in fact only protest, if necessary in court, if the executive contravenes the statutes of the foundation. The executive of an association is elected by the members, who can in this way impose changes in the policies of the executive. Accordingly, the association has a more democratic structure than the foundation. Whereas in the seventies the trend was to establish foundations, since then the number of associations has increased greatly.

Establishing and maintaining prayer-halls is only one of the explicit aims of these Muslim organizations. In general they seek to help the community follow an Islamic way of life, and they defend not only the right to religious life and worship but also the social and cultural interests of their members. General questions which arise in the context of these organizations have to do with democratic procedures; the competence of the executive and its appointment or election; the interaction between executive and members and the relationship between the executive and the *imam* whom they have appointed. In view of their general aims, the financial means of these organizations are extremely modest. In practice, each one has an active core from which, for instance, the executive is drawn, and a much wider group of members who are less active and not all of whom appear at the religious feasts. The membership is reckoned according to the number of families and unmarried men; they are in fact men's organizations though women can sometimes take part in certain activities or arrange their own. Religious organizations of Muslim women do not seem to exist in the Netherlands.

As far as is known, the Surinamese were the first to establish Muslim organizations; these appeared from the mid-sixties onwards in and near the large cities of Amsterdam and the Hague. The fact that they were the earliest can be explained by a number of considerations; the Surinamese had had experience with Dutch methods in Surinam during the colonial period; they knew the language and were less remote from Dutch society (which in a certain sense represented an ideal to them) than Moroccans and Turks were; Christian communities among the Surinamese, supported by Dutch churches, gave an impetus towards setting up autonomous organizations which could serve as models for the non-Christian Surinamese communities. A number of

Surinamese had high expectations of what could be achieved in the Netherlands, a fact which stimulated their activity. Moreover, in contrast to the Turks and Moroccans, they were not recruited to work in the Netherlands but came looking for work of their own free will. Significantly, the Surinamese in the Netherlands were inclined to stress their cultural identity for which purposes they obtained subsidies of different kinds from public funds. Surinamese cultural associations, for instance, received subsidies from the Ministry of Welfare, Health and Culture. They did not, however, receive subsidies from the government for religious purposes as the Turks and Moroccans did for a number of years. Consequently they have considerably fewer religious than non-religious organizations. It is still an open question as to how much indigenous Dutch people were directly or indirectly involved in the setting up of Surinamese organizations.

It took more time for Turkish and Moroccan immigrants to establish organizations. These arose first on the local level and in particular as religious organizations based on nationality or ethnic origin. With time, different tendencies appeared, often reflecting political attitudes in the country of origin and/or centred round a prominent personality, and this sometimes led to splits. In a subsequent phase links were established between groups from the same country of origin or sharing a common orientation, which in turn made it possible for umbrella organizations, mostly foundations, to be created. Directly or indirectly, the Dutch authorities encouraged this since they needed a representative body with whom to negotiate. The government of the country of origin, which wanted to preserve some influence on the lives of its subjects abroad, also encouraged these moves. Interestingly, it was a group of Dutch converts to Islam who took the initiative to unite all Muslims living in the Netherlands in one all-embracing foundation in the 1970s. In the end this attempt failed.

It will be difficult to write the history of Muslim organizations at the various levels because it is bound up with people who in large measure can no longer be reached. Yet, as the history of the consolidation of the Muslim communities in the country, it needs to be written. Sociological research into the dynamics of Muslim religious organizations in the Netherlands will also take time to appear, since it demands not only the mastery of certain basic research tools, for instance knowledge of the relevant languages but also the establishment of certain relationships of trust. Most researchers exhibit a remoteness towards Islam which has a negative effect; and the rare Muslim researchers tend to keep to strictly formalized procedure.

Historical and sociological research will reveal on the one hand a process of fragmentation, not only because many local organizations were founded alongside each other, but also because splits occurred through political or personal divergences. On the other hand research will also reveal processes of cohesion. The above-mentioned attempt of some Dutch Muslims to unite all Muslims in the country in one federation is a case in point. This Federation of Muslim

Organizations in the Netherlands played an important part as an umbrella organization from 1975 to around 1981, bringing together a large number of local groups of Muslims throughout the country; the Dutch Muslims defended the interests of their fellow Muslims well. When the Federation ceased to exist its staff founded the Muslim Information Centre in the Hague and took over the publication of the quarterly *Qiblah*, which had been the Federation's mouthpiece.

Among the 'national' umbrella organizations the one which deserves particular mention because of its size and efficiency is the Federation of Turkish Islamic and Cultural Associations which was founded on 10 January 1979 under the name of the Turkish Islamic Cultural Federation. This foundation brings together about eighty local Turkish organizations in Holland and cooperates with the Directorate of Religious Affairs in Ankara (*Diyanat Işleri Başkanligi*) which has been sending *imams* belonging to its overall organization in Turkey to the Netherlands since 1980; of which at present there are about fifty-five. An alternative Turkish umbrella organization is the Islamic Centre Foundation to which about seventeen local Turkish Muslim organizations belong. It is inspired by the Süleymanli movement in Turkey, will have nothing to do with the aforementioned Directorate of Religious Affairs, which represents official Turkish policies towards Islam, and consequently does not receive official recognition in Turkey.

In the case of the Moroccans the Union of Moroccan Muslim Organisations in the Netherlands (UMMON) was founded in 1978 to constitute an umbrella organization for local Moroccan Muslim organizations. The UMMON claims to represent about forty Moroccan groups but little is known about it, since it hardly ever appears in public.

Among the Surinamese the Netherlands Islamic Society (NIS) fulfilled a certain umbrella function between 1973 and 1982. This function has now been taken over by the Foundation for the Welfare of Muslims in the Netherlands, which provides some coordination between local traditional Surinamese Muslim groups of the *ahle sunnat wal-Jamaat* type.

Several umbrella organizations at present claim to represent Muslims of more than one nationality or ethnic background in the Netherlands. The Muslim Organizations in the Netherlands Foundation (MON), established in 1981 and comprising the Turkish Federation and the Moroccan UMMON, and the so-called Netherlands Islamic Parliament born in 1982 of a Surinamese initiative fit this description.

The Ahmadiyya movement with its two branches occupy a special place. The Rabwah Ahmadiyya Mission to the Netherlands from Pakistan has the Mobarak Mosque in the Hague, which was especially built for it and opened in 1955. The Lahore Ahmadiyya Anjuman Isha'at Islam, whose membership is Surinamese, has sections in Amsterdam, Rotterdam, the Hague and Utrecht. The Ahmadiyya movement is not recognized by the majority of Sunni Muslims as being Muslim in the strict sense.

There seems to be little cooperation between the various umbrella organizations, whatever claims they make, but more between certain Muslim organizations at the local level. At an estimate there are about 100 Turkish, 60 Moroccan, twenty Surinamese and five other local Muslim organizations, a total of about 185 religious organizations of Muslims in the Netherlands with official statutes. This does not include those organizations which are not specifically religious.

Other Islamic and Muslim institutions in the Netherlands

Closely connected with the prayer-halls are the *imams*. They are appointed by the executive of a local prayer-hall foundation or association, with a contract for a relatively short period. They are recruited from Turkey and Morocco; if they have studied at Turkish colleges of *Shariah* (now faculties of *Shariah* attached to the state universities) they have a good knowledge of Islam. The *imams*, who have widely varying levels of schooling and education, can be considered *de facto* as the Muslim religious leaders in the country. Their total number was estimated two years ago at about 120, that is to say around seventy Turkish, forty Moroccan and ten Surinamese (including Ahmadiyya) *imams*. During the month of Ramadan and at the time of the religious festival their number increases because then extra *imams* are invited for a short stay in the Netherlands.

The juridical status of the *imam* is at present still under discussion. He is appointed by the executive of the local organization concerned. In Dutch law one opinion considers the *imam* as being under a contract of employment and consequently falling under the provisions of employment contracts in general. Another opinion stresses that while he holds his appointment he is a religious leader, comparable for instance with a rabbi, or more remotely a minister or even priest. If he is recognized as a religious functionary, the general regulation of employment contracts does not apply and the judge can only pronounce on the formal aspects in cases of litigation between an executive and an *imam*. For the separation between church and state forbids interference by the secular authority in the internal affairs of religious associations.

Apart from leading the prayers, teaching Quran and if possible, giving further religious instruction, the *imam*'s duties are very much connected with the social welfare of the Muslim community and its members. Unfortunately the *imams* recruited abroad are not very familiar with Dutch society and conditions of life, and they usually have only a rudimentary knowledge of Dutch and spend no more than five years in the country; they cannot be considered equal to the difficult tasks which confront them. This is one of the reasons why the possibility is being mooted that *imams* be educated in the Netherlands itself at a special institution.

Another typically Islamic kind of religious institution is the Quran school, which provides for study of the Quran as well as more general instruction in the religion of Islam. Both the *imams* and the religious (Quranic) instruction started to appear when Muslim families were permitted to join their menfolk working in the Netherlands. Quranic schooling is given by the *imams* on a private basis at the wishes of Muslim parents, often alongside the regular schooling which all children in the country must receive from their fifth year onwards; this lays an extra burden on Muslim children. No less than 60 per cent of all Moroccan and Turkish children receive Quranic schooling at the moment. With respect to religious education in general there is a difference between the curricula of the state schools and those of the confessional schools (both these categories receive government subsidies). A number of Muslim children attend confessional schools, where religion is taught, though in a Christian sense; here Muslim parents would like to see special hours set aside for their children to receive instruction in the Islamic religion, but this rarely happens. In state schools ministers or priests from outside may teach religion, and *imams* would like to be able to teach Islam here, too. The new programme of Intercultural Education includes time for instruction in Turkish and Moroccan language and culture, but it is still a point of debate as to who should eventually give instruction in Islamic religion and according to what method. There is little experience of the teaching of religion in an Islamic sense in the Netherlands, nor are there materials for teaching Islam at school. But the fact remains that most Muslim parents want their children to receive Quranic schooling and broader instruction in the religion of Islam.

Imams and religious schooling are institutions inherent to Islam. Another, differing according to groups and regions but still typical, is the family. The first generation of Muslim immigrants simply brought many customs of their traditional family life with them. Though considerable changes have occurred over the last ten years, a basic pattern of division of gender and age roles remains. Together with the prayer-hall, the family may be considered the sphere of life which is specifically Muslim; Dutch laws and customs maintain a certain discretion towards it. Religion and family are the refuges where people can preserve their identity, and this holds true especially for Muslims.

The cultural background of the institutionalization of Islam

Muslims naturally have a religious motivation for creating the institutions through which their religion can take root in the country to which they have emigrated; but the cultural aspect of this process is also of interest. It seems that the Muslim culture which the immigrants brought with them forms the empirical basis for the institutionalization of Islam in the Netherlands, from prayer-halls to family customs, from the bringing over of *imams* to the use of Arabic or Turkish in the mosque.

On arrival, Muslims began a process of retaining, discarding and transforming elements of their culture. In the future third, fourth and subsequent generations will have different options with regard to the traditional culture.

They will decide which elements to retain and how to interpret them, and they will be responsible for any rediscovery of the culture of the country of origin. In the whole process of selection personal contacts and relatives on the other side of the Mediterranean have a significance since loyalties are deeper than western Europeans are accustomed to. Ideological and political factors in the countries of origin also affect the degree and way in which immigrants here are still sensitive to the cultural imperatives of their home countries.

It is noteworthy that this cultural background and the process of transforming cultural elements which is taking place are the subject of so little research in the Netherlands. Most existing studies concern processes of adaptation and the possible courses of action open to the state both nationally and on the local level. The questions at issue here — what the immigrants are making of their lives on different levels, what part their cultural background plays in this process, and what new meanings older cultural elements can acquire in the course of this process — have been gravely neglected. Strikingly little research has been done even on an amateur level into the way in which the ethnic minorities, which are cultural minorities in the first place, are developing their own forms of expression and communal life, in the spheres of proverbs, sayings, religion, cuisine, loyalty to the country of origin, ideological expression of socio-political frustrations and ideals, social differentiation and its corresponding structures (leaders and elite groups, the worlds of men and women, structures of social and political authority), the use of leisure and so forth.

In the course of this process of transformation very different attitudes towards the host country and its inhabitants develop which have various effects, either simultaneously or successively: hope, expectation and dreams on the one hand contrast with disillusionment, protest and, as yet, latent aggression on the other. An example of how research into the culture of, in this case, Turkish immigrants and their encounter with the culture of the host country can be carried out, is the pertinent study of Christoph Elsas in Berlin.

In the context of the process of cultural transformation sketched above a challenging field of study would be ethics, that is, both the ethical rules which are accepted as valid and actual social behaviour. In this, as in other research which touches on rules of Muslim behaviour, a clear distinction has to be made between those Islamic religious obligations prescribed by the *Shariah* (religious law), in particular the *ibadat*, the so-called pillars of Islam, and those elements of Muslim culture which are not prescribed by the *Shariah* but are part of the culture which the first generation has brought from home. Certain elements of this latter category may acquire new meaning and functions in the Netherlands. They may combine with new forms (unknown in the country of origin) of a properly Muslim way of life in the Netherlands in which permanent values belonging to the religious and cultural tradition are revived in the Dutch context.

Forces at work in the institutionalization of Islam in the Netherlands

We have already listed the different kinds of groups, organizations and individuals involved in the establishment of prayer-halls in the Netherlands. There are several reasons why Muslim groups have had to rely on help, in a way that Jewish communities did not since they were able to collect the necessary funds themselves.

The weakness of Muslim groups is particularly evident in the following four areas:

1. despite relatively high contributions from Turkish and Moroccan Muslims, there is too little money to pay for prayer-halls whether buying or renting them or maintaining them;
2. these groups do not have the political power to influence the Dutch authorities, the media or those sections of Dutch society who play a determining part in deciding their destiny;
3. they have too few channels of communication to Dutch society, to which they are marginal. For long they could appeal only to churches for assistance and were largely dependent on spontaneous and haphazard offers of help from Dutch society;
4. they have lacked good leaders and efficient organization to defend their interests and develop their possibilities to the utmost.

These and other weaknesses have meant that the institutionalization of Islam as a religion has been affected by a great number of forces which have little to do with Islam as a faith, religion or way of life; and particular interests and opinions bound up with these forces have tended to obscure the real problems of what has been happening and stood in the way of long term solutions. Let me give some examples of such different forces at work.

1. First of all, Dutch law has exerted an influence, for instance on the way in which prayer-halls and Muslim organizations have been established legally; the statute of *imams* as religious leaders or at least officials; and the organization of the family by excluding polygamy. It is true that the presence of Muslims in the country has already brought slight changes in Dutch law in some instances, such as the law on burial, but this is a very slow process indeed. Perhaps most fascinating to observe is the impact which the Dutch separation between the state and churches cannot fail to have on the institutionalization of Islam, conceivably with the development of a more or less separate religious domain in the future.
2. Secondly, official policies have influenced the institutionalization of Islam. In the beginning the authorities, in particular at the local level, were mostly involved in a negative sense, for example, in not granting permission for certain

buildings to be used as prayer-halls because of fire hazard or the nuisance to the neighbourhood caused by noise. Only later were the authorities more positively involved when they made certain buildings available, provided some services and even granted small subsidies.

On the level of central government, too, change has occurred. In 1973 the Ministry, known since 1982 as Welfare, Health and Culture, gave a grant towards the costs of building a mosque for Turkish workers in Almelo within the provisions of a law on grants towards the building of churches enacted in 1962 and abrogated in 1975. The same Ministry in 1976 announced general regulations for the subsidizing of prayer-halls for Turkish and Moroccan workers (thus excluding the Muslim and Hindu Surinamese who have never received government subsidies). These regulations, which first applied to the four largest cities but later also to others, were altered in 1978 to enable not only towns but also particular regions with more than 1000 Muslims to profit from their subsidies. The Ministry followed up the general regulations in 1981 with temporary regulations, under which terms subsidies could be given to Turkish and Moroccan Muslim organizations without any criterion being applied to numbers. These temporary regulations came to an end on 31 December 1983. A report submitted to the Minister on that date by a commission advised that the existing subsidy for prayer-halls be continued as long as the Minister was convinced that there was still a need for them. The report was not implemented. The granting of subsidies from 1976 to 1984 represented some form of official support for the institutionalization of Islam in the Netherlands. It implied that the demand for and presence of prayer-halls was legitimate and that a temporary policy of active support for them, in the form of subsidies, was judged to be in the long-term interests of a plural Dutch society. This policy was unique in Europe and among Muslims it obviously raised high hopes which could seldom be fulfilled. In fairness it should be added that a number of Muslim organizations did not turn to the Dutch government for financial aid for their prayer-halls.

3. A certain sector of the churches and groups of individual Christians have been a source of both practical and moral support to Muslim organizations in their efforts to establish prayer-halls. Apart from material support they have also sought to extend the existing information about Islam among Christians. Functionaries of the larger Dutch churches assigned to these tasks have been particularly active in launching a campaign against current prejudices towards Muslims and Islam. And the fact that a number of Christians have perceived Muslims as potential partners of cooperation and dialogue has also meant a significant support for the further institutionalization of Islam.

4. Although, to begin with, advice and support could be sought only from the Dutch, at a later stage Muslims themselves increasingly tended to help each other. Local organizations, and of course the relevant umbrella organizations, have held special collections for the establishment of new prayer-halls, and this has strengthened the sense of solidarity and self-help among the Muslim organizations.

5. The part played by foreign governments and international Muslim organizations is a subject apart, about which very little information is available. It is well-known that Saudi Arabia, Kuwait, Libya and other Arab oil producers have given money for prayer-halls sometimes with conditions attached and sometimes without. The workers' countries of origin send Turkish and Moroccan *imams* officially or by private arrangement, and their embassies support certain Turkish and Moroccan organizations thus ensuring that workers can maintain links with their country of origin and the governments can protect their citizens or keep an eye on them. International Muslim organizations such as the *Rabitat al-Alam al-Islami* in Mecca and to a lesser extent the London-based Islamic Council of Europe have given material support and advice on prayer-halls. It should be borne in mind that the Turkish *imams* sent out by the Directorate of Religious Affairs in Ankara have the formal status of civil servants in Turkey. There has been an increasing interference by Turkish and Moroccan authorities in existing prayer-halls and Muslim associations.

In this process of institutionalization many other forces are at work too; four of them deserve mention here, though they cannot be treated at length:

1. The appalling economic situation of the ethnic minorities plays, and will continue to play, a part in their articulation of Islam as an institution. At present 45–50 per cent of Turkish and Moroccan men in the age group eighteen–sixty-five are out of work. Possible consequences of this situation are a strengthened loyalty to the culture and religion of the country of origin and at a later stage perhaps an active ideological expression of their dissatisfaction and protest. Moreover the desire to learn more about their own background and Islam may be stimulated and attendance at prayer-halls may increase. Even if the equation 'religion = opium' is not accepted, it does appear that whenever Muslims respond to economic and social deprivation they do so at least partly by articulating their Muslim faith and way of life.

2. The forms taken by Islam in the country of origin strongly influence the forms which Muslims want to give it here; Islam at home serves as a model for its institutionalization in the Netherlands. Yet the cultural expressions of Islam to be found in Turkey, Morocco and Surinam differ from each other, and there are corresponding differences between Turkish, Moroccan and Surinamese Muslims in the Netherlands. Whereas most Turkish *imams* are recruited through official channels, Moroccans often recruit *imams* from the same region or origin as themselves or through channels or organizations in which they have confidence. At the same time, however, there is a growing tendency to adopt ideas about Islam which are current not in the country of origin but in other Muslim countries. On the whole it is through personal contacts that private groups and official organizations from abroad further the institutionalization of Islam.

3. The reaction of Dutch society to the presence of minorities which are both ethnic and religious, as expressed both through personal behaviour and in the information purveyed by the media, will become increasingly important for the articulation of Islam. Muslim groups respond intensely, in either an implicit or an explicit manner, to the attitudes which they feel the Dutch are adopting. Especially in a situation where they are threatened by unemployment and discrimination they are quick to perceive a neutral attitude as a kind of veiled distrust, while a negative attitude manifested in any form of discrimination is soon regarded as hostility. It may be predicted that if negative attitudes continue to develop among the Dutch, especially in public life and in municipal or government policies, a form of 're-Islamization' is bound to appear, whether it be religious, ideological, institutional or a combination of these. In this connection it is vitally important that government policies address themselves to the integration of the ethnic minorities into a plural Dutch society where their religious and cultural identity is recognized, maintained and further developed, and processes of emancipation are stimulated among them.

4. In determining the future the most important factor will, however, be the Muslims' own inventiveness and creativity, exercised especially in bringing people together, educating the Muslim community and deepening its sense of identity, encouraging qualified leadership, providing moral support and stimulating reflection, and developing institutions and organizations more equal to the task they must fulfil in the Dutch context. Socio-economic and political circumstances and the means available will largely determine how much latitude the groups have to apply their inborn creativity to achieving solutions to the enormous problems which exist at present and will certainly continue in the future. There can be no doubt that Islam, however it is interpreted and lived out, will play an increasingly important part in the Netherlands, particularly among the Muslim ethnic minorities. This is true whether it is in the direction of proletarization and the formation of ghettos, or in that of integration with adaptation all round and in the formulation of protests against current discrimination.

Islam and the integration of Muslims in society

Integration, defined as the participation of groups or individuals in society while retaining and developing their own identity, is opposed to assimilation, a process in which groups or individuals become part of society while playing down their specific characteristics in public life and confining expression of their essential identity to the strictly personal domain. The stress on integration as opposed to assimilation in the Netherlands is connected with the fact that Dutch society is recognized as being basically a plural society in which no one form of culture, faith or ideology may be dominant over others. The principle of equal treatment, which strengthens the recognition of a plural society, is enshrined in the new constitution of 1981. The most favourable result of a plurality of groups, beliefs and ideologies and forms of culture is to encourage the development of new ways of life and thought and thus stimulate creativity and make society more fit to live in.

What place may Muslims and Islam have in this plural society in the Netherlands? I would like to stress three points which are intrinsic to the problem of the institutionalization of Islam.

The transfer of culture and religion from the countries of origin

The first Muslim immigrants often brought with them rural traditions which were more or less religiously coloured. These traditions included both the basic religious prescriptions incumbent on all Muslims, more general norms and customs and also elements of the specific culture of their native region. Since they arrived in the Netherlands they have been caught up in a process of acculturation. There are a number of factors which complicate the study of this process and the one I wish to mention has far-reaching consequences: that is the fact that the transfer of culture and religion from Morocco and Turkey is still going on and is probably increasing on two levels.

On one level, that of the immigrants' personal lives, numerous contacts are maintained not only between members of the same family or clan but also, it seems, between groups of Muslims who share the same feelings about certain ideals of Islam. There is no doubt that Muslim groups who have emigrated receive support, moral and perhaps otherwise, from Muslim groups back home.

On another level, that of the Turkish and Moroccan authorities, a continuous transfer now takes place too. In the early years they did not bother much about nationals working abroad. Then, in the seventies, organizations sponsored by the Moroccan government set up the *Amicales* in the Netherlands and elsewhere to bring Moroccans together socially. The foreign governments concerned subsequently asserted their responsibility for the religious life of their nationals in the Netherlands. The Friday prayer in Moroccan prayer-halls should be said for Hasan II, and some kind of outline for the Friday *khutba* is apparently sent to the officially recognized Moroccan *imams*.

In the case of Turkey the Directorate of Religious Affairs has been pursuing an active policy since 1979 of sending *imams* to countries such as the Netherlands and Germany and contributing first part and later the whole of their salary. The end of 1982 saw the start of an effort to bring together the property of the recognized Turkish prayer-halls as far as possible in one foundation under the ultimate authority of the said Directorate in Ankara. In the case of Morocco, Hasan II sought to impose guidelines on the voting behaviour of the Moroccans living in the Netherlands in the municipal elections of 26 March 1986, in which they, Turks and other minority groups could take part; he was helped in this by the symbolism of the monarchy, which represents both political and religious authority. Only about 15 per cent of the Moroccan electorate departed from the king's guidelines, namely to abstain. The events of recent years lead one to the conclusion that the Turkish and Moroccan authorities' concern for the religious life of their nationals in the Netherlands has sharply increased. It may thus be assumed that the transfer of religion from these countries is increasing too, whether in the 'official' or the 'alternative' forms of Islam.

This kind of transfer of culture and religion from the countries of origin does not in my view favour the integration of Islam in the Netherlands. Furthermore, the financial support which Muslim oil exporters and international organizations have given prayer-halls in the Netherlands, even when no strings have been directly attached, favours the transfer of certain interpretations of Islam from the donor countries. To sum up, Islam in the Netherlands cannot be considered independently from Islam in Muslim countries, especially the Muslim immigrants' home countries which sustain it to a great extent.

Islam as a norm and value for Muslims in the Netherlands

The question here is what exactly various Muslim groups and individuals in the Netherlands see as sacrosanct in Islam and essential to their faith and life. It seems to me that there are at least three possibilities.

For some groups, in particular many first generation immigrants, the whole of the tradition, lore and customs which they have brought with them already has a sacrosanct character or has acquired such a character in the Netherlands. In their case religion is equated with a certain traditional way of life.

A second group, made up of people who have a certain level of education and are more oriented towards teaching and studying the Quran, holds the Quran and Sunna to be the criterion for distinguishing what is truly Islamic from what is secondary. In other words these people consider not the traditional way of life but what the Quran says to be normative. Here religion is fundamentally equated with Quran and Sunna, and members of these groups need to be able to read the Quran or at least have confidence in those who can.

A third group, less strictly organized, is inclined to combine norms taken from the Quran and the traditional way of life with 'modern' elements of life encountered in the Netherlands. Such groups implicitly take for granted that only through a combination of norms and elements of different origins can solutions be found to the problems confronting Muslims in western Europe. These groups probably constitute the greatest number.

Against this background a probable course of development can be predicted. To the extent that the children and grandchildren of Muslim immigrants seek to have a better and more intellectual appreciation of their religion they will orientate themselves towards the Quran and embark on a search for knowledge about Islam. The *imams* can play an important part by teaching authoritatively from the sources, about normative Islam, and what the Quran contains of relevance to current problems. Unfortunately some *imams* are ill-informed not only about Holland but also about Islam and they condemn their local Muslim community to a miserably low standard. Among the *imams* who have a certain knowledge of Islam at least two groups can be distinguished.

The first proposes a narrow interpretation of Islam and Quran which, moreover, is limited to the internal life of the Muslim community. It is immaterial if *imams* in this group know little about Dutch society, since their Muslim communities do not want to interact with the outside world.

A second group of *imams* proposes in their reading of Quran and Sunna an interpretation of Islam which is more universally oriented. If they have some familiarity with Dutch society they can recommend regular contact with the wider non-Muslim society, and thus encourage participation and integration.

It is clear that the teaching which the *imams* offer in the coming years is extremely important, especially for the integration of Muslims in Dutch society. For this teaching will in large measure determine the ideas of many Muslims not only about their religion but also about their place in the Netherlands.

Options in the Dutch context

The question as to what forms Islam may take in the context of Dutch society cannot be answered with certainty, but given the present processes of institutionalization, some reflections may be proposed. A general pattern does emerge in which certain specific fundamental Muslim options may be distinguished. The general pattern appears to contain the following elements:

1. The fundamental wish not to give up Islam. Despite all varieties and differences Muslims in the Netherlands all feel the same fundamental loyalty to Islam as a communal norm and ideal. All support for Islam will be accepted and all attacks against it resisted.
2. The concern of parents that their children be taught the principles of Islam and the Quran so that they can become active Muslims if they want to, and that they receive an Islamic education.
3. An increasing effort to create an institutional framework or setting (e.g. prayer-halls, associations, periodicals, a broadcasting organization) to give permanent shape to Islam in the Netherlands. This should be seen as an unambiguous process of institutionalizing Islam in the country.
4. A persistent demand for the existence of Islam in the Netherlands to be recognized if not legally, then at least intellectually and morally, and for attitudes which seem to ignore the existence of Muslims or Islam in Holland to be abandoned.

The following ways of interpreting 'being Muslim' or having a 'Muslim identity' can be distinguished as specific fundamental options against the background of the general pattern indicated above. These options are not rigorously exclusive of each other:

1. The secular option: discarding Muslim identity and perhaps even replacing it by another one: conversion to Christianity, conscious agnosticism or atheism, total assimilation to Dutch models which are sincerely believed in.
2. The cooperation option: playing down the specific features of Muslim identity in favour of commitment to a cause in which Muslims engage themselves together with non-Muslims, e.g. a social or political cause.
3. The cultural option: neglecting the typically religious aspects of Muslim identity but maintaining certain social and cultural forms of it. Solidarity with the tradition is preserved and something from the past kept alive but the door is left open to new possibilities in the future. Keeping the Muslim identity alive socially and culturally also means that Muslims retain the possibility of rediscovering their cultural background at any given time: a cultural revivification of Islam.
4. The religious option, emphasizing the religious aspects of Muslim identity at the expenses of its cultural aspects; in a sense this option is the reverse of the preceding one. It may lead to a rediscovery of the religious truths of Islam — a religious revivification of Islam. It should be noted that this religious option implies various possibilities, such as traditionalist, reformist, activist, pietistic or mystical. To identify the religious option with what is called a 'fundamentalist' attitude, this latter being opposed to a 'modern' attitude, is unscholarly. The religious option has many more varieties than the 'fundamentalist' one in any precise sense of the term.
5. The ethnic-religious option, tending to stress the religious and cultural aspects of the Muslim identity in combination with a specific ethnic identity. Here the fact that being a Muslim is a natural consequence of being a Turk or Moroccan is emphasized. Thus the desire to be a good Muslim Turk or Muslim Moroccan is stimulated.
6. The behaviour option: the expression by Muslims of their identity simply through their moral (ritual) behaviour, without their expressing any ideas about it.
7. The ideological option: in contrast to the option just mentioned, the Muslim identity and the ideals which Muslims feel Islam stands for are elaborated more or less ideologically. Muslims can adopt an ideological attitude to Islam which is identical to the official one in their home country or opposed to it. As far as alternative attitudes to Islam are concerned various possibilities exist. Broadly speaking these are either adherence to a specific alternative Islamic movement to be found in the home country, for instance the Süleymanli in Turkey, or development of a new alternative attitude in the Netherlands, as exemplified in the 'free' mosques, that is, mosques free from outside political influences. It is also possible to adhere to a Muslim group which originates elsewhere in the Muslim world, for instance by joining one of the more or less activist currents originating in Egypt, such as the Muslim Brothers.

These options are a matter of choice and should be studied as such, with respect for any Muslim's freedom to articulate his or her identity as he or she wishes. Which of these options Muslims will choose in the end and which groups will arise as a consequence, seems to be closely linked with their relations with Dutch society. Of course many factors are operative here, but we would like to submit as a hypothesis that when Muslim immigrants stress their Muslim identity in an exclusive sense — at least explicitly — this correlates with an aloofness from Dutch society. Conversely, an important degree of participation in society seems to correlate with a wider interpretation of the Muslim identity. Avoidance of contact or even verbal attacks on the existing Dutch situation which appeal to Islam are also correlated with certain options as to the Muslim identity. Further enquiry into this matter is urgently needed.

In conclusion, we contend that the forms which Islam takes in the Netherlands in the future will depend to a great extent on the relationships which develop between the various Muslim groups and the plural society around them. By now some test cases have occurred which help to indicate what the Dutch, for their part, will and will not tolerate. This of course affects the way in which Islam is articulated in Holland.

Here follow some examples of such test cases:

1. The carrying out of the *ibadat* ('pillars' of Islam) is at least in principle tolerated everywhere in the Netherlands, even though certain compromises can be found with regard to the number of *salats* performed each day and the duty of fasting.
2. To accommodate some religious prescriptions of Islam, modifications of Dutch law are feasible, for instance in the laws pertaining to slaughter, burial or custody of children in case of divorce. Such modifications are possible on condition that they do not infringe the basic principles of Dutch law, which has a territorial, not a personal, validity. Polygamy, for instance, cannot be tolerated.
3. Certain customs of the first and even the second generation which originated in their home countries have been tolerated even though they arouse irritation in the Netherlands. There have been cases, for instance, where girls could not attend co-educational schools after their thirteenth year and fathers administered severe corporal punishment to their children. Such customs which cause annoyance will have to be phased out; in fact the second and certainly the third generation themselves are less tolerant of them.
4. There will always remain a number of cases where the legal prescriptions valid in the Netherlands can be circumvented, for instance by a father who takes his children back to his home country in the case of divorce from his Dutch wife, even though she has been granted custody. If uncovered, such circumventions will be brought before a court.
5. On the other hand a number of harmless customs which many Muslims associate with Islam but which have no specifically religious connotations will probably continue to exist as social and cultural features of these ethnic groups,

provided of course that they do not explicitly conflict with Dutch law. They will remain as characteristic features of these groups, who will probably also articulate them consciously to affirm their identity. The wife and her links with the home in many Muslim families, and in general matters which concern family life and the private sphere, are examples of this point.

Islam and integration in the Netherlands

We now come to the conclusions based on the preceding remarks on the institutional aspects of the integration of Muslims in a Dutch plural society.

To start with, it must be realized that Muslims living in the Netherlands are so different in ethnic origin, language, culture and customs, and orientation with regard to Islam that it is impossible to speak of Islam in the Netherlands as if it were a single entity. This will be even less feasible in the future, given the simple fact that within the ethnic groups themselves different groups and communities develop with their own way of life which they relate to Islam. This is particularly true if the diversity in fundamental options, which we sketched earlier, is taken into account. We must consequently reject any generalizations to the effect that Islam or the Muslims will be totally incapable, or conversely totally capable, of being integrated into Dutch society. Our subject is not as simple as that, as may have become evident from the preceding pages. Among Muslims, as among other sections of Dutch society, there are many larger and smaller groups.

The problem of the relation between Islam and integration, then, must be formulated in very different terms from those in which it has usually been expressed. The question whether 'Islam' will let itself be integrated in the Netherlands should be ruled out of court; it will also to a large extent depend on the Dutch. The question, formulated in academic terms, which lends itself to future research is the opposite one: how do particular groups interpret and apply Islam, and why?

Certain groups may aim to maintain an aloofness from Dutch society through their interpretation and application of Islam; this aloofness may, however, be only implied. It may serve, for instance, to permit Muslims to preserve a completely distinctive character, as is found in Orthodox Judaism too. But it may also indicate an incapacity to participate in society at all, not on religious but on other grounds, Islam being used simply as a refuge. Conversely, when certain groups propose an opposing interpretation and application of Islam, the question may be asked whether this in fact aims precisely at bridging the existing distance, achieving acceptance by society at large and participating in it not only economically but also socially and culturally. It should be noted that an approach to society at large can also be sought precisely by not mentioning Islam at all.

A second conclusion is that a Dutch variety of Islam, that of a Muslim way of life which has adopted certain Dutch forms, is legally visible (for instance in the Muslim organizations around prayer-halls), but not, or not yet, culturally visible, except in the case of Muslim Dutchmen.

Up till now Turks, Moroccan and Muslim Surinamese have apparently clung to typically Turkish, Moroccan and Surinamese forms of Islam. It does not mean that integration will be generally rejected on Islamic grounds. This conclusion would only be justified if Islamic ideologies explicitly directed against Dutch society were to develop among Muslims. It seems certain that any such Islamic 'anti-ideology' is out of the question. Characteristically there is a general attitude of waiting to see what will happen. But this waiting attitude is dictated not by religion but by the poor economic situation, and the relative unpredictability of Dutch behaviour in situations of every-day life and in politics.

I would contend that the future may well see the disappearance not of the Muslim identity but rather of its absolute connection with ethnic identity. In other words Islam will increasingly transcend the present ethnic diversity in the Netherlands, whether it takes on a reformist, pietistic or activist form. And the better the knowledge available to Muslims about their religion, as a result of education and social development, the truer this will be.

Whether integration will be stimulated or hampered by Muslims' rediscovery of Islam as a universal faith and religion is difficult to predict. Factors such as relations with the Muslim world and especially the countries of origin will have an important influence. But at least as important will be the economic and social position of large groups of Muslims in the Netherlands. Specifically their confinement to the proletariat will make integration virtually impossible. It could even lead to sporadic anti-Dutch articulations of Islam.

Given the ways in which Islam has become institutionalized in the Netherlands, it can in no sense be seen on an intellectual level as a threat to Dutch society, nor should it be so seen on moral grounds. Dutch society has firmly decided for plurality, a plurality which can be repelled only with violence. And the democratic system of the Dutch state, based on law, guards against that.

2
Making a Place for Islam in British Society:
Muslims in Birmingham

Daniele Joly

Islam came to Britain in a very recent period. The only previous experience Britain had of Muslims in the relatively recent past had been through its empire, and it remained impervious to the influence of Muslim culture. Nothing had prepared British society for giving a home to a strong nucleus of Muslims forming communities in some of its major cities.

Britain has primarily a Christian Protestant society; this is enshrined in the composition of its institutions whereby state and church are not separated. The Queen of England is both the head of the state and the head of the church. This manifests itself in multiple facets of British society, such as the education system which makes religious education compulsory, a court of law where it is customary to take the oath on the Bible, in church, where a priest can celebrate marriages which are legally recognized. Moreover, as in most countries which possessed an empire, Britain does not have a tradition of religious or cultural tolerance of non-Christian outsiders. The past persecution of the Jews and today's prevalent racism bear witness to this.

Paradoxically, the arrival of Islam in Britain took place after the dismantling of the empire in the post-second world war era, when the economic boom demanded the import of labour which came mostly from ex-colonies. At first, no notice was taken of the introduction of new cultures and religions on British territory. The immigrants themselves initially intended to live in Britain only temporarily and thereafter return home. But as immigrant populations became settled, the Muslims rebuilt their religious institutions and increasingly felt that their religious status and rights ought to be recognized, in order to preserve their religion and culture in a minority situation. It is not simply the predominance of another religion which caused concern to Muslims; they wanted to safeguard Islam from the growing secularisation of British society.

In this chapter I seek to show how Muslims are trying to make a place for Islam in Britain, taking Birmingham as a case study. It is based on research carried out in the last two years in the Midlands. It included lengthy interviews with the leaders of mosques, councillors and headteachers, participant observation in the activities of the mosques and the results of a questionnaire which was answered by three quarters of Pakistani-based mosques. The questionnaire covered areas such as the aims and objectives of the mosque, the composition of the mosque leadership and staffing, of the people attending Friday prayer, and the mosque activities, particularly in the field of education.

The institutional framework of Muslim life in Birmingham

Statistical summary on Muslims

Muslims made their first appearance in Britain in the wake of the world wars, the majority arriving after the second world war in the shape of demobilized colonial soldiers from the Indian subcontinent and the Arab peninsula.

The economic boom of the fifties in Britain, then short of labour, combined with turmoils in what used to be the empire,[1] attracted a flow of immigrant workers from the Indian subcontinent. Most of them were young, single men who came to work in Britain with the intention of returning home after saving sufficient money to buy property in the homeland. It did not happen as planned. Whilst this immigration increased steadily, initially bringing over more and more male members of the family and/or the village, in a chain migration, its composition changed. The restrictions on immigration imposed in 1962 and 1968 limited entry almost entirely to family reunion: wives and children joined the male head of the family already resident in Britain (Nielsen 1984). This population lost its transient character and became settled as a stable feature of British society.

Statistics on Muslims living in Britain pose a problem as there is no statistical data on Muslims *per se* obtainable from the census of population. And other sources are incomplete or unreliable (Nielsen 1983). It is possible however to formulate an estimate of the Muslim population on the basis of data on country of birth or country of origin. The latest census (1981) identifies 398,624 residents born in countries where Islam is the main religion, that is 0.007 per cent of the total population in Britain. Table 1 describes the distribution by country of origin.

In addition there are Muslims from India and East Africa. People from the Indian subcontinent constitute the main group of Muslims now resident in Britain and the more detailed figures on sex and age structure that are available refer only to Pakistanis and Bangladeshis. The balance between men and women is not quite restored yet: there are 122 males per 100 females of Pakistani origin (including those born in Britain) and 119 males per 100 females of Bangladeshi origin (OPCS 1981). This population is a young one, with a large proportion

Table 1. Distribution of Muslims in Britain by country of origin

Country of origin	Muslims resident in Britain
Pakistan	188,198
Bangladesh	48,517
Malaysia	45,430
Algeria	2,417
Egypt	23,463
Libya	6,004
Morocco	5,818
Tunisia	2,037
Iran	28,068
Middle East (less Israel)	36,824
Turkey	11,848

still under school age. 46.5 per cent are under sixteen and 70 per cent under forty-four. Only 1 per cent of them are of retirement age (sixty-five for men, sixty for women). Another noticeable feature is that more and more children are born in the UK, adding to the settled character of this population. In 1981 103,000 children of Pakistani origin and 19,000 children of Bangladeshi origin were born in the United Kingdom (OPCS 1981).

In the West Midlands, the second region after London with a high concentration of Muslims, there are 52,298 residents who were born in Muslim countries, see Table 2.

Table 2. Distribution of Muslims in the West Midlands by country of origin

Country of origin	Muslims resident in West Midlands
Pakistan	38,269
Bangladesh	6,595
Malaysia	2,516
Algeria	159
Egypt	1,165
Libya	253
Morocco	113
Tunisia	40
Iran	1,232
Middle East (less Israel)	2,685
Turkey	271

Source: OPCS 1981

Turning now to Birmingham which is the specific area of interest for the purpose of this paper, the 1981 census indicated 40,565 Pakistanis and 5520

Bangladeshis[2] (OPCS 1981). An estimate for 1985 gives the following figures: 49,300 Pakistanis, 7900 Bangladeshis (Hodgins 1985). For an evaluation of the total Muslim population it is necessary to include in the total figure:

> Muslims of Indian origin estimated at 9820 (Hodgins 1985)
> Muslims of East African origin: 4100 (Hodgins 1985)
> Muslims from other countries: about 8000 (Census 1981).

Altogether these figures give us an estimate of 80,000 including British born children, that is around 8 per cent of the population of Birmingham. Within Birmingham itself, the Muslim population is concentrated in a few inner city wards: Soho, Aston, Handsworth, Nechells, Washwood Heath, Small Heath, Sparkbrook, Sparkhill and Moseley, which means that nine out of thirty wards account for 88 per cent of the Pakistani and Bangladeshi population (Census 1981, West Midlands).

Survey of the mosques in Birmingham

Following the settlement of the Muslim populations mosques were established. They are numerous and varied. My investigation shows fifty-five mosques in Birmingham and only six are situated in districts which do not contain a high concentration of the Muslim population, but are on the edge of those areas (Census 1981, West Midlands).

This figure may seem very high, but in fact new mosques continue to be created at an accelerating pace. From my survey, the mosques founded before 1970 amount to 40 per cent of the present total, whereas in the following ten years, from 1970–80, newly created mosques account for 32 per cent and from 1980–84 for 27 per cent, that is in a period of less than five years. The multiplication of mosques is a testimony to the thriving nature of Islam in Birmingham today. According to my survey all of the mosques own their own premises and in 80 per cent of the mosques, those premises are a converted family house or perhaps two terraced houses together. The other 20 per cent are the large mosques in Birmingham which can muster a few thousand people for *Eid* celebrations and more than a hundred people for Friday prayer, compared with the smaller mosques which count only a handful of people attending Friday prayer. In all cases except for the Central Mosque, the buildings do not differ from surrounding ones (as oriental designs were not permitted by planning restrictions). In the big mosques, internal structural alterations took place when three or four houses were brought together, walls were knocked down to create large prayer halls and ablution areas were installed; other buildings were bought and modified internally, such as the old swimming baths and sports centre, a spectacular and gigantic red brick Victorian building, which is a classified monument. Only the Central Mosque was purpose built (1975) and towers over Highgate with its white dome and minarets. There does not appear to have been a bid to buy old churches, as the Sikhs did.

Although mosques were generally created without registering with local authorities as places of worship, most mosques have had to apply for planning permission. The City Council in the past has shown positive reluctance to grant planning permission, imposing restrictions and conditions which were difficult to meet and do not appear necessary today. The 1970s were fraught with enforcement notices and planning refusals (Hodgins 1981). The City Council and the newspapers debated the issue, bringing it to the attention of the public in a sensational and often racist fashion. In the midst of this discussion, Mohammed Noor from the Islamic Mission promised in the *Evening Mail* (19 July 1976), that no new mosque would be created without applying for planning permission, a guarantee which in reality he was not in a position to give. As a rule mosques were granted planning permission only after several applications like the Tennyson Road mosque which applied in 1972, 1974, 1976, 1977 and 1978 and there remains today discontent over the issue among mosque leaders. It is estimated that in 1986 about three quarters of the mosques had planning permission.

Mosques are not only places of worship, they serve a variety of functions. In the main, they are frequented by men who pray there and by children who receive religious instruction. In the large mosques such as the Green Lane and the Anderton Road mosques, up to 500 children attend classes; in the smallest ones such as the Durham Road mosque less than twenty. In the mosques, the children read the Quran and commonly also attend language classes (of the language relevant to their country of origin, although not necessarily their mother tongue). Moreover the large mosques play the role of community centres and welfare and advice centres and 15 per cent offer sports facilities, 20 per cent have a bookshop and/or library. All the mosques claim to have a management committee, including a chairman, a secretary and a treasurer. According to my survey 70 per cent have paid staff, the *imam*, sometimes the secretary and one or more teachers. A high degree of commitment is noticeable insofar as salaries are kept low (e.g. £4000 per year for a secretary in a big mosque) and a great number of volunteers donate their time and efforts to the running of the mosque: an average of eleven volunteers per mosque. From my survey 75 per cent of the mosques claim that they have more than one *imam*, who in most cases was brought over from the congregation's country/village of origin. Because of the diaspora of the Indian and Pakistani people, it may mean that the *imam* came from India whilst the congregation is composed of East African Indians (such as in the Clifton Road mosque). There is, however, a developing trend to recruit a 'local' *imam*, from the congregation's community, but who is already resident in Britain (27 per cent from my survey). One mosque took this initiative a step further and founded a 'college of *imams*' in order to produce 'British' *imams* (*Darul Uloom Islamia*, in Golden Hillock Road). There is an increasing awareness that familiarity with the English language and society are useful and necessary attributes for an *imam*.

The sources of funding for these mosques remain fairly mysterious as it is difficult to extract exact information: they receive fees and donations from the faithful, they sometimes obtain a grant from the City or County Council, and it appears that substantial sums are awarded by Muslim countries, Saudi Arabia, Libya, Pakistan or others in the tide of revival of Islam in the world. The latter may have clear disadvantages as is testified by the Saddam Hussein mosque in Perry Barr, which stands unfinished because funding from Iraq was interrupted.

As was noted earlier, mosques are numerous and varied in Birmingham. It is possible to find two mosques in the same street, and not rare to find mosques within walking distance of one another. This phenomenon can be explained by a diversity of factors:

1. Although the Muslim population in Birmingham is concentrated in inner city areas rather than being dispersed throughout the town, it is still distributed over a large area. Muslims prefer to have a mosque in their vicinity to which they can walk at prayer time. This is reinforced by the fact that mosques attend to children's education, as *madrasa* (Quranic schools), and it is impossible for them, especially small children, to travel a long distance to the mosque everyday by bus, after school, particularly during winter when days are short.

2. Despite Islam's denial of recognizing national boundaries, mosques in Birmingham have been created on an ethnic/national basis. This is partly determined by the fact that chain migration brought to the same area of residence in Britain people from the same area of origin. But it is also the case that people from different areas or countries of origin often live in the same neighbourhood. It is then very possible or even likely that several mosques will be created accordingly.

The vast majority of mosques are Pakistani based, and can be subdivided according to the region of origin:

Mosques with a predominantly Punjabi congregation; one example is the mosque in Anderton Road
Mosques whose people come from Azad Kashmir (Mirpur) such as the Green Lane mosque
'Pathan' based mosques, e.g. the Woodstock Road mosque. In reality, the term Pathan here commonly includes, not only the 'authentic' Pathans, inhabitants of the North-West Frontier area in Pakistan, but also Campbellpuris who come from the extreme North West of Punjab, close to the North-West Frontier

In addition, there are other nationally based mosques:

With a congregation from Bangladesh, e.g. the Coventry Road mosque
With a Yemeni congregation, e.g. the Edward Road mosque
Finally, people from East Africa, the majority of whom originate from Gujerat in India, e.g. the Clifton Road mosque.

At the same time the ethnic national character of the congregation is often not homogeneous and can be mixed, with one group being more numerous.

3. Finally, what contributes to the multiplication of mosques is the existence of

theological differences between trends and sects in Islam, expressed at times with emphasis and hostility.

a. Most of the mosques are *Sunni Hanafi* mosques and are divided into two main groupings — Sufi and non-Sufi:

> i. The majority of followers of Sufism are called *Barelwi* (named after a village in India where the sect was founded) and are of the Naqshbandi order. The main Sufi centre is situated in Golden Hillock Road, followers of a Shaykh in Pakistan, and it is in the process of organizing a federation of Sufi mosques (seventeen mosques in the Midlands), but these do not include all the Sufi mosques. They generally refer to themselves as Sunni, excluding the non-Sufi mosques, although the latter ones may fall within the Sunni category.
>
> ii. Non-Sufi mosques of the *Deobandis*, who take their name after a village in India and seem to be the least open to British society; and the *Jamaat-i-Islami*, the politico-religious movement in Pakistan, whose founder and mentor was Maulana *Mawdudi* (who died in 1980). In Britain they are represented by the UK Islamic mission which claims thirty-five branches nationally and six branches locally. Its headquarters are the Sparkbrook Islamic Association in Anderton Road, one of the largest mosques in Birmingham. New branches are being opened in other areas. They are well organized and dynamic. In lay language one would call them fundamentalist although this term is not a satisfactory one and may have misleading connotations.

b. The *Markazi Jamiat Ahl-e-Hadith* claims sixteen branches in the UK and four branches locally. They are followers of a movement founded in Saudi Arabia. This organisation is well structured and expanding, with its headquarters in Green Lane, Birmingham.

c. Moreover there are a number of sects with a lesser presence in Birmingham. Two Shia places of worship are the Woodview Drive Imambaragh which is Punjabi based and claims 300 families; and one in Clifton Road, the congregation of which comes from East Africa.

One Ismaili mosque is in Suffolk Street, and there is one Ahmadiyya centre (the followers of the Ahmadiyya claim to be Muslims but are not generally recognized as such by other Muslims) and one Alawi *zawiya* whose followers come from Yemen. Theological divisions are further compounded by political alliances; there exist two councils of mosques, and separate groupings around some individual leaders.

Mosques and communities

The demographic map of Birmingham shows the presence of a substantial population of Muslim origin in a few areas of concentration in the inner city (Census 1981, West Midlands). This population is not homogeneous with regard to its national or ethnic origin, but the various groups have reconstituted dense networks and concomitant economic, social and religious activities, institutions and structures. The increasing number of mosques in all parts of the city bears witness to this.

The role of mosques and Muslim associations will be examined later. First it is necessary to explore the relationship between institutions and communities in terms of the observance and preservation of Islam. This interaction is a dynamic one.

1. Islam entered Britain through Muslim immigrants. The Muslim communities provided the material bases and the subjective factors that led to the creation of mosques, the people gathered funds to acquire places of worship and although in principle any man versed in Islam can become an *imam*, Muslims in Britain have often sent for an *imam* from their country or area of origin. A few individuals played a decisive role in the establishment of mosques but their initiatives could only bear fruit because they were sustained by the group.

2. It is a characteristic feature of Islam that it governs not only religious practice and morality in a narrow sense, but also social relationships, marriage, divorce, family relations, economics, politics and the most humble actions of everyday life. As a consequence, the more complete the Muslim communities, the more lively and all embracing the presence of Islam has become in Birmingham. The first single Muslim men who came to Birmingham to work founded a mosque in Speedwell Road as early as 1947. But it is the changing structure of Muslim populations, reuniting families, wives, children and even older kin, including the extended family, which has made Islam a factor to be reckoned with. Pakistanis, Bangladeshis and other Muslims established their own grocery and clothes shops, their banks, their butchers, so that most everyday needs could be satisfied within the communities in the areas populated by Muslims. This allowed for the reorganization of a way of life more akin to what used to exist in the home country, but also closer to the Muslim religion. For instance, the use of Muslim banks makes it possible not to commit the sin of taking interest from others for self-gain, and the Muslim practice of eating *halal* meat can only be observed because of the numerous *halal* meat butchers situated in the vicinity of people's residences.

3. More signficiant yet is the moral and centripetal pressure of family and social networks which re-emphasizes the necessity of religious observance, since one will be judged by kin, neighbours and fellow Muslims on one's observance. (It is for that reason, we were told, that if a Muslim man goes to a pub he will not frequent one in his neighbourhood.) The religious and moral rectitude of each individual man, woman and youth is overseen by the community. Collective practice at the mosque, such as Friday prayer or *Eid* celebrations, further strengthens the social and religious character of Islamic observance.

4. Given these circumstances, mosques are not solely passive places of worship. They fulfil many functions; the essential feature to remember is that, whilst they express and reflect the people's religious convictions, they, in turn, restructure and reinforce these convictions. The bigger and better organized mosques are the dynamic factor which campaigns for a stricter observance and wider expansion of Islam in Birmingham. Moreover, the funding and inspiration drawn from Muslim countries and the international revival of Islamic

movements have contributed in consolidating the impact of the mosques and Islam in Birmingham.

Islam: an ideological movement

Muslim leaders have expressed their concern for the development of Islam in Britain since it is subject to an alien environment. They portray western society as meaningless, aimless, rootless, characterized by vandalism, crime, juvenile delinquency, the collapse of marriages and psychiatric disorders. They postulate that Islam can provide an alternative lifestyle in Europe: Islam is presented as an ideological movement confronted with the ideology of the West and of capitalist secular society. Whereas the latter is said by Muslims to have lost its moral signposts, they claim that Islam proposes a sense of purpose with moral precepts that advocate truthfulness, justice, equality, obedience to one's parents. Islam is said to liberate man from western-like materialism, egoism and money-grabbing corruption. To the overriding selfish individualism of the West is contrasted Muslim collective responsibility, the correct appreciation of accountability to family, society, fellow Muslims, of the employer to the employee and vice-versa. To the western decadent promiscuity between men and women, sexual education at school, the mixing of sexes in all areas of life including school, the wearing of revealing feminine clothes, is opposed the modesty of Muslim women, the well-regulated interactions between men and women, in which Islam allows both for their spiritual and material needs. Moreover Islam is often presented by Muslims as the religion of measure and moderation, striking the right balance between the excesses of capitalism (extreme individualism) and communism (extreme collectivism). Islam is said to permit individual initiatives (in art, business, science) without the loss of collective responsibility.

Muslim leaders claim that Islam is flexible enough to adapt to a modern technological society; indeed, they stress that knowledge seeking and the desirability of progress are vigorously encouraged in the Quran. They only reject modernization if it aims at fulfilling material needs whilst disregarding moral matters, since that results in the disintegration of society, as is happening in the West. They argue that a good Muslim education can prevent evils such as drug addiction, gambling and drinking which afflict the young people of this society. A recurring theme in my interviews with Muslims is that Islam creates 'good citizens', and as evidence of this they point to the absence of Muslim youth participation in the recent (1985) riots in Handsworth. They are convinced of the moral superiority of Islam and believe that British society has a lot to learn from it, but they are nonetheless preoccupied with the potentially pernicious influence of westernism, which is the ruling ideology of the society in which they live.

Maintaining and reproducing Islam in Birmingham

In response to this newer environment in their country of settlement, Muslims in Britain have followed a dual strategy for the observance and reproduction of Islam outside the *Dar al-Islam*.[3] They have established the necessary institutions for the essential tenets of their religious practice, addressing their efforts to the Muslim communities themselves, and they have attempted to influence British institutions and individuals with a view to making a space for Muslims in their midst.

Measures addressed to Muslim communities

Creating the conditions for the observance of Islamic practice: the mosques

In Islam, a mosque is a *sine qua non* for compliance with one's religious duties, especially for prayers, which cannot all be performed individually. Thus arose the initial motivation for the creation of mosques in Birmingham. Though they fulfil other functions, the mosques have at least organized and structured the religious life and practices of Muslims. Numerous mosques distributed throughout the city make it possible for a number of men to be within reach of a mosque and thus to comply with the obligatory congregational prayer at noon on Friday. The smallest mosques, which were previously private houses, gather a dozen or so men every Friday noon, the biggest mosques may have a few hundred men on that occasion. Muslims are of course confronted with the problem of living in a Christian society where Friday is not a holy day, and thus most of them cannot leave their employment to attend the mosque. Muslim leaders have pointed out, however, that the dramatic increase in unemployment has made it possible for more and younger people to attend Friday prayer, whereas it would otherwise be feasible only for retired men.

The highlights of the year for Muslims and the most active periods in the mosques are the two most important religious celebrations:

> *Eid-ul-Fitr* celebrated at the end of the fasting month of Ramadan
> *Eid-ul-Adha* celebrated on the tenth of the Islamic calendar month of *Dhul-Hadj* to commemorate the sacrifice of Ishmael by Abraham.

There are also smaller-scale festivals such as the anniversary of Prophet Mohammed's birthday. On those occasions the mosques become a bustle of activity: the month of Ramadan itself attracts many people to the mosque on breaking their daily fast. *Eid* days are festive events: they constitute a family and social as well as a religious occasion. The streets leading up to the mosques are filled with entire families in their best attire, on their way to *Eid* prayers. The prayer halls in the mosques are full with numbers ranging from a few hundred to thousands, depending on the size of the mosque. In most cases, workers book a day off to allow for it, although this is not altogether unproblematic as the exact date of *Eid* cannot be known in advance as it depends on the first sighting of the moon. The mosques have now come to an agreement on the precise day of *Eid*. The great number of mosques divide the congregation which is thereby dispersed; but the Central Mosque invites *imams* from a variety of mosques to take part in the celebration and people of different trends get together in a communal celebration.

Altogether, the revitalization of Islam is well-serviced by Friday prayers, and particularly *Eid* celebrations which also fulfil a mobilizing role. It gives an opportunity to the *imam Khatib* (who in principle is well versed in Islamic theology) to address his congregation and instruct them in Islam. The issue and message transmitted vary slightly according to mosque and *imam*. The better scholars of Islam who head the biggest associations have emphasized the necessity of addressing issues directly relevant to the difficulties of maintaining an Islamic outlook and strict observance in British society, and their sermons reflect their endeavour to strengthen Muslim convictions and practices despite an adverse environment. They have also emphasized the need for an *imam Khatib* able to preach and instruct in Islam, alongside the *imam Ratib* whose role is to lead everyday prayers (apart from Friday at midday). The leaders of the better organized mosques deplore the fact that a lot of the small mosques have only an *imam Ratib*, and nobody who can really preach to the congregation. The mosques also organize the collection of alms (*zakat*) deemed to be equal to 2.5 per cent of one's income, thus accomplishing one of the five pillars of Islam. The role of the mosques as described above is directed primarily at the first generation of Muslim settlers, although the younger ones benefit all the same (but specific measures are taken towards them): to provide the basis for ensuring their practice and observance of Islam.

The mosques have also taken other initiatives:

1. Most of them have published a timetable of prayer times throughout the year, some of which are glamourous and colourful calendars, others are simple duplicated sheets. Here again they are indispensible in a non-Muslim society. In the home country, the *muezzin* call for prayer could be heard by everyone. In an attempt to re-establish this practice the Central Mosque has sought official permission for the call for prayer, and it has now been granted within the limits agreed.
2. One of the biggest mosques has published a handbook, *Haram and Halal in Islam*, giving a detailed analysis of the contents of food available on the market, indicating the make of the producer, and distinguishing between *halal* and *haram* components.
3. Another booklet has been published, this time specifically addressed to parents, warning them of all the school practices which run counter to Islamic precepts and informing them of their legal rights regarding their children in English schools (such as the right to withdraw them from religious education and assemblies): *Muslim Children in British Schools, Their Rights and Duties*.

4. There are also two monthly periodicals in Urdu, *Azan* and *Sirat-e-Mustaqeem*, published in Birmingham, and two in English, the *Straight Path* and *Al-Tawhid*.

Amongst their other functions, the mosques and their *imams* are present in key passages of life of Muslims:

1. Marriages are very often celebrated at home by an *imam* who goes to the house of the bride and the bridegroom. In this case a second marriage ceremony must take place at the registry office as well so that it is recognized by British law. As an alternative the Central Mosque in Birmingham arranges for a visit of a registrar at the mosque on weekdays and Saturday, so that both religious and civil marriages can be performed on the premises of the mosque. There are one or two such marriages celebrated at the Central Mosque every week. This is a case in which Muslims are treated differently from Christians or Jews under British law. In the case of a Catholic or Church of England priest or a rabbi performing a religious marriage ceremony, no additional civil marriage is required as the religious one is legally recognized.
2. Funeral duties are also organized in the major mosques which have a morgue with cleansing and preservation facilities. Up until now, most burials have taken place in the country of origin to which the deceased are sent by their kin. In a town like Bradford negotiations have taken place between the Council of Mosques and the Bradford City Council so that new arrangements would make it possible to conduct burial as soon after death as possible (as prescribed by Islam), outside cemetery hours and at weekends if necessary; the community would also be able to use a shroud instead of a coffin. In Birmingham, there are two burial grounds for Muslims, on separate sites within a cemetery: one is to be found in Handsworth and the other in Kings Heath (the latter generally receives children).

People are trying to widen the scope of the facilities and activities in mosques. The Central Mosque, for instance, caters for old people who have a room where they can drink tea and read religious publications. The bigger mosques run an advice centre and one of them even has a marriage bureau. Other activities fall under the general label of advice and pastoral care.

Mosques are still frequented mostly by men; women are not under obligation to perform the main Friday prayer collectively and tend to be confined at home. Although they are officially welcome in the mosque, some of the more old-fashioned mosque leaders have discouraged them from appearing there. According to my survey only 0.5 per cent of the faithful attending Friday prayer are women and 50 per cent of the mosques do not have any women attending Friday prayer. The whole family are encouraged to attend in some mosques; in one of them in particular, Sunday has been transformed into a family religious occasion where men, women and children gather to pray, listen to sermons and partake of a collective meal (men and women in separate rooms).

Most of this intense social and religious Muslim life remains unknown and unnoticed by the wider British population. There are few material signs of it. Evidence of a Muslim presence in Birmingham is provided by the characteristic oriental dome of the Central Mosque and by Arabic inscriptions on the facade of buildings that have been turned into mosques, but those remain fairly discreet as these buildings do not differ from surrounding ones. In addition a few large mosques possess shops which display and sell Muslim literature in Arabic, Urdu and English, together with a whole collection of colourful concrete symbolic representations of Islam: prayer mats, photos and woven pictures of Mecca, badges and embroidered 'Bismillah' and 'Allah' (in Arabic), and even natural wood fibre toothbrushes. Similar items can be found in many of the other ordinary shops, and in the homes, few of which do not display a picture of Mecca in a prominent place.

The younger generation

The main concern and focus of attention of Muslim populations and mosque leaders is to ensure that the next generation is not lost to Islam, thus efforts and resources are devoted to the Muslim instruction of children. Some children are sent to read the Quran in private homes where an individual takes in a small group of students. Others attend classes at the *madrasa* of the mosques. Altogether the vast majority of children go through some measure of Islamic schooling and all the mosques we visited held Quran classes at least. Some of the big mosques sent mini-buses around to collect children.

Despite unanimity on the need for Islamic instruction, the shape it takes leads to divided opinions and an ongoing debate. On the one hand some people feel that extra lessons over and above normal school hours and homework overburden the children; they would like these classes to take place within school hours; at this stage however this is wishful thinking as the issue of religious education in state schools is far from being resolved, as far as Muslims are concerned.

Another area of contention is that of teaching methods in the different mosques. Many smaller mosques adopt a traditional teaching approach, especially if the teacher is not familiar with the English environment and language. The children are taught simply to decipher the Quran which literally entails reading it without understanding the meaning of the text itself, let alone discussing it. The Quran is written in Arabic and most of these children speak Punjabi or Bengali, their mother tongue; even the minority of children whose parents come from an Arab country such as Yemen are not equipped to understand classical Arabic. The more dynamic leaders of mosques point to the danger inherent in this form of teaching: that it is totally ineffectual or even negative in effect. They are well aware of the qualitatively different environment surrounding children in European countries. It is felt that British schools lack discipline and encourage the children to seek understanding and be ready to question the teacher; this is reinforced by the attitude of the children's English peers. The undisputed respect and reverence which is expected by traditional *imams* is likely to be lacking in children brought up in the UK. Moreover, the overpowering western ideology is not only taught at school but pervades the media — television, radio, videos. These values are perceived as a concrete threat moulding the ideas and behaviour of Muslim children and which cannot be counteracted by traditional methods of reading the Quran (i.e. literally reading it through without understanding a word).

A number of mosques have launched a debate on the teaching of Islam within the new circumstances of living in British society. They advocate modifications and adaptations capable of meeting the 'onslaught of westernism'. In the first place, in those mosques, English is used as a medium of communication alongside, or instead, of Urdu and Arabic, as the children feel more comfortable using English — in fact at classes that I attended, the children would answer in English even when they were addressed in Urdu. In a few cases, a 'bilingual' Quran is used for advanced studies, with the text in English matching the corresponding page in Arabic; thereafter discussion and comments on a particular passage take place in English. In the biggest and best organized mosques the life of Prophet Mohammed, the history of Islam and Islamic law are also studied, in addition to Urdu, Arabic and/or Bengali as language subjects. The leaders of a few reputable mosques take pride in the high standard of the teaching in their institutions. Some of these classes have led to the taking of GCE O-level examinations in Urdu and Arabic. An annual award ceremony of certificates and prizes is the highlight of the year for children and parents. Birmingham dignitaries are invited. The event impresses on everyone the seriousness of the teaching and stimulates interest and efforts which are rewarded by the public recognition of achievements.

In a mosque in Coventry Road measures taken to ensure a proper Muslim education for children have resulted in the creation of a fee-paying private Muslim school for thirteen boys. It started in September 1985, and as yet it is still difficult to form an opinion on its development. But already some of the people I interviewed have expressed doubts about the standard of education. Another important mosque has established its own college of Muslim 'priests' who are boarders (twelve boys), with a view to forming a new generation of British-bred Muslim scholars and *imams*.

The vanguard of Muslim leaders in Birmingham do not have any doubts about the superiority of Muslim values over western ones, but they believe that these values have to be well explained and fully understood by youngsters and adolescents to stand any chance of being preserved. They consider that in western societies common sense and family-transmitted ideology cannot possibly be sufficient on account of the incompetence and ignorance of traditional *ulema*[4] and parents.

Issues of Concern

Through this Islamic instruction parents and Muslim leaders hope to impart the values which are essential to Islam. In addition to religious rites and practices a number of issues are worth considering as they assume particular importance in a non-Islamic society.

1. *Family life* is the basis and cornerstone of Islamic society. It is seen as an institution founded by Allah's will and going back to the beginning of the creation (Adam and Eve). Obedience and respect for parents is constantly stressed in Islamic teachings. In reality, the preservation of a tightly-knit family network has undoubtedly been an asset for the maintaining of an Islamic way of life in Britain. The basis of the Islamic family, as expounded in the sacred sources, is marriage. According to Islam, marriage is recommended as it contributes to keeping a balance between the spiritual and bodily requirements, and fulfils one's duties to Allah. The arranged marriages, which are the norm among the Muslim populations such as Pakistanis and Bangladeshis, are not the result of Muslim prescription. According to Islamic law, marriage is a sacred contract between two parties, the bridegroom and the bride, and any marriage contracted without the permission of the girl is generally invalid. Arranged marriages have a cultural basis and, on the whole, like the family system, contribute to the preservation of Islam as they ensure that no 'deviant' will be brought in who might disrupt the internal harmony of a Muslim family. Yet the family can also hinder the transmission of Islam to the next generation through the possible breakdown of communications between parents and children. Most of the parents come from rural areas and are not educated; many have kept a world outlook totally alien to the workings of the host society. It may be difficult for them to understand their children brought up in a completely different context in Britain, and vice versa.

2. *Girls and women*: in this context, the most problematic area is that of the position of girls. The mosque communities and parents show a great deal of concern for the education of girls as they are seen to be more vulnerable in British society which contravenes all the rules of good Muslim behaviour for girls, in particular because it mixes sexes in all spheres of life including school. According to my survey 1000 girls attend classes in the mosques, constituting one third of the pupils. Muslim leaders describe the girls as the mothers of tomorrow: they will be the ones who transmit a proper Muslim way of life and values to childen to come, as their prime responsibility is to be the rearing of the family. They could jeopardize the whole family structure ('the basis of Islamic society') if they did not conform. As culture intertwines with religion the whole family honour (*izzat*) can be thrown into disrepute by a daughter's behaviour. There are two main areas where a clash of aspirations between parents and daughters is likely to be sharpest: marriage and education.

In arranged marriages where these are customary, if a girl does not feel ready to marry or does not like the partner chosen by her parents a potential crisis exists in the case where no compromise can be reached. But these are still uncommon situations.

Most girls wish to pursue their education at least until sixteen and some would like to attend further education courses leading to a career. The choice of an acceptable career for a woman is itself a dilemma, but the main issue remains education. On many occasions parents withdraw their daughters from schooling as soon as it is legally possible (at sixteen) and in some cases daughters are kept at home (or sent back to the home country) as soon as they finish primary school. The main reason for this is that Muslim parents refuse to send their daughters to mixed schools: single-sex schools are very scarce and there are no single-sex colleges or universities. This is a source of great frustration for the girls and they have been known to run away from home for that reason. In some instances the mosques reinforce the parents' decision. In other cases mosque leaders have intervened in order to reconcile both parties and convince parents to be more flexible. One of the mosques has taken steps to found a women's hostel to ensure that women and girls in that situation would at least find a home in a good Muslim environment. Muslims feel that other women's hostels are inadequate, such as the one called Link House which is run by non-Muslims under the auspices of Birmingham City Council.

Paradoxically, Islam emphasizes the value of education for boys *and* girls; the biggest and more dynamic mosques, such as the *Jamiat Ahl-e-Hadith*, make a point of organizing classes for girls which go beyond Quran reading. The girls who are well voiced in Islam are then able to find arguments in Islam itself to further their insistence on pursuing their education.

3. *Leisure*: although most of the leisure time is spent amongst kin, mainly in family visits, it has become evident that alternative activities are necessary as Muslim leaders fear that the opportunities, or rather temptations, of British society might attract young Muslim people. This risk is seen to be aggravated by the high rate of unemployment which does not offer them tangible opportunities. The frustration and disillusionment they experience may lead to their greater affinity with other young people, who gather together in gangs, loiter in cafés and gambling places or discos (this applies mostly to boys, as girls are generally kept at home). Moreover the existing youth centres are seen as unsuitable because boys and girls mix freely there, drink is available, drugs may be circulated.

Muslim leaders feel that Islam can offer an ideological alternative and the better organized mosques have begun to propose counter activities. This area of work of the mosque is still fairly undeveloped as yet: they have a few items of equipment such as table tennis and snooker tables. Six of the mosques have a bookshop and/or library. A Muslim scout group was formed in Saltley. Some organize holiday trips and camps. It was stressed by one of the Muslim organizers that these camps were not designed for religious instruction but fitted in sports and games within the pattern and rhythm of life of Islam and provided opportunities for the discussion of issues. Attempts to cater for girls are fewer and less successful.

The Muslim leaders who have expressed great concern for the young people, however, still deplore the fact that the mosques are mostly frequented by very young or old people and have not yet succeeded in attracting adolescents in substantial numbers.

Interaction with British institutions

Having organized the reproduction of Islamic faith and practices within their own communities, Muslims also took into account interaction with British society. Muslim communities are in Britain to stay and they are now attempting to make inroads into British institutions so that a space can be gradually opened for Muslims.

A major area of concern is the education system as it is correctly seen by the 'first generation' as a determining factor in the formative years of young Muslims. Several initiatives have been taken by mosque representatives and a number of individual parents linked to Muslim associations, who have contacted schools in areas populated by Muslims. One specific feature of the British education system is that it gives a large measure of discretion to heads of schools. This flexibility has enabled the heads, who have recognized the need to take into account the presence (sometimes 90 per cent) of pupils of Muslim origin, to introduce adjustments despite the absence of any statutory directive. To take the example of a particular school, where 52 per cent of the pupils are of Muslim origin (Ward End School in Washwood Heath), the following measures have been implemented for Muslims:

> One visiting Muslim, from the Sparkbrook Islamic Association comes to take the assembly twice a week.
> For two weeks before *Eid* festivals the assemblies are devoted to items relating to Islam.
> The religious education syllabus includes Islam.
> Muslim pupils are given the opportunity to offer their Friday noon prayer.
> Girls are allowed to wear their own style of clothes: tunics and trousers (*shalwar, kameez*) provided these conform to the school uniform colour, this is a common practice in many schools attended by Muslims
> Girls can opt out of swimming and for physical education wear tracksuits instead of the regulation short skirt.

This example is not an isolated one. At the time of *Eid*, a social gathering is organized in some schools with the cooperation of parents who prepare the food for the event. A few school heads have also made a conscious effort to appoint a member of the community on their staff, as a teacher or as a school liaison officer. These achievements may sound impressive compared with the situation which obtained ten or fifteen years ago. This is illustrated by an incident quoted in the *Birmingham Post* (7 January 1970) headlined 'Five Muslim girls banned from school for wearing trousers'. As a result, they had missed school since November 1969.

In reality modifications that have occurred, have been on an *ad hoc* basis and have depended entirely on the understanding and goodwill of individual headteachers. Here again, the specific features of the British education system open the door to a series of demands and contentions. The Education Act of 1944 makes it a legal requirement to hold morning assemblies and to include religious education on the curriculum in state schools, yet at the same time regulations do not incorporate any guidelines which could take into account the existence of a substantial Muslim population. This has motivated the mosques and Muslim associations to form a group dealing with the issue of education. The Muslim Liaison Committee had brought together more than fifty Muslim organizations by 1983. There are now sixty-five affiliated organizations. One of its main objectives, in addition to advising Muslim parents, is to negotiate a series of measures, aimed at Muslim children in schools within the Birmingham Local Education Authority, on the basis of a thirteen points memorandum. The initial reactions of the Birmingham press expressed outrage at the MLC initiative as Mahmood Ahmad Mirpuri notes in 'The rights of Muslim pupils in Birmingham schools' where he applies himself to answer the *Birmingham Post*. A working group has been formed composed of seven Muslim Liaison Committee representatives, five headteachers from inner city areas and five persons from the City Council department of education. They have agreed on a document which is neither statutory nor mandatory but will constitute guidelines for all headteachers of schools with Muslim pupils. This document is not available publicly as yet.

One salient issue is that of religious education. There is unanimity among parents and Muslim leaders that the school curriculum should incorporate Islam. There are differences of opinion however as to whether what is needed is religious education or religious instruction. In the latter case Muslims feel that it cannot possibly be taught by a non-Muslim. In addition to the actual teaching of Islam, a whole series of issues arise:

The morning assembly
The Friday congregational prayer
The availability of *halal* food
Holidays for the main Muslim celebrations *Eid-ul-Fitr* and *Eid-ul-Adha*
Exemption from sexual education
The question of girls' education, which includes several demands for single sex schools, or at least non-mixed physical education and swimming classes, modest clothing (the uniform is unacceptable as skirts are compulsory)
The employment of more Muslim staff, there are only between ten and fifteen Muslim teachers out of 11,000 in the Birmingham Local Education Authority
The teaching of the mother tongue (this is not directly associated with religion).

We do not know as yet the extent to which these points have been met by the education authority. The negotiations between the MLC and the education authority have been protracted. Most mosque leaders declare that they have adopted a patient attitude and have deliberately discarded the confrontational strategy used in Bradford. As a consequence, the slowness of the process has begun to irritate a number of mosque representatives who are now proposing a tougher attitude. Others have expressed the view that the MLC is too big and cumbersome to constitute an efficient committee. The response to the document still remains to be seen.

One issue which is debated at the moment is that of separate Muslim schools. It has not been put forward as a vehement demand although Muslims in Birmingham would welcome them. But even some hardliners have expressed caution on that issue, insisting on the need to ensure a good academic level of education in such schools. Others would prefer to use this demand as a bargaining lever. But in any case realism is prevalent and it was stated frequently that, even if there were Muslim schools, there would not be enough of them to cater for all the Muslim children; a large number of Muslims would still have to attend state schools. The preservation of single-sex schools for girls runs counter to the process of comprehensivization undertaken in Birmingham. Within the Birmingham Local Education Authority, there are ten girls' schools left out of ninety-nine secondary state schools. A compromise appears to have been reached by the working party on this matter.[5]

Parents and Muslim leaders also deplore what they consider to be a lack of discipline in state schools. This has led a number of them to enrol their children in Catholic, Jewish or Church of England schools. Ironically, in a few cases it has reached such proportions that some of these schools have a majority of Muslim pupils. The voluntary sector school authorities have expressed some concern as to whether these schools will continue to keep their denominational characteristics.

Education is the main area in which Muslims have made concrete efforts to intervene and interact with British society. But it is not the only one. As part of their pastoral work, *imams* or mosque representatives visit hospitals and prisons. They are also in contact with the social services and provide an informal advisory service. Some of the mosques have established contacts with churches in their area with which they hold regular meetings. For example in Highgate the Central Mosque entertains a particularly friendly relationship with their neighbourhood Baptist church and its very open-minded minister. The Islamic Resource Centre takes part in multi-faith encounters; such as religious celebrations comprising Muslims, Jews and Christians. It also collaborated with the Selly Oak Colleges and Birmingham University to organize a series of lectures on Islam. The bigger associations also pay attention to public relations such as inviting dignitaries like the Lord Mayor and Mayoress to preside over the prize-giving ceremony at the *Markazi Jamiat Ahl-e-Hadith*. The Sparkbrook Islamic Association organizes *Eid* parties for a variety of guests including the neighbouring school and church staff, social workers, and councillors.

Altogether, one feels that changes and progress remain very slow, and Muslims display a remarkable patience. Despite their repeated assertions that Islam does not distinguish between political and religious worlds, Muslims have been least incisive in their efforts to intervene in the political arena. Mosques and Muslim associations have approached local authorities for planning permission and grants, mostly under the inner city urban partnership scheme. Most of the grants accorded were destined for mother tongue teaching programmes or community centre activities. Muslims are remarking that there is a reticence on the part of the authorities to award grants for religious projects and some have voiced their discontent on this matter, from my survey 68 per cent of the mosques felt that local government authorities are unhelpful. Nevertheless Muslim organizations have not cut themselves off from British political and local authority institutions. They currently approach city and county councillors or MPs for advice or for help. From my survey only 5 per cent of the mosques had never approached a councillor or MP. The few Muslim city councillors in office have not been elected as a result of an organized Muslim lobby. Although Muslim organizations will state that it would be useful to have more Muslim councillors or MPs (there is no Muslim MP in Birmingham), they have not attempted to sponsor any candidate to further their interests. Both councillors of Muslim origin consider this a weakness partly due to the lack of unity of Muslims and partly due to a lack of political will.

This paper has shown that Muslims cannot be ignored in Birmingham in 1986. They have already been successful in setting up numerous mosques in order to create better conditions for Islamic observance. Islam is thriving and its followers are attempting to install structures for the continuation of their religion. A great deal of effort has been devoted to measures addressed to the younger generation. Muslims have been capable of creating facilities for religious instruction within their own communities. They are also endeavouring to make a place for themselves within British institutions, in particular the education system. Progress is very slow, but, certainly, progress there will be. And there are already indications that the next generation, when it takes over, will make use of its better knowledge of and participation in British society in order to ensure a place for Islam.

Notes

1. The partition of India and Pakistan (1947) and the building of the Mangla Dam in Mirpur (early 1960s).
2. These figures include people born in Pakistan or Bangladesh and those who live in a house whose head of household is Pakistani or Bangladeshi.
3. Literally, the house of Islam, i.e. a Muslim country.
4. Muslim scholars.
5. A document pertaining to this matter was released in November 1986.

References

Hodgins, H. 1981. Planning permission for mosques — the Birmingham experience. *Research Papers: Muslims in Europe* 9:11-27. Birmingham: Centre for the Study of

Islam and Christian-Muslim Relations, Selly Oak Colleges.

———. 1985. Ethnic Minorities in Birmingham: Populations Statistics. Unpublished paper. Birmingham Community Relations Council.

Nielsen, J.S. 1983. UK Statistical Sources: Religion. Other Religions. Unpublished paper. Birmingham: Centre for the Study of Islam and Christian-Muslim Relations, Selly Oak Colleges.

———. 1984. Muslim Immigration and Settlement in Britain. *Research Papers: Muslims in Europe*, 21. Birmingham: Centre for the Study of Islam and Christian-Muslim Relations, Selly Oak Colleges.

3
Muslims in Britain and Local Authority Responses

Jørgen S. Nielsen

There have been Muslim communities in parts of Britain for over a century, and before that numerous individual Muslims visited or settled in this country.[1] The diversion of the sea routes between Britain and India into the Red Sea with the opening of the Suez Canal in 1869, was the immediate cause of the first communal settlement of Arabs from Aden and its hinterland. Recruited for work on ships, some made their homes in the main sea ports of Britain. Together with people with other backgrounds, including British converts to Islam, they formed the nucleus of small Muslim communities in places like Liverpool, Cardiff, South Shields, and London. Some moved inland, and by the 1930s Birmingham had its first mosque, frequented mainly by Yemeni Arabs. After the second world war, the growth of Islam in Britain became an integral part of the whole process of immigration of labour from various parts of the empire and its successor states. The enormous growth of immigration from Pakistan during the 1960s and early 1970s was added to immigration of traditionally Muslim groups from parts of East and West Africa, Cyprus, parts of the West Indies and Guyana, as well as India and Bangladesh. Although other groups have arrived since, in particular from the Arab world and Iran, the public face of Islam in Britain is still very much dominated by Muslims of Pakistani and Bangladeshi background.

Although estimates of the total Muslim population in Britain vary according to source from half a million to two million, the most reasonable estimates lie between three quarters and one million. As is to be expected, they are concentrated in the big conurbations, London, the West Midlands, South and West Yorkshire, and Greater Manchester with smaller groups in many other towns. Compared with populations of Muslims in some other countries of Europe there is in Britain a noticeable proportion of professionals, merchants, and small independent businessmen, who provide a leadership resource which is, on the whole, not available to, for example, that part of the Turkish population in West Germany which identifies itself as Muslim. Two other distinguishing factors apply to most of the Muslim community in Britain; namely, the comparative legal security of citizenship or the residential status of Commonwealth citizens, and the relatively lengthy period which the major proportion have lived here. Both factors mean that the communities have made a greater investment in their presence here. This applies particularly to the community leaderships, which have found their role here, and to the approximate 40 per cent of Muslims who have been born in Britain, an increasing proportion of whom are now moving through secondary school and into family life and higher education.

For a long time Muslims have been making their own demands on the public structures of British society. These demands have taken the form of individual claims for respect towards their religious requirements, expressed sometimes in basic forms like the withdrawal of children from religious education lessons in school. At the other end of the scale have been demands that central government adopt policies or arrange for legislation to meet Muslim needs which have been particularly expressed; for example, the introduction of Muslim family law. Some Muslim organizations have concentrated their efforts on lobbying central government, parliament and political parties. The polite expressions of support they sometimes receive is occasionally reported in the Muslim press abroad as a change in policy. Thus, last year one newspaper published in Pakistan mistakenly reported that the British government had agreed to allocate land for mosques in several major British cities.

This incident is symptomatic of a basic misunderstanding of the way in which much of government in Britain has, at least hitherto, worked. The decentralized nature of public authority in Britain is unusual compared with many other countries, not only in Africa and Asia but also in Europe. Many aspects of public control and organization are in the hands of local authorities, and even those which are in some way controlled by central government are often administered by local government. It is at this level that one should look for adaptation to Muslim requirements, and there has been substantial anecdotal evidence to suggest that in many areas working relations between local government and ethnic and religious minority groups have existed for some time.

This study presents the results of a simple survey carried out during 1985. Based on a crude reading of tables, relating to place of birth in the 1981 census, I identified local authorities in Britain which had a significant (roughly 2 per cent and over) Muslim population within their boundaries. Forty-six district councils, fifteen metropolitan district councils, and sixteen London boroughs fitted this criterion. As some London boroughs are not responsible for education, the appropriate education authority, that of Inner London, was added. For similar reasons eight county councils and the Strathclyde Regional Council were also brought into the survey. The total number of authorities thus contacted was eighty-seven. The authorities identified were sent a first letter on 19 December 1984 asking for information on the following points:

1. *Burial.* (a) Are particular areas of cemeteries set aside for Muslim burial? (b) Are Muslims permitted to inter their dead according to their customs, e.g. with cloth rather than coffin?
2. *Slaughter.* Do Muslims have access to (a) cattle and (b) poultry slaughter according to their religious requirements?
3. *Worship.* Do Muslims in the employ of your authority have the right (a) to days off on religious festivals, and (b) to time off for Friday noon prayer?
4. *Education.* (a) Is there a policy on the part of the authority regarding making school facilities available for Muslim religious instruction? (b) What is the authority's practice regarding mother-tongue teaching? (c) How do school meals make allowances for Muslim dietary rules? (d) What is the authority's policy on school uniforms for Muslim girls? (e) What is the authority's practice regarding sex education? (f) What is the authority's policy on racism and/or multicultural education?
5. *Voluntary schools.* Has the authority been approached regarding the possibility of establishing a Muslim voluntary school? If so, when? What is the current situation of the approach (rejected, accepted, under discussion)?
6. *Planning permission.* (a) What are the authority's policy guidelines on planning permission for mosques and places of private Islamic instruction? (b) How many mosques are known to be functioning with and without planning permission?
7. *Literacy.* (a) Does the authority have a literacy programme directed specifically at Asian women; how does it function? (b) Does the library service have a policy of encouraging Asian language users?

Two reminders were sent during 1985, one in May and one in October, so the responses do not have a common reference date. In some instances, therefore, policies which were under consideration at the time of response may have been accepted or rejected since. All in all, seventy-nine authorities responded.

Table 1. Responses from a 1985 survey of local authorities with significant Muslim populations

	Number approached	Number responded
County Councils	8	8
London Boroughs	16	12
Metropolitan District Councils	15	14
Inner London Education Authority	1	0
Strathclyde Region	1	1
District Councils	46	44
	87	79

In the following sections I shall be surveying the response to those questions which concern Muslims most and have the greatest direct relevance to local authority policy-making. The areas thus covered will be planning permission for mosques, access to time off for worship, burial, slaughter and education. Multicultural education will be mentioned only in passing, and literacy and library provision will be omitted, since all of these affect much wider areas and bring in issues wider than the immediate concerns of this paper.

Planning permission and mosques

'All the world is a mosque' is apt in the sense that a Muslim can prostrate himself in prayer anywhere. All that is required is a demarcated cleaned space. At its simplest, this is achieved by laying a prayer carpet on the ground at the required time. The sight of a truck driver praying thus by the side of the road is familiar to those acquainted with the Muslim world. But as Islam is a religion which stresses community, the ritual prayer (*salat* or *namaz*) is ideally to be performed in congregation, particularly at Friday noon, the so-called *juma* prayer. For this reason there have been special buildings for the purpose of worship since the time of the Prophet Muhammad. The term mosque is derived from the Arabic *masjid*, meaning a place of prostration. Another common term is *jami*, a place of congregation, often translated 'Friday mosque'. In Britain, the distinction between the two terms is generally reflected when the term '*jami* mosque' is used for a central mosque.

The function of the mosque in Britain is not limited to the set prayers, and this also reflects the fact that mosques historically have been the gathering places of the Muslim community in all its activities. Where there is a mosque it should be expected that Islamic instruction also takes place, usually for children but often also for adults. Some mosques have begun to offer social facilities for the elderly and for young people, although the availability of space in smaller premises places limitations on such projects. Larger mosques will try to have facilities for the necessary washing of the dead before burial (see below). A very few have managed to incorporate a morgue, so that a body can be kept in decent conditions until burial is possible.

First and foremost, though, is the role of the mosque as a place of worship. The set prayers take place five times a day according to the position of the sun (Ahsan and McDermott 1980; 24ff). A number of Muslim organizations around the country regularly produce prayer timetables specifying exactly what these times are. As most mosques serve quite localized communities, worshippers will normally walk to the mosque, an action which is, in any case, recommended for the devout. Only the larger central mosques, serving wider areas or the business communities in city centres, are likely to need car parking space of the level associated with many Christian churches.

The call to prayer is part of the ritual requirement of prayer and is usually performed inside the prayer hall of the British mosques. Very few mosques have sought permission to call to prayer over outside loud speakers. Such permission was granted to the Birmingham Central Mosque in the spring of 1986 in the context of a debate which attracted the attention of the national press.

As far as public authorities are concerned, mosques can exist in two ways. A building may be certified as a place of worship under the 1852 and 1855 Places of Worship Registration Acts. The register is maintained by the General Register Office (GRO) in England and Wales (a different system applies in Scotland) and is published at irregular intervals by the Office of Population Censuses and Surveys (GRO 1981). From the accounts of officials at the GRO it seems that most applications for registration are made with the purpose of getting a reduction in the local rates (property tax). A building can also be granted planning permission to function as a place of worship or education (or both) under the Town and Country Planning Act 1971 which, as far as mosques are concerned, is administered by district councils and London boroughs. It should be stressed that while registration is not a legal requirement for function as a mosque, planning permission is.

On this basis it is possible to give an estimate of the number of mosques in Britain and their growth (see Table 2).

Table 2. Mosques registered with the GRO 1970–85

Year	Annual	Accumulated
1970	10	51
1971	8	59
1972	8	67
1973	8	75
1974	8	83
1975	16	99
1976	21	120
1977	18	138
1978	20	158
1979	16	174
1980	20	194
1981	31	225
1982	21	246
1983	22	268
1984	31	299
1985	30	329

These figures are based on inspection of the Register; no account is taken of buildings taken off the Register since 1980.

Many of the local authorities surveyed responded either that they did not know of any mosques functioning in their areas, or that their files did not allow them to distinguish the denomination of any particular place of worship. But fifty-one authorities out of a possible seventy-one among those responding (the eight county councils do not deal with this area) gave numbers of mosques in their areas. Several mosques were operating with temporary permission, and others had been given permission on specific conditions. There were known to be mosques operating without permission in thirteen authorities. In the areas surveyed the overall number of mosques with some form of permission was 217, while a further 35 mosques without permission were known.

The boundaries of local authorities and registration districts do not always coincide, so it is difficult to make a simple comparison between the two sets of data. But it can be done in some areas (see Table 3).

Table 3. Mosques in selected areas in 1985

Area	Survey	GRO
Birmingham	26	28
Blackburn	13	21
Bolton	9	8
Bradford	26	18
Bury	4	4
Manchester	8	10
Peterborough	3	4
Scunthorpe	2	4
Sheffield	13	7
Walsall	8	12
Wandsworth	4	5
Westminster	1	3

The discrepancies may be due in part to slight differences of boundary and to different reference dates. The one or two major discrepancies suggest that some authorities are not fully aware of the situation, that some mosques may be registered but not have planning permission, and that some mosques have not been registered.

Experience has shown a number of authorities that the Muslim requirements and the nature of mosques differs sufficiently from that of existing religious buildings to warrant some form of re-evaluation. This process has been very uneven across the country. Most authorities, in fact, responded that applications would be considered on their merits in the same way as other applications. A few authorities reported that they have decided to develop a new approach (e.g. Waltham Forest). Calderdale stated that they did not differentiate except that 'a condition would normally be included with any permission restricting any amplification except for the midday call to prayer.' Compared with the practice of most councils, this is quite permissive despite the wording. Some authorities have approached the problem not by developing special guidelines but rather by investigating the needs of the various communities and on that basis adopting an active policy of meeting those needs particularly by helping in identifying suitable sites. Thus Crawley states that:

> Specific sites are now being examined for a number of these groups, and in the event of these sites being mutually acceptable . . . applications for planning permission will be sought and terms negotiated for leasing the sites.

A similar process was considered by Leicester but it came to the conclusion that the responsibility for finding appropriate sites rested with the communities concerned. The report did, however, encourage the churches to consider a more efficient use of existing premises with a view to joint operations thus freeing some buildings for the use of other religions. The document concludes by adopting new guidelines for dealing with applications for religious buildings.

In this way Leicester joined the other authorities which have changed policy in relation to minority religious needs, particularly those of Muslim communities, in all fourteen of the authorities surveyed. Some of these policy decisions amount to no more than a brief paragraph or two stating intent. Thus the draft city plan of Southampton says:

> Within Southampton is a variety of religious and minority groups, and the City Council will continue to attempt to accommodate these through the provision of suitable sites or buildings wherever possible. To ensure good accessibility these are generally likely to be located within the Central area.

The experience of other authorities suggests that the preference for the central area is not likely to satisfy the Muslim community.

Lambeth declares its sympathetic treatment of applications and in the context of its local plan states its preference for the conversion of redundant churches for use by other religious communities. Slightly more detailed guidelines are applied by Scunthorpe, although without the status of adopted policy, and by Brent. Scunthorpe accepts that religious use is suitable for a residential area as long as due consideration is taken of possible noise nuisance to neighbours. It is stressed that experience has shown little need for car parking space, as most worshippers arrive on foot. Brent prefers main road locations to avoid the problem of noise to neighbours and prefers that a religious building should retain its function. Planning officers are to be flexible and actively help applicants. Coventry, in a policy statement of 1983, 'actively welcomes the establishment of facilities for religious and cultural groups'. Temples and mosques are suitable for residential areas, while cultural buildings are to be encouraged 'primarily in non-residential areas'. In both cases it is judged that residential property is not appropriate. Hounslow (policy adopted December 1981) encourages religious minority groups but refers them to the 'normal planning requirements' and specifies that the premises be detached. A relatively strict requirement of car parking space of one car to five persons of accommodation is imposed. The policy does, however, allow for exceptions especially when no social or educational activity is envisaged or where the building is surrounded by followers of the relevant religion, and there is no 'overwhelming' local objection.

There remain eight local authorities which have adopted detailed policy guidelines. The earliest of these was Birmingham. The initial policy, adopted in November 1973, was restrictive in a number of ways (Hodgins 1981: 16ff).

Permission was temporary, limited to use between the hours of 08.00 and 22.30, car parking was to be satisfactory, the property was to be detached, and no material alterations to it allowed. This created a situation where numbers of applications were unsuccessful, application proceedings became lengthy and complicated, and eventually the policy was in effect overruled in certain aspects when the Secretary of State on appeal allowed applications which had previously been rejected by the local authority. The import of these decisions was to allow the use of residential property, to reduce the importance of the requirement for off-street car parking, and to stress the importance to a local community of having a local place of worship. In 1981 a new policy was thus adopted which allowed a much more flexible approach. The new policy distinguished:

a. Purpose-built prayer houses, generally with a wide catchment area.
b. Small prayer houses serving a local area, usually created by a change of use.
c. Local educational, social and cultural facilities. The first two types of facility will often be in the same place.

Quite strict requirements were imposed on buildings in category a), including consideration of local amenities, car parking, and traffic. It is worth noting though that flexibility continues to be central as, for example, when the parking space necessary is suggested as somewhere between ratios of 1:5 and 1:20 of cars to regular worshippers, depending on local circumstances. It is worth noting also that there is now allowance for flexibility of design: 'The site must be capable of absorbing a non-traditional design, of non-domestic scale.'

It was categories b) and c) which had created the main problems under the 1973 policy, and it is here that the major changes were introduced. Semi-detached properties and end-terrace houses are now regarded as acceptable, especially if the religious official is resident in the neighbouring property. Only when a mosque is situated on a main road should off-street car parking be a consideration. Normally noise will only be a factor when the property is also used for instruction of children who 'are usually noisier as they arrive and leave and as certain lessons may be relatively noisy'. Restrictions of use to certain times of day will not normally be imposed. In its response to the survey, the Birmingham planning department notes that before the adoption of the 1981 policy there was only one purpose-built mosque and thirteen permitted house mosques, a further twelve were known in unauthorized use. Since then a further three purpose-built mosques have been granted planning permission, and nine of the unauthorized cases have been resolved, evidence of the improvement brought about by the new policy.

Whether the Birmingham experience was consciously adopted as a model by other authorities is not known. It is, however, typical of some. Kirklees adopted a similar policy in 1978, which, in the light of experience, was later amended to conform more closely to the Birmingham model — especially on the type of property, neighbourhood, and car parking. However, these amendments were in the form of exemptions in particular circumstances from the continuing general rules, and were to be applied in the form of only temporary permission for two years to allow the community time to find more suitable premises.

The policy adopted by Wellingborough in February 1979 takes the form of guidelines for applicants and is in several ways similar to the original Birmingham policy. Flexibility over parking is noted although there is a general car parking ratio of 1:10. There is an insistence that only detached property can be converted to religious use in residential areas, and new buildings should be designed so as to be integrated with the surrounding area.

In 1979 the planning department of Walsall undertook a review of the 'needs of ethnic minority groups', which reported in February the following year. The report explicitly took into account the experience of a number of other local authorities. The recommendations on policy subsequently adopted by the planning committee are in essence similar to that of Wellingborough. Permanent use basically has to conform with general planning rules but exceptions can be made in the form of a two-year period of temporary permission while the community finds more suitable premises. The following circumstances would assist in obtaining such temporary permission:

1. If the neighbouring houses are wholly or predominantly occupied by members of the same religious community.
2. If the use is restricted to worship and religious activities with the specific exclusion of social activities and education, when these can be accommodated in other buildings such as local schools.
3. If no material alterations are to be made to the building which would prejudice its return to previous use.
4. If the applicants can demonstrate a genuine inability to obtain more suitable premises in the area.

Birmingham's policy appears also to have been the model for the guidelines published by Leicester, Stoke-on-Trent and Sheffield, although they all take a more restrictive view about the necessity for off-street car parking, appear more reluctant to permit conversion of semi-detached or end-terrace housing, and are less prepared to accept the educational and social activity accompanying worship. If these activities are intended, then premises are preferred in areas of mixed use, usually in the vicinity of shopping districts. Just as Birmingham's policy has become a model for a number of other authorities, so might the guidelines published by Sheffield (Sheffield 1983) justifiably be advanced as a model for public presentation and guidance.

Prayer and festivals

In this as in other areas, there is great variation among Muslims as to how strictly they will abide by the religious requirements. In the matter of the five daily prayers there is, in any event, a good deal of flexibility in the timing. The exact times listed on the various prayer timetables available apply to prayers said in mosques in congregation and to those who are not legitimately hindered by other considerations:

> Winter: The winter months . . . do bring the midday, the afternoon and the after-sunset prayers very close together, but there is quite a degree of flexibility in which these prayers (of about ten minutes duration) can be given. The midday prayer can be timed at schools and work places to coincide with the lunch break between 12 noon and 1.00 p.m.; the afternoon prayer between 2.30 p.m. and 3.30 p.m. and the after-sunset prayer between 4.00 p.m. and 5.00 p.m. The morning prayer can, in most cases, be said at home from dawn to about 7.30 a.m. and the night prayer . . . can be said any time till dawn of the following day, though before midnight is strongly recommended.
>
> Summer: This provides little real difficulty as the time gaps between each prayer are quite long; in schools and colleges the midday prayer is the only one that needs to be arranged and this can be between 1.00 p.m. and 4.00 p.m., as there is usually sufficient time to return home before the late afternoon prayer. At work, arrangements are certainly easier in the summer than in winter. The morning prayer (except for night workers) can be said at home, the midday prayer as for schools, between 1.00 p.m. and 4.00 p.m., and the afternoon prayer up to 30 minutes before sunset. The total time involved in winter is about 35 minutes per day; in summer it is considerably less (Ahsan and McDermott 1980: 38ff).

The festivals in question are normally the two main ones. Eid al-Fitr starts at the end of the month of Ramadan and marks the end of the fast, one of the five pillars of Islam. Eid al-Adha, the feast of the sacrifice, coincides with the ninth day of the rites of the annual pilgrimage at Mecca, the *hajj*, another of the five pillars. Both occasions are usually marked by a two-day holiday.

Problems arise out of the festivals because they follow the lunar Islamic calendar and therefore move through the solar year in a 33-year cycle. Each month starts at the sighting of the new moon which cannot be predicted with absolute certainty, and as there is not yet agreement among Muslims in Britain about a common authority to follow, Eid al-Fitr can be a source of confusion. There will usually be nine days notice for Eid al-Adha.

The code for employers produced by the Commission for Racial Equality includes the statement that practice of religious obligations should not be used as a reason for discrimination. The only legal guidance on this matter is an unsatisfactory decision by the European Commission on Human Rights in the case of Mr Iftikhar Ahmed. The plaintiff had claimed unfair dismissal against the Inner London Education Authority, because it would not allow him to attend the midday congregational prayer on Friday afternoons while he was in full-time employment. The Commission said, in effect, that Muslim employees were entitled to time for Friday prayer in principle. But in this particular case, the complaint could not be upheld because the plaintiff had not informed his employers that his religious obligations might conflict with his duties, until six years after employment.[2]

The response of the authorities to this question showed enormous variations. Ten stated that they had not had a request for time off and a further sixteen that they do not have or are not aware of having Muslim employees. In some cases "the authority does not, therefore, have a policy for this matter" (Walsall). In other cases the response envisages scope for flexibility within existing arrangements, especially in the growing practice of working to some type of flexitime system:

> Although there are no Muslims currently employed by the Council, the working arrangements are based on a flexible hours system which would be able to accommodate their needs, e.g. by taking an early lunch break from noon day prayers, and by taking one day's leave (in lieu of hours worked in excess of the basic 37 hour week) each month for religious festivals (Oxford).

Oxford's response regarding religious festivals is unusual, in that most councils suggest that flexibility can be achieved by allowing days to be taken from annual leave entitlements rather than by saving up hours as part of a flexitime system. In fact, seventeen authorities report that they operate a flexitime system which would accommodate time-off for Friday noon prayers, while thirty-one say that festivals have to be taken out of annual leave entitlement. Leicester has adopted an official system whereby Muslims are allowed half a day on each of the two main festivals or one whole day on one festival as extra-statutory leave. But they have to give notice in February of each year that they intend to make use of this provision. If they do not, or if they fail to take the notified leave, they revert to general leave arrangements.

In most local authorities, terms of employment vary in practice among departments, and in some, departmental chief officers have discretion in the granting of time off. The requirements of different types of work have also contributed to such differences of practice. Teachers and other staff in schools have restricted scope for flexibility during term. However, some councils have found it possible to accommodate them. Strathclyde Regional Council has agreed to allow three days unpaid leave annually to school and nursery teachers, specifically for religious festivals, who otherwise could only take their paid annual leave during school holidays. Muslim teachers have been granted similar official arrangements in Barnet. Brent have also allowed employees bound by school terms a specified number of days leave for religious festivals, two days for Muslims and Hindus, three days for Jews. This arrangement has been put to the Council's Establishment Committee and the trade unions as a model to be extended to all council departments.

Local transport is a different matter because of the needs of bus timetables and complicated shift systems. Three authorities comment particularly on this, but with mixed results. Northampton says that time off for Friday noon prayer "could be permitted within the flex-time arrangements which apply unless impracticable in the case of a particular employee such as a Corporation bus driver operating to a published timetable." Cardiff views this rather more positively: "The City Transport Department employs a significant percentage of Muslims and operates a flexible working roster which, with the cooperation of non-Muslims and the use by Muslims of some of their annual leave quota, avoids any real problems with time off . . ."

A similar view is taken by Hyndburne, where religious festivals can be taken off in exchange for working on public holidays.

In general, the combination of flexitime working hours and use of annual leave entitlements to cater for Muslim needs would seem to justify the comment by Tameside: "It appears that most Muslim employees find the present arrangements satisfactory. This view has been confirmed by representatives of the local Council for Racial Equality."

Burial

According to Islamic requirements, the community owes four duties to the dead (Darsh 1981): washing of the corpse, its wrapping, funeral prayers, and burial, in that order. The first three can be performed at home, but it is preferred for obvious practical reasons, as well as for religious reasons, that facilities for these steps are available at a mosque. Purpose-built mosques will usually have such funeral facilities incorporated in their plans. Some larger converted buildings are also likely to have such facilities.

The dead should be buried as quickly as possible, and there is a widespread expectation that this means within twenty-four hours. In fact, if a mosque has morgue facilities, the urgency is less. Islamic law lays down quite specific requirements for a grave. These requirements differ according to whether the soil is solid or loose, dry or wet. Where the soil is wet, as in Britain, a coffin may be used — a shroud only is required in dry, desert type conditions. The grave should be aligned so that the body can lie on its side facing Mecca, in other words the alignment in Britain should be in the general direction south-west to north-east. Mourners are required to throw the first handfuls of dust on the coffin before the grave is filled in.

Two practical questions have arisen for local authorities out of these requirements, namely availability of space in cemeteries allowing the required alignment, and availability of graves at short notice. The solution adopted in most instances has been the allocation of special areas within cemeteries for Muslim burial, a practice which also meets the community's understandable wish to have Muslims buried in close proximity to each other. Of the authorities responding to the survey, fifty-eight stated that they make or are willing to make satisfactory arrangements. Several of the remaining authorities are not responsible for cemeteries or have not been faced with requests for special arrangements. Woking reports the existence of a privately-run cemetery which serves much of southern England and is used mostly by Muslims.

Although the question was not specifically asked, a number of responses included reference to the fact that Muslims might need burial at short notice. In most cases, a notice of at least forty-eight hours is normally required for burial in council cemeteries, and some of the regulations also specify that payment of the required fees has to be made at least twenty-four hours in advance of interment. Such conditions explicitly apply to Muslims in Southampton, where an area in a local cemetery was allocated to Muslims in 1969, but with the attached conditions which still apply:

1. The Right of Burial to be purchased in each grave.
2. Burials to take place betweeen the hours of 9 a.m. and 4 p.m. on Mondays to Fridays.
3. The time for each service not to exceed thirty minutes.
4. At least forty-eight hours notice of a burial to be given to the registrar excluding Saturdays, Sundays and bank holidays and any other public holiday when the cemetery is closed for burials.
5. A properly constructed coffin to be used.
6. All fees to be paid twenty-four hours prior to the burial taking place.
7. A suitable screen to be provided to ensure privacy if the coffin is to be opened at the graveside.
8. All funerals to be arranged and carried out by either the Society or a bona fide Funeral Director.

The remaining three conditions relate to other administrative matters.

Middlesbrough report that they have been asked to accommodate a number of customs, including burial at less than the usual forty-eight hours notice, correct alignment of graves, filling in of graves by mourners, and roofing over of the coffin to prevent direct contact with the soil. All these requests have been agreed to.

Manchester is another authority which has been faced with a variety of requests from the Muslim community. In February 1985, its Leisure Services Committee responded to a report from its officials by deciding to discuss with "the appropriate trade unions with the possibility of extending normal working hours on Fridays to 4.30 p.m., these discussions to include the possibility of employment of Muslims financed by Section 11 funding". Agreement in principle was given on other items including the mounding of graves. The practice of other authorities is to be investigated, as is the possibility of drawing up a formal agreement parallel to one already existing with the Jews.

Response to the question of burial in a shroud is mixed. For many Muslims, who are used to this practice from the country of origin, it is clearly very important — burial customs are often among those defended with the most vigour. Most authorities have a clear response that it cannot be allowed on grounds of health and hygiene. A small number report that they have not been faced with a request of this kind. Bradford and Kirklees allow burial in a shroud in one cemetary in each authority, and Bradford consider individual requests in other cemeteries favourably. Blackburn and Newport have similar arrangements.

It is to be expected that some urban authorities, like those four, should have acceded to Muslim requests. More surprising, perhaps, are the further three authorities which allow the practice, namely Waverley, Aylesbury Vale, and Windsor and Maidenhead. There is no indication in the responses of the process by which this situation has been arrived at.

In general, it is not possible from the responses to determine the extent to which this has been a significant issue. In some areas, Muslims have clearly not asked for shroud burials, while in others they have asked and been refused. Only in a very few cases, seven in all, is the practice permitted, although one or two further councils are considering the matter. More important has been access to cemetery plots allowing the proper alignment and the necessary privacy. This seems, on the whole, a matter which has been resolved — at least from the point of view of the local authorities. Plots are available, although in some instances under-used. Access to burial at short notice still remains, it seems, an unresolved issue. Most authorities continue to expect in the region of forty-eight hours notice, and weekends and public holidays remain out of bounds.

Education

As a number of practical problems facing Muslims have been sorted out to differing degrees of satisfaction, attention has increasingly turned to the educational scene. Schools and local education authorities (LEAs) in England have been faced with varying requests for special consideration from Muslims for about two decades. A survey published in 1971 (Townsend 1971: 61ff) suggests that during those early years, the main requests were for exemption from religious education (RE). Related to this were a few requests for schools to allow provision for Muslim religious instruction under school auspices. The second main area at issue until 1970 would appear to have been dress, both as concerned school uniforms (in particular for girls) and physical education and sports.

In the years since then, these particular issues have continued to surface but have become part of a larger complex of issues. It has become increasingly common to find schools in certain parts of the country where over half of the pupils are Muslims — indeed there are schools with over 75 per cent Muslim pupils. At the same time as the increase in pupil numbers, parents and community leaders have grown more familiar with the way in which LEAs and schools operate. Muslims have been settled in the country long enough to be aware of the ways in which they can apply pressure to achieve changes to their liking. At the same time, movements in the Islamic world have opened a discussion on Islamic concepts of education which are becoming a resource for formulating demands from the British educational system.

Over the last couple of years, these various developments have coincided, producing a series of determined efforts to gain changes in the schooling of

Muslim children. Given the decentralized structure of education, the form of these efforts have varied greatly from area to area. In a number of LEAs, Muslims have concentrated their energies on preventing the closure of the remaining girls' secondary schools. In other areas, the prime concern has been to influence either individual head teachers or the LEA to produce directives giving more flexibility on specific practical points. And then there are groups which in some areas have sought to establish Muslim voluntary schools.

An example of a Muslim approach, which is not untypical if, perhaps, more categorical than most, is a two-page paper originating in the South London Islamic Centre in Streatham, which has achieved a wide circulation in the Inner London area. It lists "the duties Muslim children MUST observe while they are at school and the provisions that the law of this country allows for them to carry out their duties". Parents are reminded that they may withdraw children from the daily assembly required by law. Prayer rooms should be provided in school for the daily prayers, and children should be allowed to attend the Friday noon prayer at the nearest mosque. Children are entitled to a holiday on the two main Muslim festivals, and it is suggested that schools with a large proportion of Muslim pupils should make the festivals official holidays. Special attention is paid to provision of *halal* food, and parents are advised to withdraw children from school dinners if it cannot be provided. Dress remains a particular concern, especially in swimming and physical education, and the paper provides detailed guidelines. Likewise, relations between the sexes is an issue. There should be segregated swimming and physical education lessons, and Muslim children should be withdrawn from sex education lessons. Finally, music and dancing are judged to be un-Islamic activities.

The concerns raised can usefully be divided into two categories, practical matters and curriculum, where the first mainly relates to food and dress, and the latter to teaching content, especially religious education, sex education, and multicultural education. The question of Muslim voluntary schools will be dealt with as a distinct theme.

Practical matters

Two issues dominate this area and have done so for a long time. Although all the local authority responses to the survey suggest that movement towards resolutions has been significant, they also indicate a good deal of variety across the country. The questions of dress would appear to have progressed the further, although in a manner which does not preclude the possibility of more local conflicts in the future. The basic Islamic requirement is for female dress which covers the whole body leaving only face, hands and feet free; and for male dress which covers the body from the navel to the thighs, in both cases in such a way as not to emphasize the shape of the body, i.e. loose fitting. These rules continue to apply in a single-sex environment, although here the dress may be closer fitting. This has implications for school uniforms, physical education and swimming lessons.

With its traditional insistence on school uniforms, the British education system creates problems which continuously surprise mainland Europeans. For a variety of reasons, seldom to do with the presence of ethnic or religious minority communities, the prevalence of school uniforms has fallen quite markedly in recent years. Only Sheffield states unequivocally that it has abolished uniforms altogether. In the majority of authorities, the decision remains with the head teacher and the school governors. Many urban schools have individually abolished the requirement for uniforms and do not, therefore, experience particular problems, as in the case of Haringey: "There is no Authority policy on school uniforms and the majority of schools, even at Secondary level, do not insist on special uniform. However, any request from parents to permit their children to wear clothes reflecting their Muslim background would be sympathetically dealt with."

The situation might be different in an area where uniforms are still widely used, even though the authority does not have a policy, as in Buckinghamshire: "No published policy. No problems in schools were uniform is voluntary. In others girls may wear trousers sometimes they have to fit in with the uniform colour scheme. Some schools allow traditional dress in school colours."

In three out of the twenty-eight responding LEAs, guidelines have been issued to head teachers, and in a further six the LEA has a policy of allowing Muslim girls to wear trousers, *shalwar* and *qamiz*, or other suitable attire. Brent reported that it was in the process of considering the adoption of such a policy. The picture is similar as regards dress for physical education and swimming where seven authorities indicate that they guide or tell their schools to permit girls to wear some form of acceptable dress, such as leotards or tracksuits. Kirklees is among these, although it has no policy on school uniforms.

In all the remaining LEAs the decision lies with the head teacher or the governors. This seems, on the whole, to have been a pattern which has worked well, although it does, on occasion, suffer the odd hiccup when misunderstandings or misjudgments take place, as they apparently did in a Derby school in 1985 (Fullerton 1985). This approach requires that head teachers should show flexibility and that experienced guidance and advice be available from education department officers when questions arise or are anticipated.

The second practical matter relevant to this discussion is the kind of menu which is made available for school meals. The Islamic requirement for *halal* (permitted) food is straightforward: no pork or alcohol or derivatives of those products at all, and other meat must be slaughtered in the correct way. All the LEAs responding have made arrangements for alternative menus for Muslim children. The practice has been for these to be vegetarian — by avoiding all animal products the question of whether the animal has been slaughtered correctly is also avoided. Several authorities have used the opportunity of introducing new menus to give their school meals staff further training so as to make them more sensitive to the dietary and cultural requirements of children from different backgrounds. Only Bradford reports specifically that it has introduced *halal* meat, served twice a week in schools where there is demand, in addition to the usual vegetarian alternatives. Lancashire and Sheffield state that *halal* food is available in schools where it is needed. Brent and Bedfordshire are both investigating the possibility of introducing *halal* meat into their menus.

Curriculum

Because the information was easily accessible elsewhere, the survey did not include a question about the local RE syllabus, the so-called Agreed Syllabus which each authority is obliged to produce according to the 1944 Education Act. For many years such syllabuses amounted to a continuation of previous practice, namely a Bible-based religious instruction aimed at nurturing Christian faith. As late as 1962, the City of Birmingham's agreed syllabus could state: "We speak of religious education, but we mean Christian education . . . the aim of Christian education in its full and proper sense is quite simply to confront our children with Jesus Christ . . ."

But in the late 1960s the pattern changed, primarily for educational reasons (Howarth 1983, 8ff). Research had shown how little such traditional syllabuses achieved and had argued for more child-centred approaches. So we began to see new syllabuses, initially still Christian in content, which stated their aims and objectives in terms of children's perceived ability to comprehend religious experience. They had titles like *Religion and Life* (Lancashire 1968) and *Learning for Life* (Inner London 1968). In this context it was, at least in educational terms, natural also to take note of the growing presence of non-Christian children in class rooms. The 1966 West Riding of Yorkshire syllabus was the first to include a reference to other religions because of immigrant children. Birmingham 1975 was the first properly multi-faith syllabus, where other religions were intended to be studied for their own sakes and on their own terms, and not from the perspective of Christianity. The syllabus generated controversy because of the initial inclusion of Marxism and humanism — they were toned down in the final published version to 'stances for living'. But Birmingham had set the pace and other authorities followed. The Hampshire syllabus of 1978 has been particularly successful, having been adopted by at least eleven other LEAs.

For many Muslims the original state of affairs was in some ways preferable; here was a system which was explicit about its purpose, namely Christian nurture, which was familiar from the missionary schools in the country of origin, and from which one had the right to withdraw one's children. The new multifaith syllabuses were more problematical. Muslims share with many other communities, including many Christians, a good deal of hesitation over apparent implications of the new concepts. They seem to imply that all religions are equally open to questioning, that the absolute of the deity is actually only relative. The approach appears subversive of traditional religious teaching authority. There is theoretical acceptance that children should know about the religion of others, for the sake of better community relations, but the desired emphasis is on instruction in the child's own religious tradition by someone from within that tradition. For a while Muslims were willing to participate in the statutory syllabus conferences which drew up these documents, including the controversial 1975 Birmingham one. But the experience of one of the most recent ones, Inner London 1984, suggests that such cooperation can no longer be taken for granted — all the major London Muslim groupings issued a joint statement condemning the basic secular and relativistic assumptions of the new syllabus.

The other main area of curriculum concern is sex education. The view of one Muslim parent is typical of many: "It is in the nature of men and women to know what to do when the right time is blessed by marriage — for a Muslim, explicit guidance on morality, marital relationships, love and affection are clear in the Qur'an. Sex education and sex aids are for a society of people sick and disenchanted by their own promiscuity." Very few schools do, in fact, schedule separate lessons in sex education. Most include the subject as an integral part of human biology, health education, or moral and social studies. The response of Kirklees is representative of many LEAs:

> We do not differentiate sex education from health education. It is seen as part of three curricula areas: health education, personal relations and biological studies. It is felt that sex education is not the appropriate term to use and can best be dealt with through the three areas above. Staff are aware of pupils' cultural backgrounds and would not offend deliberately — they are sensitive to both, to the teaching of the home and of religious groups.

At the other end of the spectrum is the situation as described by Coventry: "Sex Education is a subject on the school curriculum and all pupils are expected to study it, and any parents with particular concerns are encouraged to discuss them with school staff."

There is the general practice that parents are informed in advance when an element of sex education is due to appear on the timetable. Ten of the responding LEAs have either a policy to allow parents to withdraw their children from such lessons, or they advise the schools to allow this. The remainder, on the whole, state that this decision is at the discretion of the head teacher. The guidance given by Lancashire may be worth quoting:

> Sessions with parents and children together have been successful in some schools, and schemes have also been evolved where teachers and parents jointly prepare beforehand for work with pupils. Good liaison with parents must have a high priority in all such school planning.
> Although we must accept our responsibility to help pupils to come to terms with the personal values, problems and demands of a sophisticated society, we must offend neither the consciences of the parents nor the sensibilities of the pupils themselves.

The general context of these more detailed questions is one of the attitude of education authorities and individual schools to the increasing cultural plurality of the communities they serve. The political test often applied in recent years has been the extent to which the LEAs have been prepared to make 'multi-culturalism' or 'anti-racism' official policy. This is not the place to enter into the related debate, but merely to record the responses of the survey. Only Surrey and Strathclyde do not report the existence of a policy as such, although both state their opposition to racism and support for equal opportunities. Many of the remaining LEAs produce general statements of principle, and occasionally reports of good local practice as encouragement to other schools in the area. A few authorities have gone further, developing strategies for the implementation of anti-racist and/or multicultural policies in schools and the education service generally.

Separate schools

Whatever takes place within schools, it has long been established practice among the various religious communities to organize their own classes for religious instruction, the so-called supplementary sector. The earliest Muslim organizations set up in Britain had the instruction of the community among their priorities. Most Muslim supplementary teaching takes place in mosques and homes, but there remain numerous instances where the organizers of such classes want to run them on ordinary school premises. They may be the most convenient, but this location also avoids the problems of children roaming the streets between two different locations outside the control of teachers, parents or chaperones. So far as LEAs are concerned, requests for such facilities are seen as part of wider community needs. Seven of the authorities surveyed left the decision on letting of school premises for community education purposes to the individual schools, in several cases encouraging lettings at concessionary rates. One of the county councils, Berkshire, has a policy of free lettings, and two others, Lancashire and Leicestershire, were in the process of considering such a policy. Four of the London boroughs had also adopted such a policy, as had six of the metropolitan district councils. The detailed account given by Waltham Forest may stand as a model for most of these:

> The authority receives sympathetically applications from community groups to use suitable school accommodation free of charge between 4.00 pm and 5.30 pm, weekdays. The aims of the organisation must be broadly educational, including social, education, religious and cultural objectives. Examples of this type of use of schools, which is usually during school term times, are language teaching and studies of the Koran and associated customs. Studies of Islam is therefore included. The types of facilities made available are largely at the request of the groups who approach the Authority, e.g. for classrooms. Except for ensuring that safety regulations are observed, there is therefore little restriction placed on the use of school premises for broadly educational activities at these times. Use of schools at other times is subject to the usual criteria, including the levying of a subsidized charge by the Authority.

One of the Muslim groups arranging such religious instruction on school premises is the Muslim Educational Trust, who in their 1984 report stated that their teachers visited sixty-one schools. When contacted, twenty-eight of the schools responded. Two reported that such visits had taken place in the past but had ceased. Four had only received courtesy visits to explain the work of the Trust, or could not recall having had any visits at all. However, the remainder had regular arrangements involving teaching either during the lunch hour, immediately after school, or occasionally immediately before school. A few had arranged for Muslim pupils at the written request of their parents to have a separate assembly with the visiting MET teacher. In all cases such visits took place once or twice a week. Inevitably, there were problems, such as the odd unreliable MET teacher, incompatibility of teaching methods, and occasionally resistance by Muslim pupils and parents. But in the majority of cases such visits appear to run smoothly, and in some cases they are being used by the school staff to put relations with the local Muslim community onto a more constructive basis of cooperation.

A more thorough application of the concept of separate Muslim education has occasionally surfaced in the form of requests for schools of Muslim foundation with voluntary-aided status, i.e. with a degree of independence from the LEA but with extensive public funding, on a par with Jewish, most Roman Catholic, and many Church of England voluntary schools. At the time when a government commission on the education of ethnic minority children, the so-called Swann commission (DES 1985: ch.8) reported, this was a question of some public debate. Bradford had for more than a year been considering a request for five such schools, a request which was ultimately rejected. The National Union of Teachers had issued a discussion paper arguing against the idea (NUT 1984), and the Swann Report itself came out against it, although six members registered their dissent, the only point of dissension in the final report.

Anecdotal evidence suggests that pressure for Muslim voluntary schools is in part related to local single-sex provision at the secondary level. Thus when the closure of a girls' school was being discussed in Reading (Berkshire) a few years ago, the Muslim community started thinking of the option of a voluntary school, although no application was, in the end, submitted. The immediate reaction when Bradford rejected the five applications in 1985 was the establishment of an independent Muslim girls' school. Birmingham has decided to retain a small number of girls' schools and to consider Asian applications favourably, and the Muslim Liaison Committee here, while pressing for other things, has decided specifically not to press for voluntary schools. The authority itself says in its response:

> The Muslim Liaison Committee was established partly as a result of Muslims requesting changes in the school curriculum. There have been no approaches for the establishment of a voluntary aided school, but underlying the consultations with this group has been the knowledge that if schools do not accommodate Muslim wishes various organisations may well make a request for normal voluntary-aided status.

Sheffield was approached about voluntary schools, but discussions on a number of issues of concern has led to practical compromises (e.g. on dress, sex education and food) which appear to have won general acceptance. Derbyshire was approached in 1983 regarding the possibility of establishing a LEA secondary school for girls, but there has been little follow-up. When faced with a similar situation, Lancashire assisted a Blackburn Muslim group in its approaches to the Department of Education and Science to establish an independent girls' school in 1984. Hounslow reports retaining two girls' schools and there must be several other authorities which have done the same.

In addition to Sheffield and Bradford, two other authorities report formal approaches concerning the establishment of a voluntary-aided school. Kirklees have been approached by the London Mosque[3] with a proposal for a primary school for about 150 children, but discussion has remained at the preliminary stages. Brent were in discussion for some time with the Islamiyya Primary School established and funded by the former pop singer Cat Stevens, now Yusuf Islam. The LEA finally gave its approval in early 1986, but as of June 1986 the decision of the Secretary of State for Education, who has the final word, is not yet known. Eight other authorities report that they have not been formally approached, suggesting that initial explorations or suggestions have been made at some time. Only twelve LEAs state specifically that they have not been approached.

Slaughter

Under English law there is a requirement for humane slaughter of animals for human consumption. This means that some form of stunning of an animal, including poultry, is required before it is killed. Exemption from this rule is granted on religious grounds, traditionally to Jews but today also to Muslims. At various times animal welfare groups have sought to have this exemption withdrawn. In 1985, the Farm Animal Welfare Council, a body set up by the Ministry of Agriculture, Fisheries and Food, in a review of the subject, proposed that stunning should be required without exception, and that the religious communities be given three years to get used to the idea (FAWC 1985). Muslim reactions against this have been very strong, and a consultative group, coordinated by the Islamic Cultural Centre in London, issued a detailed rebuttal of the proposals in the spring of 1986.

The role of local authorities in this highly emotive area has at the legal level been marginal, limited primarily to questions of planning, health and hygiene. In a number of cities, licensed Muslim slaughtermen have been granted access to slaughterhouses at certain times or for certain consignments of animals so as to carry out the required form of slaughter. In a few places, the Muslims have agreed to carry out the required slaughter after stunning of the animal. The survey suggests that some half dozen privately owned Muslim slaughterhouses are in operation in various parts of the country, and that the greater part of *halal* meat on sale through the numerous Muslim retail outlets comes from those few meat companies. This applies to beef, sheep and poulty. However, poultry slaughter appears to be spread over many more localities than beef or sheep, partly due to the practical ease of storing and transporting live poultry and partly because the law is less stringent as regards poultry slaughter. Some authorities, including for example Birmingham, would like to limit the number of sites where poultry is slaughtered, to make health and hygiene control easier. This is a process where it may be difficult to find an acceptable balance between negotiation and enforcement in achieving results.

Conclusion

At one level it is virtually impossible to reach any conclusion from this survey, other than to restate that the response of local authorities to local Muslim needs has been sporadic and varied. The survey provides only circumstantial evidence of coordination of response, or at least some degree of learning from others' experience. Equally, it can be said, particularly with reference to burial and educational matters, that the Muslim approaches to local authorities have been varied in emphasis, although it is not possible to judge how far the variation is due to the difference in local perceptions of what could realistically be gained as opposed to what is needed.

Equally, a more refined analysis of the responses, involving a follow-up correspondence to clarify points of vagueness, which I have not undertaken, would be necessary to determine to what extent changes of policy and administrative flexibility have come about specifically because of a Muslim presence. It is clear, for example, that the issue of school uniforms has been defused in some areas primarily because the general trend has been against uniformity of any kind. That it still remains, in fact, an issue is evidenced by the example I recently heard quoted by a Birmingham head teacher, who stated that he had had to ban any form of head covering, because some of the "West Indian kids had started wearing Rasta-style head gear to school", which was an unacceptable challenge to authority. Some of the changes which have come about have been achieved because several different communities have challenged the inherited system. This may be said in part of the whole question of multicultural education and, more certainly, of uniforms and burial. In some fields specific changes have been implemented because of Muslim demands, as in the area of planning permission for mosques and, to a certain extent, as regards burial.

One result of the survey, although again to a great degree impressionistic, is an indication that we might be dealing with three distinct types of response. A basic response is that of rejection. This is most explicitly stated in a covering letter from the chief executive of one district council (which I shall leave anonymous):

> I notice that . . . you thanked me for responding to your request for information. However, I did this merely to supply the information and not in any way to support this study. The reason I say this is that Muslims have an anti-Christian attitude and, in many parts of the world, are responsible for and promote persecution of Christians.
>
> I, therefore, consider that it is wrong to promote relations with these other religions in this Country unless they were clearly with the intention of conversion to Christianity. There is far too much of other religions in this Country and belittling of Christianity.

No other rejoinder is so explicitly negative, and this one is, of course, also quite personal. Some of the other letters received do, however, show indications of a similar attitude of rejection. Several of the replies were brief to a degree of curtness. Only further exploration would indicate whether this betrays harassed civil servants or attitudes of rejection. The substance of a number of responses suggest, more seriously, the existence of local councils whose policy has been one of minimum concessions.

On a more positive note, I would suggest that the majority of the councils surveyed have adopted policies more accepting of the changes which are taking place inside their boundaries. This is, of course, no guarantee that the bureaucrats responsible for interpreting and implementing those policies are applying them positively, nor does it say anything about the way the recipients of the policies, in this case the Muslim communities, view the matter. But in adopting policies of acceptance, I suggest that councils fall into two main categories. On the one hand are those whose particular policies are adopted in the context of a general anti-racist or multicultural policy. Some of these operate with an explicitly secular ideology, often of the political left, which in certain circumstances can result in specific Muslim demands being rejected. When this happens in the context of a previous pattern of general acceptance of Muslim needs, a consequent sense of surprise and frustration on the Muslim side is to be expected. On the other hand, there are councils whose policy can best be described as one of ad hoc flexibility, where requests are met with a response of practical negotiations on a case-by-case basis. This seems on the whole to have worked, until one group or other in the community suddenly decides that its concerns have been neglected and in turn voices its own demands. In terms of local politics, both categories are vulnerable to popular backlash.

A different kind of result suggested by the survey is the fact that particular, on the face of it minor, practical issues are major symbolic tests of acceptability — someone, somewhere probably has the appropriate technical jargon for this. This is a phenomenon well-known on the Muslim side. Where there is a wide measure of agreement, individual Muslim movements have marked out their distinctive character by selecting particular smaller markers as exclusive to themselves. Such markers can be a special form of dress; the symbol of the beard as a marker of piety has appeared throughout Islamic history; head gear has played a similar role, in, for example, the Kemalist reform in Turkey. One sees something similar in the science of hadith-criticism, where the outward behaviour of individual transmitters is a major test of reliability.

In the response of European structures to the presence of Muslim communities, a similar phenomenon is perceivable. In West Germany, head covering worn by Turkish girls and women sometimes appears to have become the exclusive test of integration in the public mind. The recent question of amplified public call to prayer from Birmingham's Central Mosque, for the immediate neighbourhood a primarily practical issue, became increasingly symbolic of more fundamental matters as the issue was debated in the higher echelons of local structures, and as it was reported and discussed further afield.

A number of points arising out of the survey could be explored further in this context. In relation to planning applications, to what extent are car parking restrictions and considerations of noise being used as cover for other reasons for rejection, reasons which are currently not considered legitimate in the language of public debate? The same may be asked in reference to Muslim desires to bury their dead in a shroud — since some councils have not found this a problem, and since it is not a strictly Islamic legal requirement, it would seem a classic example of such a symbolic test, viewed from both sides. Time off for festivals and Friday noon prayers, questions of school uniform, attitudes to sex education, all these can clearly in some circumstances be imbued with such a role. Similar considerations are to be found underlying, at least in part, the issue of access to slaughter of animals without pre-stunning, an issue which surfaces at intervals in Britain as well as elsewhere in Europe. But these are all suggestions arising out of this small survey, suggestions which would need other research methods and additional resources.

Notes

A full report of this survey, including a systematic summary of the responses of each local authority, is published in *Research Papers: Muslims in Europe*, no. 30/31, June/September 1986. I am grateful to the Islamic Council of Europe who supported the study.

1. For more detailed material on Muslims in Britain and their history, see Daniele Joly and Jørgen Nielsen (1985), *Muslims in Britain: An Annotated Bibliography 1960–1984* (Centre for Research in Ethnic Relations, University of Warwick). On English law as relevant to the themes of this paper, see S.M. Poulter (1986), *English Law and Ethnic Minority Customs* (London: Butterworth).
2. European Commission on Human Rights, 'Decision of the Commission, application no. 8160/78'; see also *The Times* (London), 23 March 1977.
3. The London Mosque, Gressenhall Street, is one of the main British centres of the Ahmadiyya, a movement declared non-Islamic by many Muslim organizations and countries.

References

Ahsan, M.M. and McDermott, M.Y., 1980. *The Muslim Guide for Teachers, Employers, Community Workers and Social Administrators in Britain*. Leicester: The Islamic Foundation.

Darsh, S.M. 1981. *Islamic Health Rules*. London: Ta-Ha Publishers.

DES (Department of Education and Science). 1985. *Education for All*. Cmnd 9453. London: HMSO.
FAWC (Farm Animal Welfare Council). 1985. *Report of the Welfare of Livestock when Slaughtered by Religious Methods*. London: HMSO.
Fullerton, M. 1985. The Muslims of Derby. *New Society*, 13 September 1985: 389-90.
GRO (General Register Office). 1981. *The Official List*, Part III. London: Office of Population Censuses and Surveys.
Hodgins, H. 1981. Planning permission for mosques — the Birmingham experience. *Research Papers: Muslims in Europe* 9:11-27. Birmingham: Centre for the Study of Islam and Christian-Muslim Relations, Selly Oak Colleges.
Howarth, R.B. 1983. Agreed Syllabuses of Religious Education 1975-1982. Unpublished M.Ed. thesis. University of Birmingham.
NUT (National Union of Teachers). 1984. Religious education in a multifaith society. *Circular*, 414/84(E), 10 October 1984.
Sheffield, Department of Planning. 1983. *Religious Meeting Places for Ethnic Minority Groups*. Sheffield: City of Sheffield MDC.
Townsend, H.E.R. (Ed.) 1971. *Immigrant Pupils in England: The LEA Response*. Slough: NFER.

4
The Religious Life of Muslims in Berlin

Hanns Thomä-Venske

In the year 1777, the envoy of the Sublime Porte, Resmi Ahmed Effendi, who in 1763–4 paid an official visit to Berlin, sent a report to the Sultan Abdul Hamid I in which he described the friendly reception in Berlin with enthusiasm. He said, a bit too optimistically, in his report that "the population of Berlin recognizes the prophet Mohammed and would not be afraid to accept Islam".

The visit of Resmi Ahmed Effendi took place at a time when the Ottoman state and Prussia were attempting to build better economic, political and military relations. The Berlin population, however, did not adopt Islam. Nevertheless, since that time there have existed small Muslim groups in Berlin. In 1798, on the occasion of the death of the Ottoman envoy Ali Aziz Effendi, a Muslim cemetery situated at the Columbiadamm was opened, which still serves the Berlin Turks as their burial ground. Organized Muslim community life developed in the 1920s.

The Islamic community in Berlin was founded in 1922 and Muslims of forty-one nationalities joined it. It regarded itself as a "union of all male and female Muslims living in Berlin and Germany, in order to serve Islam" (Abdullah 1981: 27). The attempt of this community to build a mosque on the Kaiserdamm failed for financial reasons. The newly founded Ahmadiyya community, however, laid the foundation stone for a mosque in 1924 in the Brienner Strasse, and it began functioning in 1926–7. Even now this mosque is used by the members of the small Ahmadiyya movement.

Because of the immigration of Turkish workers to the Federal Republic and West Berlin, the number of Muslims has increased since the middle 1960s. Today, about 1.7 million Muslims live in the Federal Republic, including about 2000 German converts to Islam. These Muslims come from more than forty countries, most of them from Turkey (roughly 1.5 million), and from Yugoslavia (some 120,000). About 90 per cent of the Muslims living in the Federal Republic are Sunnites, and 95 per cent of these belong to the Hanafitic Law School. There are approximately 700 mosques and prayer rooms, most of them located in tenement houses, factories or warehouses. There are actual mosques only in Berlin, Hamburg, Frankfurt, Aachen and Munich. The number of Muslims in religious associations is estimated at 340,000 (Abdullah and Gieringer 1980).

In West Berlin, there are at present about 248,000 foreigners, some 130,000 of whom are Muslims. Among these, the approximately 108,000 Turks are by far the majority. Estimates indicate that about 97 per cent of the Turkish population are Muslims (John and Caemmerer 1986). With a total West Berlin population of 2 million, Muslims constitute 6.5 per cent.

Problems in maintaining a religious tradition

The presence of a significant number of Muslims in a secularized state with Christian traditions poses questions for which, until now, answers have not been found, neither in the political nor the religious traditions of the parties concerned. While Christianity came into being as a minority religion, which from the beginning had to develop forms of religious practice which were suitable under unfavourable conditions, often in fact in hiding, Islam today for the first time faces such a situation in western Europe. At the same time, the process of preservation and change of religious tradition is complicated by a number of adverse factors.

1. The Islamic way of life of the Turkish working families is a mix of popular religiosity, national customs, Islamic rules of conduct, mysticism, folk knowledge, folklore and magic with Islamic elements — all welded into a traditional interpretation of Islam which has grown organically in Turkey. It is, however, an unsystematic and unmeditated religious and cultural tradition, barely accessible to arguments and discussions. It is difficult for reform-oriented theologians and pedagogues to introduce new interpretations, which would be more suitable for the Turkish working families in the Federal Republic into this stable system of religious tradition. Often those attempting to do so have to defend themselves against accusations of 'modernization' and 'westernization'.
2. In the Federal Republic the religious symbols and rituals of Islam are no longer affirmed by the social environment, and they thus lose their character of certainty which underpinned their existence in Turkey. The maintenance of tradition therefore demands interpretations and explanations which respond to the societal realities of Turkish working families. However, few of the Turkish migrants are able to explain to their children the traditional religious customs and symbols and how and where they originated. This, in turn, would have made a conscious processing possible. As it is, Islam becomes a matter essentially related to the past of the parents and the societal circumstances in the countries of origin.

3. Islam is a religion which is dependent on public and communal celebration and which thrives on the right religious behaviour of the believers, rather than on religious dogma. Orthopraxis is more decisive than orthodoxy. This emphasis on public action in Islam makes religious life strongly dependent upon external conditions facilitating religious practices. These external conditions are not favourable for Muslims in the Federal Republic.

4. The diaspora situation of the Muslims in the Federal Republic complicates the development of more 'open' forms of belief. At the same time, Islam gains greater importance as a defence against social discrimination and as a positive identification mark. Therefore, traditionalistic interpretations have a better chance of succeeding than reformatory interpretations, as the former represent a superior morality in the eyes of the Muslims. Hereby the social hierarchy with the 'guest workers at the bottom' and German society at the top is subverted in the moral and religious sphere.

Muslim organizations

In this situation, discussions about religious associations and institutions, about theological and political interpretations, about the control of rituals and about who is entitled to speak on behalf of Islam take on increased significance. These discussions are rendered difficult by the fact that the mosques and the Quran schools are not controlled by the local communities but by political groupings and movements, and that international Islamic organizations and individual countries exercise a distinct influence on the building of mosques and the financing of community activities.

The efforts by Muslim organizations towards an institutional consolidation have made progress in the past years. The main issues in this process are the recognition of Islam as a 'body of public law' (*Körperschaft öffentlichen Rechts*), which would lead to Muslims having the same legal status as other religious communities, the introduction of Islamic religious education in German schools, discussions about the Quran lessons, and the attempts to find buildings for mosques and cultural centres.

At the beginning of the recruitment of Turkish manpower in the 1960s and 1970s, the Turkish government did not take any measures for the religious care of the families living abroad. However, radical sects and parties, forbidden in Turkey partly because of their militant and subversive character, founded religious associations, financed the building of mosques and organized the Islamic community life and out-of-school religious instruction in the ill-reputed Quran lessons. "In Germany organized Islam . . . shows more radical, fanatical and militant traits than would be tolerated in Turkey", judged the expert on Turkey Petra Kappert (*Frankfurter Allgemeine Zeitung*, 9 September 1982). For a long time, this was of no concern to the Turkish authorities, who were of the opinion that this was a matter for the German authorities. Only since the beginning of the 1980's has the Turkish state developed a strong interest in the creation of religious care in the Federal Republic, and then in competition with the already existing Islamic associations.

These mosques and cultural associations stood and still stand in more or less close connection with parties and religious movements in Turkey. Many of them have in the meantime formed national associations. In Berlin, the most important of these are the following:

1. In the early 1980s, seventeen mosque associations and Islamic student associations founded the Federation of Islamic Associations and Communities in Berlin, the so-called Islamic Federation. These fundamentalist Islamic groups work militantly for an 'Islamic system' of a trans-national character. Most of the associations were closely related to the former National Salvation Party, MSP. In this federation, the Turkish associations clearly dominate, but it also has German, Arab, Iranian and Iraqi members. The Islamic Federation today has twenty-six member organizations. In 1980, it organized thirteen of the eighteen largest mosques in Berlin. The *Statistisches Jahrbuch 1985* (*1985 Statistical Yearbook*) for Berlin lists it as the only Islamic group among the religious communities. According to the Yearbook (145ff.), it has 47,250 members or interested people, twenty-six meeting halls, thirteen ordained and fourteen non-ordained clergy and 130 other employees, including ten teachers, working in the community. The Islamic Federation has striven for recognition as a 'body of public law' in order to be able to conduct Islamic religious education in Berlin schools, but its application for this has been refused. It is also struggling for permission to build a mosque according to Islamic concepts.

2. The Süleymanli movement which is united in the Islamic Cultural Centres has, since the 1970s, represented the largest and best organized association of labour migrants in the Federal Republic and probably in Europe. According to a statement of the former speaker M.S. Abdulla in 1980, the Islamic Cultural Centres had built up — within a few years — 134 communities with more than 160 preaching places and mosques. Furthermore, about 75 communities were associated with them. They thus organized nearly 60 per cent of all Muslim organizations in the Federal Republic. Outside of the Federal Republic, there were in 1980 fifteen Islamic Cultural Centres in the Netherlands, one in Belgium, one in France, six in Switzerland, nine in Austria, two in Denmark and one in Sweden. In March 1979, the central office of the Islamic Cultural Centres in Cologne applied to the Minister of Culture in Nordrhein-Westphalia for recognition as a 'body of public law', but this application was subsequently refused.

The Süleymanli movement is forbidden in Turkey. As an underground sect, it is alleged to have developed a camouflage ideology. The followers are encouraged, it is said, to infiltrate other groups and also, for tactical reasons, to be able to mimic views they do not really hold. The German Trade Union in 1980 accused them of advocating Islamic fundamentalist and ultra-right positions in their Turkish language publications while in their German publications they stress their will for integration, their readiness for partnership and cooperation with the state authorities and their recognition of the constitution of the Federal Republic (*Frankfurter Rundschau*, 4 March 1980). In West Berlin, however, the Islamic Cultural Centres do not play as prominent a role as they do in the Federal Republic. Three mosques belong to them. One of these is located in a factory, and its 1000 square metres include a library, a school and other rooms.

3. At the beginning of 1982, the Turkish-Islamic Union for Religion (*Diyanat Islerli Türk Islam Birligi* — DITIB), was founded in Berlin as an official representative of the Directorate of Religious Affairs in Ankara. President of the Union and its first honorary president is the president of the Directorate of Religious Affairs. The statutes of the association assure the decisive influence of the Directorate on all important issues. The association, which one also finds in the Federal Republic, represents the official laicistic and nationalistic direction of Islam in Turkey. Its aim is 'to care for the Turkish community in Berlin in all affairs relevant to the Islamic religion . . ., to establish and keep up suitable rooms for religious devotions and education, to educate lay preachers, to conduct language courses as well as social and cultural activities, to prepare and conduct programs for the Islamic religious education in Berlin schools.' It also plans to organize pilgrimages as well as distribute training and university scholarships.

In its disputes with the Süleymanli movement, with the Islamic Federation and with some smaller groups, it seems that Islam, as furthered by the Turkish state, has consolidated its position in Berlin very rapidly. To date, fourteen newly-founded or already existing mosques have joined this association. Since the school year of 1984–85, it has organized Islamic religious education within the Consulate's mother-tongue lessons programme. About 12 per cent of the Turkish pupils participate in the mother tongue 'additional' education, and about 90 per cent of these have attended the religious education lessons in the 1984–85 school year.

4. The foundation of an association called the Turkish Community in Berlin was aimed at a broad representation of the interests of the Turkish population within German society. It is a union of political, cultural and religious organizations ranging from right-wing (nationalist, conservative, fundamentalist) to centre and left-wing (liberal, social democratic). The three above-mentioned Islamic organizations were also members of the Turkish Community. Internal disputes at the beginning of 1986, however, led to the withdrawal of the Islamic Cultural Centres and the Islamic Federation from the Turkish Community. As a national organization, the Turkish Community has taken a laicistic and pluralistic stand on religious issues. It did nevertheless support the mosque projects of its member organizations and it has also worked on issues related to Quranic studies and religious education. With the withdrawal of the Islamic Federation and the Islamic Cultural Centres, which are in opposition to the religious policies of the Turkish state, the religious–political influence from Ankara may have increased in the Turkish community.

The description of the Islamic associations and their organizational power does not really give a true picture of the religious spectrum of Muslims in Berlin. As already indicated, the majority of Turkish Muslims orient their religious practices towards 'folk Islam', and are little interested or actively engaged in theological and political issues. By and large, there is a tendency to join the nearest mosque, no matter which view it represents. According to a poll which the Emnid Institute conducted on behalf of the Berlin Senate at the end of 1983, 84 per cent of the Turks who were questioned wished to educate their children in Islamic ways. On the question of the best representative of Islam in Berlin, 58 per cent did not give detailed answer, 16 per cent mentioned the Islamic Cultural Centres of the Süleymanli movement, 13 per cent the Islamic Federation, 8 per cent the Turkish-Islamic Union (DITIB) and 4 per cent the Turkish Community in Berlin. Since this poll was taken, the figures may have changed in favour of the DITIB.

In dealing with German political and social institutions, it is still unclear who can legitimately speak for the Muslims and with what authority and with what degree of representativeness. On the German side it is taken for granted that Islam has institutions comparable with Christian churches and other religious communities, which can maintain the status of 'body of public law' and thus be able to act as legitimate partners. It is extremely difficult for the authorities to relate to the different Islamic groups. The dilemma is described by the Berlin Senate's commissioner for foreigners. John and Caemmerer, in an article entitled 'Turkish Muslims in Berlin' (1986), wrote that the original folk Islam of the Anatolian rural regions to which the majority of the Turkish Muslims in Berlin adhere, is as such neither able to organize itself, nor articulate itself, systematically. The administration is thus faced with the dilemma of not being able to communicate with the Muslim majority as such, but only to meet with separate sect-like groups or self-appointed national associations. An alternative is to meet with the representatives who are commissioned from the outside (i.e. the Turkish state) and who often only inadequately and in a politically-stereotyped manner reflect the needs and concerns of the Muslim majority. None of the larger organizations, the article also claims, "is content-wise acceptable to the Senate or the administration" (John and Caemmerer 1986: 10ff.).

Although the question of a valid Muslim representative has still not been answered, a noticeable consolidation of the Islamic communities has taken place in the past few years. This will be elucidated in the following case concerning Islamic religious education.

Islamic religious education

The first discussions about introducing Islamic religious education in German schools took place in the 1970s, occasioned by the disputes over the Quran lessons and their obstructing effects on the integration of Turkish pupils. Apart from the accusation that right-wing parties tried to propagate their political views in the Quran lessons and to train new recruits for their organizations, the teachers pointed in particular to the negative effects of such education on their pupils, such as an over-taxation of time and energy, learning impediments due to a mixture of teaching styles, social isolation, animosity and anxiety towards the German environment, lack of ability to integrate, lack of independence, stultification and one-sidedness, impediments in personality development, discrimination against girls.

Parents sent their children to the Quran lessons because there was no other religious education offered and because they learned traditional norms such as discipline, obedience, and a traditional sexual morality. Also, since they were looked after during the Quran lessons, they were less exposed to the street pressures. Additional motives on the part of the parents were group pressure and the expectation that a traditionally-oriented education could stabilize the Turkish-Islamic identification of their children and reduce the sharp family and generational conflicts (cf. Thomä-Venske 1981: 140ff.).

In the debate over this problem, there were calls for the prohibition of the Quran lessons, and demands for qualified Islamic religious education in German schools, from the German and also, to some extent, from the Turkish side. Firstly, it was hoped that regular Islamic religious education would counteract the negative effect on integration of the Quran lessons. Secondly, because of the large participation of Turkish pupils in the Quran lessons, according to some estimates around 50 per cent, the parents' pressing concern for an Islamic religious education had become a fact that could not be neglected. The first educational, theological and organizational preparations for Islamic religious instruction were made in Nordrhein-Westphalia and Hamburg at the beginning of the 1980s.

The Conference of Cultural Ministers of the Federal States instituted a commission to examine Islamic religious education, and effect a "coordination of basic fundamental questions occasioned by an introduction of Islamic religious education in public schools". In their report of 20 March 1984, the commission dealt with legal and organizational issues and presented different (ideal) models for instruction in Islam. These models differed according to organizational criteria:

a) Islamic instruction in the mother-tongue can be the responsibility of the diplomatic missions, as in six Federal States, or the responsibility of the school administrative departments, as in five Federal States.
b) Religious education can be provided within the normal schooling structure according to the German curriculum, in German, and be performed by specially trained German or foreign teachers.
c) Religious education can be provided within the normal schooling structure according to a Turkish curriculum or a German curriculum or according to a curriculum coordinated with Islamic religious communities.

In some Federal States, different models of Islamic instruction in the mother-tongue are presently being tested. Islamic religious education as a regular class, as in Belgium and Austria, has not as yet been instituted.

In Berlin, an agreement between the Senate and the Turkish General Consulate resulted in the establishment of a weekly two-hour voluntary religious instruction course in Islam, beginning in the 1984–85 school year. It is conducted within the additional mother-tongue schooling programme provided by the Consulate and financially supported by the Berlin Senate. The courses are taught by teachers attached to the Consulate and the school books come from Turkey. The curriculum has been discussed with the Berlin Senate. The Turkish-Islamic Union, DITIB, organizes the further education of the teachers and also functions as subject supervisor.

Before this form of Islamic religious instruction was established in Berlin, the Islamic Federation had, in May 1980, made an application to the Senator for Education, Youth and Sports for authorization to conduct Islamic religious education according to paragraph twenty-three of the Berlin school law. According to this paragraph, religious instruction is "the issue of the churches, religious and ideological associations". The Federation offered to pay the expenses of the teachers. Four suitable teachers with certificates of qualification from the High Islamic Institute in Turkey were already in Berlin. Three more were also ready to conduct such courses. It was promised that books suitable for religious education would soon be developed.

At the same time, a draft for 'basic rules of a framework curriculum for the Islamic religious instruction in the Berlin primary schools' was presented, which in its style, arguments and formulations closely reflected the corresponding document for Protestant religious education. It can be assumed that this parallelism would serve as a means of legitimization for the school authorities. The application of the Islamic Federation was rejected by the Senator for Education, Youth and Sports on the grounds that the Islamic Federation did not fulfil the criteria of being a religious association. In view of the fact that Islam has no organizational form comparable with that of the Christian churches and that the Muslim communities in general are decentrally organized, one has to ask for how long Muslim organizations can be denied the right to conduct Islamic religious education on these grounds.

Islamic education within the mother-tongue classes, conducted under the auspices of the Turkish General Consulate, does not correspond to a religious education according to the school law and therefore does not request the sponsor to fulfil the criteria of a religious association. In practice, however, this organizational model operates in a similar manner to how an Islamic organization would if it had permission to act as a sponsor for religious education: the preferred grouping can extend and consolidate its institutions and obtain considerable advantages over other interested parties.

The religious instruction offered by the Turkish–Islamic Union reached 2691 of the 2971 pupils who in the 1984–85 school year participated in additional mother-tongue lessons. In the long run, the better educational organization will strengthen the official nationally-engraved influence of Turkish Islam over the Muslims in Berlin. This imported Islam, taught by teachers who have little knowledge of daily life of Turkish children in Berlin, will have an alien and probably nostalgic character for the children. It is associated with a society in which the Berlin Turks do not live. Moreover, it has nationalistic elements which are marginally consistent with educational goals such as integration and tolerance. An example is the programme for grade two of the primary school, where points four to eight read (Milli Egitim Bakanligi, Tebligler Dergisi — 7.6. 1982 — Cilt: 45/Sayi: 2114):

> My fatherland is Turkey. I love Turkey more than my life. I love the beautiful banner with the crescent and the star. I love Mustafa Kemal Atatürk, our saviour, our founder of the Republic and our great hero. I love all our great Turkish personages.

In other Federal States there exist curricula which avoid the confinement to only one Islamic direction, as the German school authorities take over the supervision of the Islamic religious instruction and discuss its content with the Islamic groupings. In Hamburg, Turkish teachers are employed by the German school districts to provide Islamic religious instruction. They take part in advanced training seminars conducted by German and Turkish Islamic experts and religious pedagogues. The curriculum and the educational aids have been developed in co-operation with Turkish teachers on the basis of religious instruction books from Turkey. In the revisions, elements not suitable for the instruction of Muslims living in Germany were omitted. In 1985, 1800 young Turks attended this kind of religious instruction, 24 per cent of the total (*Volksblatt Berlin*, 20 August 1985).

Such a curriculum avoids the problem of the German school authority's self-incapacitating actions in dealing with Islamic religious education, when it turns down, on the one hand, applications for sponsorship on the grounds of unclear representativeness on the part of the Islamic groups applying and decides, on the other hand, in favour of one group to the exclusion of the others.

The form of institutionalization of the Islamic religious education in the German schools will also help determine whether Islam in Germany becomes an integral part of the cultural, social and religious life of the country or whether it will remain a foreign element related to life abroad.

References

Abdullah, M.S. 1981. *Geschichte des Islam in Deutschland*. Graz: Styria.
Abdullah, M.S. and Gieringer, F. 1980. *Die Präsenz des Islam in der Bundesrepublik Deutschland*. Cologne: CIBEDO-Dokumentation Nr. 9.
Abgeordnetenhaus von Berlin. 1984. *Kleine Anfrage Nr. 3121* (25.1.84), 'Einführung

einer islamischen religionskundlichen Unterweisung im Rahmen des türkischen Konsulatsunterrichts.'

———. *Kleine Anfrage Nr. 3316* (8.3.84), 'Islamischer Religionsunterricht.'

———. *Kleine Anfrage Nr. 4350* (3.12.84), 'Ausländerregelklassen, Ausgleichsmassnahmen und muttersprachlicher Ergänzungsunterricht.'

———. 1986. *Kleine Anfrage Nr. 1307* (21.1.86), 'Einführung des islamischen Religionsunterrichts.'

Elsas, C. (ed.), 1983. *Identität: Veränderungen kultureller Eigenarten im Zusammenleben von Türken und Deutschen.* Hamburg: Rissen.

Emre, G. 1983. *300 Jahre Türken an der Spree: Eine vergessenes Kapitel Berliner Kulturgeschichte.* Berlin: Ararat Verlag.

Harnisch, U. and Ayanoglu. 1985/86. *Mit-Bürger-Beteiligung am Gülizar Bahnhof: Studie über Notwendigkeit und Funktion eines türkischen Kulturzentrums mit Gebetsraum in Berlin-Kreuzberg SO 36. Im Auftrag der Internationalen Bauausstellung Berlin 1985/86.*

Islamische Föderation in Berlin. 1980. *Reden Sie mit uns.* Berlin.

———. 1982. *Reden wir miteinander.* Berlin.

———. 1986. *Leben wir miteinander.* Berlin.

John, B. and Caemmerer, H. 1986. 'Türkische Muslime in Berlin'. Unpublished manuscript.

Sekretariat der Ständigen Konferenz der Kultusminister der Länder in der Bundesrepublik Deutschland. 1984. *Möglichkeiten religiöser Erziehung muslimischer Schüler in der Bundesrepublik Deutschland: Bericht der Kommission "Islamischer Religionsunterricht".* Bonn.

Statistisches Landesamt Berlin. 1985. *Statistisches Jahrbuch 1985.* Berlin.

Thomä-Venske, H. 1981. *Islam und Integration: Zur Bedeutung des Islam im Prozess der Integration türkischer Arbeiterfamilien in die Gesellschaft der Bundesrepublik.* Hamburg: Rissen.

Ucar, A. n.d. *Die religiöse Erziehung in der Türkei: Der Religionsunterricht nach der Verfassung 1982 und dem neuesten Lehrplan für Religions- und Moralkunde. Materialen zur Lehrerfortbildung im Ausländerbereich Nr. 5.* Berlin.

5
Religion and Ethnicity:
Orientations, Perceptions and Strategies among Turkish Alevi and Sunni Migrants in Berlin

Czarina Wilpert

A diversity of traditions and potential minority identities within Turkey have come to the fore in international migration. The largely homogeneous structural position of the Turkish migrants in German society is not matched by a comparable internal cohesion and a unity of world views. The minorities I refer to here are those ethnic and religious groups whose legitimate claims to a collective life have been submerged within the secular Turkish nation state. Of these, the largest Turkish religious minority in Berlin are the Alevis.

In this chapter religious affiliation among Sunni and Alevi Turkish nationals in Berlin will be looked at primarily as a factor of identification which has implications for group solidarity and involves concern for group survival. Religious affiliation may be used among Turkish migrants abroad to relate to one another as Muslims or to differentiate themselves — Alevi from Sunni, or Muslim from Christian. Less attention will be given here to the actual content of religious beliefs and the institutional form of religion.[1]

The focus will be on the meanings Turkish emigrants attach to outward symbols of appearance and significant markers of behaviour to assign persons to certain religious categories or to evaluate their qualifications for social interaction or social exclusion. In this respect one cannot disregard the cleavages in Turkish society which maintain to a certain extent a symbolic significance abroad. Two prominent examples are the proscriptions and meanings attached to women's dress, especially the wearing of the headscarf and participation in the sectarian non-state Quran courses run for young people. As is often suggested, Turkish secularism, or laicism, may be considered in some sense as an ideology which competes with religious belief for the loyalty and core identity of the citizens of the Turkish nation state. Part of Atatürk's effort to laicize Turkey also included divesting Turks of many symbols of traditional behaviour and substituting these with a new western code. Religious dress became a red flag aggravating ideologized Turkish secularists (Olsen 1985). Thus, one finds that the manner of dress, especially that of women, is a normal topic of conversation amongst the immigrants in Berlin. And, one's evaluation of women's styles of dress tells much as well about a person's identification with one of the religious-ideological segments of Turkish society.

The attendance of children at the 'unofficial', (non-Islamic Union)[2] Quran schools has acquired a similar significance. In Turkey, Quran instruction outside the control of the Turkish state with its officially trained teachers is formally forbidden. Divergencies on a regional or local level exist, nonetheless, and privately run courses are considered subversive by secularists. In Berlin the meaning attached to both the headscarf and the Quran courses extends beyond this group to a much wider circle. Early on in the migration of families abroad, German teachers in the public schools also became sensitized to the significance of these symbols for the highly politicized Turkish society, where religious orthodoxy and political extremism are considered to be linked.[3]

Here the question arises about the extent to which religious affiliation continues to differentiate interaction and solidarity patterns among Turks. Has international migration neutralized or further polarized these patterns of categorization and evaluations? Is there a transfer of entrenched markers from Turkey? And, if so, what indications are there of an attenuation of these categorizations from one generation to the next?

According to modernization theory one might generally expect international migration to encourage increasing secularization and greater distance from the dictates of religious exclusiveness, at least with the transition to the second and third generation. One might also forecast a model of identity change comparable with that which occurred among emigrants with strong village and regional identities, such as the Sicilians, Sardinians, or Corsicans, who only became aware of being Italian through ascriptive processes in the United States. Does the urban industrial setting, regardless of structural constraints, forge new experiences and new group formations which counteract the recourse to long-standing traditional ethno-religious ties? Another position, however, with similar unifying results, but in another direction, might argue that the structural marginality, denigration, and stigma attached to Turkishness in Germany, would provide enough common experience to encourage the formation of a homogeneous Muslim population with a common Islamic ideology out of an ideologically heterogeneous micro-society. It would seem, however, that it is still too early to reach clear-cut conclusions. Instead I will elaborate on some divergent trends.

Before entering into an analysis of social categorizations and conflicting symbols to be found among Turks in Berlin, it is necessary to situate these within the broader context of international migration, guest-worker policy and the history of ethno-religious differentiation basic to Turkish society. These contending forces have produced a particular blend of Turkish life in Berlin which is exemplified in the vitality of its economic institutions, the diversity of formal associations, and the complexity of social networks. This broader picture must be kept in mind when one interprets the mutual evaluations and interaction preferences expressed by first and second generation Turks.

The Immigration Context: The Stratification of Foreign Nationals

Certain conditions which are specific to the Turkish migration to Germany set the scene within which alternatives to ethno-religious identification may occur or be perceived. These include two factors. Firstly, the guestworker system has created a situation of institutional marginality, which in turn has reinforced an ideology of temporariness. The result is not ethnic but national stratification into the second and third generation. This has determined perceptions in both the receiving society and amongst the foreign nationalities about the possibility of settlement. Boundary setting has been formalized and institutionalized bilaterally. There exists accordingly no legitimate right to citizenship, but more officially the opportunity for citizenship has been formulated as a call for assimilation or return. Germany does not consider itself a country of immigration, not even for the recruited workers and their families. This is further kindled by the stigma attached to Turkishness.[4]

Secondly, there are several other factors which lead to contradictory policies and a confusion of interests among Turks and Germans. These have to do with the rights accorded to nationality in the European Community and the related question of the role of Turkey in the Western Alliance.

The first issue means that a European Community migrant has the right to settle and work abroad without being forced to give up his original nationality, that is, to 'assimilate or return'. The second factor means that Turks abroad are an important element in negotiations between Germany and Turkey, whether in the Turkish bid for European Community membership and military aid, or with respect to Germany's representation of the interests of the Western Alliance to guarantee Turkey's loyalty to NATO. Finally, the Turkish government needs and wants to keep the flow of remittances from their citizens abroad (Deutsche Bundesbank 1985) which have not decreased substantially since 1980.[5]

Thus, it becomes obvious that it is not only the German state through its guest-worker system which has marginalized Turks, but the Turkish state is also vitally concerned that these Turks in Germany maintain their ties with Turkey. The labour migration of Turks to Germany is anything but a simple case of classic immigration, acculturation and assimilation. Let us now return to what Muslim Turks bring with them and how their perceptions are altered through international migration and life in the diaspora.

Differentiation in Turkey: The Sunni-Alevi Divide

It is common practice to use geographical origins to distinguish Turkish migrants, implying that those from the West are 'modern' or possibly more secular and those from the East more traditional, meaning more conservative, religious, rural and peasant. These distinctions are legitimate to the extent that certain regions and rural areas in Turkey are underprivileged with respect to natural resources, economic development, and social infrastructure, and as a result access to educational opportunities is also limited. Beyond this, however, important distinctions exist in the cultural and religious traditions of Turkish migrants, which cannot be easily classified according to geographic origins.

This is true particularly for the eastern part of Turkey, which historically has been the home of a myriad of ethnic, linguistic and religious affiliations (Yalman 1969, Karpat 1976). This is explained in part by its geographical characteristics, rugged mountains, deep valleys and its distance from the centre of national — that is, imperial — power. According to Yalman (1969), this is also due to its location on the borders of the Persian and Ottoman Empires which was the marker of the religious division between the Sunni and Shi'a.

Ethnic and religious diversity and antagonism between the Turkish minorities and the majority is further complicated by histories of nomadism, tribal structures, internal labour migration (Karpat 1976) and the forced resettlement of the Kurds into other areas of Turkey (Engelbrektsson 1982). Most important is probably the discrepancy between the aspirations of the young Turkish nation state to a modern secular and culturally homogeneous society and its actual achievement.

The Kurds are the largest linguistic and cultural minority in Turkey. Originally at home in Central East and South East Anatolia, a large number of them have been forced for political and economic reasons to resettle in other regions. Where they are resettled they may be linguistically but not necessarily socially assimilated (Engelbrektsson 1982). They speak two major distinct dialects and are primarily either members of the Sunni or the Alevi branches of Islam. There are, however, also smaller numbers of non-Muslim Kurds who have chain-migrated to Berlin.

Some authors feel, however, that it is the religious distinction which draws the most rigid boundary between the Islamic Turks (Yalman 1969). The major split occurs between the Sunni and Alevi, and it has significance for ethnic Kurds as well as ethnic Turks.

The Alevi, as followers of Ali, are usually considered to belong to the Shi'a branch of Islam. But, as Yalman (1969) notes, their practices and beliefs are rejected as heresy by Shi'a as well as Sunni Muslims. Elements of a folk religion separate them distinctly from classical Shiism. Some scholars find their rituals and customs closer to ancient Turkmen traditions. For our purposes, their most important features are to be found in their less rigid practices of Islamic ritual. They neither visit mosques, send children to Quran schools, pray and practice ritual purification five times a day, nor fast for a month during Ramadan. They have as well a rich mystic and folkloric tradition, which has influenced Turkish folklore music and poetry. They consider themselves as politically progressive, socialistic, and more liberal than their Sunni fellow-countrymen. Their women are not necessarily veiled, and interact more freely in public surroundings. Tribal structures and ritual kinship play an important role in their social organization.[6]

This description, which approximates to their self-perception, is not, however, the image held by the conservative Sunnis who view them as heretical, incestuous, and impure. The Alevis have their counter-image as well. For them, "Sunni-Muslims are 'fanatic, degenerates' and they disapprove of what they perceive to be extreme segregation and oppression of women practised by Sunnis".[7] On the more positive side, both Dubetsky (1976) and Karpat (1976) find religious affiliation among the Alevi to be one of the major means, along with the *Landsmannschaft* (approx. 'fellow nationality') system, of social organization among internal migrants in the Turkish urban areas.

Turkish Life in Berlin

The more than 100,000 Turks in Berlin account for over one half of the foreigners. They constitute about 6 per cent of the population and are considered to be the largest settlement outside of the home country. Due to the Berlin urban housing structure, the renewal patterns, the return orientation of the migrants and their large families — not to speak of the discrimination against them — the Turkish population is concentrated primarily in the five most dense inner city districts. Certain schools, playgrounds, youth centres and street corners are filled with predominantly Turkish adolescents. Elementary and secondary (*Hauptschule*) schools in these areas often have student bodies with over 80 per cent Turks. A professional and para-professional stratum of Turkish teachers, social workers, psychologists, youth project directors, etc. is developing there as well. As a result, the majority of Turkish youth in Berlin are socialized in a primarily Turkish albeit German-Turkish environment.

Over 4000 small shops and businesses have mushroomed in these neighbourhoods: grocery stores, restaurants, cafés, hairdressers, repair shops, tailors, travel agents, video shops and second hand stores are the most common. These have created a Turkish infrastructure and territorial base in Berlin. Their success can be attributed to the desire for familiar cultural products. The need for *halal* meats has especially stimulated the link between business chains and religious movements (Gitmez and Wilpert forthcoming). Not long after the success of the first shops, when the future potential for Turkish goods immediately became apparent, wholesale companies were formed. They not only established a number of dependent retail shops with German names and delegated these to Turkish shopkeepers, but they provided all supplies as well. This line of development was significant for the establishment of Turkish business in

Berlin, because it laid the foundation for other large scale chains which in turn were able to exploit the traditional religious needs of a section of the population.

Between the early 1970s until about the mid 1980s, a series of religious business chains emerged, expanded and declined. These often had their own mosques, sport clubs, and Quran schools. Until about 1980, they competed among themselves and were often politically aligned with nationalist or conservative or political parties and movements, which were then primarily oriented toward an Islamic re-vitalization within the secular Turkish state.[8]

In addition to an economic infrastructure, Turks have established numerous (over 100) formal associations in Berlin. These express the full range of ideological diversity latent in Turkish society. Some of these associations, due to their controversial character, were first officially established in Germany. Until the early 1980s the majority of Turkish associations could be categorized according to their place on the continuum of the extreme poles of Turkish society. There are the most radical Maoist and Marxist splinter groups on the left through to the socialist worker associations with their affiliations to the then existing Turkish political parties, and at the other extreme the religiously oriented rightist parties. The religious movements among Turkish Muslims are also diverse. Movements and mosque associations have been identified which extend from the fundamentalists to Sufi mystics, from the secular state-espoused Islam to the most orthodox, ranging from conservative to progressive (Elsas 1983) to the Alevi.

Little information exists on the exact numerical significance of these groups. The scant available data comes from the reports issued by the associations themselves, which can thus be presumed to be influenced by their competing to appear as the legitimate representatives of the Turkish Muslim population. Here it is sufficient to know that there are several divergent tendencies among what is considered to be the majority Sunni population (Gitmez and Wilpert forthcoming).

Formal religious organizations are less significant for the Alevis. To our knowledge there exists only one in Berlin; but nothing, however, is known about the number of their members. Since their religious organization is not based on mosques and Quran courses instruction and their religious leadership is often tied to a hereditary family system and traditional tribal structures, it may be especially difficult for the Alevi to evoke new kinds of formal institutions abroad. On the other hand, their religious-ethnic identity lends strength to their informal social networks which appear to be extremely efficient despite the extensive mobility and fragmentation caused by migration. In Berlin there have been some attempts to recreate the traditional communal prayer ceremony, the Cem, attracting Alevis of very different regional and ethnic composition.

The Social Background of the Turkish Population in Berlin

It has taken at least two decades of Turkish life in Germany for the complexity of its internal structure to emerge. Until now, the internal heterogeneity of the Turkish population has been considered as having little significance for the establishment of a 'Turkish' way of life in Germany (Kudat 1976). However, with the increasing permanence of a Turkish enclave in Germany, the heterogeneity of origins may begin to increase in importance. Meanwhile, the balance of the original population structure has begun to shift. In order to evaluate the relative weight of the mutual perceptions found in the following observations it is opportune to provide some indications of the background of Turks in Berlin. Using material from earlier studies we have found that, on the other hand, the commonly held stereotype that the majority of Turks are East Anatolian peasants is not justified (Kudat 1976). Nevertheless, by 1974 a little less than one-half of the Turkish emigrants living in Berlin were born in villages in the East or West (Wilpert 1983).

Studies of the children of emigrants attending Berlin schools support these observations. Since 1974 it has been the villagers, who because they tend to have larger families have been the most capable of enlarging their presence in Berlin (Wilpert 1983). And, among the villagers it has been the religious and ethnic minorities who have been the most engaged in chain migration.

There are two distinctions of primary importance to be made about Turkish emigrant families in Germany. The first is whether or not they belong to the Sunni religious majority or to one of the religious minorities, here, the Alevi.

Table 1. A Typology of Characteristics of Turkish Migrant Families in Berlin

In this typology the signs indicate tendencies: + indicates relative common/high, – indicates relative weak/low, + / – and – / + indicate both characteristics with a tendency toward the first. The diagram is by definition extremely dichotomized. The 'Others' column includes such other minorities as Christians, Yezidi and Assyrians.

	RURAL/PEASANT FAMILIES					URBAN FAMILIES	
	Sunni		Alevi		Others	Sunni	Laicistic
	Turkish	Kurd	Turkish	Kurd			
Chain migration	– / +	+ / –	+ / –	+ / –	+ / –	–	–
Individual family migration	+	–	+	–	– / +	+	+
Large families with three or more children	+	+	– / +	+	+ / –	+ / –	–
Extreme fragmentation	+	+ / –	– / +	– / +	– / +	–	–
Educational level of parents beyond primary school	–	–	– / +	–	– / +	+	+

The second distinction is, whether or not they have participated in chain migration. The distinction between individual and chain migrants gains its significance from the role chain migration plays in the types of social relations and interaction patterns maintained in Berlin. Chain migrants tend to be more intensely involved in family, kin and village networks. Due to the nature of the situation, the individually migrating families are more subject to the broader Turkish community for their social and cultural needs.

In addition to these major classifying categories, obviously a number of other factors may contribute to the explanation of the extent of orthodoxy or the criteria employed for evaluating the social position and origins among Turks. Until recently the level of education and a person's urban as opposed to rural origins were thought to indicate the extent of more 'modern' secular belief systems as opposed to the more traditional among Turkish Muslims.[9] Table 1 gives a rough picture of the social structure of the Turkish enclave in Berlin.

Religious Affiliation as a Criterion for Social Interaction

Observations made by a Turkish emigrant from the Black Sea area exemplify some aspects of the question of religious affiliation among first generation Turks in Berlin. Our informant, who is referred to as a Kurd by his fellow *Landsmann* from the Black Sea, explains the chain migration of persons from his village. He speaks first about the solidarity among Kurds, how they help one another find a job, and how, once they have one, immediately send for their relatives and friends and thus appropriate all work. As it turns out, he means only certain Kurds, his kind, who are Sunni Muslims. He distinguishes between his fellow *Landsmänner* from the Black Sea, whether they are Kurd, Laz or Circassian, and 'Eastern' Kurds. As a Sunni he feels that he has more in common with other Black Sea migrants than with the Kurds from the East. They are "backward". "They can't even speak Turkish." However, contradicting the common image held about the division between East and West, "they" have also "become more westernized — they dress like Europeans", "their women have discarded their scarves".

These remarks mirror distinctions, symbolized by dress and outward appearances which reflect deep-seated cleavages central to Turkish society. His evaluations have nothing to do with being a Kurd, but reflect instead his Sunni sense of orthodoxy, which is disturbed by the less strict practice of traditional clothing customs for women by some Alevis. Outward appearances, especially the clothing styles of women, retain an important symbolic function in a strongly polarized Turkish society (Olsen 1985). These symbols and some characteristic responses are also at work among Turks abroad. Religious affiliations may also continue to maintain its ethnic-like quality among Turkish emigrants. And, as in the case of this informant from the Black Sea, signs of ethnic and religious identification may also become confused.

Chain Migration, Religious Identification and Social Interaction

Chain migration is built upon group solidarity, and evidently the ethnic and religious minorities have been the most active chain migrants. Many persons were able to enter Germany between 1973 and 1981 through marriage transactions. In some cases, as is common in some parts of rural Turkey, children's marriages would be arranged with cousins from their place of origin.[10]

Chain migration permits at least the partial reconstruction of family and village networks abroad. Depending on its extent of efficacy, chain migration may also tie the migrant and his family into interactions back home. The village community, then, though geographically distant, continues to exercise a certain social control over its members abroad. As one young man explains: "Even most of the young people primarily have to do with people from the same area". Rural origins in themselves are not sufficient to motivate interaction across ethno-religious boundaries. However, experiences of ascription and denigration as well as identification and solidarity patterns from Turkey are transmitted most easily through chain migration, where outward appearances may be more easily controlled or continue to be sustained by the group of fellow villages. Similarly, the intense interaction patterns of some village chain migrants may also cause others to dissociate from them. Nonetheless not only common village, but also common regional, cultural, or religious origins assume an additional dimension of shared identity in the foreign setting.

Marriage and Endogamy

Returning to the first case of Black Sea emigrants in Berlin, they do socialize, for example when looking for work, across ethnic groups following the solidarity patterns of the *Landsmannschaft* system. However, with respect to marriages of their children, the majority of first generation villagers prefer to practice endogamy. As our informant explains:

> These people from the village keep close ties among themselves. They form their own groups. Marriage is only possible within these groups. The Laz, Kurds and Circassian only marry among themselves. Sometimes, a Kurd takes a wife from the Laz. But, they don't give their own daughters to marry outside the group. The Circassian only marry among themselves.

These are all Sunnis, however, and their reluctance to intermarry is even greater with regard to Turks of another religious faith. Even if they are of the same ethnic group endogamy within one's own religion is the norm among rural Sunnis and Alevis.

Similarly, although Alevis consider themselves tolerant and open-minded, emigrants from Alevi villages in the East also apparently prefer endogamy. As expressed by the son of a village emigrant:

> We have a custom that the wish of one's father must be followed. And my father did not want someone outside the village . . . I only wanted what my parents desired, so we married. Families do not marry their children outside of their own circles. And marriages are not contracted with Sunnis. Among our villagers abroad there is only one woman who came from a Sunni family.

In these areas, marriages between cousins were always traditionally preferred. Rural families may, however, at times consider marriage with an outsider, but not with someone from another religious affiliation. One second generation Alevi and Kurd put it this way:

> Marriage with a Sunni is seldom. In general, we think that we understand ourselves better. After a certain point we have difficulties with Sunnis. Even if we can get along with one or the other, we cannot get on with their parents or their environment.

This claim is well illustrated in the following case of an Alevi family, who to the outside observer would appear 'well integrated' into life in Germany. Here, however, it is possible to observe the transformation of identification patterns from one generation to the next.

Both parents originate from a Kurdish village in East Anatolia, and were not educated beyond minimal literacy level. Their eldest son now attends university, their second is making similar plans. They live in a rather middle class section of Berlin. The mother, especially, has worked since her arrival in Berlin in 1967 to provide the family with what it needs. Due to the market for women in Berlin industry it was easier for her to find a job here. She was the first to migrate, but she was soon able to organize work for her husband. The four children were sent for two years later. At that time the daughter, Aysel, the second oldest in the family, was nine years of age.

The discussion which takes place between Aysel, now twenty-one, and her mother, Sema, centres on the daughter's future and the conditions a suitable spouse will have to fulfil. What makes this case interesting is both the high achievement orientation and solidarity of this family, as well as the mother's shifting identification between being Alevi and Kurd.

The narrative of the mother reflects her own perception of belonging to a Turkish minority, especially the experience of being discriminated against and looked down upon in Turkey. She also stresses the importance of her own ways, underlining their family values. Above all, Sema wants to make clear that, as an Alevi, she is liberal and humanitarian. She has nothing against other ethnic groups. As far as other Turks are concerned the Sunni are acceptable as long as they do not regard Kurds or Alevis in a condescending manner. She rejects the *hoca* bunch.

> You can look at the religious of the *hocas* among us, they're also going the wrong way. They have no respect for people . . . They're always saying we're [the Alevis] backward. In truth, they are the most backward of the backward . . . Look, in Beylerbey [near Istanbul] we've bought a huge villa and a piece of land, three

thousand square metres. But nearby are living people from Konya and Nigde. They wear headscarves. They are loud and peculiar people. It's a nice piece of land, but as long as these people are there, I'm not going to live there. We'll have to look for an apartment somewhere else.

On the other hand, Sema will allow her daughter to remain in Germany only if she marries, since parents are only free from the responsibility of their daughters when these are settled and in the care of a husband. Preoccupied with the qualifications of an eligible spouse for her daughter, Sema argues that the partner should at least be a liberal Turk since he would not look down on the Alevi if not an Alevi himself. Once, earlier, she used to insist that he be an Alevi, but "now I don't care anymore . . . The main thing is that he is well brought up . . . As long as he is from Turkey . . . But someone progressive like us . . . Most Sunnis don't like us. His family shouldn't disapprove of Alevis". Most important to Sema is that Aysel should marry a Turk:

> . . . we'd rather be together with people whom we know and who appreciate us. When our qualities and traditions are different, then there are a lot of problems . . . When someone is a good person, doesn't discriminate, he's okay for us. But when one wants to marry you, and says, 'You're just a Turk' or 'You're just an uneducated Alevi', or when parents say that — what can we do then?

Germans look down on them for being Turks, Sunnis denigrate them for being Alevis. It's not, however, solely discrimination which concerns Sema, she is also worried about marriage to a non-Turk, because of the difference in their "moral values". This is why she threatens to reject her daughter if she marries a foreigner. Marriage and the family have less meaning for Germans. If her daughter marries a European, she may one day find herself on the street. All the cases she knows of where Turkish girls have married foreigners have ended in divorce.

But, unlike the foregoing Alevi chain migrants living in a tight network of villagers, twenty-one year old Aysel has completely different reference groups from her parents. Her nuclear family remains, however, the central object of her loyalty and affection; on the other hand she also expresses a great deal of distance to Turks. Aysel is ambitious, and she has been relatively successful. She did well in school, but dropped out for personal reasons.[11] Her ambition and the achievement orientation of her family explain her relative job mobility. Despite the general negative ascription felt by Turks in Germany, Aysel has experienced personal opportunities for herself, and she plans to take further advantages of these.

She views the Turkish women at her place of work and the Turkish peers of her parents, here and in Turkey, as malicious gossips, condescending and socially manipulative. She has to keep her comings and goings a secret. At work she serves as a translator and a spokeswoman for her fellow workers. She defends the rights of the "conservative, scarved Sunni" women, but pesonally she cannot relate to them.

But, to her, Germans are not much better. Although she shares many interests with them, she does not trust them. They are not loyal. They feel superior to Turks, even although she does not have any qualities that irritate them. And, above all, German men are not to be trusted as they have a different value system. In contrast to her mother, however, she does not seem to be concerned about being an Alevi or a Kurd.

It is not nationality, or religion, but rather personal autonomy, material and emotional security which Aysel most values. Continuity with her family is found in her desire to respect and maintain her ties with them, but her own best friends are other foreigners, Portuguese, Spaniards, Americans.

This story illustrates some aspects of the transformation of religious and national identification among some Turkish women of the second generation, who like Aysel, prefer to remain in Germany because of the value they place upon personal autonomy. Germany provides the social space which according to Aysel's experience allows the manipulation of social identities as needed. Nevertheless, she remains loyal to her family of origin who continue to be a source of warmth and security.

This case only highlights some conditions and issues involved which may influence individual shifts in ethno-religious identification. This family and their daughter are not typical of village or chain migrants. The parents socialize with other 'liberal' Turks, whether Sunni or Alevi but not with Germans. And they live outside the Turkish enclave. Their children, especially the males, have been successful in their education and have attended schools with Germans. Aysel perceives occupational opportunities and freedom to manipulate her identity in Germany in ways not possible in Turkey. Moreover, she is not regarded by the Germans as a Turk, she has 'no qualities which irritate' them. In this case it looks as though Aysel and her mother are hoping for her entry into an 'enlightened' Turkish milieu, where religious affiliation and ethnic categorizations will no longer play a role in their lives.

The potential change or conservation of the primacy of religious affiliations among Alevis expresses itself, however, in other ways among the Sunni. For the traditional Sunni, non-Muslims and Alevi are never candidates for marriage with their daughters.

Attendance of the Quran School — A Conflictual Symbol of Muslim Identity and the Problem with Generalizations

The ability to read the Quran is a highly admired quality, which should earn esteem and reverence within the Muslim community. In Turkey a special religious office appoints and supervises religious education, in keeping with the submission of Islam to state authority. This has only been possible to a small extent in Germany, so that the majority of the *hocas*, teachers organizing Quran instruction, are affiliated to and supported by the movements alluded to earlier.

The emigrants referred to in this section are all Sunni Muslims, none of whom were involved in chain migration.

The Quran school instruction of children has been both a challenge to the authority of the Turkish state, and often knowingly linked to extremist political movements. Good practising Muslim parents who desire the maintenance of religious belief, customs and practices are faced with a dilemma. If they want their children to learn their faith, 'someone to pray for them when they are gone', to protect them from the dangers of 'German moral values', or ensure their acceptability to the reference groups in the settings they plan to return to in Turkey, religious practice and the discipline of Quran lessons are a logical alternative. If they live in predominantly Turkish neighbourhoods, there may even be additional social pressures to send their children to Quran courses.

In Turkish neighbourhoods such as Kreuzberg, the outside observer is struck by the increased visibility of the most traditional display of Muslim dress. Distinctive features such as long coats, veils, scarves, full beards were not as apparent a few years back as they are now. Here one would expect that pressure to send children to the Quran school would be the strongest. Our field work also verifies this. In 1975, we found that about 20 per cent of the school children we interviewed had at one time or another attended the Quran school (Wilpert 1980), while in a larger study in 1981 at least 30 per cent of those interviewed fell into this category (Wilpert 1983). From interviews with parents and children involved in both studies, we gleaned some insights into the need for and reaction to Quran instruction.

For those parents who are not necessarily the most militant members of a mosque community, the value of attending the Quran school is viewed primarily as a means of securing traditional beliefs and values. A father from a small town in Central Anatolia explains why he has not sent his children:

> My only worry is that the children may get into trouble. Here a lot of bad things happen and I would like to protect the children from them. Some families send their children to Quran school so that they do not get into trouble. I would have liked that too so that at least one of us after our death will read from the Quran. But here even Quran courses are not good — even there many things are happening. That's why I haven't sent them.
>
> We have neighbors here; their children go to the Quran course. Since our children are not going, they do not want them to play with our children, and when they see us they ask us why don't we send our children to the Quran course. I didn't want that our children would be burdened by that.

Other parents are very anxious to explain why they have decided to send children to Quran courses, as have the father and mother in the next case, a family with five children from a village near Giresun. This family experienced extreme fragmentation. Parents were separated from the children for three to five years — the eldest son was left with grandfather between the ages of nine and thirteen, and during this time he became extremely independent from the authority of his parents. First the father presents his reasons for sending his children to Quran school:

> Actually, Germany is not of value to a Turkish child. Their school and life situation is no good here. People are coming here from all parts of my country. The children like the life here. They begin to oppose their parents. You're not even allowed to hit your children here. The laws are on the side of the children, so of course it's easy for children to oppose their parents. Of course we should not become like Germans. We have our own customs that we have learned from our parents; we cannot just throw these customs away. My wife, for example, prays and covers her hair. In order that the children do not forget these customs we sent the two eldest to the Quran course. Actually, it was their mother who wanted that. But that doesn't help either, the children still go their own way here.

The mother interrupts:

> I wanted the children to attend the Quran course, but then they were hit by the *hoca* and that's why they don't go anymore. In the summer I will send my little one — of course, he has to go.

But their youngest son speaks up, claiming:

> I'm not going to the Quran course. Our teachers don't like it either. Learn German, learn English and then Arabic; it just gets you all mixed up in your head they say. That's why I don't want to go.

The older son at twenty, after seven years in Berlin, is rebellious, articulate and politically aware, but with all ambitions for his own advancement frustrated. It is he who sets the example for the younger children and can best explain why many young Turks have become alienated from the Quran school system.

> That's all that they do in the Quran courses. They say: Don't go to the German schools — they're Christians or Communists — that's what they say. If I wanted to I would do a lot against that, but right now I am not concerned with politics anymore. I went to the Quran school, I went there in Turkey because my grandparents wanted me to. But of course I didn't go regularly; I always ran away. And when I came to Germany my mother wanted me to go, and here the Quran schools are even stricter. No laughing, no talking, not even the slightest movement do they allow you to make. If you say a word they beat you. The iman stands in front and prays. No, I said, I can't continue with that. I told my mother that I'm not going to go anymore. My sister was going with me and I didn't let her go any longer either. To attract the youth they try every means possible: first they open a discotheque and then, next to it a Quran course to attract the youth. You can't achieve anything with a Quran course. Of course, my parents are a bit responsible. A relative or somebody from our area comes and says: Our children have already read the Quran twice, and what has your child done? My mother always takes their children as an example, and then I say to her: First we have to learn Turkish and then German and then we still have time to learn Arabic.

The repetition of this last refrain is significant since it has become standard rhetoric among youngsters who attend Berlin schools. These boys articulate the concern they have heard from school teachers, Turks and Germans, about the influence of Quran courses on school children.

These interviews were carried out in 1980, before the military coup in Turkey. It was also during the height of political activism among Turks in Germany. Another father of five children from a small town in the Province of Kütahya complains that at that time children were being 'brainwashed' in the Quran courses.

> For example, in the Quran course, they brainwash the children. Our children went there for quite a while, but we didn't insist, and they thought the situation was bad there, and they didn't want to go any longer. In fact, they went to the Quran course because other friends of theirs went. Our youngest child didn't go because we didn't allow him.
>
> It begins with the Quran and stops with weapons. They make religious fanatics out of them, in fact, even by the holy day prayers that's the case. If you are in the key party — the party of religious fanatics — you don't need to pay any contributions, but if that's not the case, then you have to pay ten DM every month.
>
> Besides that, in any case, I didn't want to let the children go. The children don't learn any morals or customs, and they don't learn it there either, when they go to the Quran school. The children don't know our customs and they don't know the German customs. They just behave like they feel. According to the ways of clothing, they adapt here — but of course, not quite. For example, they're not quite so liberal in their clothing. In fact, my wife dresses the same as when she came — she lives here as she did in Turkey.

His wife intercedes:

> Of course I've changed. If we would have been in Turkey, I wouldn't be sitting here talking with you. I only changed when I came to Germany. I've become more open. Of course, I still put on a scarf, but not as tightly as previously — you can still see some of my hair. My husband says that I should go around without my jacket and with short sleeves in the street, but I don't want that — after all, we're used to our ways.

This father's narrative illustrates a number of contradictions symbolized around the issue of Quran school instruction. Obviously aware of its political significance and referring to its ties to 'the party of religious fanatics', he feels one argument in favour of Quran courses would be that his children would learn 'morals and customs', but they don't learn them either. Religion, formerly taken for granted, assumes an added importance as a result of the helplessness of many families in the socialization of their children in the diaspora.

It is clear that these evaluations do not represent families who are active in Islamic organizations. Nor are they representative of the reaction of all children to the objectives and methods of instructions in Quran courses. Nonetheless, they do indicate some factors which make it difficult for the most zealous religious organizations to keep a hold on children educated in German schools with a completely different educational style. This is further complicated by migration conditions of extreme family fragmentation where parental values have as a result of alienation lost much of their former power. It also appears that this dilemma is most extreme for the conservative Sunni families of rural origins. Our interpretation is that family structure and its transformation through special patterns of migration also has an impact on affiliation and the transmission of values.

Conclusion

This article has attempted to cover quite disparate aspects of Muslim and Islamic affiliation in the social organization of the lives of Turks in Germany. These observations remain elements in the completion of a mosaic. The focus has been on ethno-religious affiliation as a means of social identification, the categorization of one's own group — or the other, which includes implications for social interaction, and the evaluation of the outward symbols of Muslim Alevi or Sunni or non-Muslim, German behaviour. In the narratives of first and second generation Turks we see that the way women dress is also an important ethno-religious symbol.

The picture of mutual categorizations and identification is so complex, that in this respect, I can identify with the comments of Bruno Etienne (1984) when he speaks about the existence and practice of Islam in Marseille. According to Etienne, his observations could provide evidence for both extremes: either to prove that Marseille is the centre of an Islamic network, or that there are no longer any practising Muslims living in Marseille. Etienne observes a tremendous cleavage between his study of Islamic institutions, networks and the messages they preach, and the daily lives and practices of the second and third generation youth from Muslim cultural backgrounds.

On the other hand I would not care to generalize about second and third generation Turks in Germany in a similar way. Some youth may be alienated from their families, but there exists a vast matrix of micro-contexts, as Table 1 indicates. It does not allow sweeping generalizations about relations between parents and children, or the second and third generation to their ethno-religious groups of origin.

Our observations illustrate a variety of relationships between religious identity and ethnicity. And some of these are based on a history of subordination and ethno-religious group consciousness. Particularly among the Alevis the confusion between ethnic and religious belongingness (Kurd or Alevi?) appears to become more critical abroad. First generation Alevis who are attempting to restructure and preserve religious rituals abroad, especially the practice of the Cem in Berlin, are concerned about losing the second and third generation to political extremism and ethnic movements. In fact, the family and its social networks in Germany and in Turkey continue to play a crucial role in the transmission of solidarity patterns as well as values.

Concern for religious and ethnic affiliation may be observed time and again among first and second generation Turkish migrants in Germany. And, as some of the above cases illustrate, there are shifting references to 'we' and 'they', as categorizations may overlap and interchange depending on the sphere of life or the ethno-religious distance from one's family of origin.

It is too early to answer fully the questions we raised at the outset, whether there is a polarization or attenuation of entrenched markers transferred from Turkey in the transition from one generation to the next. Although to be a Turk means to be a Muslim, for a large minority (the Alevi) it does not mean identification with the Sunni. The Alevis and the laicists are unlikely candidates for Islamic religious movements. At this stage it is difficult to evaluate whether Alevi solidarity will gain momentum to become in itself an ethno-religious movement abroad, or whether the modern Turkish ideology of laicism will counter-balance the Islamic or ethnic Kurdish causes to mobilize and unite Turks. Good arguments may be made for each case, but the trends are not clear. It appears that ethno-religious affiliations persevere. For the second generation Alevi and Sunni youth there is more than one source of authority putting claims or disclaimers on their ethno-religious identity. The first and most legitimate claim may be the state, until now the Turkish state, which refuses to recognize minority identities. And, to be a Turk, still means to be a Muslim, stratified accordingly in Germany.

Notes

1. Sections of this paper are revised versions of a chapter I have written with Ali S. Gitmez to appear in Rex *et al.* (forthcoming), which is particularly concerned with the structure of the Turkish migrant 'community' in Berlin. This work is based on several years of research with Turkish migrants in Berlin and returnees in Turkey (Gitmez and Wilpert 1979, 1983; Kudat 1974, 1976; Wilpert 1983, 1986). Within the context of a research project about the future prospects of migrant families at the Berlin Technical University, Ali Gitmez has collected a series of migration histories of first and second generation Turks in Berlin. In the same study, foreign youth and families were interviewed about their future aspirations and social networks. Preliminary results are reported in Wilpert (1983).
2. The Islamic Union is the official representative of the Islamic religion sponsored by the Turkish state.
3. Thomä-Venske (1981: 140–56) presents clearly the development of this controversy in Berlin.
4. One example of this is the position of a high administrative school official in Berlin (Bath 1982) who coined the phrase "a sneaking territorial invasion" with reference to Turkish settlement in the city. This educator speaking about integration went so far as to question whether "the naturalization of people from a Muslim culture is at all possible or bearable" (see also Wilpert 1983).
5. According to the most recent data from the Deutsche Bundesbank (1985), the amount of remittances transferred from Germany to the sending countries has not noticeably wavered between 1981 and 1984. Turks have transferred an annual average of DM 3.35 billion in this period, with a slight decrease in 1983, the year that

the German government offered the limited repatriation scheme. Remittances began to drop between 1975 and 1978, but increased sharply thereafter.
6. For a detailed ethnographic study of the customs and ritual of a Bektashi community in the West of Turkey which is akin to the Alevi, see Gökalp (1980).
7. This is quoted from Mandel's (1986) description in her thesis about relations between Alevi and Sunni migrants in Germany and Turkey. Ruth Mandel and I have done field work together among Alevi Turks in Berlin and summer returnees in Turkey.
8. Some of these continue to exist, on a smaller scale. A number of the diverse orientations among the splinter groups with mosques became affiliated with the Islamic Federation in 1981. New chains with a laicist orientation and the support of the Turkish secular state are now also being formed.
9. Toprak (1981) and Olsen (1985) comment on recent events to do with the public involvement of intellectuals, students and professors in the fight for the right to religious dress in public which would qualify such sweeping generalizations.
10. Although there are also instrumental attitudes among village chain migrants as well, as in one of the cases collected above (note 1). Many village males have entered Berlin through 'paper' and real marriages arranged by relatives usually with German women.
11. Relatively successful in school, this young woman dropped out at fifteen due to the pressure she felt from the protective and controlling behaviour of her elder brother. She then went to Turkey, increased her age on her papers so that she could receive a work permit, and upon return began to work in a factory. From the conveyor belt she has worked herself up to sales and part-time translation. She is ambitious to improve her occupational position through further training.

References

Bath, H. 1982. Integration: Chance oder Schlagwort? *Kritik der Ausländerpolitik.* Berlin: Hochschulpolitische Gesellschaft e.V.
Deutsche Bundesbank. 1985. Überweisungen ausländischer Arbeitsnehmer in ihre Heimatländer. *Ausländer in Deutschland* 3:4.
Duben, A. 1982. The significance of family and kinship in urban Turkey. *Sex roles, family and community in Turkey: an anthropological view.* Kagitcibasi, C., ed. Bloomington, Ind.: Indiana University Press.
Dubetsky, A. 1976. Kinship, primordial ties, and factory organization in Turkey: an anthropological view. *International Journal of Middle East Studies* 8: 433–51.
Elsas, C. 1983. Religiöse Faktoren für Identität: Politische Implikationen christlich-islamischer Gespräche in Berlin. *Identität. Veränderungen kultureller Eigenarten im Zusammenleben von Türken und Deutschen.* Elsas, C., ed. Hamburg: Rissen.
Engelbrektsson, U.-B. 1982. *The Force of Tradition: Turkish Migrants at Home and Abroad.* Göteborg: Acta Universitatis Gothoburgensis.
Etienne, B. 1984. L'Islam à Marseille ou les tribulations d'une anthropologue. *Les Temps Modernes* 40: 1616–36.
Gitmez, A.S. and Wilpert, C. 1979. *Disgoc Oykusu.* (The Myth of External Migration) Ankara: Maya Publication.
———. 1983. *Disgoc ve Donenler: Beklenenler, Gerceklesenler.* (External Migration and Return: Expectations, Fulfilments) Istanbul: Alan Publishing.
———. Forthcoming. A Micro-Society or an Ethnic Community? *Immigrant Associations in Europe.* Rex, J., et al., eds. Aldershot: Gower Press.

Gökalp, A. 1980. *Têtes rouges et bouches noires. Une confrérie tribale de l'Ouest Anatolie*. Paris: Société d'Ethnographie.
Karpat, K. 1976. *The Gecekondu: rural migration and urbanization*. Cambridge: Cambridge University Press.
Kudat, A. 1974. *International Labour Migration: A Description of the Preliminary findings of the West Berlin Migrant Worker Survey*. Berlin: Wissenschaftszentrum.
Kudat, A., et al. 1976. *Internal and External Migration Effects on the Experience of Foreign Workers in Europe*. Berlin: Wissenschaftszentrum.
Olsen, E.A. 1985. Muslim Identity and Secularism in Contemporary Turkey: 'The Headscarf Dispute'. *Anthropological Quarterly* 58:161-71.
Rex, J., et al., eds. Forthcoming. *Immigrant Associations in Europe*. Aldershot: Gower Press.
Thomä-Venske, H. 1981. *Islam und Integration*. Hamburg: Rissen.
Toprak, B. 1981. Religion and Turkish Women. *Women in Turkish Society*. Abadan-Unat, I., ed. Leiden: E.J. Brill.
Wilpert, C. 1980. *Die Zukunft der Zweiten Generation — Erwartungen und Verhaltungsmöglichkeiten ausländischer Kinder*. Königstein/Ts.: Hain.
———. 1983. Wanderungen und Zukunftsorientierungen von Migrantenfamilien. *Bedingungen und Folgen internationaler Migration*. Wilpert, C. and Morokvasic, M., eds. Berlin: Technische Universität Berlin.
———. 1986. Zukunftsorientierungen von Migrantenfamilien: Türkische Familien in Berlin. *Gastarbeiter*. Reiman, H., ed. München: Goldmann Verlag.
Yalman, N. 1969. Islamic Reform and the Mystic Tradition in Eastern Turkey. *Archives européennes de sociologie* X: 41-60.

6
The Islamic Presence in France

Rémy Leveau

The development of social attitudes in French society when people are faced with a visible Muslim presence brings to mind the argument concerning antisemitism proposed by Léon Poliakov. It was when the Jews became citizens like everybody else that hostile reactions became manifest.

"Before, they were not afraid because the immigrant spoke pidgin, and that was enough, he did his work. But today there are his children, this new youth speaking like their own children and in some cases having the same diplomas as their own children or other diplomas and thus other occupations than that of a labourer. This makes them feel threatened," explains an Algerian woman, born in France, twenty-five years old, secondary school diploma, secretary (Enquête 1985:454ff.).

The comparison with the Jews makes it easier to understand the sometimes ostentatious assertion of a separate identity. Since the end of the last century, western society has been accustomed to seeing organized groups formulate their demands in terms of Messianic political or social ideologies. Religion became a private matter and it was easy to note the decline of the church in urban and industrial societies. But it has been observed that the Jews in France, after the periods of persecution during World War II, returned to their religion as an assertion of their collective identity (Schnapper 1980:231). The presence of Islam in France provides a means of asserting a collective identity that is comparable to that of Judaism and is derived from the importance attached to practices of everyday life (dietary regulations, a rhythm of time marked by prayer and religious celebrations, ritual fasting). But, contrary to the rebirth of Jewish religious practice which was connected to a kind of reconquest of the religion from above based on intellectual reconstruction and support for the state of Israel, the affirmation of Islam assumes, rather, the form of "politics from below" (Bayart 1985). Social actors who are deprived of other legitimate means of asserting their collective presence, have recourse to the means of expression that are closest to them at their cultural level. French society — which for a variety of reasons does not accord them open access to its controlling and decision-making mechanisms — cannot, by virtue of its own principles, deny them the freedom of practising their religion which nevertheless, in being practised, is felt to be an assault on its secular social organization.

In a more profound sense, the idea that the manifestation of a collective identity in the middle of the twentieth century would assume religious forms, comparable to those of the Reformation and the religious wars, clashes with the conception of modern political procedure, organized and institutionalized both with respect to the demands of its participants and to the response of those in power. In the second half of the nineteenth century, after some violent events, the proletariat submitted to this procedure, having recourse to mass parties and unions. The first waves of Italian, Jewish and Polish immigration fell into the same pattern and negotiated in a classical manner their integration into the French system. Suddenly, one discovered that the Communist party, also in this context, no longer played the role that it had made its own during the 1930s and in the aftermath of World War II (Wihtol de Wenden-Didier 1986). The unions seemed bypassed and colonized by Maghrebi immigrants. Fearing the formation of a Muslim labour union, they went as far as to demand space and time for prayer in the factory. Television broadcasts in 1984 of striking workers praying at Poissy or Aulnay made all levels of French society aware of an overt Muslim presence. The Prime Minister even talked of sabotage actions against French industry carried out by Shiite extremists, thereby expressing a diffuse fear in the collective unconscious of a connection between the events in Iran and Lebanon and this new form of Islamic assertion in France.

Who are these Muslims? How many are they? How do they live their religion? Does their life in France influence their attitudes and their beliefs? A survey made during the month of Ramadan (May–June 1985) of a sample of some sixty persons, Maghrebis, Turks and West Africans, allows us to offer some rudimentary answers.

The Muslim population

During the times of the colonial empire, leading politicians did not hesitate to declare France a great Islamic power. It was in this spirit that the Mosque of Paris was constructed by the end of World War I, in recognition of the sacrifices made by the Muslim soldiers who had died for France. The Algerian immigrants have thus reappropriated this religious site that had been conceived in the spirit of the colonial exhibition of 1930, rather than in that of multi-cultural France. It was already at stake at the time of the struggle for the independence of the Maghreb. The French authorities were for a long time anxious to keep control over it before finally ceding it to an Algerian *imam*. Islam did not become visible until the 1970s, when it was associated with hunger strikes against expulsions, with demonstrations against raised rents in the Sonacotra housing complex and, above all, with the gradual transformation of the immigration of single individuals into an immigration of families. The assertion by a group of people of control over their daily life at the workplace and particularly in the residential area is linked to a conception of a long-term presence. During the first phases of immigration, Islam formed part of a set of practices and behaviour that remained associated with the country of origin. The immigrants often had their vacation coincide with Ramadan, if the employer accepted a certain flexibility. When unable to be absent a whole month, they arranged to spend the Id al-Kabir in the family environment, as much to make the celebration meaningful as to avoid unpleasant conflicts with neighbours over the sacrifice of a sheep in a dwelling shared with non-Muslims.

The settlement of families in France during the 1960s emphasized the need for a religious frame of reference for the education of the children, both those born in France and those who arrive while still very young. These children no longer benefit from the modes of collective socialization provided by a dominant Muslim community. On the contrary, they are subjected to the multiple demands of the environment which tend to make them lose their personality.

The transition from a situation where Muslims spend some years of their working life abroad but continue to anchor their religious life in their country of origin, to a situation where there is a community settled in France and negotiating its presence as a Muslim minority — this is a process occurring gradually and without the different groups concerned having a clear idea of the issues at stake and the objectives sought. The first immigrants to use Islam as the basis for an assertion of their identity, incidentally, were the former *harkis*. In the beginning, this group numbered some hundred thousand persons. Family members who joined later and numerous children have increased the number to approximately 400,000. Violently rejected by Algeria which continues to close its territory to their children, and being victims of racism and lack of understanding in their French environment, they were the first to find in an ostentatious Islam a means to assert a legitimate social identity that can be challenged neither by their Maghrebi fellow-believers nor by their French fellow-citizens. The former officers of the colonial army who continue, through the intermediary of various associations, to contribute to the integration of the *harkis* into the French system, seem from the beginning to have been in favour of this assertion of identity, organizing the participation in pilgrimages and the construction of mosques in community centres.

The Algerians, numbering more than 800,000, are the most numerous group among the Muslim immigrants. Either at the time of the Evian agreement or, later, simply through the workings of the regulations concerning French nationality — as in the case of previous waves of immigration — the existing legislation has allowed the integration of a large number of persons born in

France or who have lived there a long time. Although it is not possible to present precise figures, this group of French Muslims of Algerian origin can be estimated at more than 400,000 persons. Their position on the question of French nationality is often ambiguous since its adoption would correspond to a *de facto* cultural integration, which for some of them would entail a feeling of betrayal of their Islamic culture and of their past struggle for the independence of Algeria. To become French means in practice, for many, to become Christian since it entails adapting to a society that is deeply permeated by a secularity of Christian inspiration, and thus doubly removed from the spirit of Islam. In spite of this, the passing from one nationality to the other is accomplished in ways approximating those of the old immigrations, and the different degrees found in the practice of Islam lessen the barriers of nationality.

Similar comments could be made regarding the Tunisians (approx. 250,000) and the Moroccans (approx. 450,000). But we are here dealing with a more recent immigration, less integrated into the French system and more marked in various ways by the culture and society of the country of origin. The Tunisians seem, to a larger extent, to have been single migrants, to have a strong belief in the return to their country and to share, at the same time, a certain secular view of society which makes the French model more acceptable.

Like the Tunisians, the Moroccans have migrated as a result of the concern by the French rulers to diversify their sources of manpower after the independence of Algeria. They have often experienced, within a short span of time, the three stages that the Algerian immigrants have gone through since the 1930s. They have been worked on by the movements opposed to the government of Hassan II for a long time, and they remain very oriented towards their country of origin.

To these groups one must add approximately 120,000 Turks and 100,000 West Africans (mainly from Senegal and Mali) who have recently immigrated. In these two cases, a significant number of clandestine immigrants must be added. Whereas the Turks live mainly in families, the majority of the Africans are single, and experience Islam as structured by the brotherhoods of their country of origin, sometimes with a vague attitude of proselytism in relation to the receiving society.

To complete this brief survey of the groups who constitute the Islamic presence in France, we must mention the Middle Eastern Arabs (Lebanese, Syrians, Egyptians, Palestinians), but in most cases they have a Christian cultural background, and their wish to settle for a longer time is not so marked. Being middle class, they often engage in activities linked to the Arab and international world. There are also other categories of immigrant workers, like the Yugoslavs and the Pakistanis, who include a not insignificant number of Muslims. The French converts to Islam distinguish themselves more because of certain personalities than because of their numbers (approx. 30,000). They are now beginning to associate themselves with the activities and demands of their immigrant fellow-believers.

Relations to Islam

Without raising much concern, Islam has thus become the second largest religion in France and no doubt also the second religion of the French people. (According to figures quoted by Jacqueline Costa-Lascoux at a conference in Göteborg in April 1986, there are 2,800,000 Muslims in France, among them 1,500,00 Franco-Maghrebis. The 'sociological' Protestants and Jews were estimated to number 800,000–1,200,000 and 600,000–800,000 respectively.) It is, however, not a question of a homogeneous block but of a social group marked by a certain cultural and religious heritage within which the national currents and the individual itineraries in the midst of an alien urban and industrialized society allow for a wide diversity.

Maghrebi Islam is the tradition that has influenced the majority of the Muslims in France. It can be considered as homogeneous in spite of national divisions and rivalries. Next to it, the Turkish and African Muslims form sets that can be clearly distinguished and which are rivals in certain respects. But the greatest differences are certainly not attributable to national heritage. With some modification one could apply to the Muslims in France the categorization presented by Dominique Schnapper (1980) concerning the Jews.

Muslims who judge their life impossible in France because it interferes with their practice of Islam are very rare. A preference for the return to a country where Islam is the religion of the majority is often expressed, for individual and collective religious life is easier there, as a seventeen-year old Turkish girl, who has lived for ten years in France explained (Enquête 1985: 15). But this often constitutes a variant of the idea of return which tends to assume an increasingly mythical hue as the residence in France is prolonged. If departure is considered, it is mostly due to rejection by French society, to racism, to the economic crisis, rather than for religious reasons. On the contrary, a rigorous Muslim might justify his emigration in terms of *jihad* in the sense of bearing witness:

> My country is the country of Islam and of Muslims. The best is to live among Muslims, but he who has a very strong faith can lead a better life in non-Muslim countries. It is a kind of sacrifice. It is not a violent war, but the war to spread God's message, the voice of Islam and its image. One's education should be Muslim and one should be a model for others. Jihad should not be with a sword to kill people or to blow up something. That is a mistake, and that is not Islam at all.

This comment is by a thirty-three year old Moroccan, a bookseller who has lived in France for ten years (Enquête 1985: 333).

Similarly, for a Turkish tailor, a small entrepreneur in the clothing sector, who has been in France for seven years, "It's more important to live Islam in France than in Turkey, to be able to follow one's own ways and customs in a society that is different from one's own is a more important achievement" (Enquête 1985: 30). Numerous Muslims thus practise Islam in a minority situation with a certain ease and a sense of ordeal. But worries are easily aroused. Is there not a risk that life in France results in a long-term fusion with a non-Muslim population?

These concerns come to the fore, first, in connection with citizenship, since the identification between nationality and religion seems sometimes total and absolute. For a thirty-four year old Tunisian labourer who has lived in France for seventeen years, "to become French is to become Christian" (Enquête 1985: 505). Others express with more modification the same uneasiness without denying the advantage of a change of citizenship. "There are many people who for various reasons have become French citizens. As far as I am concerned, I will not change my nationality. I would feel that my religion had lost in importance, I would feel as if my faith had diminished." Often the refusal to change nationality expresses itself through the rejection of a way of life: "The French way of life is very different from that of a Muslim. It's not possible for a Muslim to take on French nationality. The French eat everything. They don't marry, they don't cover themselves. French nationality is good for work, for the papers, but not for customs," explains a fifty-two year old Turk, having lived for nineteen years in France (Enquête 1985: 120).

Indirectly, since Muslims reject the French political system, they appeal to an influential protector who can command respect for the Islamic rules. Often this will be the country of origin, but perhaps even more often a powerful country like Saudi Arabia which regards itself as invested with a general mission in the name of the *Umma*. It is asked to help in the construction of mosques, but also to serve as a spokesman for and, in fact, a protector of the Muslims in their host country.

The rigorous interpretation of Islam among intellectual believers appears to be a strategy for coping with French society. In some cases this may result in the return to Islamic countries and the obliteration of Occidental symbols. In others the rejection may be less absolute, but it may be necessary to constitute a separate group which has two needs to survive: either the external protection of the Muslim states, or a vigorous proselytizing effort to enlarge its base to encompass all Muslims in French society, or even beyond if circumstances allow. The ultimate dream is to find oneself again within the framework of an Islamic majority and thus rid of the present contradictions.

Muslim identity is asserted through the public practice of religion, the education of children and, in a very strong sense for a significant number of those surveyed, the keeping of the dietary prohibitions that assume an importance comparable to that observed among Orthodox Jews. This point is especially sensitive since the Muslims complain about not having at their disposal safe and recognized institutions — on equal terms with the Jews — which allow them to consume meat that has been ritually slaughtered. They are therefore forced, if they want to respect the prescriptions of the Quran, to act in an almost delinquent manner which marginalizes them, and makes them fear the authorities and the attention of the common people. "We go to the countryside to slaughter a sheep, a chicken. We have never bought in the store . . . We go to the country saying 'Bismullah' and everything.'' (Interviewer:) "Is it your father who does the slaughtering?'' (Informant:) "Yes, it's my father who does the slaughtering'' (Enquête 1985: 15). The problem is particularly acute at the time of Muslim celebrations, if the father himself wants to cut the throat of the sheep in front of the assembled family. "Among French municipalities there is not one that provides some kind of slaughterhouse where Muslims can cut the throat of a sheep . . .'' (Enquête 1985: 191).

The dietary restrictions inhibit contact between those observing them and non-Muslims. Some refuse contact totally, but one may speculate to what extent this constitutes a reaction to a rejection met within the context of work and residence. The cultural level, the linguistic fluency, the economic and social success seem, in a classical fashion, to play their parts as intervening factors.

The education of children is an area in which the concern to maintain one's identity, with varying degrees of openness to the surrounding society, is particularly manifest. In this context the dietary restrictions also justify, in the eyes of some, their hesitation to have contacts with the outside. Invitations are not accepted for fear of coming into contact with impure food. In other cases, visiting non-Muslims is accepted if there is certainty that they will respect the dietary restrictions which will be conscientiously recalled. "I may well accept the invitation, but I will not eat any meat . . . Why shouldn't I go? He is also a human being. If they invite me, I will go to them, but without eating their meat'' (Enquête 1985: 98). "I eat, as God has said, with the Catholics and the Jews (the food of the 'People of the Book' is permitted), but not with the atheists'' (Enquête 1985: 332).

Next to food, the school has an important place in the assertion of a Muslim identity. There is a great fear of seeing young Muslims exposed to ideas and to contacts that would rapidly make them French. With rare exceptions, the accusations against schools are not connected with the mode of teaching, but with the absence of educational responsibility and the conflicts arising from the mixed classes or from not respecting the dietary restrictions. "To be in France is a loss to Islam, since the majority of the children born here will be non-Muslim'' (Enquête 1985: 143).

"Here, if anywhere, the children need Muslim culture. Besides, I have decided to return permanently to Turkey for that reason. Here, the culture is totally contrary to Islam. The schools seem to be like brothels,'' says a thirty-seven year old Turkish woman who has lived in France for ten years (Enquête 1985: 143).

"An immigrant will not go to a private school. He goes to a secular school where he is taught Napoleon, the French Revolution, the Rights of Man. He will not be given any religious education'' (Enquête 1985: 560).

Others are of the opinion that all teaching, even of mathematics and natural sciences, should be Islamic in content in order to preserve the cultural authenticity of the children. Many, without going to these extremes, think that the principle of mixed education is unacceptable after the girls have reached puberty.

Rigorous Muslims also wish to assert their identity by building mosques that will allow them to practise their religion openly. The height of the minaret and the call to prayer appear to some as the very conditions for the exercise of the cult in a manner comparable with that of a Muslim country. "Muslim communities are obliged to construct mosques that are a proclamation of Islam wherever they go. It is an obligation, a necessity for the religion" (Enquête 1985: 55). "It's good to construct mosques and prayer halls, because there are millions of Muslims in this country. At the moment, there is not even the voice of the 'Ezan' (the muezzin). When we go to our country, at five o'clock in the morning there is the voice of the Ezan, it is not necessary to set the alarm," explains a twenty-two year old Turkish worker who has been in France for four years (Enquête 1985: 67). More often the presence of the mosque is justified on the grounds of the education of the youth, the morals, a certain form of civic spirit. Since it is thought that mosques contribute to the general order and the common good, their construction should, in the eyes of those holding a rigorous view of Islam, be funded by the government or the municipalities of the host country. In the view of others, they should be agreed upon by both immigrant Muslims and the countries of origin. Many complain that the construction of mosques is being obstructed by the municipalities, although there is recognition that progress has been made.

The mosque appears as the symbol of the reconstituted group, of its ties to the *Umma*, the community of believers. It is also the symbol of the durable presence of the group, and of its desire to sanctify the place where it finds itself. A Muslim on the move can pray anywhere, make up for Ramadan later if he has not been able to observe it, or even gain dispensation from it if he is on a journey. Settled in more permanent quarters, he can no longer be content with leaving religion behind in his home country, only practising it during holidays. He finds it necessary to meet with other believers, to procure the legitimate foodstuffs, to circumcise the boys, and to teach his children Arabic and the Quran. In providing these services, the mosque also helps to resolve his everyday problems and creates networks of solidarity in case of sickness or unemployment. It permits the women and children to break out of their isolation while ensuring that their socializing is acceptable. It organizes pilgrimages to Mecca and holidays in the countries of origin. It also provides funeral arrangements through mutual help associations linked to the mosque which may be charged with the repatriation of the body to the country of origin, or the interment in France according to the demands of Islam.

All these services have the effect of structuring the community, of organizing it as a separate group and assuring it a dignified presence in France. In this regard, they constitute a factor of integration not on an individual but on a communal basis.

Proselytizing is also widespread among settled Muslims. There are few persons among the interviewers — with some familiarity with the countries of origin or with the Arabic language — who have not asked themselves, at one time or another, about their own relation to Islam. Settled in France, the Muslims seek intermediaries with French society and they wish them to be Muslims. French Muslims also offer the advantage of being situated outside national and geographical divisions affecting the immigrant communities. If the immigrants think of the Arabs as belonging to the inner circle of Islam, they will readily think that French Muslims could further their participation in the French system. But one does not find a wish for, or an illusion of, a massive conversion.

This will to effect a religious penetration of the surrounding society can be put alongside a pronounced desire for dissociation from the French political order. It is regarded as secular and therefore contrary to Islamic principles which do not make the distinction between religion and politics. The secularity of French society obliges these believers to situate their politics elsewhere, in the countries of origin or in the protector countries, who thus have the mission of seeing that the French system respects the rules of the Muslim community in its midst.

With Ramadan and prayer, we approach a domain where the behaviour of practising Muslims is dependent as much on public as on private life. Some would emphasize the necessity of the testimony constituted by the observance of fasting, on condition that one works as usual. The same principle applies to prayers in the work place. Others find that they cannot achieve a satisfactory state of ritual purity for fulfilling their religious duties at the work place, or they feel that they should not steal time from the employer. Rigorous religious observance can be accompanied by a retreat to the family environment. This may have as a consequence the gradual movement towards another category of Muslims that one could call private believers. For the latter, there is a basis for a social secularism in the sense that they recognize the exterior law of the state or the employer.

> Here we practise religion, it's good to do that, but you can't force everyone to practise the way we do. You have to practise where you are because you have to be there . . . We are not required to practise the same way we do in a country where everyone is a Muslim. We are required to practise our religion where we live, without bothering about the others.

This is the opinion of a forty-year-old Moroccan, a qualified worker with twenty years' residence in France, married with four children and living in a low-cost housing complex in a Parisian suburb (Enquête 1985: 524).

> When I'm working, God does not require me to practise my religion formally. Because I'm under the order of my employer, he comes first. That means that if I want to practise my religion, it must be with the consent of my employer . . . This is why you have to make all the prayers when you are free. You can do them before going to bed . . . As for Ramadan, it's even better to be lighter, you work better, you are calm. But the last days it gets a bit hard . . . Still, Ramadan is something that has to be observed without making it a catastrophe for the body, for the person . . .

The same person would accept his children becoming French, provided that they remained Muslim and that their religious choice was respected, like that of the Jews, and that it would not be shameful to be called Muhammad or Ali.

These Muslims make a choice of the obligations they will observe, for example the food and drink prohibitions relating to pork and alcohol and partially also those relating to Ramadan. But one notices among them a clearly different attitude with respect to politics in the French context. The end of the traditional conception, according to which politics constitutes a direct and necessary expression of religion, leads to a new attitude. There is a willingness to participate in French political life, an attitude coupled with a concern to be recognized, individually and collectively, as members of French society. Some of them still decide to make their activism a function of the Muslim community in general, and usually with a reference to Islam in the country of origin. Others are especially concerned about the place of Muslims in French society. The former are often students or intellectuals who have come to France with the intention of staying for a limited time. They prolong their stay through various jobs that do not normally measure up to the ambitions which their education may have led them to expect. Still, they do not abandon this prolonged waiting situation. Instead, they transfer their sense of injustice at their status as *déclassé* intellectuals to the relation between Islam and the Occident. Their militant attitude does not concern France, except to the extent that it places them in a vaster and less degrading context.

Since Islam is viewed by them, first of all, in its historical and political dimension, the battle must be fought even inside French society. Obtaining the right to vote would not only signify the recognition, individual and collective, of the Muslim immigrants; it would also give these active and knowledgeable militants the means to wage a much more effective struggle for their identity expressed by Islam. According to this view, French society is a society whose political system is legitimately constituted according to its own rules, whereas for the traditional believers the only legitimate society is the one conforming to the religious rules. If necessary, the protection of an authentic Islamic regime may permit a Muslim to live in the environment provided by a heathen society.

To these militants, the talk about the right to vote, the citizenship and the nationality is above all a step towards integration. This stance is balanced by an affirmation of identity that has abandoned references to the countries of origin, but tends to idealize the Palestinian cause.

The group of private believers is characterized by a long stay in France, by a certain integration with respect to occupation and family, and by the intention of staying in France to see their children achieve the goal of upward mobility that they themselves had in the beginning.

The non-practitioners

The survey also revealed the existence of a large group who do not practise their religion and to whom Islam is often but a distant background. Most of them belong to the group of Maghrebis born in France who tend increasingly to present a secularized version of Islam as an ultimate point of reference, much influenced by the French environment. During the 1985 survey we encountered persons in this category who refused to answer questions. It was explained by comments like: "Islam, that was something for my parents." Sometimes a reference would be added about a brother or a cousin still considered to be a practising Muslim, but whom the survey would often reveal to have only a certain religious restlessness. When they became aware of their distance to religious practice, they often made maximalistic declarations of principle on the following themes: "The new *beur* generation will return to Islam." Or: "One should build mosques and allow Maghrebi workers to perform their prayers at the work place." These declarations would be the more peremptory, the more their education and aspirations showed that they were little concerned about these facilities. Speaking poor Arabic and not reading it at all, they would have no access to the traditional religious culture. Moreover, their rational approach learned in school and in French society would be applied equally in the religious domain and most often hinder them from benefitting from the simple initiation that their illiterate parents could have provided. To believe or to practise, they have to construct a justifying argument. If not successful in this endeavour, they tend to escape into militancy, idealizing their country of origin, Kabylian culture, or the diverse movements within the second generation. For them, the passage from religion to traditional politics is accomplished through the demonstration of a marked interest in the right to vote in France, although they may hesitate on the question of citizenship and justify it — not by religion this time — but by the racism or the rejection shown by French society.

It is in people with this pattern of behaviour that one finds a favourable stance taken towards the Palestinian cause. On this question there is a continuum stretching all the way from wearing the keffiye to an intellectual and emotional interest, in principle similar to the reference to Israel that, with many Jews, takes the place of religious practice. In the French environment, this attitude among the youth of Maghrebi origin is associated with an anti-zionism that is sometimes difficult to distinguish from anti-semitism. The presence in France of what they regard as a powerful and organized Jewish community, occupying important positions in the world of politics, business and even the church, seems to them an almost insurmountable obstacle to their ambiguous wish for integration. At one extreme, the existence of the Jewish community is used to justify their hesitation to take the step of naturalization, for their efforts would be blocked by the Jewish community. It is taken for granted among Muslims in France that to accept integration would require, first of all, renouncing the political protection of the Muslim community. If the endeavour to enter a secularized Christian system leads to the submission, in fact, to a social authority exercised by Jews, then the endeavour is judged impossible. Through a series of imperceptible displacements, the defence of the Palestinian cause becomes, thus, an important element common to both groups of militants. For those who see their future in France, the difficulties encountered in their efforts of integration remind them of the fate of the Arabs in Israel and of the desperate struggle of the Palestinians in the Middle East.

This reaction seems especially exaggerated since, unlike the Jews, the Muslims in France have a very small elite. Their settlement is of recent origin, and their reticence concerning citizenship prohibits them from entering public office, otherwise a source of dignity and representation. The members of the free professions still have a better chance of succeeding in their countries of origin. Those who have settled in France wish to distinguish themselves from the labouring immigrants. The merchants, who form a substantial group, played an important role supporting the Front de Liberation Nationale, but many wish to have French customers and take great care in their relations with the wider society. Their role in the black economy and in the illicit money-changing networks also puts them in a position which is unfavourable to political engagement. The proliferation of associations, the youth of their cadres, and their inability to join forces in action that would be significant for the environment — all seem to indicate the emergence of a self-mandated elite. This elite is for the moment totally against any involvement with political parties, labour unions, or organizations like the SOS Racisme. The countries of origin have little more success, in spite of a few spectacular examples such as the election of Akka Ghazi, leader of the CGT, at Aulney-sous-Bois, to the Moroccan parliament in 1985.

But the problem for this new elite remains its relation to the French system. Organizational life, relations to local or national authorities, to the media, and to the churches have contributed to their relatively smooth integration following models of recruitment to political action which reject the institutional game where they would feel 'trapped'. The 'foyer' strikes, the manifestations in the factories associating Islam with statutory revendications and the hunger strikes against the expulsions or the modifications of the rules for acquiring French nationality have inserted them into the French system without forcing them to embrace it or to formulate general goals. But their problems can no longer be dealt with in their absence, without knowing with whom to engage in dialogue.

A good number of these militants belong also to the category of children of Muslim immigrants who have passed through the French school system and are today usually called *beurs*. Their religious practice has been weakened and the acculturation to French society has carried them far from their origins. In particular, they have adopted the idea that religious notions and practices belong in the sphere of private life.

Some typical answers will illustrate these attitudes. This is an Algerian secretary, unmarried, who arrived in France at the age of five, talking about Islam:

> I admit that I don't know very many [persons speaking of Islam]. I don't even know anyone. I belong perhaps to the great majority of young *beurs*. I have never really been interested in that kind of problem. We talk about it in the family, but outside of it I would never call my friend to say: Hallo Islam. What can one say about it, where can one talk about it? In these matters I think there is a certain shyness. I have been able to read the Quran, in the French version . . . I did not learn the prayers. I asked to be taught them, but I must say that my parents are illiterate . . . But I did go through with Ramadan once to prove to my parents that there were other things that could make us fast. This was to explain my conviction that it is not necessarily a superior being that gives you the power to fast (Enquête 1985: 445-59).

To a French architect of Algerian origin, the distance from Islam is even greater:

> I don't feel Muslim in the religious sense of the term. On the cultural level, say, it's clear that I have got something . . . It's something of an asset. I feel I have something positive in spite of the fact that for me it has always been something negative, because my education at school was complicated for a number of reasons. But now I feel it has become an asset . . . Yes, now I eat pork, I drink wine and I like it . . . All religions are the same to me . . . but I think that for a worker of Muslim origin, the only support in this society, the only thing he can master, that belongs to him, is his religion . . . So, of course, I understand his attitude completely (Enquête 1985: 370-5).

Still, they refuse French citizenship. One might think that the attachment to their parents, the memory of the war in Algeria, which they themselves mention, would prevent them from full participation in French political life, the only one they know and are interested in, and yet demand French citizenship. But it is possible that they still unconsciously merge the notion of nationality and the Islamic community. This would give legal and political naturalization a connotation of betrayal of the family and, in a wider sense, of the Maghrebi community. The Algerian war, mentioned in the interviews, has in this way reactivated the Islamic tradition.

But today, the young *beurs* do not show less attachment to France than French youth in general. One may even ask whether the perception and the celebration of France as a country of freedom, of openness, of the meeting and mixing of different cultures does not constitute the new expression of patriotism in accordance with the values expressed by the whole of their generation.

In trying to circumvent the problem of nationality on account of their parents, the *beurs* do express a desire for political participation shown, for example, in their activism within the movements defending immigrants or combating racism. One may view anti-racist activism as a contemporary reinterpretation of the values emerging from the republican tradition and understand this militancy as an expression of internalized democratic values.

The problem of the relation to France is at the heart of their own search for themselves. The discovery of cultural differences and the quest for their own origin follow similar procedures. The identification with French society begins with the school, the sports, the general culture of the big cities and suburbs. Today, the media and the consumer society have taken over and extended the role of the school.

The countries of origin do not count for much: a place for sunny holidays and couscous on Sundays, a sentimental link of the same kind that Bretons and Corsicans living in Paris have with Bretagne and Corsica. But the entry into French society is not made without difficulty due to the economic crisis and especially because the French fear Islam on account of its international, mainly Middle Eastern dimension. The risks for a confrontation derive more from this perception than from an Islamic reality embraced by the second generation. On the contrary, the *beurs* reproduce a distorted and not very orthodox version of Islam without real connections to the behaviour that gives rise to the delusions of the host society.

This Islam of the militants and the *beurs* demonstrates a search for a collective identity. One may advance the hypothesis that it is a provisional identity, a passing discourse which serves the special purpose of breaking away from the society of origin. One does not yet dare to proclaim oneself French, because the memories of the war in Algeria are still too close, and one fears the parental curse. One also fears the very real rejection on the part of a society that has no need of you and makes you feel it.

This Islam is, however, essentially an imaginary Islam having little relation to the Islam of living communities experienced by the parents and still constituting the frame of reference for Muslim believers. It is practised in French, without much regard for the rules which one ignores, reinterprets or transgresses at will.

In less than twenty years, the transformation of immigration in France and in the countries of Europe (especially West Germany, Belgium, the Netherlands and England) has created a new situation through the permanent settlement of a Muslim minority community. The social existence of this community has more often borrowed the means for expressing its identity from religion than from class position. The French example is not unique (cf. Bastenier and Dassetto 1985) and, in spite of its particularity, Islam reminds one of the behaviour observed within the Jewish community (Schnapper 1980). The analysis of the survey of Islam in France shows, in fact, that there are very few cases expressing the impossibility of living in France according to one's religious principles. A significant number of immigrants of the first generation choose Islam as a way of affirming their identity. They do so with the aim, it seems, of negotiating their integration and also, no doubt, because they lack access to alternative legitimate channels of expression and representation. In return, the religious practice of the young people of the second generation is much influenced by the secular character of French society. Their behaviour with regard to Islam is similar to that of the 'Israelites' analysed by Dominique Schnapper (1983) with respect to Judaism. The less they are concerned with their own religious practice the stronger is their demand for religious rights for others. They find ways of socialization that owe more to sports, media or associations than to religion.

Their Muslim sensibility tends to be affirmed in terms of political solidarity with the Arab nation, the Palestinian cause or the new forms of struggle against racism that occupy a position for which the political parties and the labour unions have not been able to find a place within their frame of reference. Faced with this new situation, the traditional social forces have shown only hostility or incomprehension. They continue to act as if they believe that the immigrants will return home or as if one can integrate them more or less like the old waves of immigration. The fear that the events in Iran or Lebanon will spread makes them instinctively place the Islamic fact outside the domain of French politics for as long as possible.

As for French society in general, it reacts to the crisis by seeing 'Islamic fighters' where the militants use essentially non-violence, hunger strikes, and symbolic manifestations addressed more to French public opinion, French media and French authorities than to the external Muslim world. They prove to be more anxious to obtain the support of the Christian churches and the Primat des Gaules than that of the Shaykh of al-Azhar. The sudden concern of the countries of origin for the second generation is a sign both of this rift and of their confusion. The efforts of Algeria by means of the Amicale or the Mosque of Paris (over which it obtained control from the French authorities in 1982) have been joined by those of Morocco and to a lesser extent by Tunisia. They send teachers of Arabic and preachers to recruit the immigrants and not to leave the field open to preachers from neighbouring countries or from the Middle East. In addition, the countries of origin fear the development of an agitation against them that would be based on Islam. They are ready to collaborate with the French authorities in controlling the activities of Islamic movements seeking support among the immigrants. The risk for conflict is undoubtedly more real in this sphere than in the sphere of French politics. However, one should not exclude the possibility that violent action will occur borrowing Islam as a mobilizing theme. But it would then be the case of a reconstructed identity, comparable to the black Muslims in America. This entails precisely the risk of introducing, as parties in the negotiations for a settlement of the conflict, state actors or religious actors who have little interest in facilitating a compromise.

It is only in considering Islam as one of the permanent constituents of the social, religious and political system of France and Europe that it will be possible to escape from the ambiguities characterizing the present situation of immigration. The other inevitable outcome would be violence, which has already occurred in some reactions and practices of a socially marginal nature — violence on the part of the immigrants as well as the dominating society.

References

Bastenier, A. and Dassetto, F. 1985. Organisations musulmanes de Belgique et insertion sociale des populations immigrées. *Revue européenne des migrations internationales* 1 (septembre): 9–21.

Bayart, J.-F. 1985. L'énonciation du politique. *Revue française de science politique* 35:3 (juin): 343–74.

Enquête CERI-INSP. 1985. *Culture islamique et attitudes politiques dans la population musulmane en France* (mai–juin).

Schnapper, D. 1980. *Juifs et israélites*. Paris: Gallimard.

———. 1983. Les jeunes générations juives dans la société française. *Etudes*, mars: 323–37.

Wihtol de Wenden-Didier, C. 1986. *Les immigrés et la politique*. Thèse. Paris: Institut d'Etudes Politiques.

7
The Second Generation:
The Children of Muslim Immigrants in France

Annie Krieger-Krynicki

The expression 'second generation' has now become a standard one, although it is somewhat inappropriate since it is already the third generation knocking at the doors of the labour market. There are in France 1.5 million Muslim immigrants with their origin in the Maghreb, and close to 200,000 Turks and 5000 Pakistanis. To this category must be added the Muslims from black Africa. The second generation Muslims, however, consists mainly of daughters and sons of Algerian workers settled in France. It is difficult to give exact figures, since the legislation on information and freedom of 1978 prohibits the listing of religious denomination. Those younger than twenty-five years are estimated to number around one million.

This second generation is uneasily positioned between a society that integrates them poorly and a country of origin towards which their parents maintain an increasingly vain hope of return. It was noted, in 1977, that only 867 workers out of 14,000 wanted to make use of the legally provided assistance to return. Mohammed, a young unemployed man, declares: "I have a French identity card but I have never time to show it to the employer. My curly hair and my brown skin have already intervened to my disadvantage." A young Algerian woman, returning from the country of origin of her parents, is devastated at having been treated as a tourist and as a lost woman because she was wearing jeans.

Rootless, members of the second generation have tried to express their protest by turning their back to society. Says Cherif: "I'm a citizen of the world of work. I'm not afraid of racism, but of unemployment. My country will be the Europe of work." He is a nomad without borders and without roots.

The legal and social position of the young 'Beurs'

One million of the young Beurs have a double nationality, which only complicates their situation without increasing their opportunities. These are Algerian children born in France after 1 January 1963. They are claimed by Algeria, but also by France which does not want to lose her nationals easily. An act of 9 January 1973, requires a statement of renunciation or a verdict of loss of citizenship. Young people born after 1963 must, at the age of eighteen, ask for the national identity card. If they want to remain Algerian, they have to obtain a certificate of residence in Algeria, where they may never have lived.

In 1981, the French Minister of the Interior, Gaston Deferre, declared that the Algerians should be considered foreign workers and not immigrants and that consequently the young born in France should not get French citizenship automatically. This idea was taken up in the political programme of the new government, that wants citizenship to be a consequence of a voluntary and informed choice. The opinion of the young is in this respect as ambiguous as is their situation. During a colloquy in Lyon in 1983, they rejected the right to participate only in municipal elections, which would have recreated the system of two electorates, one French and one Muslim, that existed in their countries of origin during the colonial era — a disturbing reminiscence. At the same time, they demand double citizenship and full voting rights. There is a potential danger here. One can imagine the consequences of a successful national election of a candidate who had claimed to be in favour of Polisario, and consequently had been supported by the Algerians and opposed by the Moroccans. The result would be a disruption between the Algerian and Moroccan communities.

After having initiated the illustrious March for Equality in 1983, and the March for Convergence in 1984, the young Beurs wanted in 1985 to sensitize the public to their marginal position by a celebration at the Place de la Concorde where they would demand the right to be different. It was planned to take place in 1986, but apparently in a changed spirit, — one of integration into the national community.

The attitude towards the right to vote goes as far as a total rejection on the national level. It is explained by young people to be caused by a kind of embarrassment in relation to their parents, who are not allowed to vote. In a curious way, to achieve voting rights in France would in their minds be an indication of social promotion. One is led to believe that we are dealing here with a rational attitude. Many young people admit in confidence that they are afraid to hurt their parents by abandoning their nationality, to hurt them in their patriotism and to destroy their hope of return.

This prospect of return is dreaded by the women who are in no rush to lose the little independence that exile has accorded them. It is also feared by the children, who would almost like to be absorbed into France. Speaking French with the accent of Marseille, Lille or Paris, they will go as far as making their first names French. Warda becomes Dora, Djenane becomes Gina or Anne,

Mohammed becomes Medi or Maurice. Jeans and anorak are the uniform of the most conformist, whereas the most daring girls create an extravagant fashion for themselves. This is just one example of how the refusal of others creates a whole range of attitudes. Delinquency leads 20 per cent of the young Maghrebis to prison or special homes. Protests against forced marriages places young women in dead-end streets, leading to run-aways or suicides. Resignation, poorly coped with, leads to educational failures and to unemployment.

The father distrusts the shining and cold world of consumption, and tries to keep his children away from its temptations. A taxi driver settled his family in a small village far from Paris and without any means of communication. This way, his children will not be 'contaminated', will not be attracted to and subsequently rejected by French youth, and will respect him without rebellion. Modern urban society makes one lose one's sense of honour, but he, the father would never receive back a delinquent child. It is the mother who would take the steps to soften this harsh judgement. He would retreat in shame. Naturalization, modernization, delinquency — there are so many risks. It is understandable that the atmosphere in certain homes is heavy and oppressive for the young.

Some interviews point to the difficulties of transition, like Malika's, who has arrived from Lille to watch Maghrebi films in Paris. She prepares for the *baccalauréat B* (a secondary-school degree with emphasis on economics and social studies) and does research at the library of a cultural centre, compiling documents in anticipation of a presentation. Her professor has advised her to talk about Maghrebi novels written in French. A friend goes with her. She is well versed in Arabic and has chosen books in Arabic, not to be found in Lille. She reads and writes proper Arabic, whereas Malika only speaks Arabic at home and does not write it. Her friend envisages an initial university spell in Algeria, and perhaps a permanent return. A male sitting close by watches Malika intensely. She blushes. If she encourages him, perhaps as a joke, it would be just a game. Although she is perfectly westernized intellectually, the family taboo is too strong. There could be neither adventure nor marriage. She dives back into the books, her only escape. From this stems the success in schools and universities for girls who have nothing but this pursuit as a loophole.

One student is Algerian, from Tlemcen. He has a degree from Paris VIII, and prepares a doctoral thesis. His project concerns the translation of works on linguistics and structural grammar into Arabic. He makes his living through teaching Arabic in the immigrant associations. Emotionally, the future seems bleak to him. If he marries a French girl, he does not envisage a return to Algeria, where he now spends his holidays. If he finds a student of Maghrebi origin who is cultivated enough, will he be able to obtain the consent of her family, who may have attitudes rooted still in the seventeenth century?

Ahmed comes out from the Centre Georges Pompidou where there has been an exhibition about the artistic creativity of the second generation. He is twenty years old and he is upset about what he calls "cultural fetishism". "Look at that old man! He has been working for twenty years, but he will have to go back since he is unemployed. We don't care about all that, the right to vote, films, paintings," he explains. "We want to come and go, and work wherever it is possible." He does not think about returning, as he feels the hostility on the part of the Berber against the Arabization and he finds Algerian socialism oppressive. As for religion, that is something he ignores. Somewhat embarrassing to him, a youngster intervenes: "Religion, one shouldn't mock it. But work is also a serious matter." Saddock declares "I'm a Muslim and I'm French. When I tell my name, no-one gives me a job." Nevertheless, he has chosen the French identity card.

It is difficult to elaborate a theory on the basis of the hundreds of similar cases studied. One can only confirm the diagnosis of the second generation as not 'lost' but as being 'shoved around', and in danger of moving from failure to failure.

The condition of failure

The condition of failure is, of course, due to an unfavourable social and economic context, to the atmosphere of unease which has been described, to a complex attitude of the young with regard to their parents who are poorly integrated into French society and therefore held in disrespect. A young boy admitted that on Sundays, to walk behind his mother in her neckerchief and Maghrebi dress and his father in his outdated jacket and with the swarm of brothers and sisters was becoming quite an ordeal. At his age, shyness and fear of non-conformism is unbearable.

The feeling of humiliation is shared by the children of the *harkis*, the Muslim soldiers who — having fought on the French side in the Algerian war for independence — fled to France after 1962, and are now 'living dead' in a society of which they are nevertheless full members. Their children are seriously handicapped in educational achievements and social advancement. This impression is reinforced by the fact that foreign Maghrebi students from a non-French speaking but otherwise more advantageous environment, often have a considerable rate of success in French schools and universitities.

For some sociologists and psychologists, the remedy for the loss of self-esteem described above would lie in a recognition of Muslim culture. This would allow for the rehabilitation of the attitudes of the parents otherwise considered obsolete and inconvenient, not to say ridiculous. This recognition is the aim of a large number of organizations, not least those which work to make the Maghrebi woman come out of her subservient position — a heritage of a tribal and agricultural society and not emanating out of the Quran. It is simultaneously a question of raising the value of her handicraft and cultural traditions as well as allowing their transmittance to French women and other immigrant women. The exchange is thus two-sided and strengthening for both parties.

This effort at raising self-esteem and also aiding integration works through televised broadcasts that constitute the basis for the culture of immigration. It is significant that televised programmes such as 'Mosaiques', produced by the Agence pour le développement des relations entre les cultures. (Agency for the development of relationships between cultures) and operating under the auspices of the Ministry of Social Affairs which also publishes a magazine called *Insertion*, constantly play the card of integration while maintaining the differences. Even more significant is the fact that a Beur magazine, launched in 1979 under the name *Sans Frontière* (Without Boundaries), now has the name *Baraka* (blessing, good wish): best wishes, in other words, to the second generation in its efforts at integration.

In school, these efforts at integration most frequently prove to be in vain. The Ministry of National Education has created introductory classes, up-grading courses, and adaptation classes for non-French speaking children. Some twenty Centres de formation et d'information (Training and information centres) for teachers were created between 1975 and 1980, but the teachers were too young and inexperienced to be able to handle classes where 50 to 80 per cent of the children were of foreign origin and without any contact with French children. The secularity of teachers was put to a serious test by the presence, prescribed by international conventions, of teachers of Maghrebi origin, paid by their home countries and teaching Arabic and the Quran during regular school hours. To avoid this discrimination, which was taking a religious character, it was proposed in 1985 to extend the language courses as well as the courses in Islamic civilization to all children. In addition, the immigrant parents themselves were afraid that their children would be confined to a new educational ghetto, and wanted them instead to learn English. Instead of watching pictures of their own country and making visits to an exhibition of Arab-Muslim art, they prefer their children to visit castles on the Loire. Since 1986 the very modest aim is to achieve perfect command of written and spoken French in elementary school, with the help of introductory classes and shortened programmes in other subjects.

To persons who reject traditional ways of teaching, the municipalities have created centres where basic skills are taught by means of computers. These teach reading and writing in the guise of modern games, suited to those with mobile and volatile minds, who have been discouraged by bookish methods since they come from an agricultural environment with an oral cultural tradition.

A feeling of incomprehension on the part of young people is also evident with respect to the necessities and constraints of collective living. This explains the outbreaks of vandalism in large housing complexes. The subsequent reactions of violence and vengeance mobilize the young anew, as against the murderous gunmen in the notorious town of Minguette, close to Lyon. The ambiguous feeling on the part of the second generation concerning the society where they have been called to live thus gives rise to outbreaks and rebellions when they do not understand the too remote values of this society. The members of this society react by reinforcing their ostracism. This reproduces the Greek society with its *métèques* excluded from civil rights and its 'barbarians' who did not speak the language.

To break this vicious circle, Sheik Abbès, the director of the mosque in Paris, voiced these ambivalent feelings and reactions in front of a congregation of French Muslims assembled in Lille on 27 April 1985:

> In a territory that is becoming an adopted territory and that will become yours, you, Muslims, should become acceptable, and thus accepted without loosing your identity. You must not make yourself accepted without being Muslim, but on the contrary accepted because you are Muslim. You must not be the object of disapproval by being lazy or violent. Islam is the opposite of this. We live in France, the country of the values of brotherhood, equality and liberty, and the majority of the French subscribe to these.

It is also possible that the idea of brotherhood is not extended to the young Beurs. They definitely have the impression of being rejected as Muslims. They feel that there is a fear among the French over the rebirth of a society that would mix the sacred and the profane as propagated by doctrinaire and proselytizing Muslims. The distinction between the sacred and the profane has been made in France since Philippe le Bel, it was reaffirmed during the Renaissance and secularity has been a governing principle since the Third Republic. But the Quran — revelation, cosmology, book of ethics — is also a social, legal and religious code. (It may be added that young Frenchmen of Ismailian confession have not had the same problems of integration, as their spiritual leader Agha Khan II has advised them to melt into the receiving society, to live like the French in France and like the Burmese in Burma.)

However, the problems of the youth are not of a religious order. Their unease with life is not metaphysical, but social. They believe, but they do not practise. The refusal to eat pork is constant, and the fasting during Ramadan is adhered to by some, but mainly to please their parents. On the other hand, superstitions are adhered to rather tenaciously. A young woman technician with upper secondary education, feared that she had been bewitched with crushed scorpions by her mother-in-law. A marabout disenchanted her, she gave him a blank cheque and was almost ruined. The experience left her dissatisfied but at the same time relieved. Incidents like these explain the vogue for marabouts, coming mainly from black Africa and proudly claiming to possess a 'Quranic ritual' to help their clients.

It is only when the agony of exile becomes unbearable that the immigrants, mainly those of the first generation, turn to religion. But the young are also susceptible to missionaries, some of whom come from Pakistan to preach the return to the sources of the Quran. The mosques grow like mushrooms at the initiative of the faithful. There are now 410 mosques with prayer halls, creating a climate of religious competition.

If French society, in spite of some incidents at the construction of these centres of worship and religious education, is essentially open to all religions, one may nevertheless note a certain hesitation regarding the demands for a multi-cultural society made by the members of the second generation.

The ambiguity of the concept of a multi-cultural society

All cultures consist of multiple and exterior contributions and none is completely pure. A striking example of such cultural syncretism, in this case the osmosis of Islam and the Occident, was given in a theatre performance in Paris.

In June 1984, the company belonging to Tayeb Saddiki, a Moroccan from Mogador-Essaouira, played at Maison des Cultures du Monde a piece called 'The Book of Delights and Pleasures'. The title is deceptive, as it is not a frivolous extract from *A Thousand and One Nights* but a staging of a religious and political work by a persecuted author who lived in tenth-century Baghdad, at the time of the Buyid caliphs who made Shiism prevail. However, the book defends another heresy, one which was hostile to the cult of Ali and was a kind of syncretism of several religions, including Hinduism. The author was condemned and burned to death after a trial conducted by a judge, 'Iradatoullah', depicted as an irascible ayatollah, and 'Lalla Fkithi', a ferocious woman acting as prosecutor.

Various coloured masks overflowed the scene: vizirs and town people in turbans, veiled women, filthy beggars, a yellow felt camel in the style of Bob Wilson but with less naivety and more winks to the public which explodes in laughter at the social criticism, barely veiled by the evocation of the tenth century. The narrator of the play displays Arabic eloquence, mixed with phrases in French slang. The choir echoes quotations in Latin. The Moroccan, Algerian, French and Beur spectators cry with laughter at the quotes from Aristotle, used at random by the pedantic officers of the court. The alert comedians, who relate to the style of the Commedia del Arte, turn everything into derision: bigotry, intellectual pretentiousness, egoistic politicking, superstition and fanaticism.

This is reminiscent of the truculence of Rabelais and the implacable powers of observation of Molière. Nevertheless, even if the Arab intellectual is not duped by anything and does not take himself seriously — not even in his return to his cultural roots — he remains a prime example of a *homo religiosus*. His critique of society, be it amused or bitter, is inserted in a metaphysical dissertation. He has not adopted the French culture, nor is he bi-cultural, but rather tri-cultural if one considers the Greco-Latin heritage which he takes care to preserve. This makes him even more of an anachronism, as this particular heritage has been recklessly eroded in France since 1967.

Some Beurs sincerely believe that multi-culturalism is an illusion. Farid Chopel, a young comedian who abandoned his medical studies for the stage, thinks so. He does not enquire into his roots. His mother left Kabylia when she was eight years old. "I feel Parisian all the way to the earlobes," he claims, "and then French." He explains the marginalization of the young with reference to their disadvantaged social and economic position. "But multi-cultural society does not exist," he claims, "because what is the culture of the second generation? The same as that of the French of the same age." This means among other things television, cinema, comic strips and rock music. Farid Chopel claims that he has no Arab culture except the music.

Karim Kacel is today a famous singer, and speaks only French and sings in French. His mother made him read the works of the Comtesse de Ségur (1799–1874) as a child. His father advised him not to forget that he is a Kabyle. "I am a mutant," he declares. The painter Rachid Khimone dismembers Arabic letters he does not know in order to decorate the gutter plates he exposes, marking the itinerary of the Beur along the devious paths of the French city. In the film *Thé au Harem d'Archi Ahmed*, Mehdi Charif depicts the story, comparable to *Satyricon*, of two suburban hooligans who have broken with school and family. The Maghrebi and the French are here united in the same lack of culture.

In a book by the writer Leila Sebbar, the liberated heroine leaves to find the country of her parents' dream after a long journey in the sulphuric Parisian underground. Her parents look for her everywhere, except at the library of the Centre Pompidou, where she is reading everything that comes under her eyes, like many other young people.

To be an artist is an envied profession among these young people, irrespective of origin or religion. Maybe this is a more obvious way out for those who are rejected by the regular educational system. This is the reason for the fortunes made by the agencies run by young Beurs and casting other Beurs for films intended for a large public. The films by Charif and *Baton Rouge* by Rachid Bouchared are considered to be too confidential. The short-film festival of young immigrants was viewed as a ghetto by its participants as well as by the association of film directors. Music has produced an intercultural breed with an increasing number of groups like 'Babouch Rock', whose members want to stay Algerian, 'Mohammed Travolta', 'Carte de séjour', 'Bossa-Nova Kabyle'. The names speak for themselves.

One could conclude with the song by Lounis Lounès: "My country, it's a bag in my hand, ready to go, although French is written on my card." But he adds: "They won't erase me from here, Paris, city of my troubles."

Contradiction, ambiguity, expressions of disenchantment by lonely youths distanced from their parents and basically not claimed by any country. They are not undesirables. They are simply not desired, which may be worse. However, the country of origin of their parents chooses to work on them at the very moment they want to be included, perhaps even integrated, in French society.

The policies of the countries of origin to attract their nationals

The policies of the countries of origin have developed gradually. After the associations and the friendship meetings, cultural centres were created. Since 1984, teachers from Tunisia, Algeria and Egypt have been in charge of literacy programmes. One centre for the learning and relearning of Arabic can function only due to Egyptian students who are working on their masters theses in French. These teachers devote part of their time to teaching Maghrebi youngsters to read and write so that at least they will be able to communicate with their families. With assistance from the associations, they have created a library as well as a painting and drawing studio.

For the Algerians, a very important cultural centre has been created in Paris with a library holding newspapers and some 12,000 books in French and Arabic. Showings of films from the Third World, Maghreb and France attract youth who receive perspectives other than those fragmented and parochial ones provided by their parents. A set of lectures in French by university teachers or Algerian administrators makes it possible to expose the economic, social and cultural situation of their country. Exhibitions of work by African or second generation artists attract the Algerian community, whereas the language laboratory for Arabic drains Lille and Lyon of their students. Some of the participants admit to being flattered by the dimensions of their own culture, but it will be their French teacher who will have initiated them to the Maghrebi authors in French!

Basically, it is a question of providing the young people with enough options to enable them to make a free choice. The Charter of Alger in 1964 had as one of the objectives the repatriation of its nationals. On 10 November 1983, President Chadli Bendjedid declared in front of 2000 members of the Algerian community in Paris that had welcomed him: "You are all ambassadors of Algeria. French law must be respected, but the aim of each one of you should be to return to your country."

The leader of the Pakistan People's Party, Benazir Bhutto, has the same aim of wanting to give a boost to her country by allowing the immigrants in the Emirates and in France to return. After 1981, since the closing of immigration to England and the introduction of limitations on entries in the Gulf States, some 20,000 immigrants have arrived clandestinely. The problem of the younger generation has not yet arisen, the community is turned inwards, and closed off by a total ignorance of French. The people of this community have been attracted by the hope of getting rich, or at least of making a modest living. But the idea of an El Dorado has vanished rapidly. The disappointment is deep. They would like to return to their country, but with empty hands this is impossible.

It has been shown that attitudes vary with different communities and environments. For the young of the second generation who have become doctors, lawyers, teachers, administrators, the problem of a multi-cultural society does not exist. They have been assimilated into French culture, but they will retain a certain curiosity, sympathy and interest in this original culture, which they may wish to know about and retain. But scorn is the only thing left to those who feel rejected by the social system. Rachid Khimone interpreted this in a tragi-comical way in his exhibition at the Algerian Cultural Centre in May, 1986. One painting called *Ali False News* showed a figure with two pieces of gutter instead of eyes. The exhibition had a telling title: 'The Suitcase-men, Men of Nowhere and Everywhere . . .'.

8
Islam in Belgium:
Contradictions and Perspectives

Albert Bastenier

Immigration to Belgium from countries of Islamic culture is rather recent. Beginning in the first half of the 1960s and consisting mainly of Maghrebis and Turks, it constitutes the latest migratory wave. These migrants arrived to join others of foreign origin who had been massively mobilized since 1945 to perform subordinate manual tasks from which indigenous labour had deserted or was too scarce to manage. The relative lateness of the Maghrebi and Turkish immigrations has not prevented these migrants from growing rapidly and acquiring an important position among the 900,000 foreigners in this country. In 1960, they numbered 1200, in 1970 some 65,000, and in 1985 about 200,000 (of whom 130,000 are Maghrebis and 70,000 Turks). In terms of size, the immigrant category with Muslim background is in second place, after the Italians (approx. 320,000) and before the Spaniards (approx. 58,000). They constitute almost 2 per cent of the total population in the country, but, due to unequal regional distribution, this figure is misleading. Whereas they do not constitute more than 1.1 per cent of the population in the Flemish region and 1.3 per cent in the Wallonian region, they amount to almost 8 per cent of the population in Brussels, where their presence has become increasingly manifest in the course of the last few years.

Islam has become a widely-embraced, collective reality in the midst of Belgian society. Quantitatively, it represents the second largest religious category of the country. But one should also note the qualitative aspect of the situation which has thus emerged. Since it is necessary, generally speaking, to regard immigration as a powerful demographic phenomenon with a heavy formative effect upon human societies, one may claim that Belgium has witnessed, during the last forty years, one of the most significant demographic events in its entire history. From the moment its durable character became evident, the Muslim component of this phenomenon could not be minimized. The consequences of this migration passed unnoticed, no doubt, in the beginning of the period when Muslims established themselves in Belgium, when they were still uncertain as to the future of their settlement and when they accepted the relegation of their religion to the category of realities pertaining to their countries of origin. It is not at all the same today. Increasingly conscious of the long-term stakes of their settlement, they have reached the point of exhuming the symbolic attributes of their faith and culture which had been buried or maintained clandestinely. Through the specific case of Islam, one is thus forced to pay attention to one of the long ignored implications of the settlement of populations of foreign origin in Belgium. Since it is an irreversible social phenomenon, the very definition of the 'migrant' and his status must be changed. For many years, the migrant was looked upon as an individual in transit or as an 'immigrant' expected to make his distinct features disappear after some time. Now, however, he tends more and more to be defined and to define himself as a new citizen but also as a member of an ethnic minority maintaining a specific identity.

Nonetheless, the fact that the expression of a collective identity can assume religious forms goes against the conceptions generally held of modern social and political life. Even in a country such as Belgium, where legislation has accorded the great religious traditions a relatively privileged status, this goes against the tradition of situating religious convictions in the private domain of life and regarding them as regulated by the secular state only to the extent that they enter the public realm. This is also the reason why the affirmation of the identity of the Muslim community by means of the only thing that really belongs to it and that it has the power to master — the religion — has led finally to the demarcation of the limits to, if not the failure of, the model for integrating foreigners that has been operating for a long time in this country. One is led to say in retrospect that, perhaps, the assimilation of the Poles, the Italians, the Spaniards and many others took place at the expense of a mutilation of those concerned. Until today this has not been recognized. This holds true unless assimilation (or that which has been considered as such) of these categories of immigrants is infinitely less real than has been commonly thought and unless the too harsh demands of society have caused a tendency to rely on an underground network for the expression of a still inveterate identity. But awareness of these matters required the experience of the immigration from Muslim countries.

The decisive question that has to be faced is the one concerning the place accorded cultural and ethnic minorities in societies which consider themselves democratic. Having become in fact multi-cultural and even multi-religious, will they demand that these new segments of their population not make any perceptible signs — which could be judged troublesome or even intolerable — of their specific character or intimate convictions? Or, on the contrary, will these societies abandon such injunctions, which, in the final analysis, are perceived as abusive demands requiring the abandonment of certain human rights upon which democratic regimes are considered to be founded? So far, this question has not received any convincing, definite and clear answer. Its various implications are only beginning to be grasped. The case of Belgium proves to be especially interesting to analyse and this for a very particular reason. After a period in which the Muslim minority appeared to operate without major difficulties according to the institutional scheme in force with respect to religion, there arose evident tensions between the minority and the indigenous public opinion on the one hand, and between the Belgian authorities and the official representatives of the minority on the other hand.

The study which we have carried out attempts to delineate the sociological realities of Islam transplanted to Belgium, especially with regard to the immigrants originating from Morocco and Turkey.[1] It is limited, however, to the analysis of organized Islam such as it appears in the mosques, in religious instruction, in the movements and brotherhoods, and in the state apparatus. We have deliberately left aside the question of Islam as a system of values and orientation for conduct in other than religious domains of life.

The visible basis of Islam: the mosques

For a population of some 200,000 persons, there are in Belgium approximately 130 places of Islamic worship. We are here dealing with a relatively recent phenomenon, as half of them have been established during the last five years. Thus, although the population originating from Muslim countries has multiplied by approximately 2.8 between the years 1970 and 1981, the number of mosques has increased tenfold. This has resulted in an infrastructure of mosques in Belgium with a density that is almost comparable with that of the countries of origin.

The creation of a mosque reveals the existence of unshaken social skills. From the moment the decision is taken to organize a place of worship, the responsibilities are rapidly established according to codified rules. These are relatively standardized and hierarchical. Nevertheless, there are two types of social of organization from which mosques emerge.

The most common type is created by heads of families on the basis of nationality, residence, village of origin and, often enough, close kinship links. The function of these places of worship is limited to the area where they are situated. Sometimes these places of worship are created through the fission of a preexisting mosque for religious, political and ethnic or kinship reasons. Other places of worship, less numerous than those discussed above, are created by religious movements, be they traditionalist or reformist, with or without political connotations. They have a local anchorage but their sphere of influence is more extended, reaching members and sympathizers of the movement in Belgium and sometimes even in other European countries.

Even if we find these two types of organization in the origins of the mosques, their final configurations are a good deal more complex. These places of worship, and particularly those with only local influence, are rather rapidly surrounded by agents with religious interests of another kind. There is, for example, the Directorate of Religious Affairs of the Turkish government attempting to preside over the organization of mosques. Likewise, although in a less explicit manner, the Moroccan consulate seeks to intervene. On its part, the Centre Islamique et Culturelle de Belgique tries to coordinate and supervise the entire cultural organization and to educate the *imams*. The religious movements, furthermore, make attempts at proselytizing in the mosques by visiting them regularly and providing guidance. The social basis of the mosques is a result of their becoming the meeting place for different religious interests, whether conflicting or converging, but this also provides considerable vitality to the social life of these places of worship.

In our research, an attempt has been made to delineate the profile of the people visiting the mosques and to specify, from a qualitative perspective, what in the beginning appeared to be merely a quantitative reawakening of Islam. Two important characteristics have emerged. Firstly, it is obvious that with few exceptions the mosques are organized as national entities, incidentally a fact that is denied by the believers themselves in the name of the universality of Islam. Secondly, the mosques are frequented mainly by adult men over the age of eighteen years. The mosque is thus expressive of a masculine Islam. As regards the feminine Islam, it belongs to the private sphere and is even conceived of as heterodox. This tendency, already current in the countries of origin, becomes vigorous in emigration. The organization of the places of worship and the pattern of frequenting them belong above all to the adult male society and in particular to that of the married men. One may perceive a certain evolution of this society: whereas it is the heads of families who are dominant in the local mosques and in the oldest ones, the young men seem to appear in greater numbers in the recently established mosques and in those connected to the movements. This is due, it seems, to the fact that the new mosques and the movements foster a reflexive attitude to Islam using codes that are not limited to a simple reproduction of traditional models.

The places of worship are seldom equipped with a separate entrance for women, or a special area in the prayer room according to custom. Even when these particular arrangements have been made, female participation is not very high. In a mosque in Brussels where we carried out a census, the proportion of women did not exceed 5 per cent. In general, the percentage of women among the people visiting a mosque is between 2 and 3 per cent. In a recent investigation in Casablanca, the proportion of women in the places of worship was found to be less than 10 per cent. Such a figure would seem to lend support to our findings and also to indicate a tendency for the masculinization of the places of worship under the conditions of immigration. If this tendency can be further confirmed and if the frequenting of the mosque can be regarded as the public pole of the public/private polarity, it would confirm once more the increased circumscription of immigrant women.

Quranic schools are almost always attached to the mosques. According to our survey, they are frequented by some 15 per cent of the children of Muslim origin. A considerable pedagogical uncertainty is noticeable in the transplanted Quranic school. One may find both the most traditional pedagogical model (children seated on the floor, tablets, learning the Quran by heart through recitation) and more modern schooling methods, as well as various mixtures between the two. Yet, these various methods all retain a very authoritarian conception of the teacher which is in stark contrast to the pedagogical model usually advanced in Belgian schools.

How is one to understand this development of the mosques? The creation of the mosques is a result of the demands articulated by their potential users. But the proliferation of mosques is still not comprehensible without taking into account the organizations offering these services. These offers are the result of the activities of various agents. They may emanate from individual religious agents who kindle religious needs and somehow or other stimulate the organization of the demand. They may also emanate from religious groups making use of the social force deriving either from the tradition or from their own capacity for recruitment and mobilization. The offers may, moreover, emanate from state or interstate authorities to which the political and religious powers delegate the task of organizing Islam. In addition to the activities of bodies belonging to each emigration state, there has also been the development of the new and potentially universal role of the Muslim World League with the prestigious backing of Saudi Arabia. The last element is, finally, the Belgian state itself to which we shall return later. But it is clear that the success of these offers, as well as the proliferation of spontaneous initiatives to create places of worship, would not be possible without the existence of a pressing demand and unless these places really did fulfil certain functions.

There may be multiple and converging hypotheses for explaining the growth of the mosques. One hypothesis would postulate that the mosque is a meeting place allowing the reconstitution of social networks disrupted by emigration. If so, is this a case of an old model in a new social context, in other words a dysfunctional social organization? This is, some would argue, evoking the ghetto.

A second hypothesis would focus on the psycho-social functions of the mosques interpreting their development as a consequence of the search for a functional substitute in a situation of marginality and frustration. To illustrate this hypothesis, let me mention two examples. The mosque could be the answer to the search for 'Muslim space', a pure enclave as opposed to the polluted and polluting environment which lacks respect for the Islamic rules. The mosque could also be a place of certainty of truth as opposed to the uncertainty and doubts arising out of a situation of change and cultural rupture.

A third hypothesis derives rather from a theory of identity. Islam would, according to this hypothesis, permit the reaffirmation of the identity of a marginalized immigrant group. The mosque becomes a place for the reaffirmation of the identity of a community of adult (and unemployed) men whose position of authority is threatened today as much on account of the activities of the youth, as on account of the new roles for women.

Finally, the development of the mosques can be interpreted as an indication of a modification of the migratory project in the sense of an orientation towards stabilization. Somehow, the creation of the mosques coincides with the massive process of family reunification and a concern with the socialization of the children which is an essential part of this process.

A vertical cut through Islam

Beyond the immediately visible part of Muslim organizations, observable especially at the time of prayer, there is a vast network of religious organizations of various kinds, less obvious and sometimes striving for secrecy. As a preliminary measure, one may classify them into, on the one hand, those organizations deriving from the traditional brotherhoods (*tariqa*) and, on the other hand, those movements which have emerged within the framework of Islamic reform during this century.

It is beyond the scope of this chapter to provide a detailed analysis of each of these movements. Suffice it to say that some of those proposing a 'political' approach to Islam, such as the Muslim Brotherhood and the Association d'Etudiants Musulmans, are marginal to the majority of the immigrants and have gained a foothold mainly in intellectual circles. Others, such as the Tabligh, the Sulaymancilar and the Alawiyya, are centred at the very heart of the immigrant population. Whereas the Alawiyya develops a kind of modernized version of classical Sufism attractive to the youth, the Tabligh[2] is characterized by the intentions of setting up a practical and proselytizing Islam presenting itself as apolitical but at the same time reinforcing identity symbols such as the beard, the *jellaba* and spatial rearrangements of the home.

One may venture a classification of these movements using two axes. One runs from the 'traditional' to the 'modern' pole, and the other from the 'political' to the 'isolationist'. From the organizational point of view, the movements orientating themselves towards the traditional pole develop personal ties to leaders of a charismatic and authoritarian type. It may occur, moreover, that these movements are based on community foundations and are grafted onto already existing social networks. The modern movements recruit their followers rather on the basis of adherence to Islamic ideology and doctrine and through the mobilization deriving from the vigour of this adherence.

State activities

The organization of transplanted Islam brings with it new political actors related to the new political framework within which Islam has now got to function.

The states from which the immigrants come undoubtedly seek to maintain their tutelage over their expatriate citizens. They are not inclined to watch passively the attenuation of the migrants' links with their home countries which could well lead to the ultimate stabilization of the immigrants in the new country. This attitude has both ideological and economic reasons (such as the need for continued remittances). In various domains of the life of the immigrants — associations, culture and religion — there is thus an attempt at 'forging allegiances' in the transplanted population.

Morocco intervenes in a rather disorganized and ultimately limited way, operating more through the infiltration of informers than through actual organizational procedures. More important are the activities of the General Directorate of Religious Affairs of the Turkish government, represented in Belgium by an official with diplomatic status. Moreover, an international association has been constituted that is supposed to provide a firm institutional base for the organization of Islam under immigrant conditions. The desire to create an institutionalized framework for Muslims of Turkish origin is easily seen here. One may actually speak of a diffusion of a national Islam so that the shifting relations between the Islamic religion and what the Turkish state expects from it are extended into Belgium itself.

The principal organization, however, aiming at coordinating and guiding the future of Islam in its new political and territorial circumstances is, in fact, the Centre Islamique et Culturel de Belgique. This is an international organization linked to the Muslim World League operating under the aegis of Saudi Arabia. Although contested on many sides by competing associations, the Centre has acquired actual power over the organization of mosques, the education of staff and the nomination of teachers. It derives its power first of all from the considerable means put at its disposal by the League. It should be added that Brussels is the seat of the League's department for promoting the establishment of mosques in Europe. In addition, the Belgian government has conferred upon it the privileged role of being the official Muslim voice on all matters rising out of the law of 1974 concerning the "worldly aspects" of Islam in this country.

We should therefore consider another actor intervening in Islamic matters — the Belgian state. The Belgian constitution does not recognize official religions, but guarantees that the state will assume part of the financial burden of the infrastructure and some of the current costs for certain 'recognized' religions. Since 1974, this provision has applied to Islam on the same grounds as to other religions already benefiting from this advantageous treatment. Moreover, within the field of public education, the state pays the salaries of the teachers giving religious instruction while abstaining from intervening in the appointment of these teachers or in the content of the courses. This is considered to fall within the competence of the authorities of each religion.

Since 1974, the Belgian state has thus recognized the Centre Islamique et Culturel de Belgique as spokesman for the Muslims in the appointment of religious teachers and in the organization of 'mosque committees' charged with the practical management of the mosques and the financial support of the *imams*. In the case of the mosques there have still not been any concrete effects of the law of 1974. In the case of education, on the other hand, one can observe a considerable and progressive development of courses in Islamic religion. For the school year 1984/85, more than 300 Turkish and Arabic speaking teachers of religion were appointed in Belgian schools. Some 20,000 pupils in primary school and some 9000 pupils in secondary school attended such courses (that is about 50 per cent of all those potentially concerned).

The motives of the Belgian government for adopting the law of 1974 were fairly ambiguous at the time. Even if some of the promoters of the law were inspired by respect for the freedom of religion, this law was meant to maintain good relations with the oil-producing countries in the context of the first oil crisis and at a time when Belgium was negotiating commercial contracts with them. Once this recognition of Islam had been hastily accomplished, it was followed by complete uncertainty as to the implementation of the law. In practice it turned out to be problematic, for example, to appoint religious teachers. Taking into account the existing rivalries concerning the exercise of religious leadership within the Muslim community, the authority given to the Centre Islamique et Culturel de Belgique to appoint religious teachers was highly controversial. Incidentally, this criticism extended beyond the confines of the Muslim immigrant communities. Within the 'progressive' faction of the indigenous public opinion voices were raised questioning the exclusive position maintained by the Centre Islamique. Was not the Centre primarily the spokesman for the Islam of the powerful? And did not its practice in the sphere of education run the risk of being nothing but a political and religious tutelage aimed at channelling and controlling the aspirations and the ideological orientation of the transplanted Muslim masses? Moreover, the Belgian state itself had, paradoxically, become one of the principal organizers of Islam in the country. The system of appointing religious teachers permits foreign governments to select personnel, according to their own criteria, who are to function within the Belgian framework. By relinquishing to other states part of its own prerogatives in such a sensitive area as education, did not the Belgian government somewhat hastily give away the possibility of evaluating correctly the actual role played by the teachers in the process of cultural and social integration? Surely children of immigrant parents are entitled to expect such an assessment from the educational institutions? Behind this issue, as is evident, there is the question again of the 'forging of allegiances' within the immigrant population. The fact that the teaching of Islam in the schools has been conceived, so far, by the religious authorities concerned as a way of shaping Muslim immigrants with the help of a staff essentially imported from outside Belgium, was certain to raise some anxieties.

Nothing more was called for in order to make some people evoke the 'fanaticism' of certain teachers of the Islamic religion. This trend started at the beginning of the 1980s when international events were increasingly marked by the effects of the Islamic radicalism of the Iranian revolution. The reference to a dangerous breakthrough of Islamic 'fundamentalism'[3] in Belgium has been facilitated by the increasing visibility, in recent years, of symbols of the Islamic presence in urban Belgium. These include not only the proliferation of mosques, but also the physical appearance (beard) and the clothes (*jellaba* and veil) of a small part of the population, and furthermore, some barely tolerated cultural and religious practices (ritual slaughter of sheep, insistence on segregation of the sexes in certain school activities). Public opinion obviously does not make the fine distinctions between that which derives from the cultural and religious traditionalism of the population of Muslim origin and that which derives more explicitly from a religious radicalism with political overtones that could be classified as 'fundamentalism' or better as 'Islamism'. Such a mixing of categories comes all the more easily as some local politicians grappling with ethnic minority problems, more cultural and social than religious, believed they could discern in 'fundamentalism' the major source of integration difficulties.

The discussion of migration policies in Belgium have thus been dominated in recent years by issues related to Islam, a religion that is nowadays viewed as a specific source of problems and as the major factor of resistance to integration on the part of this immigrant population. Events forced the government to review the terms of the application of the law of 1974. The patent inconvenience of having the Centre Islamique et Culturel de Belgique designated as the sole spokesman for the Muslims forced the authorities to aim at the establishment of a new representative body for the Muslim community, the Conseil Supérieur des Musulmans de Belgique. This council would comprise, apart from spokesmen for the Muslim World League and Muslim diplomats accredited in Belgium, persons representing the immigrant population itself.

Prospects for the future

Although Muslim immigration has been a massive reality since the early 1960s and although the Belgian state has legislated in principle to normalize relations with this new confessional community, their religious dimension did not become really apparent to the indigenous population until about 1980. During the past ten years, the Muslim immigrants' affirmation of their identity through religion has not been exempt from internal tensions, or contradictions deriving from their heterogeneity and the adjustments inherent in a period of transition. This affirmation of identity has not always escaped external influences from an Islamic world in full effervescence. In some regards, these wider events have reinstated pride in those whom Belgian society relegates to the lowest level of its status hierarchy.

But the appearance of this ostentatious Islam has released sentiments of fear and even opposition among the indigenous population. The Belgian state, for its part, is entangled in the contradictions, produced in large measure by its own ignorance of Islamic realities and the opportunism evident in the 1974 legislation.

It attempts to reduce its responsibility by tacity endorsing the notion of the disastrous influence of 'fundamentalism' within the Muslim community.

It is true that the recognition of the Islamic fact in Belgium does upset some received notions about the parameters of religion in social life. Even in a country such as Belgium, where the religious denominations enjoy a rather privileged status, the fact that the expression of a collective identity assumes religious forms and encroaches upon public life — in principle secularized — is clearly offensive to current conceptions of what modern social and political life should be like. But the defensive reaction of Belgian society in this respect has become so affected and passionate that it prevents a composed reflection on the new social system of which the Islamic presence constitutes a durable feature. At best, the Islamic reality is only tolerable, in the eyes of some persons, on condition that it assumes the privatized form characteristic of the other Occidental confessions today. If this kind of reduction or secularization of Islam seems acceptable to a smaller or larger group of individuals of Muslim origin, one should not forget that — for the moment at least — its general imposition would be tantamount to demanding that the majority of the immigrants, who see no reason to question their religion, abandon it. The task for the years ahead is thus to search for the means to adapt to this new situation in which Belgian society will be afraid to retract what it considers as achievements in its mode of collective functioning and in which it will be demanded of Muslim immigrants that they start reflecting on what form their religious practice should take in a secularized social context.

The Belgian experience is an eloquent example of current contradictions and impasses, but also of the demand and the necessity for facing up to the new social reality constituted by the stabilized presence of a Muslim minority in Europe. The Belgian experience shows rather clearly to what extent, so far, one has been satisfied to improvise solutions to these issues, while one is far from ready to really face them. What seems certain, in any case, is that the solutions must be sought with the people actually concerned in the various European countries in mind. It is imperative to cease delegating to foreign states, foreign movements, chancelleries and embassies the question of the future of Muslim populations transplanted by migration.

Notes

1. Cf. Dassetto and Bastenier (1984). This study is part of a research programme designed to elucidate the effects of Islam on the social dynamics of groups of foreign origin. It continues today in, first, a study of the teachers of Islam in Belgian schools and, secondly, a study of the ways of social integration of the so-called second generation.
2. See Dassetto's contribution to this volume.
3. Editors note: The author uses the French terms *intégrisme* and *intégriste* which have no precise equivalents in English. Among the many words used to label the contemporary Islamic resurgence in English we have chosen, following Dekmejian (1985), 'fundamentalism'. It comes close to the Arabic concept *al-usuliyyah*

al-Islamiyya denoting 'a search for the fundamentals of the faith, the foundations of the Islamic polity (*ummah*), and the bases of legitimate authority (*al-shariyya al-hukm*)' (Dekmejian 1985: 4). The other term used by Bastenier, 'Islamism', evokes the term Islamic fundamentalists usually apply to themselves, *Islamiyyin*, 'Islamists' (see further Dekmejian 1985: 5).

References

Dassetto, F. and Bastenier, A. 1984. *L'Islam transplanté: Vie et organisation des minorités musulmanes de Belgigue*. Anvers-Bruxelles: EVO/EPO.

Dekmejian, R.H. 1985. *Islam in Revolution: Fundamentalism in the Arab World*. Syracuse, New York: Syracuse University Press.

Part II
Migration and Changes in the Religious Experience

9
Migration and Religiousness

Werner Schiffauer

The basis of this chapter is a comparison between the religiousness of the peasants of Subay[1] — a village in North Anatolia — and that of the migrants from the same village now living in Germany. In the process, I grapple with a question raised by Gellner (1969) in 'A Pendulum Swing Theory of Islam',[2] a question which, as far as I am concerned, has not been dealt with further or expanded: the question of the connection between societal context and religious attitude.

In this paper, religiousness encompasses: 1) the manner of ritual practice; 2) the relationship to religious and societal order — or, more precisely, to the *Şeriat* (Turkish for *Shariah*); 3) the direction of religious thought and 4) the attitude to one's self. My hypothesis is that the changes which can be observed in this regard are the result of a restructuring of the religious community into a secular society. Due to the communal nature of Islam, this restructuring has far-reaching consequences.

Islam in Village Society

In Subay, the village society is, at the same time, the Islamic community. Those with whom one stands in a reciprocal political–legal as well as economic relationship are always brothers in faith, the same people seen Fridays in the mosque and with whom the great religious feasts are collectively experienced.

This means that the village society oscillates between two states according to a present rhythm dictated by the Islamic calendar. During secular times, the village appears to be comprised of a group of largely autonomous households which base their relationships on the values of honour (*namus*) and respect (*saygi*) and observe the reciprocal exchange of offerings and provocations.

During sacred times (the five times of prayer, Friday mornings, the month of fasting, the holy nights, the great religious feasts), this society changes into a religious community. Through the Islamic rituals, a social structure is established in which one does not stand in opposition to one's fellow man but rather beside him; in which one does not preserve one's honour against the others but collectively honours God; in which one does not exchange but shares; in which goods are given not because of mutual obligations but because of need; in which not competition and conflict but unity reigns.[3]

The oscillation between a secular and sacred order demonstrates that all mutual relationships not only possess a societal (i.e., political–legal) but also a communal (i.e., ethical–moral) character.[4] Both elements stand in a complementary relationship to one another; they augment and correct each other. The peasants are unanimously convinced that a true community cannot be based solely on one element or the other. A community in which only mutual relationships of a political–legal nature were valid would collapse since everyone would feel responsible only to his own family or group. The powerful would triumph and there would exist no possibility to end a fight or a feud. It is said: 'Only he who fears God recognizes your rights as well' and 'Fear those who do not fear God'. Yet just as doomed is a community based solely on communal thoughts. It would be illusory to believe that one could live in legal security simply because all others are Muslims like oneself. One appeals to this (and says: 'Why do you do that to me? I am neither a *gavur* (unbeliever), nor a Christian.') yet knows that, in the end, one can exist only when reciprocity is established, when one provocation is answered by a counter-provocation. As beautiful as it would be if the structure of the community could be sustained by the mutual fear of God, daily life shows that the fear of one's neighbour must enter in as well.

The complementary relationship of secular and sacred order is expressed by the fact that the individual must have a status within both systems in order to be recognized as a person in Subay. One must be a Muslim as well as the member of a family whose honour and reputation are indisputable. If either of these is lacking, the individual becomes an outcast.

This relationship between religious community and society determines the peasant form of religiousness.

Ritual Practice

Let us now turn to ritual practice. From what has been said, it is clear that participation in rituals is never solely the expression of an individual's relationship to God; for, at the same time, the individual formulates a claim to membership in the community. I do not want to go so far as to assert that this political meaning of ritual fully pushes the religious one aside; nevertheless, it often seems to eclipse it and to be primary. Let us note the following statement by a young man raised in Subaỷ:

They go to the mosque because everyone else goes there. They see: The people go to the mosque. So they go as well. When they pray, they pray without concentration or contemplation; instead, they think about their livestock and about what they want to buy . . . When the intention is lacking, then the *namaz* prayer [ritual prayer, *salat*] is nothing more than an exercise. That's the case with almost everyone. They're only Muslims in the following sense: If somebody comes along and ploughs under a piece of their land, then they say: 'Why do you trample upon my rights, the rights of a Muslim?' They're only Muslim as long as their rights are in question. For the *Kurban* [Turkish for *qurban*] feast, they make excuses and say that they had no money for a sacrifice. When the *Hoca* forbids something, they say: 'But everyone else does the same thing' and so they continue to do it.

In accordance with the political meaning of the ritual, value is placed on each household documenting its membership in the Islamic community. At least the head of the family, who represents the family in extra-familial affairs, must participate in the ritual. Occasionally the other members of the household even seem to consider it their duty to give him time off to participate. This was especially noticeable in 1977 when the Ramadan fell in midsummer. The threshing work and fasting were seen as incompatible. The solution, embraced by the majority of families, was to require the sons to break the fast and to carry out the work alone. In this way, the older men were freed to perform their ritual duties.

In this manner, ritual practice is seen not as the task of the individual but more as the task of the household as a whole. It therefore often seems extraordinarily external and formal. It is more important to demonstrate externally that one's own group is Islamic than it is to adopt a particular inner attitude.

The Attitude Towards the Şeriat

The complementary relationship between the two orders prevents the sacred order from becoming independent of the wordly order. I would like to clarify this by means of an example.

The *Bayramlaşmak* ritual — literally translated: 'to offer congratulations on the occasion of a feast' — is performed twice a year, namely at the time of the sugar feast (*Şeker Bayrami*) and the sacrificial feast (*Kurban Bayrami*). Following the service, the men of the community form a circle, taking their places according to their advancing ages. The youngest man then starts to work his way along the group and greets everyone — those only slightly older with a handshake, the others with the traditional kiss on the hand which shows respect. Then comes the second youngest, the third youngest, etc. until the group has been rolled up, so to speak. The ritual is considered an atonement ritual: The conflicts which threaten to disrupt the religious community are ritually ended and the ideal order of the brotherly community (represented by the circle in which the younger men demonstrate their respect for the older men) is once again established.

During a discussion about this ceremony with Mustafa 'the Snail', I asked him how he deals with his longstanding enemy, the tobacconist, in such a situation. His reply was simple: 'I just pass him by.'

To me, this attitude seems characteristic of their ways of dealing with the two orders. Their oppositional nature and their contradictions are clearly recognized. But they cannot be resolved. The divine order cannot assert itself over the reality of the wordly order; after all, the conflicts in the secular sphere determine the course of the ritual as well. Nevertheless, the divine order is not questioned because of this. The ritual continues to be practised and is taken seriously. It displays the ideal which must be firmly upheld, despite reality, if the society is not to disintegrate. It is not reality . . . and yet it is anything but an illusion.

For me, this knowledge determines the peasants' attitude to the Şeriat. Hardly a soul in the village opposes the notion that the reintroduction of the Şeriat would be desirable for Turkey. Yet there are no lofty hopes linked to this. In a conversation with a republican-minded migrant, he was not contradicted when he claimed that it would set the country back fifty years. The reactions were rather defiant: 'And even if, then at least it is an Islamic country.' An attitude which, in its matter-of-factness, differs markedly from the hopes for a theocracy, as we shall see during the discussion of the situation of the migrants.

The Direction of Religious Thought

In this context, religious thought mostly takes the form of collective self-certainty. During the religious conversations, one constantly imagines the communal possession of norms, values and assessments. In the process, the classification of acts is usually central: Which ones are necessary (*farz*) or merely recommended (*eftal*), which ones frowned upon (*makruh*) or forbidden (*haram*). Discussed are questions such as whether the sin of eating pork is greater or less than that of drinking Raķi, or how one can accumulate the most religious merit (*sevap*). The consequences in the hereafter for disregarding rules is just as avidly dealt with. Religious talks often sound judicial. They are marked by no pensive search for the meaning of a text or rule, no speculation about God and the world; it is much more central to them to swear to uphold the laws and the instructions for carrying them out — the basis of the communal order. Usually, very familiar and obvious points are discussed, as if a collectively inherited treasure is removed from a chest, held up to view for a moment and then put back: an undertaking both satisfying and communally supportive.

The Concern With One's Self

Given the ritual practice and the form of religious thought, it should come as no surprise that the individuals see their religious obligations as a mountain of debts which are to be paid off as completely as possible during their lifetime. These obligations, especially the *namaz* prayer (ritual prayer) and fasting, are generally considered to be a burden. That does not rob them of value but, on the contrary, bestows importance upon them. Anyone who thinks he will be able to be redeemed without completing these unpleasant tasks is met with utter disbelief. He is accused of being interested in only the pleasant side of religious life, so to speak. "You Christians have only *dua* prayers (prayers of supplication) and no *namaz* prayers. Do you really believe you'll go to Heaven if you make it so easy on yourselves?"

The attitude which is biased against the obligations is also evident in the peasant interpretation of the institution of *kaza* (Turkish for *kada*), the main possibility in Islam of 'catching up' on religious duties. The younger men make ample use of this possibility; they avoid fasting and prayer with the intention of making up what they have neglected when they are old (when, one has the impression, the interest in sinning naturally dies out, anyway). With increasing age, the feeling of being in God's debt constantly grows. One starts praying regularly in order — as they say — 'not to die still owing a debt to God'. Countless elderly men rise early to make up the prayers they neglected in their youth.[5]

Islam Abroad

Within the complex society in which the migrant worker finds himself, the relationship between the individual, the Islamic community and society as a whole has a totally different structure. The relations in the religious community are no longer identical with the totality of the economic, political and social relations of the individual. They exist as specifically religious alongside other societal relations. In the religious community, one no longer encounters the person with whom one has societal exchange relationships but a person of similar mind. Consequently, the specifically peasant experience of an oscillation of one's social world between the states of religious community and society is no longer present. During sacred times, society no longer changes into a religious community but, rather, one leaves the society and enters the religious community — if possible, we must add, since the opposition between secular and sacred times is now determined by the more fundamental notions of the working day and leisure. Membership in the religious community is therefore irrelevant for one's societal standing; it no longer bestows any political-legal status but becomes a private affair.[6]

Although this is also the case in the urban centres of Turkey, one still notices that this change of structure is especially entrenched among those residing abroad in Europe. Added to this, the religious community often becomes a counterweight to the secular society as well as a place of retreat, a haven.[7] It becomes a counterweight insofar as it is the place where, in a Christian environment, the Islamic (as well as the Turkish) norms and values are maintained and tended to. Such a place naturally gains importance if one wishes to pass on these norms and values through the socialization process. When the peasants from

Subay send their children to a Quran course, their concern about a Turkish upbringing plays just as great a role as their concern about their children's religious education. The religious community becomes a haven insofar as it is a place where one is treated with respect and esteem, a place where the value and dignity of the individual are recognized — as opposed to the external society in which one often feels discriminated against and humiliated.

Especially in Germany, the religious community and the society no longer stand in a complementary relationship but rather in opposition to one another. That is why the specific character of the respective relationship is more pronounced than it is back in the village. On one side are the 'cold' societal relationships characterized by exploitation, discrimination and injustice; on the other side are the 'warm' and brotherly relationships characterized by mutual respect and esteem. In this religious community of the similarly minded, one no longer needs the tricks that Mustafa 'the Snail' had to resort to back in the village: societal reality, so to speak, stops at the door.[8]

In order to describe the consequences of this fact for religiousness, I will concentrate primarily on one migrant in particular, namely Yaşar Fuad who lives in Augsburg.

Ritual Practice

Given the new position of the religious community in society, ritual practice changes its symbolic value as well. One no longer expresses, as in the village, affiliation with the society as a whole but, through ritual practice, one bears witness to one's place in a minority group. The ritual is no longer demanded by the general public but, rather, ridiculed and quite often it has to be carried out despite outside opposition.

> Today in the Islamic community, it is absolutely essential that a self-aware (*kendine bilen*) Muslim uphold his Islam. Today it is necessary for a Muslim to perform the *namaz* prayer and to obey fasting and — how can I put it? — to shun what is *haram* (ritually forbidden). To do all that here is very difficult, since none of it is considered normal.

Active membership in this minority group often means a denial of all those who do not belong to the group. However, not everyone goes so far as Yaşar who refused to visit a migrant from his own village with the following reasoning: "He doesn't pray, he doesn't fast. Why should I see him?" Through ritual practice one also dissociates oneself from German society: this is especially obvious (and especially serious) in the case of the socialization of the children. Yaşar, for example, does not send his children to kindergarten. On the one hand, he is afraid they will become estranged from him through the influence of the German teacher; moreover, his concern that they will receive sausage there (i.e., pork) also plays a role. His nine-year-old son already embodies the father's dissociation to a large extent. His father told me that his son does not play with German children because he doesn't like them — they smell of pork. In the children's centre where he goes for tutoring and help with his homework, the boy refused to make a plaster mask. "We Muslims don't do such things." Yaşar is proud of his son's attitude.

This encourages the development of purely religious motivation. When the rituals are performed by the diaspora, they are usually against the society and mainly out of concern for one's fate in the hereafter.[9] Mahiye Eren's statement is illustrative in this regard: "In this world, the Germans laugh about our head-scarves; in the next world, they will regret it." This shows a more individualized approach to religion where social control is replaced by individual responsibility for one's fate. Yaşar Fuad:

> As a Muslim, I prefer the Islamic path. I live in accordance with this path. I follow this path. But if others do not walk this path, I don't care. Each person has a mind and common sense; each person must decide for himself . . . Each must consider how he wants to spend his lifetime.

A result of this is that, in terms of religious practice, the migrants vary much more among themselves than do the peasants in their native village. Some heads of households are negligent to an extent that would never occur back in the village. For example, Mahiye Eren's husband: "He says: *Burası Almanya* — 'This is Germany' — and doesn't fast and doesn't go to the mosque." Others, like Yaşar, take religious practice much more seriously. Especially noticeable, however, is that, to women, religious practice increases in importance within the migrant situation. In the Eren family, the traditional roles in this regard are totally reversed: there it is the woman who attends to Islam and no longer the man.[10]

The New Attitude to the *Şeriat*

The transformed structure of the relationships between religious community and society is evident in the attitude towards order demonstrated and actualized in ritual. In the village, the vision of a brotherly and just society stands in a reciprocal relationship to societal reality. The two orders correct and augment one another. With the separation of religious community and society, the vision becomes autonomous as well. Now it is placed only in opposition to the existing society. In rituals, what is shown is no longer what the society *also* is but what it *not yet* is. A radiant future is anticipated. This leads to criticism of the present. Under the conditions of a complex society, Islam becomes, as Waardenburg formulated it, a "vehicle of protest" (Waardenburg 1984). From the ideal is born a utopia or, for the more sceptical migrants, an illusion.

Now millenial hopes can embrace the idea of the reintroduction of the *Şeriat*. Yaşar Fuad believes that, with its reintroduction, the present situation will turn into its opposite. In long statements, he saw the lack of the *Şeriat* as the root of all evil in the world. Two passages are telling in this regard:

There is unrest today in all the countries of the world. Why? Because Islam is not alive. Islam is not practised, the commandments of Islam are not heard; that's why the countries, the people, the rich, the poor — all are restless . . . The representatives, the heads of state have a responsibility. The people vote for them . . . But as soon as they become representatives, they are no longer interested in us. All this unrest is present because people no longer live according to God's laws, because people no longer use and apply them.

Since people do not know Islam, they know no humanity. They think only of themselves. Take the employer of today, for example. An employer has to respect my rights as long as he employs me . . . But, unfortunately, he doesn't do that. He's always thinking only of his pocketbook, not about his workers. He doesn't think about you, whether you have children, a wife, children to educate or not. Yet that's really his human responsibility and duty. Islam teaches us about this. Islam says: 'A shepherd is responsible for the flock he is tending.'

While Islam is also the 'vehicle of protest' in urban Turkey, residence abroad still fosters a more precise and more concrete form of criticism. From without — and in comparison with Germany — some faults in Turkey are seen more clearly. The logical problem which arises for a Muslim fundamentalist when he finds the institutions of a Christian country admirable was solved by Yaşar by means of two arguments. The first is based on the thesis that Germany has taken up and furthered the traditions of the Ottoman Empire:

If we turn and look at [public relations in] official public offices and hospitals for example, the Germans today display, in their behaviour and activities, what we had under the Ottoman Empire. In Turkey today, no one can expect similar treatment . . . For example, a German walks into an office and unloads his problem. The official helps him; he does his job. But that's not the case in our country. With us, the officials have better things to do . . . [11]

This rationalization allows the experience in Germany to be used for the formulation of the ideal of an Islamic republic. The second argument can be summarized in the following way: if something is already practised in Germany, a Christian country, then it is opportune that it be practised in Turkey as well:

In Germany, taxes are collected for all churches. In Turkey we have mosques, but no taxes are collected for them. The government doesn't help the mosques. They have to rely on the people for their financial support.

A variation of this argument suggests that if certain modes of behaviour or patterns of dress are already allowed in Germany, then they should be allowed in Turkey as well.

Here, for example, we can wear veils or grow a beard. We can live freely in every sense. In Germany there is no law regarding dress as there is in Turkey . . . That's why we can't dress there like we want to as Muslims. So, in this sense, we can live better in Germany.

Utopia clamours to be actualized; it entails a political mission. Yaşar tries to carry out this mission by voicing his position publicly. He is aware of the convincing power of openly-practised prayer. Consequently, he tries to win the fight to be able to pray at work. The Germans would then come over, look and say: "What kind of faith is that, that's practised with such conviction?" They would inform themselves and convert to Islam. "If all Turks who have come here were serious Muslims, then the Germans would have converted to Islam by now."

The Direction of Religious Thought

One of the most basic consequences of the new relationship between the religious community and society is that one no longer automatically belongs to a given community; the community (and the religious leader) can now be chosen according to how convincingly it (he) represents Islam.[12] In the process, everyone sees that the differences in the religious communities do not affect the cult but rather political questions — how the utopia is to be actualized — and normative questions relating to the individual aspects of one's lifestyle:

> I was a member of the *Milli Görüşcü* [National View]. I left the group. Now I'm a member of the *Tebliğ* community [Announcement group]. The aim ... of the *Tebliğ* community is the following: We want to live according to God's commandments and to tell others about them. Nothing more. The others, however, have a specific goal: They support a particular party's political line. Besides that, there's no difference; the Quran courses are the same. The Quran is taught the same way in the *Süleymancı*, *Nurcu*, *Milli Görüşcü*, and the *Tebliğ* communities. There's no change ...

Yaşar left the *Milli Görüşcü* and joined the *Tebliğ* community because of his political pragmatism. He was convinced that an Islamic republic could be established only through a mass movement similar to the one in Iran, not through supporting an Islamic party which, because it is tied to the constitution, is forced to compromise itself.

Yaşar's decision shows a new form of religious thought. The individual's search for truth takes over from collective self-certainty. Yaşar is very well aware of this. He sees his search for the right community and the right path as far from over. As we were watching a video tape of a sermon by Cemalletin Kaplan — one of the foremost religious leaders of the *Tebliğ* movement — he exclaimed:

> I'm searching for the truth. That's why I left the *Milli Görüşcü*. I'll keep searching. Perhaps one day I will leave this man (pointing to Cemalletin Kaplan) as well and turn to another.

The succession of religious communities one joins in the course of one's life thus becomes a type of special religious biography:

I woke up in the city. When I came to Istanbul . . . what was in Istanbul? A religious community existed there . . . I found good people there, made good friends, went with them to hear the *Hocas* [religious teachers] and to pray the *namaz* in the mosque . . . Later, when I came to Germany, I took a second step. Here I've gotten to know religious communities that are outlawed in Turkey.

The Concern With One's Self

The individualizing of religious practice and the new form of the religious quest corresponds to a changed relationship with one's self. Let us once again listen to Yaşar:

> Back in our village . . . the parents are uneducated; they also don't send their children to someone who knows more. Look, when I was young I went with my father to the mosque. But only after I came to Istanbul did the love of faith begin for me. Then, for example, I bought books about faith . . . I went to the mosque to pray the *namaz*; I educated myself in this way. But how are those in the village supposed to educate themselves? (*Kendimi öyle yetiştirdim. Ama onlar nerede yetişecek köyde.*)

The key phrase here is: "I educated myself." This bespeaks a totally new concern with the self. In the village, the aim was to reduce an objectively existing mountain of sacred debts, so to speak; in the process, little importance was placed on one's inner conviction. Yet that is now precisely Yaşar's point. For him, prayer is no longer merely an obligation which has to be 'paid off' but, instead, primarily an exercise in the "Islamization of one's self" (Nagel).

First, this is shown in a changed interpretation of the *kaza*, the possibility of making up prayers. The natural acceptance with which it is utilized in the village is no longer valid for Yaşar. For him, there is a marked difference as to whether the prayer which one makes up was neglected for a good reason or simply because of a lack of interest and desire:

> But did I neglect the *namaz* prayer on a whim or was I forced to neglect it? Only when I was forced to neglect it is my debt paid by a *kaza* prayer. If, however, I neglected it out of a lack of interest or desire — then it is in God's hands. There's a big difference between neglect out of necessity and neglect out of self-interest.

Consequently, Yaşar criticizes the swiftness with which the peasants in his native village have an excuse at hand to relieve them from praying.

> What they say [about work leaving them no time to pray] is no excuse. The *namaz* prayer takes ten minutes. Ten minutes! One prays the *namaz* five times a day, and three of these times, if need be, at work.

Decisive for me is that Yaşar lives the consequences of this critique in his daily life. He does not make it easy on himself. For example, even against the will of most Turkish co-workers, he tries to see that one may pray at work. As of now, he still has to perform his prayer there in secret. Whereas in the village the prayer is neglected when it could well have been performed, Yaşar tries to perform it under the most difficult of circumstances.

This much more methodical lifestyle means that religious practice has shifted from a question of which phase one finds oneself in to a question of lifestyle in general. The decision to embrace Islam becomes an existential question which is posed without reference to one's age:

> They say: 'We're still young . . . when we're over forty we'll fulfil our religious duties.' That's what you always hear . . . For example, there are people who say to me: 'Why do you wear a beard when you're still so young?' But Islam does not differentiate between young and old. One must say: 'Perhaps I will die tomorrow' . . . Would I then have time to grow a beard? I also regret that I've not yet been able to go on the pilgrimage. Since I was sixteen, I've seen the *hac* [Turkish for *hajj*] as my duty.

Not only is the concern about performing prayers more intensive but also the attitude which is adopted during prayer. Unlike the peasants, Yaşar concentrates hard when praying. Likewise, he criticizes the village practice of talking in a relatively uninhibited manner when in the vicinity of someone praying. He considers this to be distracting for the person demonstrating his faith:

> Yes, that's not right. Your talking upsets the thoughts of the one praying. If we talk while a brother is over in the corner praying the *namaz*, then we distract him. Either we have to talk very softly so he'll not be able to hear us or he'll have to go elsewhere to pray the *namaz* . . .

This consideration shown to the praying person, unheard of in the village, portrays very clearly the new meaning of prayer. Whereas in the village it is done to pay off one's debt, it is now to educate one's self.[13]

In this chapter, I have tried to demonstrate the importance of the migration process for the development of religiousness. It should be clear that, above all, I understand the migration of workers as a process of urbanization. Consequently, the development shown here would not be markedly different in Turkey itself as opposed to in Germany. However, the unusual quality of life abroad contributes to an accentuation of this process. Under these conditions, the development of specifically urban (and modern) structures of consciousness can be more clearly observed than in the native country.

Notes

1. All proper names have been changed.
2. The thesis was subsequently taken up and expanded in *Muslim Society* (1981).
3. Among others, T. Nagel refers to the representation of Islamic order through ritual: *So hat das rituelle Gebet, das am Freitag im gemeinschaftlichen Gottesdienst ausgeführt werden soll, nicht nur den Charakter einer Zwiesprache des Menschen*

mit dem Schöpfer, sondern auch einer Demonstration der Mitgliedschaft im islamischen Staat. Im Freitagsgottesdienst wird das Gemeinwesen veranschaulicht (1981: 15). In this connection, I consider above all the rules regarding the distribution of alms and the sacrificial animal to be important as well (compare Soymen and Schmiede 1960: 52-3).
4. I use the terms religious community (*Gemeinschaft*) and society (*Gesellschaft*) here in Weber's sense (1972: 21 ff.).
5. Regarding the concern with paying one's religious debts, which dominates religious life in the village, see Schiffauer 1984a.
6. See also Sayad 1983.
7. This structural change is especially pronounced when it concerns an individual form of migration (as in the migration from Subay) so that the (partial) reconstitution of the original community, characteristic for the *chain migration*, does not occur. For a comparison of the two types of migration see, above all, Engelbrektsson (1978). The pattern of the migration from Subay strongly parallels the migration from Alihan, one of the two villages studied by Engelbrektsson.
8. By this I don't want to imply that the religious community is a sphere without conflicts. However it seems to me that the character of conflicts changes considerably in the context of migration. The conflicts in the village community bear, so to say, a societal stamp; the conflicts in the urban community have a much more 'immanent' character: they centre usually around questions concerning the correct interpretation of Islam. This shows in a certain readiness to accept splits of the community for dogmatic reasons. Compare for example Waardenburg's representation in this volume of the processes of fusion and fission of the Islamic communities in the Netherlands.
9. Shop owners, especially grocers, are possibly an exception. As diaspora, they can also (or just) earn symbolic capital through religious practice. Compare Blaschke 1984.
10. In another article I have extensively portrayed Mahiye Eren who joined the *Nurcu* community in Berlin (Schiffauer 1984a). Despite all the similarities with Yaşar Fuad who is chiefly discussed in the present paper, there are still characteristic differences which can be linked to the varied social situations of men and women. Consequently, for Mahiye, the political differences in the individual groups are less important than for Yaşar; instead, she, more than Yaşar, is concerned with a basis and justification of her daily life.
11. In this argument strategy, one notices again a widely used motif: . . . *(Es) hat sich in der islamischen Welt ein umfangreiches Schrifttum entwickelt, das sich die Aufgabe stellt nachzuweisen, daß alle die Errungenschaften der modernen europäischen politischen Kultur längst durch die šari'a vorweggenommen worden seien, die westlichen Verfassungen also nur in äußerst unvollkommener Form — sie sind doch Menschenwerk — dazulegen versuchten, was seit eh und je den Kern islamischen politischen Denkens ausmache.* (Nagel 1981 (II):257).
12. This moment of individual choice of the religious community by the faithful runs throughout Islamic history: it is a moment at which the attempted control of teachings by the state has often failed. Thus in the ninth and tenth centuries, the traditionalists asserted themselves against the Mutazilites who were backed by the Abbasids. (Nagel 1981 (I):179-81). In more recent times, the movement of the Muslim Brothers serves as a good example. (Compare, for example, Hanafi 1984).
13. The connection between life abroad and the education of one's self has been recognized by the Sufi teachers. Consequently, travel for a mystic like Sulami plays a great role. *Es wird als Möglichkeit angesehen, Stolz und Dünkelhaftigkeit der Seele zu brechen. Man rät den Brüdern in die Fremde zu wandern und sich dort aufzuhalten, wo man verachtet wird, weil man unbekannt ist.* (Nagel 1981 (I):409).

References

Blaschke, J. 1984. Islam und Politik unter türkischen Arbeitsmigranten. *Jahrbuch zur Geschichte und Gesellschaft des Vorderen und Mittleren Orients, 1984. Thema: Islam und Politik in der Türkei*. Blaschke J. and Bruinessen M. V., eds. Berlin.

Engelbrektsson, U. B. 1978. *The Force of Tradition*. Göteborg: Gothenburg Studies in Social Anthropology/Acta Universitatis Gothoburgensis.

Gellner, E. 1969. A Pendulum Swing Theory of Islam. *Sociology of Religion*. Robertson, R., ed. Harmondsworth: Penguin Books.

———. 1981. *Muslim Society*. Cambridge: Cambridge University Press.

Hanafi, H. 1984. The Origin of Modern Conservatism and Islamic Fundamentalism. *Islamic Dilemmas: Reformers, Nationalists and Industrialization*. Gellner, E., ed. Berlin, New York and Amsterdam: Mouton Publishers.

Nagel, T. 1981. *Staat und Glaubensgemeinschaft im Islam: Geschichte der politischen Ordnungsvorstellungen der Muslime*. Two volumes. Zürich und München: Rissen.

Sayad, A. 1983. Islam et immigration en France: Les effets de l'immigration sur l'Islam. Paper presented at the conference "L'Islam en Europe à l'époque moderne", organized by Associations pour l'Avancement des Etudes Islamiques, Paris, at Collège de France, 30 September — 1 October 1983.

Schiffauer, W. 1984a. Mensch, Gesellschaft und die Vorstellung vom Sakralen im dörflichen Islam. *Begegnung mit Türken, Begegnung mit dem Islam. Teil IV*. Brandt H. J. and Hasse, K. P., eds. Hamburg: J. B. Mohr.

———. 1984b. Religion und Identität: Eine Fallstudie zum Problem der Reislamisierung bei Arbeitsmigranten. *Schweizerische Zeitschrift für Soziologie* 10 (2): 485–516.

Soymen, H. and Schmiede, H. A. 1960. *Kleiner Islamischer Katechismus*. Ankara: Veröffentlichung der Behörde für religiöse Angelegenheiten.

Waardenburg, J. 1984. Islam as a Vehicle of Protest. *Islamic Dilemmas: Reformers, Nationalists and Industrialization*. Gellner, E., ed. Berlin, New York and Amsterdam: Mouton Publishers.

Weber, M. 1972. *Wirtschaft und Gesellschaft*. Tübingen: Directorate of Religious Affairs.

10
The Tabligh Organization in Belgium

Felice Dassetto

Among the numerous Muslim religious groups that have emerged in Belgium, particularly in the past fifteen years,[1] the Jama'at at-Tabligh no doubt holds a special position by virtue of the strength of its presence and the impact of its activities. This article attempts to answer the question of whether we are witnessing today an increasing influence of the Tabligh over the Arab mosques in Belgium. But the basic orientation of this chapter is to study the Tabligh primarily from the viewpoint of the sociology of organizations and of social movements. There are two reasons for this endeavour. One of them is theoretical: the intention being to assess the relevance and fruitfulness of sociological tools with respect to a Muslim religious grouping. The other derives from an analysis of the Tabligh as such, and consists of the hypothesis that its success is due as much to its cultural and ideological appropriateness to the situation of immigrant populations as to its capacity to develop a complex organization capable of responding to the demands emanating out of multiple contexts.

The Jama'at at-Tabligh

The Jama'at at-Tabligh is a kind of religious organization which was founded by Muhammad Ilyas (1885–1944) between 1920 and 1940 in the north of India.[2] The present centre of this movement is in Nizam Ud-Din, close to Delhi, where the founder's grave is also located. He died in 1944 and was succeeded by his son Yusuf. Since the death of the latter in 1965, the movement has been directed by In'am ul-Hassan, the founder's cousin.

The Jama'at at-Tabligh, while being modern in organization and mode of operation, has traits which emanate from the Sufi tradition to which Muhammad Ilyas was closely linked. He was shaykh of the Shabiriyya brotherhood, a branch of the Čistiyya.

Muhammad Ilyas was in fact a descendant of an important Sufi family which originated in Kandhala in the Muzaffarnagar district in Uttar Pradesh. After a period of apprenticeship where he came into contact with, among others, the Deoband, Muhammad Ilyas engaged in the educational mission which had already been started by his father among the Meo in the Mewat region, a rural population south-west of Delhi. They were poor, socially marginal and only superficial adherents of Islam. It was during his second pilgrimage and a long stay in Mecca (1924) and during his third pilgrimage (1932) that Muhammad Illyas decided to organize a missionary campaign among the Meo people in order to strengthen their faith and to purify their life practices. It is in this area that the organizational principles and the new techniques of religious activity which characterize the Tabligh were elaborated. They are built around itinerant preaching groups, which in turn engender new preaching groups.

Muhammad Ilyas himself tried the effectiveness of this mode of action — teaching and propaganda — which forms an alternative to the madrasa model. The aim is to create 'mobile madrasas' in order to teach mainly poor and uneducated people whom the classical educational techniques have in reality neglected.

In the mid-1930s, the movement became very popular and highly successful in Mewat. Hundreds of mosques as well as madrasas were constructed. Non-Muslim manifestations were eradicated from daily life.

After his last pilgrimage to Mecca in 1938, Muhammad Ilyas extended his preaching to the rich merchants of Delhi among whom he achieved considerable success, asking them to give a part of their time to missionary activity and to purify their commercial practices.

Official Islam was indifferent to the activities of Muhammad Ilyas and looked down on this popular form of Islam, inspired by simple and uneducated Muslims indulging in propaganda activities. In 1944, Muhammad Ilyas published a kind of manifesto addressed to the Muslim leadership in India summarizing his missionary project.[3] This project correspondended closely to the principles which govern the present activities of the Tabligh. According to Ilyas, the success of missionary activity requires the total adoption of Islam on an individual level and strict obedience to God's commands. Moreover, the activities of the missionary should be guided by certain rules. A true missionary spirit like that of the Prophet should animate the Muslims of today who are plunged into apathy. This activity requires an acquisition of knowledge which is indispensable to its transmission. For the action to be successful all internal divisions within the community must be silenced and it should be governed by a spirit of altruism and solidarity.

The aim of the missionary action is to reach the hearts of the believers and affect their personalities. Muhammad Ilyas forwarded this aim in opposition to that which presupposes the seizure of power to impose Islamic behaviour on people. That method should be abandoned, since, according to Muhammad

Ilyas, a religious act can never be prompted by force.

Yusuf, the son of Muhammad Ilyas, succeeded him in 1944. It was between 1944 to 1965 (in which year Yusuf died in Lahore) that the activities of the Jama'at at-Tabligh were dispersed not only on the Indian subcontinent but also in the Arab countries, Turkey, Great Britain, the United States and Japan. The idea of missionary activities among non-Muslims was developed, and large international reunions were organized. The movement is at present deeply entrenched in the north of India, in Bangladesh and in Pakistan. It is also widespread in the Maghreb, in European immigration countries[4] and will probably be increasingly so in the United States and Canada where important meetings were organized in Michigan and Ottawa in 1983.[5]

The Tabligh is part of a momentum which revives the idea of propagating Islam among Muslim populations. This project is not alien to the Christian idea of missionary action which was learned and experienced during the colonial period.[6] This trend of ideas underpins the activities of the Tabligh, but it nevertheless exhibits some traits of its own. In fact, it addresses itself primarily to Muslims, working by way of a missionary action of re-islamization which implies the adoption, as we will see, of a particular pedagogy which can strike roots in a previously Muslim territory. The Tabligh, moreover, addresses itself primarily to the less educated in the Muslim world, thus showing that it takes into account the situation of the majority of Muslim adults. One finds in the Tablighs a critique, more or less explicit, of the elitism of other Islamic movements like the Muslim brotherhoods. More precisely, one could postulate that the Tablighs constitute a meeting ground for the old urban middle class — commercial and public servants among others — who seem to play a leading role in the movement, and the lower layers of the urban proletariat. This junction would provide Muslim life with a modern social framework after the breakdown of the old.[7] Finally, the Tabligh groups, which were created in the context of Islam in India, seem capable of acting — regarding themselves as a minority group — on the religious and political level. This implies the development of an autarkical missionary activity organized according to a logic which requires limited means and an attitude of strict neutrality with regard to power and politics. The Tablighs have also learnt lessons from the failure of the Islamic political movements and avoid by their neutrality all confrontation harmful to the movement.[8]

The Tablighs intend to place themselves — as in reality they actually do — at the very heart of orthodox Islam.[9] Thus they have to develop their specific activities without rupture and without separation. In the continuity of Islam, they suggest a cyclical interpretation of its history. After the missionary expansion of the first centuries there was the consolidation in the times of the empires, followed by a period of decadence. Only at the beginning of this century did Muslims start to consider the shortcomings of Islam, the reasons for its degradation and the consequences for society. For the Tablighs, the renewal of Islam is accomplished mainly through personal adherence to the founding principles and to emulating the life of the Prophet and his followers. The Tablighs defend a practical Islam in contrast with the excessive intellectualism that they find in other movements. Their activities are based on a few simple rules: to have faith in God, to pray, to act with modesty, to learn the word and transmit it, to follow the right way, to receive all believers. These are the virtues of pious Muslims, accompanied by the idea of the transmission of knowledge and the invitation of believers.[10]

Belief in God is translated into a strong projection into the other-worldly and expectations for life after death. This can be deduced from expressions such as: "Here there is just earth." "Life is a prison. There are prohibitions that must be adhered to. After that, its's finished . . ." Someone would add this paradoxical argument: "Now it's God who decides . . . afterwards it will be everyone." This total faith is extended into an attitude to politics which is as neutral as it is radical. The Tablighs call themselves apolitical. They even say that it is prohibited for them to "make" politics. Since politics cause divisions in Islam, their reference model is derived from the origins of Islam. But the very radicalism of their faith and their models of reference are powerful elements in a critique of political systems, particularly those defining themselves as Islamic. Everything suggests that the Tablighs, far removed from power by virtue of their position in society, instead of attaching themselves to it engage in challenging its legitimacy. They go to the heart of the problem of power in 'Muslim' countries without touching it.

Prayer governs strongly the life of the Tablighs: their mosques are among the most visited and in the typology that we have constructed,[11] they belong to the category of 'devotional' mosques. To learn the knowledge and transmit it constitutes another rule of the Tablighs. To know Islam, as opposed to merely engaging in repetitive and conformist religious practice, is their response to the lack of knowledge of Islam among the common people and to the excessive specialization of religious erudition. From this knowledge emanates the duty to proclaim the way for Muslims to follow which is translated into missionary activity. This duty is incumbent on each believer as a continuation of the successful prophetic activity by the Prophet.

Individual modesty, moral improvement and openness to all believers are rules which guide individual attitudes and characterize the atmosphere of the Tablighi mosques. In this way the Tablighs really emerge as pious Muslims.

From project to organization

The aims of the Tablighs consist thus in the enrolment of members adopting the Tablighi principles as particular modalities, but which are not separated from adherence to Islam. This adherence is generated by the secular society, particularly in the socially and culturally more marginal sectors. The Tablighs maintain a relative distance to the political and religious powers and exercise a certain autonomy. Tablighi activities do not aim at a simple reproduction of existing religious fields but are innovatory and expansive and do not hesitate to confront new social and geographical areas. In consequence the Tablighs must handle, from an organizational point of view, a large amount of uncertainty. In addition, there are multiple segments to consider, due to the differing social, political, and religious environments, and the situation confronting prospective members.

My hypothesis is as follows: the Tablighs have created a complex organization which is capable of handling at the same time all the relations with these multiple environments. It remains faithful to the objectives and the missionary principles established by the founder, and it makes use of the human resources provided by secular society which also constitute the human material considered by the founder as targets for Tablighi action.[12]

In summary, it seems that the success of the Tablighs consists not only in the appropriateness of the structure and function of the organization in relation to the goals set. It is also a result of the fact that the structure and the function are juxtaposed to the objectives — this means that the organization of the Tabligh is both the means of action and its aim. Moreover, since the organization values and uses human resources, which at the same time constitute the target of its activities, its very principles hold a capacity for self-expansion.

To describe the Tabligh, one could use the image of concentric circles. At the centre, true Islam is located, viewed as a personal attitude in perfect imitation of the initial prophetic era. Moving outward from this centre, there are different levels of adherence that go all the way to a position of exteriority in relation to the centre, with respect to Muslims, or of 'otherness' with respect to non-Muslims. These multiple circles belong to a global interpretation which constitutes the worldview of the Tabligh. The organizational reality of the Tabligh handles each of these circles in a simultaneous and varied manner by deploying different resources.

The relationship to the exterior Muslim environment and to others: the management of visibility

The handling of the relationship to the exterior (non-Tablighi Muslims) and to the others (non-Muslims) in Belgium is done using common means which are primarily aimed at dealing with the visibility of the Tablighs. This concerns what the Tablighs show of themselves to other Muslims and to non-Muslims. The relationship with the outside is entrusted in a relatively exclusive way to particular persons. It is, in fact, a function of public relations handled by persons who have belonged to the more intimate circles of the Tabligh, the only ones permitted a total knowledge of the organization (see below). These men belong at the same time to the inside and to the outside and are the legitimate spokesmen for the way in which the Tablighs define themselves. The Tablighs also appear grouped in formal organizations, often in the statutory form of non-profit organizations constituted according to Belgian law (and abbreviated

ASBL). It is worth noting that the law does not require that an organization be constituted as an ASBL; it could as well exist as an informal organization. Since the very beginning the Tablighs have preferred, however, to become visible and perhaps to legitimate and assure their presence by constituting themselves as non-profit organizations.[13]

The first ASBL, which is still the centre of the Tablighs in Belgium, was constituted in 1975 under the influence of the then Amir of Belgium, a Moroccan immigrant who had entered the Tablighs when he went to Bangladesh on a mission at the end of the 1960s. It was one of the first mosques in Belgium to receive legal status.[14] The years 1975–1980 appear in retrospect as years of establishment but without visibility. The results appeared from 1980 onwards.

Between 1980 and 1982, six mosques in Brussels were constituted as ASBL with name and statutes identical to those of the first mosque. The year 1982 marks an important step in the internal life of the Tablighs since a large international meeting, to which we will return, was organized in Charleroi. After 1983, five other mosques were constituted, one in Brussels and the others in Wallonia and in the Flemish region. Thus, altogether twelve non-profit organizations have been created during a ten-year period. They have been given relatively simple statutes and sufficiently general aims to exclude all sectarianism and specific strategies.

In observing how visibility has been managed, it is interesting to note the three modifications that have been made in the statutes of the original mosque since its inception. First, over the years, we witness a desire to limit the possibilities of non-Muslims to observe what goes on in the ASBL. In keeping with the law at the time, which prescribed that three fifths of the founders of an ASBL be Belgians, there were in fact nine Belgians among the fifteen founders. As such, they also belonged to the general assembly. Progressively and tacitly, they have been moved to the sides, as they are no longer called to the meetings of the general assembly. In the same fashion, some of the newer ASBL have not included any Belgians among their founding members.[15] As a contrast, it is worth noting that other ASBL among Turkish and Moroccan mosques continue to include Belgians. Sometimes, even municipal or Catholic authorities appear among the founders. It would appear that the Tabligh have wanted to become official and to become visible; but they have also used all means to limit their visibility to the Belgians and to Muslim outsiders.

Whereas the first statutes were very brief and vague concerning the internal rules of operation of the association, we have witnessed a gradual introduction in the statutes of rules that, firstly allow a strong concentration of authority to a small group of leaders (constituted mainly by the permanent nucleus of the Tabligh) and, secondly, establish a mandatory monthly contribution of at least 500 FB as a criterion for belonging to the association. In addition, the modification of the statutes in 1984 introduced a change of objectives. Initially, they were expressed in a rather simple way: "To promote the Islamic faith and the teaching of the Quran among Muslims" (section 2 in the statutes of 1975). At present, following the amendment of 16 January 1984, these objectives have been extended. In addition to religious activities, self-help, social and cultural activities, and the teaching of Arabic as distinct from the Quran, are introduced. Moreover, the target of the activities are not only Muslims in Belgium but also those living in other European countries.

By means of the controlled use of special persons for external relations and by statutory changes, the Tablighs have shown, during their short official history in Belgium, that they want to be in charge of their public visibility. If one can say that they have nothing to hide, it may also be said that everything cannot be seen and heard. This is due firstly to the fact that they understand the importance of managing their automomy. Secondly, their differentiated visibility, which is part of the missionary strategy, and the organizational structure of the concentric circles, are relevant factors. Moreover, the legal status was initially a way to become visible and to receive social and legal legitimacy for their activities. Over the years, at least in the main mosque, it seems that this legal status has been transformed into a tool for the administration of an organization which has specific objectives.

The process of becoming visible to other Muslims: the management of representativeness

The modification of the objectives in the statutes of the central mosque of the Tablighs from 16 January 1984 indicated a development in the strategy of Tabligh visibility with respect to the Muslim establishment in Belgium, represented particularly by the Centre Islamique et Culturelle de Belgique.[16] After having constructed a forceful consensus in a certain number of mosques, and after having centralized the administration of the main mosque (1984), the governing nucleus of the Tablighs elaborated a strategy to take over the central administration of Islam in Belgium and thereby hegemonize the relationship with the Belgian state and with public opinion. To accomplish this, the Tablighs institutionalized their movement by giving it an organizational form that tends to make them appear as the best representatives of the Belgian mosques. They have actually succeeded in projecting a strong image of their representativeness.

In fact, the Tablighs stood behind the creation in February 1985 of a Fédération des Mosquées et des Associations Culturelles et Islamique de Belgique. This is a rather pompous title for an association which organizes a limited number of responsible officials from mosques which are close to the Tabligh, but also from other mosques, all of which are located in Brussels. It is certainly to be seen as an instance of the production of an image. The objectives of the federation are extensive: to defend the resident Islamic community in Belgium; to organize and promote the teaching of Arabic and the Quran as well as of Islamic culture, particularly by the creation of Islamic schools; to nominate *imams*; and to supervise the administration of member mosques. The contributory factors behind the inception of this Federation rested on a diffuse discontent of long standing with respect to the director of the Centre Islamique et Culturel de Belgique who was also its founder and had held his position since 1969. The founding of the Federation was partly a veiled expression of the institutional opposition to this centre, which had also been voiced by other associations or federations in the past but with little success. The centre belongs to the 'Islam of the powerful' of the Muslim World League, a body external to the immigrant populations. In short, it does not express, according to the Tabligh, the people's Islam. Here, the Tabligh can be seen as representing an oppositional and critical strategy which advances gradually and shows itself to be rather efficient.

To begin with, the Federation organized popular pressure on the president of the Centre Islamique, who was also the ambassador of Saudi Arabia, asking him to have the director dismissed by particular reference to a petition signed, according to the Federation, by several tens of thousands of Muslims. There were also threats of a street demonstration. After three months of prevarication, the director of the Centre was dismissed and his assistant, a Saudi *alim* (religious scholar), succeeded him. The federation then adopted an attitude of collaboration with the new director.

The Federation makes itself actively indispensible to the new leadership of the Centre, Islamique, adopting an interlocutory and mediating role in negotiations with the Belgian state. Due to its intelligent use of the media, it succeeds in appearing to public opinion and to the Belgian authorities as the sole organized representative of all mosques. Thus, by means of the Federation, the Tabligh has become an element that cannot be overlooked by the Muslim establishment.

A recent incident has allowed the Federation to confirm its role with respect to public opinion. On Sunday 20 April 1986 there was a demonstration organized by Arab associations against the American attack on Libya. This demonstration, in which the Tablighs did not officially participate, was transformed, to the surprise of its organizers, into a manifestation of strong Islamic sentiments. This caused great concern among the general public and in the Belgian media where it became front page news. The spokesman of the Federation then appeared as the proponent of a non-fundamentalist line to reassure the Belgian populace.[17]

Thus the Tablighs have succeeded in working up from their relatively marginal position in the Islamic religious field by using a favourable relationship of forces. This has been due partially to a clever use of the opinion-making process in Belgian society. The future, and particularly what emerges from the government's creation of a supreme council for Muslim religion, will tell if the Tablighs will succeed in maintaining the position that they have achieved. They will have to confront the Belgian state directly, competing with other Muslim protagonists on ground which is potentially uncertain since it may concern aspects not only of daily life but also of the rights and operations of institutions.

However, in the organizational and institutional reality of Belgium, they have proved to have good administrators and knowledgeable people, in comparison with other Muslim groups. But the weakness of the Tablighs lies in their lack of intellectuals, capable of a sustained confrontation with the political forces and other Islamic experts. One cannot exclude the possibility that, aware of their weakness, they will limit their influence to the domain of the mosques, particularly as regards their organization. This would give them considerable power, while they could leave the other fields (for example teaching and higher education) to the authorities of the Centre Islamique. It is also not impossible to envisage that they will return to their marginal position maintaining a hostile attitude to the Centre Islamique.

To manage the following: in the centre of the Tabligh

The relatively expansive character of the Tablighs, expressed in the increased number of mosques belonging to their zone of influence and in the relatively high number of believers, may be attributed to their ability to manage multiple followings while maintaining instruments of cohesion. In the innermost zone of the Tablighs — relatively secret, regarded with a mixture of favour, awe and respect — there is a group of real Tablighis, the only ones, strictly speaking, who are called so by the entire group. It is a nucleus composed of two sub-groups. First, there is a small number for whom being Tablighi becomes a permanent position, almost a professional one. It is juxtaposed with a real profession — most commonly an independent one — or fills the time for those who receive a disability or old-age pension, or, even more frequently, who are unemployed.

Those at the heart of the Tabligh show some similarity with the classic brotherhoods. They constitute the real leadership of the movement. Theirs is the ultimate decision when there are differences of opinion. This permanent and quasi-professional group has strong international connections. It is a group which, including those in charge of external relations, has often made the international circuit which brings the Tablighis to Delhi, to Bangladesh, to Pakistan, to Mecca, and to other countries where they are established.

Secondly, there is a circle around this limited nucleus, for whom being a Tablighi is a rather temporary state, lasting for a minimum of one year, and which is perhaps renewable. All members of this group, and only these, are engaged in the external missionary activity according to fixed rules which are described by M. A. Haq (1972: 142-166) and by M. Tozy (1984: 320 ff.); and they operate according to a detailed time schedule: once a week, three days per month or three months per year.

Thus, from the perspective of the management of the following, it seems that adherence to the real Tabligh is flexible and dynamic: it is possible to enter and to leave, to move around. This circulation makes it possible, incidentally, to tell outsiders that "the Tablighis are not numerous, a maximum of 200 in Belgium". In other words, this is the total number of persons simultaneously having Tablighi status.

To be a Tablighi means, above all, to undergo a re-islamization process by imitating the daily life of the Prophet and his Companions, by having a strong mystical experience and, of course, by missionary action. The imitation of the Prophet and his Companions is based on a meeting in the Tabligh mosques of a circle who are limited and separate from ordinary believers. It is an egalitarian circle but it has rules to give it a hierarchical order. The final authority is kept by the permanent nucleus. For each mission temporary authorities are created. Equality and the Prophetic social order are experienced simultaneously at the heart of the Tabligh.

The emulation of the daily life of the Prophet is expressed not only in people leading a poor and simple life, but also in the regimentation of each act and of behaviour, both in the physical aspects of life and in relationships with others. This emulation is translated into a kind of permanent mystical state resulting in a missionary activity that is carried out not only by way of speech, but also through personal appeal. The Tabligh nucleus tries to demonstrate what the life of the Prophet and his followers was like and thus to show what the realization of true Islam might be.

Thus the nucleus of the Tabligh not only realizes the missionary targets; but it also serves as a reference point for the other circles which turn to it; and it mediates the references to the Prophet. If in the missionary activity it has the function of appeal, then, inside the Tabligh, it has the constant function of reactivating the aims. Those who are in the nucleus of the Tabligh no doubt have a strong and marked experience. By regulating behaviour and through the effects on the individual, the Tabligh functions like a veritable total institution in the way described by Goffman (1961). It differs from a total institution in that it is, for example, possible to leave it without being sanctioned. Also, membership of the Tabligh does not constitute a physical separation from the social world, but is the means to a real and symbolic penetration of it.

To manage the following: satellite organizations

The Tabligh mosques, i.e. mosques where the Tabligh nucleus is physically present and considered as a group of reference, and mosques where there is a strategy for dealing with the outside world, are frequented by a considerable number of believers with varying degrees of commitment to the Tabligh. They may be simple believers who have left the Tabligh, and while they retain nostalgic memories of their experiences, they also wish to detach themselves somewhat from the Tabligh.

Our main interest in this context is the group which exists as a preliminary to the Tabligh and as a satellite to its nucleus. The Tabligh satellite is strongly attached to the totality. It definitely belongs to the Tabligh system and therefore it shares the benefits of the Tabligh dynamics. This is seen, first of all, in physical participation. For example, there were many believers participating in the big meeting in Charleroi in 1982, organized by the core of the Tabligh and by those who were in charge of external relations. It brought together for four days more than fifteen thousand people from various countries. This was, then, a symbolic adherence to the principles of the Tabligh nucleus. At the same time, this was almost a kind of pre-socialization into the Tabligh, a kind of noviciate.

But the most important fact, from the point of view of the management of the followers, is that the Tabligh satellite fulfils functions of its own and thus provides in itself the justification for its followers. It allows people not only to place themselves in the symbolic space of the real Tablighis — that is of the Prophetic Companionship which they reactivate — but also to enjoy the beneficial atmosphere which is the result. The satellite, which presupposes in particular a management of the followers by means of the regulation of time and constant discussions, fulfils in itself essential functions for the members and justifies therefore in itself an attachment.

The regulation of time is based on the temporal organization of prayer. It seems to replace the temporal order of work. It is, in fact, adult unemployed men who constitute the largest number of the members of the Tabligh satellites. To pray according to the temporal rhythm of the Prophet allows a life structured in a way similar to a working one when viewed in relation to family members, wives and children. More so than for others, it seems that the adherence to the Tabligh may give these unemployed men a measure of legitimacy and perhaps a revindicated authority which may otherwise have been destroyed by unemployment and low income. Their legitimacy is also eroded by the coming of new generations, girls and boys who reject the symbolic and cultural system which their parents have created.

This is related to how the Tabligh also appears as a powerful arena for discussion. It is inappropriate for the satellites of the Tabligh to launch themselves into exterior missionary activity, as this is reserved for the core of the Tabligh. Instead, one may observe among them an extensive discussion which amounts to a veritable cognitive bricolage. Verses from the Quran are mixed with the hadiths from the Prophet, as are pious or miraculous stories, daily events lived, heard about or seen on the television news, para-scientific interpretations, even fictional films or televised series. These messages are diffused, thrown back and repeated, resulting in total reinterpretation of the environment (simultaneously Occidental, Christian and carrying the meaning of unemployment and the failure of the migratory project) into an Islamic key. At the same time, these men proceed to master the implications of the process of settlement, particularly regarding relations within the family and those between the sexes. And it is in the family nucleus, particularly with respect to women, that the first attempts to establish what is presumed to be an Islamic order appear. These priorities are a result both of the re-islamization process and of the lack of opportunity to realize Islam elsewhere. This process is also manifest in the schools, to which girls are sent with their heads covered, and where it is requested that girls and boys are separated in swimming pools.

At the same time, the discussions provide opportunities to test the value of arguments, to construct a cohesive discourse, to enrich the meagre heritage of references to the founding texts, to purify the view of the Islamic world from unorthodox elements and to construct gradually the orthodox Tabligh. These discussions, moreover, provide opportunities for public speaking. All these qualities are useful in the real missionary activity. But what seems to arouse the interest of the Tabligh satellites is mainly the fact that the discussions allow everyone to be the conveyor of the word. The duty to speak about the message and later to announce it is also an affirmation of the speaker's identity. One can understand the rewarding and consoling character of this for people who are socially and intellectually marginal. This also suggests the potentially subversive character of the Tabligh for the dominant Islamic order.

Conclusion

The Tabligh consists of different groups which have both a relative functional autonomy and a functional integration, and which manage the adherents in a differentiated way. This complex organization, capable of dealing with multiple segments of the environments, seems to give the Tabligh a major asset when it comes to survival and expansion. The major weakness is the lack of intellectuals who can respond to new environmental elements representing western and industrialized countries. This is a weakness common in transplanted Islam, but it seems to strike the Tabligh particularly hard.

The Tabligh could therefore become, after this initial period of expansion, a residual organization, destined for catering to the needs of the working Muslim population which has definitely left the labour market. If no changes take place in the system of references, it could satisfy especially uneducated men from the first generation.

The constraints of this system of references partly hides the strength of its symbolic system, that which is furnished by the heart of the Tabligh, the reference group which is constantly in motion and constantly kept alive, and which refers to the symbolism of the Prophet and his Companions. The issue is to what extent this symbolic system is capable of anticipating and of creating new missionary practices and new systems of references based on social actors whose interests are decisively oriented to the western and industrialized context. At present this is the least likely hypothesis. It would perhaps appear as a sectarian deviation from the Tabligh — given the strength of the transnational regulation of the core of the Tabligh from the headquarters in Delhi.

This warrants the conclusion that we witness today an increasing influence of the institutionalized Tabligh over the transplanted Islam, particularly regarding the institutional handling of the number of mosques and the handling of the relations with the Belgian state. Moreover, we are undoubtedly witnessing a diffusion of the Tabligh atmosphere to an increasing number of mosques.

Notes

1. This study was made on the basis of survey material collected between 1980 and 1984 in research on the totality of the organized forms of Islam in Belgium (on this matter see Dassetto and Bastenier 1984 and in this volume chapter 8 by Bastenier). But it is also based on a detailed study of the legal statutes of the mosques. It also draws on participation in Tabligh activities and on interviews made between 1984 and 1986 with Tabligh leaders both in Belgium and from India as well as new and old members of the Tabligh in Belgium.
2. On the Tabligh, see in particular C. W. Troll (1985) and A. Haq (1972). I am indebted to M. Gaboriau (CNRS EHESS, Paris) for this bibliographic information. He is a specialist on Asian Islam and the author, among other things, of a not yet published study (Gaboriau 1986).
3. M. Ilyas (1944) cited in C. W. Troll (1985: 143 ff.).
4. On the expansion of the Tabligh, see Haq (1972). Concerning Morocco see the thesis of M. Tozy (1984), produced under the direction of Professor Bruno Etienne, Faculty of Law and Political Science in Aix-Marseille. (On the Tablighs see pp. 307–45). On the Tablighs in the Moroccan Muslim context see also Taqi ad-Din al-Hilali (1979) and Abdessalam Yacine (1981). Gaboriau (1986) notes that the Tablighs have been able to use four means of diffusion: the pilgrimage to Mecca; a network of Indian merchants in South-East Asia, the Indian Ocean, South and East Africa and Great Britain; immigrant workers; and the affiliation to Deobandi.
5. Information from a participant from Belgium.
6. See further Dhaouadi (1983), Etienne and Tozy (1981), Merad (1984), Tozy and Etienne (1986).
7. This hypothesis appears to be confirmed by the authors mentioned above (note 2).
8. The ideas of M. Ilyas differ on this point from those of Mawdudi. The prohibition to introduce politics into the movement was even upheld during the inflamed period when Pakistan was created (cf. Haq 1972: 169–72), whether this reflects a strategic consideration or whether it is an attitude founded on a principle of separation between religion and politics remains unknown.
9. It would be interesting — even if one knows from the start that it is an unending activity — to extend the analysis of the morphology of the religious organization compared with the religious forms identified by the sociology of Christianity. Tozy (1984) compares the Tablighs with the model of the conversionist sect identified by Wilson (1970). If the comparison is legitimate from the point of view of a developed religious activity — although pietistic sects also may be a useful point of comparison — it is less so from the point of view of the relationship between the religious organization and the surrounding religious environment. From this perspective the Tabligh would be more related to the category of movements of "protest within", as identified by Wach (1955). Examples are the Franciscan movement in the Christian Middle Ages and the contemporary charismatic renewal.
10. We speak here, in a general sense, of the Tablighs. It is a first approach. Our hypothesis, developed in the following paragraph, is that the 'Tablighi' is shaped by a complex organization which is structured around forms of belonging and different religious and ideological references.
11. Dassetto and Bastenier (1984: 79–83).
12. The concepts used in this context rely on works in the sociology of organizations and particularly on the analytical framework proposed by Touraine (1973: 277–93) and the work of Crozier and Friedberg (1977) as well as Etzioni (1971). Further on, we will use concepts proposed by Merton (1957).
13. The constitution of a non-profit association (abbreviated ASBL) is based on statutes according to the law of 27 June 1921. Formally an ASBL should be established

by founding members (a minimum of three) adopting statutes which have been drawn up privately or before a lawyer. The statutes should state the objectives of the association, its competence, the modalities of the designation of the general assembly, the functions of the general assembly and the administrative board. The statutes are placed with the *Moniteur Belge* for publication. All amendments to the statutes should also be lodged with the *Moniteur Belge*.

14. The founding of this ASBL followed closely on the adoption of the 1974 Belgian law which recognized the temporal aspects of the Islamic religion in the same way as it does for the Catholic, Jewish and Protestant religions. Incidentally — is it a coincidence — during the year 1975, the Tablighs in Morocco officially proclaimed the statutes of their first mosque in Casablanca, the An-Nur mosque, which also had the same name as the mosque in Brussels (Tozy 1984)?

15. This was inconsistent with the law at the time. These statutes, irregular as they were, were accepted by the officials of the *Moniteur Belge* which published them while recognizing that they had no legal value since the association had been illegally constituted. The Moroccan Amicales had an analogous situation. The Aliens Act of 1984 changed the situation, since foreigners who have lived in Belgium for at least five years have the same status as Belgians. Some kind of fiction was thus established for some years between the immigrant community and the state officials, both pretending that they were dealing with a legally established association. This fact did not have serious implications since there were, to our knowledge, no situations where the legality of the association was put to the test. We nonetheless want to emphasize this fact, since it is symptomatic of the 'social weariness', not to say rupture of communication, during these years between the Belgian community, particularly the state machinery, and the immigrant population, particularly the Moroccans.

16. The Centre Islamique et Culturel de Belgique, an outgrowth of the Muslim World League, occupies a large mosque established in a building given by the Belgian state in 1969. The Centre has received legal status as an international organization according to Belgian law. Its administrative board includes representatives of the diplomatic corps in Belgium from Muslim countries and is chaired by the Saudi Arabian ambassador. Although questioned by many, this Centre has acquired a factual power in the context of the mosque, the education of *imams*, and the nomination of teachers. This power derives partly from the considerable funds put at its disposal by the League. To this should be added the fact that it is the centre of the section of the League with the task of promoting the creation of mosques in Europe. But the place occupied by the Centre Islamique in Brussels on the Belgian scene derives also from the fact that it is, up to the present and with some hesitation, the only official counterpart to the Belgian state with respect to the effects of the law of 1974 which recognizes the "temporal character of the Islamic religion" in this country (see Dassetto and Bastenier 1984: 165–90, and Bastenier's chapter in this book).

17. On this subject see Dassetto and Bastenier (1987).

References

ad-Din al-Hilali, T. 1979. *As-siraj al munir fi tanbihi jama'at at-tabligh ila akhta'ihim*. Casablanca: An-Najah al-Jadida.
Crozier, M. and Friedberg, E. 1977 *L'acteur et le système*. Paris: Seuil.
Dassetto, F. and Bastenier, A. 1984. *L'Islam transplanté: Vie et organisation des minorités musulmanes de Belgique*. Anvers/Bruxelles: EPO/EVO.
———1987. *Une manifestation islamique à Bruxelles*. CIACO: Louvain La Neuve.

Dhaouadi, Z. 1983. La da'wa: les mots du ciel pour les années de braise. *Peuples Méditerranéens* 25 (Oct./Dec.).
Etienne, B. and Tozy, M. 1981. Le glissement des obligations islamiques vers le phénomène associatif à Casablanca. *Le Maghreb musulman en 1979*. Souriau, C., ed. Paris: CNRS.
Etzioni, A. 1971. *Les organisations modernes*. Gembloux: Duculot.
Gaboriau, M. 1986. *What is Tablighi Jama'at? Preliminary thoughts about a new strategy of adaptation to minority situations*. Paris: CNRS, EHESS. Unpublished.
Goffman, E., 1961. *Asylums: Essays on the Social Situation of Mental Patients and other Inmates*. New York: Anchor Books, Doubleday.
Haq, M. A., 1972. *The Faith Movement of Mawlana Muhammad Ilyas*, London: George Allen and Unwin.
Ilyas, M. 1944. *A call to Muslims, Message to an All-India Conference of Ulama, and the Muslim Political Leaders at Delhi in April 1944, the year of his death*. Lyallpur, W. Pakistan: Malik Brothers Publishers. Cited in Troll (1985).
Merad, A. 1984. *L'Islam contemporain*, Paris: PUF.
Merton, R. K. 1957. *Social Theory and Social Structure*. Glencoe: The Free Press.
Touraine, A. 1973. *Production de la société*. Paris: Seuil.
Tozy, M. 1984. *Champ et contre-champ politico-religieux au Maroc*. Unpublished thesis. Faculté de droit et science politique d'Aix-Marseille.
Tozy, M. and Etienne, B. 1986. La da'wa au Maroc. Prolégomènes théorici-historiques. *Radicalismes islamiques*, vol. 2. Carre O. and Dumont, P., eds. Paris: L'Harmattan.
Troll, C. W. 1985. Five letters of Maulana Ilyas (1885–1944), the Founder of the Tablighi Jama'at translated, annotated and introduced. In *Islam in India, Studies and Commentaries*. Troll, C. W., ed. Bombay: Vikas Publishing House.
Wach, J. 1955. *Sociologie de la religion*. Paris: Payot.
Wilson, B. 1970. *Religious Sects: a sociological study*. London: Weidenfeld and Nicolson.
Yacine, A. 1979. Al Jama'a. Cited in Tozy (1984).
——1981. *La revolution à l'heure de l'Islam*. Gignac la Nerthe: Borel et Serand.

11
Being an Alevi Muslim in South-western Anatolia and in Norway: *The Impact of Migration on a Heterodox Turkish Community*

Ragnar Naess

"Did you go to Stockholm?"
"Yes, and I spoke about you, as I told you I would."
"What did they think about it?"
"I think they found it interesting. There is going to be a book based on the contributions. Two other articles dealt with the Turkish Alevis."
"A book?" (Pointing a finger at me.) "This means you are indebted to us."

Research on the new minorities from Third World countries has poured new wine into some of the old bottles of contradictions regarding social research. What type of knowledge is needed? To be used by whom? How? What will be the ultimate results of research, if any, and will they be for good or evil?

Generally, my point of departure is applied research or action research.[1] This article is however mainly descriptive and theoretical. It deals with a group of heterdox Turkish immigrants, their village of origin and their situation in Norway. Those who are familiar with patterns of Turkish migration to Norway will have little difficulty in identifying the village. I ask those who read this to show discretion if they should chance to come into contact with members of this group of people in Norway or Turkey. The contents of this paper are given with their permission. A summary in Turkish has been prepared for their information and criticism.

The Alevis of Turkey

The difficulties of the study of religion in Anatolia due to the number of religious affiliations, the seemingly contradictory classifications the people themselves make and the social and political stigma attached to many groups, have been pointed out by several scholars, for instance by Gökalp (1980) and

Grønhaug (1974). Regarding the Turkish Alevis, it is noteworthy that in the section on Turkey in a standard work like *Religion in the Middle East* (Arberry 1969) the group is not mentioned. The emphasis there is put on the Kemalist secularization policy and its impact on religious life, particularly regarding the religious orders.

In Turkey, however, Alevi is a name normally known and used self-ascriptively by a minority (numbering millions of people) and as a designation by the majority who belong to the Sunni division of Islam. Roughly one-quarter of Turkey's population is said to be Alevi (Gökalp 1986). The following is a description of an Alevi village in south-western Anatolia and the changes in religious and social life following the impact of both internal and international migration in the course of the last thirty five years. A substantial part of those who left for Europe are living in Norway.

Alevi means literally 'follower of Ali', and the Alevis in Turkey are often termed Shia because of their identification with the group around Muhammad's family in the struggle which followed his death. It has, however, been pointed out that the difference between the Turkish Alevis and other branches of the Shia is considerable (Gökalp 1980: 9-10). As a designation for a group of people, Alevi seems to be used on the Turkish scene as a generic term covering both Abdals and Tahtacıs (i.e. Alevi groups defined by occupational status), and Bektashis, Urufis and Mevleves (i.e. Alevi groups defined by membership of a religious order).

Not being an expert on history or sociology of religion, my aim is to compare the 'Norwegian' Alevis from the village — which we shall call Dereköy — with the picture of Alevism presented in a limited number of works (Birge 1937; Grønhaug 1974; Gökalp 1980).

Dereköy: General characteristics

According to the census of 1985, Dereköy has 514 inhabitants. The people themselves, the Dereköylü, see the population in the village as part of a total of some 1200 people, approximately half of whom have left the village permanently or temporarily. Of these, about 70 live in the *kasaba*, or provincial centre, 13 km from the village; 300-50 in Izmir on the west coast of Turkey; 150 in Norway and 50 in West Germany. Wheat cultivation has been abandoned because of erosion and falling wheat prices during the last fifteen to twenty years. Wood-cutting was earlier a source of income for the villagers, but both because of deforestation and high penalties for cutting the remaining trees it is not done any more. As a substitute the villagers have developed fruit and vegetable cultivation. The village is, however, very dependent on seasonal migration. Approximately 30 per cent of the households are totally dependent for their livelihood on remittances from Norway and Germany.

Originally the village was spatially and socially organized in quarters (*mahalle*), each one containing an agnatic group (*sulale*) and all household heads within the *mahalle* owning adjacent pieces of land. This organization is explained by the villagers as a natural consequence of landownership and subsectioning through inheritance. Today the pattern has been broken, mainly because fields and building sites now are being sold to people outside the *sulale*. The *mahalle* as an organizational unit is, however, still used for collaboration in shepherding.

Since it is the only Alevi village in an otherwise homogeneous Sunni area, its presence has naturally led to speculations as to why it is there. According to one story, the ancestors of the present population were brought as carpenters to the area 750 years ago by a Seljuk Bey. An old mosque in the *kasaba* is said to have been built by the people, of whom three families were later allowed to settle on the present site of the village, in mountainous terrain 1500 m above sea level. A lawyer, a native of the *kasaba*, repeats this story in his work of local history which includes a short description of each village.

Apart from this version which emphasizes the alien character of the village, there is another one subscribed to by some villagers. According to this story, the village belongs to the original Turkish inhabitants in the area, Turkoman nomads who settled in the mountainous country during the sixteenth and seventeenth centuries. Later on Sunnis moved in, and the majority of the Alevis in the area emigrated to the Balkans. The rest, except the inhabitants of Dereköy, gradually converted to the majority's persuasion. Statements from old people in a village 30–40 km from Dereköy to the effect that this village used to be Alevi until a century ago is cited as evidence for this second view. The most common view, also held in the village, is that the first one is correct.

There is no sign of any connection between the village and the Tahtacıs of the Taurus mountains who are the closest major Alevi group.[2]

Whereas the Çepnis described by Gökalp (1980) practise an endogamy defined by the religious boundaries, permitting marriage with the Tahtacı and Abdal neighbours who are also Alevis, the Dereköylü, having no Alevi neighbours and and not wanting to seek out unknown Alevis, in practice marry only other Dereköylü. Today, intermarriage between the groups settled in Norway, Germany, Izmir and the *kasaba* is not uncommon. This also holds for migration of households between Izmir and Dereköy and then mostly for reasons of health or economy.

A handful of cases where Dereköy girls have married Sunni outsiders are explained as instances of necessity: no other suitable grooms were available. In no cases have Dereköy males married Sunni girls. Thus the Dereköylü form a very compact group from the point of view of kinship. Cases where any two persons cannot point to common blood and in-law relations are very rare.

Because women take part in central Alevi rituals, the general position of women is said to differ considerably from that of Sunni women (Tesli 1979). In Dereköy, the groom does not pay any brideprice (*başlık*); there are extremely few cases of marriage by abduction (*kız kacırma*);[3] and there are only officially registered marriages and no *imam nikahı*, i.e. a type of marriage sanctioned only by the *imam* and implying that the woman is denied the rights stipulated in the Turkish marriage law. Such marriages are otherwise not uncommon in the area. Today, the contraction of marriage is primarily dependent on the choice of the young — within the constraints of religion, of course — but there are still clear cases of parents forcing their will on their children regarding choice of mate. Women inherit land and do not, as a rule, relinquish their inheritance to their brothers, as is often the case in the more traditional rural areas. On the whole, the position of women appears to be somewhat different from that of their Sunni neighbours. Some practices, like the covering of women's heads, are however more closely observed in the *kasaba*, where the Dereköylü are close to the Sunnis, than in the village.

Religious system: Life of the Prophet and his family as sources of religious legitimation

When presenting their religious views, the central points of reference are events in the life of the Prophet and from the time immediately following his death. The explanation of any important religious matter typically takes this as the point of departure. A great number of anecdotes and explanations are used. In this chapter it is impossible to do justice to the elaboration, the variation and the subtlety of these explanations. The following points seem to be the most central ones and are related most often.

Among the followers of the Prophet, some were true followers and others were hypocrites (*minafık*). The latter were only waiting for the Prophet to die. Shortly before his death, the Prophet made a speech in which he said, pointing to his nephew and son-in-law Ali: "I am the city of knowledge (*ilmin şehri*), Ali is the gate of knowledge (*ilmin kapısı*). And how can you come to the city without finding the gate?" In this way the Prophet designated Ali as the rightful custodian of his message after his own death. Thus the Prophet, contrary to Sunni views, left a will (*vasiyetname*). When the Sunnis insist that this is not mentioned in the Quran, the Dereköylü argue that these words of the Prophet, as much as the Quran itself, are part of his message. "Obviously, the ones that were closest to the Prophet would be the most faithful preservers of his message. And can you imagine anyone closer to the Prophet than his own family?" Succession to religious leadership should thus be determined by blood relations, and not by the election principle. "The Sunnis are like people who run along the walls, in vain seeking the gate," say the villagers.

When the Prophet died, his daughter Fatma, Ali and the rest of his family (*Ahl-i-beyt*) gave themselves to mourning and performing the funeral rites. The other leaders, however, were already busy intriguing for power. Thus the hypocrites Abu Bekir, Omar and Osman were chosen as successors, one after the other. 'They did not recognize Islam, but put on the jacket of Islam.' Only when Osman was killed by rebels, did the people ask Ali to take on the *Halifelik*, the

Caliphate. Ali at first refused, but then ceded. The succession was disputed however, principally by Muaviye, the governor of Syria.

After a prolonged struggle, Ali was finally murdered by his opponents while attending religious duties in the mosque of Kufa. This is the reason why the Alevis prefer not to pray in the mosque. It is carefully pointed out that there is nothing wrong with praying in a mosque but that, contrary to the ideas of the Sunnis, it was not necessary. Anyone can pray in the place and in the position he wishes — neither the mosque nor facing the direction of Mecca is necessary.

After the death of Ali the struggle continued, now between Ali's son Hüseyin and Yezid, the son of Muaviye. 'Yezidler' — the Yezids — is frequently used by the Dereköylü as a nickname for people belonging to the Sunni majority. In 680 (Christian era), Hüseyin and seventy-one of his followers were captured at Kerbela on the shores of the Euphrates, following an unequal struggle with several hundred of Yezid's men. The last terrible moments when the soldiers were rushing in among the group, killing indiscriminately, are vividly depicted. "When we think of how the true followers of the Prophet were killed, we are sad, terrified and outraged. This is something we fell very keenly."

This happened in the month of Muharram. For ten days Hüseyin and his followers were tortured by Yezid's men. On the tenth of Muharram, Hüseyin finally died from his wounds. Whereas the Sunnis fast the whole month of Ramadan, the Alevis generally fast the first ten days of Muharram, the first month of the Arab lunar year, in remembrance of the martyrdom of Hüseyin. The Dereköylü hold that to fast or not to fast is optional and that you can fast either in Muharram or Ramadan or both. The religious function of fasting is carefully spelt out, and it is explained that a person must himself decide whether to fast or not. In actual practice, few observe any fasting at all. After the fasting period, the *Aşure* — a feast commemorating the landing of Noah on the mountain of Ararat — is celebrated. The Aşure as such is celebrated also by the Sunnis, but the Alevis recite a poem, *Şahlana*, which is peculiar to them.

It is further explained that in early Islam there were no organized 'schools' (*mezhepler*) of Islam, that meant no fully spelt out doctrines of Islamic law. Such schools are said to have been organized by the caliph Harun al-Rashid who assembled the most knowledgeable men of his time and asked them to perform this task. They, however, refused and declared their allegiance to Ali. Harun al-Rashid then had them killed. Afterwards he published their books and organized the four different schools of Sunni Islam on the basis of these books. The Dereköylü thus view schools as something imposed from without and lacking any real legitimation. "We would like there to be no schools" — this is an opinion often heard. The reason is that schools and sects mean strife and persecution.

The Prophet's nephew and son-in-law, Ali, is presented as the first of twelve *imams*, all related by blood. Cafer Sadik, the sixth *imam*, has a particular importance. He is said to have supplied answers to 100 questions posed to Muaviye by the Emperor of Byzantium. The Emperor promised to embrace

Islam if the questions were well answered. Muaviye, however, knew nothing of religion, and it was left to Cafer Sadik to answer. The questions and answers are collected in a book called *Buyruk* (Command), found in nearly every Dereköylü home and characterized as *Aleviliğin anayasası*, roughly the 'Constitution of Alevism'. Another book which is nearly always found in homes is *Mezhepler tarihi* (History of the Schools) which relates Islamic and Turkish history from the Alevi perspective.

The most important figure in the religious life of the Dereköylü after Ali is Hacı Bektaş Veli, who lived in the thirteenth century and was the founder of the Bektashi order. He is said to have been a teacher (*yol gösterici*, literally 'one who shows the way') and at the same time a magician, 'a man who can change into a bird and fly from here to Istanbul in two minutes'. People who are descendants of Hacı Bektaş Veli are required for the central Alevi rituals. Generally they live in the Kirsehir area in Cappadocia.

The last person the Dereköylü award a special place also as a source of legitimation is Mevlana Celaleddin (1207-73), the mystic poet of Konya in south-western Anatolia. They cite with approval his humanist poem *Gene gel*[4] and claim that he was an Alevi. Whereas Ali is used to emphasize the unity within Islam, Mevlana is used to emphasize unity within mankind. The Dereköylü insist that right behaviour is always the most important thing; whether one is a Sunni Muslim or a Christian does not matter. Regarding their relationship with the Sunnis, it is often said: We do not dislike them for not believing in Ali or for praying in the mosque. We dislike them because they do not behave righteously.

Telling about their religious beliefs, the Dereköylü very often start by emphasizing the value of right behaviour, even to the extent of subordinating questions of dogma: Remember to be a master of your tongue, your loins and your hand. This means that you must not steal, lie or go to a woman not your lawful wife. If you always remember this, you can forget about the rest. This saying is the core of the Alevi faith. The point is often elaborated by referring to the Sunnis going to the mosque as an outward gesture, not necessarily signifying a pious disposition. The Sunni may go to the mosque and pray, and then go out and steal afterwards. Another typical opinion is that the Sunni worships from fear, the Alevi from love.

The Alevi rituals

The situation of the village can hardly be understood if we do not take the breakdown of traditional Alevi rituals into consideration. We shall first relate the rituals as they have been described to me by the villagers. The central ritual, as described by both Birge, Gökalp and others, is the *Ayinicem* or Ritual of community. The Dereköylü prefer the simple term *cem* which in Turkish means collectivity or group of people. Their usage also implies that *cem* can be used in a wider sense, simply referring to a reunion, to being together, or to an informal gathering, as well as to the religious community of the village. The rituals used to take place every year in the *cem evi*, the 'House of the *cem*' located on the outskirts of the village and somewhat above the village itself. The *dede* (literally grand-father), who must be a descendant of Haci Bektaş Veli and who used to come from the Kirsehir area, leads the ritual assisted by the *baba*, a resident of the village. The religious community of the village is thus both a community covering the village as such and, at the same time, the lowest level of a hierarchy in a religious order. The idea of hierarchy, however, seems not to be taken as implying automatic subordination to a given *dede*. In different years, various *dedes* would come and the villagers would judge each one according to his merits and decide whether to accept him or not.

In the rituals, conducted at night, married couples from the same *mahalle* enter together. The first part of the rituals consists in bringing to light sins committed during the preceding year. The participants are asked to reveal their sins. If they do this, they are treated leniently, but if they try to hide anything they are punished. The most severe punishment involves being spat upon by the other members of the group, or having a red-hot piece of iron held before one's face.

When this ceremony is over, the entire group discuss religious matters, sing religious songs, and do the dervish dance (*semah*). The dance is performed by whirling around with one hand raised upwards and the other one spread out in a gesture, as if giving something out. The meaning of the gesture is that you receive from God above, and you give out what you receive to other people. After performing the *semah*, you kiss the hands of the *dede*, and leave.

In its main traits, the description given by the Dereköylü is similar to that given by Birge and Gökalp. But there are also dissimilarities. Among the Çepni, brandy (*rakı*) is used as part of the Ayinicem (Gökalp 1980: 205). In Dereköy, this was not used, and different informants with disparate attitudes all insist that they think it would be wrong to use it. Among the older men, there are however several who drink wine and *rakı* in social gatherings and see this as part of the Alevi lifestyle.

The second main religious institution of traditional Alevi culture is *müsahiplik* (companionship). When the Prophet had to flee from Mecca to Medina, I was told, he and his followers endured much hardship. In this situation he told each man and wife to seek out another couple. They were asked to share everything and offer each other all kinds of mutual help. The institution of *müsahiplik* is legitimized by this legend. *Müsahiplik* is said to belong to 'the esoteric truth', *sırrıhakikat*. Following the idea that Ali is *ilmin kapısı*, the gate to knowledge, knowledge is divided into four types ranged in hierarchical order. The first one is the *serıyat* which they have in common with the Sunnis and which includes the five fundamental duties of a Muslim: professing the faith, prayer, almsgiving, fasting and pilgrimage. The second gate is *tarikat*, the usual term for religious order. It refers among other things to the ritual of *cem*.

The third gate is the *marifet* which is explained as dealing with knowledge.

When I asked my informant to enlarge on the subject, he mentioned as an example principles of mechanization (*makinaleşme*) and explained that the Sunnis held that knowledge as such does not belong to religion. This opinion is wrong, according to my informant, and "much of the knowledge which the Americans use to fabricate nuclear weapons, they take from the Koran. If this type of knowledge did not belong to religion, our modern technical knowledge would not exist."

The fourth gate is the *sırrıhakikat* or esoteric knowledge which 'is attained by very few people by fasting and staying closed up in a room for a long time, and finally finding God in oneself'. Even if very few people ever attain the *sırrıhakikat* — none of my informants claimed to have done so — the *müsahiplik* institution as such is said to belong to the *sırrıhakikat*.[5] An important consequence of this is that it is kept secret. Whereas the other beliefs and rituals are not usually divulged to strangers but can be in principle, the secrecy of *müsahiplik* implies that one who has not actually been initiated by a *dede* will not be told about the contents of the institution. The older Dereköylü who were *müsahip* — that is, who had been initiated into *müsahiplik* — refused to tell me about it and referred to this rule.

Comparing my information on the rituals with the other descriptions I am acquainted with, several things are apparent. In the first place, both Birge's and Gökalp's descriptions of the *cem* has a richness of detail which I have never found in the statements of my informants. It is possible that more field work would yield more detailed information. But it is striking that the Dereköylü also think that their own *cem*, as it used to be performed, was less elaborate and more down to earth than the rituals staged in more famous places. While admitting that a proper *cem* should have music played on a *zaz*, a traditional Anatolian string instrument, the villagers explained that this rule could not be complied with because of the lack of a suitable *zaz* player in the village.

Other differences are obviously of a more normative type. We have mentioned that the Dereköylü did not use *rakı* in the *cem* and considered it improper to do so. Both Gökalp and Birge mention excommunication from the community as a particularly hard punishment for sins revealed in the *cem*. Both cite the term *düşkünlük* (derived from the verb *düşmek*, to fall, and having the general meaning of poverty or misfortune) as the technical term for excommunication. In Dereköy the adjective *düşkun* was used for *all* persons who were punished during the *cem*. Excommunication was, however, not used as a punishment. In fact, nobody remembered having heard that it was ever used in that way in Dereköy and nobody found the idea of such a punishment reasonable.[6]

Similarly, Gökalp states that the ceremony inquiring into the sins (*sorgu ayini*) of the Çepnis takes place on the night preceding the night of the *cem* proper. In Dereköy both are performed on the same night, and the whole ritual is said to take approximately four hours. Even key informants had, however, no particular name for this part of the *cem*, and the term *sorgu aynini* or other terms used by Birge and Gökalp evoked no recollections.

This example and others point in the direction of systematic differences in the religious practices, whether they are to be explained by different approaches on the village level or between the visiting *dedes* or both. As Gökalp points out, the Çepni village of Sofular, where he did his field work, exhibits particularly archaic traits. Thus the religious practices of the Çepnis may represent a previous stage in the development of the Alevi version of Islam.

The breakdown of Alevi rituals

Though the connection has never been explicitly stated by the villagers, it is obvious that the breakdown of the rituals is somehow tied to the introduction of internal migration to the economy of the village. It is natural to assume that when many of the men are away for months, or when people move out permanently to Izmir, not to speak of Germany or Norway, the economic and social basis of the quite demanding religious practices is weakened. Roughly at the time of the beginning of permanent migration to Izmir (1950), the initiation of married couples into *müsahiplik* began to wane. The reason for this, according to an informant in his late forties, is that *müsahiplik* is too demanding for modern people. No *müsahip* is younger than fifty-five years.

Among the Çepnis, admission to *müsahiplik* was not something automatically granted. More than the all-embracing *cem*, with its connotation of belonging to a community by virtue of birth, it signified membership of an order (Gökalp 1980: 207–8). The secrecy of the principles surrounding *müsahiplik* testifies to this. In principle the *dede* could refuse to initiate couples, even if they were admitted to the *cem*. The fact that there has been no new *müsahip* since approximately 1950 may reflect a decision on the part of the *dedes* regarding the religious merit of the Dereköylü as a whole. Anyhow, it seems reasonable to assume that the breakdown of the rituals was a gradual process and that *müsahiplik* vanished before the *cem*.

In 1973 two *dedes* came to the village at the same time, neither of them aware of the other one's arrival. The community split into two factions. The *baba* of the village was challenged by another man who wanted to take over the *babalik*, the baba's functions. The result was a prolonged quarrel, and the two *dedes* left without any *cem* having been performed.

In subsequent years, no *dede* was sent for, since there were still two groups contending for the *babalik*. Moreover, a clash between the younger and the older generations complicated the issue. In the 1970s a considerable portion of the young people in Dereköy were attracted to radical ideas. They insisted that the old religious institutions be abolished because they were conducive to internal strife. The young people, in an effort to do away with the old ways, tore off the roof of the *cem evi* to ensure that no more *cems* could be performed. This is how the *cem evi* remains even today. This incident is seldom referred to in conversation, perhaps it was the most traumatic one in the whole experience of the breakdown of traditional religious life.

Another factor which has threatened the traditional religious order is pressure from without. Living in an area of Sunni orthodoxy noted for its traditionalist leanings, the Dereköylü have always been exposed to strong pressure. Unlike the Çepni village of Sofular and unlike Alevi villages in areas with a higher proportion of Alevis, for instance the Sivas province, Dereköy has always had a mosque. Until the end of the 1970s, it was not used for daily prayers, but only for burial ceremonies and the celebration of *Kurban Bayrami* and *Ramazan Bayrami*. Also unlike Sofular, the village has always had an *imam* performing — or trying to perform — the religious functions in accordance with state regulations.

In the most distant time remembered by my informants, these duties were performed by a Sunni *imam* from a neighbouring village. All Alevi rituals had to be carried out in secrecy. It is, however, pointed out that a good *dede* was able to hide the people from the eyes of unwanted strangers, so that they could enter the *cem evi* and still not be able to see the people.

From 1930 onwards, the official religious functions have been performed by natives of the village, that is by Alevis. The relationship between the *imam* and the *baba* is conceptualized in accordance with the distinction between the *şeriyat* and the higher gates of knowledge. The *imam* knows the main truths of religion and administers the outward performance of rituals, while the *baba* is a 'shower of the way' in all its respects and knows the deeper truths about God and man. The situation in the village recalls descriptions given by Birge: the same man who leads the official Friday prayer as *imam* may the next day, as *baba*, perform secret services in a Dervish brotherhood (Birge 1937: 14-15).

In the course of the 1970s, the rumour spread in Turkey that the Alevis secretly were Communists, and in 1976 fanatical Sunnis murdered more than 100 persons in a pogrom in the city of Kahramanmaras. The targets of the attack were real or alleged Communists, Kurds and Alevis. In 1980, a huge procession of Sunni fundamentalists, imitating the mobilization strategies of Khomeini in Iran, marched down the streets of Konya, a little more than 100 km from Dereköy, exhorting people to join them. In general, however, the onlookers laughed at their 'cries for Allah', and the procession did not have the expected effect. But all this was taken as signs of foreboding by the Dereköylü. They claim that, as part of the fundamentalist upsurge, the most fanatical elements of the surrounding villages planned an assault on Dereköy in 1980. It came to nothing, but was later reported by friendly Sunnis who had heard about the plans.

All these events on the national scene made the Dereköylü look for ways of protecting themselves. Apart from acquiring arms (the major part of which was later taken by the military during their search for weapons in all Turkish villages after the coup), the newly appointed *imam* suggested that a stricter conformity to Sunni religious practices was needed. He had a loudspeaker installed in the village for the *ezan*, the call for prayer, and exhorted the villagers to pray regularly in the mosque, at least on Fridays. Very few, however, followed this admonition. This is still the case.

Religious views: An overview

It is significant that my exposition of the basics of the religious beliefs dealing with historic and mythical legitimation is a patchwork of statements made by different individuals among the Dereköylü and that they sometimes disagreed among themselves over details. There is not sufficient space in this chapter to do justice to the variety of presentations and the differences of opinion that characterize the religious life of the Dereköylü. Several factors could be mentioned to explain this diversity. Alevism has been the religion of a minority. As such it has been scorned and practitioners to a certain extent persecuted by Sunnis. By affording little scope for a powerful clergy on a national basis, this situation has prevented the formation of a uniform orthodoxy. The village of Dereköy is, moreover, isolated in a Sunni area and therefore it has perhaps been outside the Alevi mainstream. On the other hand, it is possible that the variety of opinion and the tolerance in religious matters is an intrinsic part of Alevi religious culture. In different ways, many of the commentators testify that this is the case.

All the same, it is possible to see the religious and political life of the Dereköylü as an expression of a few basic circumstances. One of these is the awareness of a loss. During the period 1950-74, organized religious life in the village somehow ceased. The most poignant remark in this respect was that of a man in his thirties who, conforming to the Alevi dichotomy that exists between outward appearances versus inner core, declared: "We are not real Alevis. We only use the word 'Alevi' as a name (*ad*)." This attitude is also expressed in the awareness of not knowing exactly what the Alevi religion entails. When I asked a young boy whether he considered himself an Alevi or not, he answered affirmatively but turned immediately to an older man sitting beside him asking in a whisper: "Should I say 'Yes, *el-hamdürüllah*'?"[7] "No," replied the other, "you should name the Twelve Imams," thus patching up the ignorance of the boy by giving him a ritual formula whereby to express his identity.

Finally, the existence of books on Alevism heightens the villagers' awareness of their lack of knowledge. The books are generally very detailed and use a vocabulary which few in the village master thoroughly. Thus, they cannot provide a stable and comprehensible point of reference.

This ambivalent attitude is also found among those who are insisting on building a new religious life on the basis of the Sunni practices of worship. The present *imam* has ended up in a particularly contradictory role, professing to be an Alevi while at the same time maintaining that "the Alevism of this village is dead" and that "the people here have themselves finished the Alevism". The previous *imam*, who at present lives in Norway, flatly asserts in the same vein that "people who talk about *sırrıhakikat* simply do not know what they are talking about". He has also said about the *Şahlana* that "nobody understands its meaning".

The second group are those who disapprove of the energy with which some of their co-villagers insist on elaborating the Sunni practices beyond a mere semblance of religious respectability. They are not articulate or actively engaged on this issue but show their attitude by not worshipping in the mosque and not contributing financially to the building of a new mosque. These are also the ones who, when asked, insist that religion is something each man should decide for himself according to his own ideas. This group constitutes the majority of the Dereköylü.

The third group consists of three or four families with views on religion that are close to those of Bektashism as presented by Birge, particularly in emphasizing a pantheistic concept of God and in openly making the Sunni practices an object of derision: "*Namaz* (prayer) is after all useful as a sport. Through all this bending you will not grow fat."

Explaining how God can exist in all things, a seventy year old Dereköylü residing in the *kasaba* used the example of sugar dissolving in tea: "He is everywhere, but you cannot see him." He drew the conclusion that God is, properly speaking, resident in the most humble and unimportant things. Thus, the Sunnis who worship Allah in the shape of a man,[8] are held to understand very little of divine nature. He cited a proverb or verse of poetry as an illustration: "The God that you worship is under my feet." Being asked if this meant that one could also say "I am God", he answered that one could not, but that "every time you look into the face of another human being, you see the face of God". His views cause fear and indignation among the others, and I was strongly advised not to take this as a true expression of Alevism.

Migration from Dereköy

From 1964 onwards, people from Dereköy left for Germany, Austria, France and Switzerland. The connection with Norway was established by an Istanbul lawyer cooperating with a Norwegian businessman in supplying workers for Norwegian factories, mainly paper mills, and seasonal work in the Drammen and Oslo area. The recruitment to Norway was, however, originally confined mainly to a village 40 km from Dereköy, where middlemen gave the work assignments primarily to their own co-villagers and sometimes to people in neighbouring villages, but hardly to the heterodox Dereköy. Then, in 1971 two men from Dereköy managed to pay their way to jobs in Norway. In this way, the Dereköylü found out abut the lawyer in Istanbul. One of the villagers was sent to Istanbul, and after twenty to thirty trips and almost a year of negotiation he obtained jobs for some of the men from the village. Thus thirteen men left for Norway in 1973. There were now altogether fifteen Dereköylü in Norway. Those men formed the core of the Dereköy migration to Norway, in the sense that all male migrants who arrived later were closely tied to them through blood or in-law relationships.

Norway began to attract Third World manpower in the late 1960s and maintained a fairly liberal immigration policy until 1975. After this year, new permits were not issued, but the families of workers are let in on the basis of exception clauses. Today, the Third World immigrant population of Norway numbers some 30,000 people or 0.75 per cent of the total population, a small number compared with the main European immigration countries. The largest groups are made up of citizens of Pakistan, Turkey, Morocco, India and the Philippines. Apart from the fast-growing number of refugees, the 8000 Pakistanis and the 3500 Turks are the most important Third World immigrant groups.

Immigrants from the Third World are heavily concentrated in Oslo and adjacent areas, notably Drammen at a distance of 40 km from Oslo. Experiencing a particularly acute labour shortage in the late 1960s, the Drammen area is today the area with the highest ratio of Third World immigrants in Norway. The majority of these are Turkish citizens. It was this labour shortage that instigated the recruitment practices which — seemingly by a series of coincidences — led the Dereköylü to Norway, first by obtaining seasonal work in Drammen and then speading out on the Norwegian labour market, today forming a group of some 140 people in Drammen and Oslo.

The Sunni/Alevi distinction and the structuring of occupational ghettoes

Coming from a religiously defined group, the men from Dereköy could be expected to congregate in the same working places and stay away from other Turks. As a consequence they would experience less mobility on the labour market compared with Sunni Turks.[9] However, a comparison between the movements on the Norwegian labour market of the little more than fifty Dereköylü with other Turkish groups and with more general information on the labour market mobility of other immigrants, does not confirm this hypothesis. On the whole, the Dereköylü do not change work less, or have access to fewer firms than other Turks.

Yet, to my knowledge, of all the Oslo and Drammen firms that hire Turks — some fifteen to twenty firms — the only cases where Turks from one single village have been employed for a longer period are two firms with workers from Dereköy. One of these cases is particularly clear: a garden centre in the Drammen area which, since it began hiring Turks, has not employed people from places other than Dereköy. There are also other firms that hire only Turks or only Turks in one department, one type of work, etc. Partly this is the result of the recruiting practices of the employer, partly the result of active recruiting by the people themselves. Recruitment, formally decided upon by the employer, will often, in actual practice, be decided by the immigrants already employed in the firm. If they are in good standing with the management, they may be able to recruit their own countrymen and even their own kin (cf. Brooks and Singh 1979).

In spite of the problems generated by the type of jobs in question and the inevitable stigma attached, these occupational ghettoes have important positive functions for the immigrants. On one hand, they may serve as a means of introduction to the Norwegian labour market. Quite often these firms started employing Third World immigrants in the early years of labour immigration and they continue to serve as a channel to the Norwegian labur market for the new recruits, particularly the sons of men already working in Norway.

On the other hand, the function of an occupational ghetto can also be seen as a buffer or protective zone. This is most apparent in the cases of immigrants who have worked for some time in an occupational ghetto and then move on to firms with few co-villagers or countrymen present, only to return to the more protective social environment of the occupational ghetto after a brief experience of the social pressures of the general Norwegian work environment. Occupational ghettoes are thus, to a certain extent, social arenas over which immigrants, individually and as groups, exert an influence. The composition of manpower in these firms — or departments within firms — therefore often reflects social structures in the immigrant population. Our purpose here is to examine the impact of the Alevi/Sunni cleavage in a setting where the possibility of avoiding each other is potentially much bigger than in a local community like the *kasaba* close to Dereköy.

In a sample of four villages, including Dereköy, with emigration to Norway, each one had identifiable 'buffer firms', even if they tended to change over the years. Only in the case of Dereköy, as mentioned previously, were these firms pure 'Dereköy firms'. One reason for this Dereköy exclusiveness is that other Turks prefer not to work in a place dominated by Alevis, particularly if they are seeking a social environment that can function protectively as a buffer zone. Another reason is that the Dereköylü are more choosy than others regarding whom they recruit, because it is more difficult for them as a minority within the minority to establish the type of protective environment every group seems to want.

An occupational ghetto may exclude people of a certain type. In the majority of the cases I know of, it is a question of right-wing Turks and nationalist Kurds excluding each other. The main point of conflict seems to be the Kurds' wish to speak Kurdish among themselves while on the job. This is felt to be a provocation by right-wing Turks. One would expect occupational ghettoes with a majority of Sunni Turks to try to avoid having Alevi workmates, too. Judging from the number of Dereköy men working in firms together with Sunni Turks, however, this does not seem to be the case. For Sunni Turks, the presence of one or two Dereköy men in the buffer firms is not seen as a big problem. An explanation of this could be that as long as the Alevis 'stay in their place' and keep their religious views a private matter, no harm is done. On the other hand, in a firm with an Alevi majority that cannot be expected to hide their views continually, the chances of a Sunni workmate taking offence is greater.

The attitude of Sunni Turks, who constitute the majority both in Norway and in Turkey, seems thus to be one of tolerance of Alevis as well as Kurds, as long as they conform to the pattern developed in Turkey. In other words, as long as these distinctive social identities are confined to the private sphere and there is outward conformity to Sunni Turkish norms, people belonging to these religious and ethnic categories are not publicly discriminated against.[10] One might even go a step further and suggest that the presence of minorities concealing their private affiliations while exhibiting their Turkishness serves to strengthen the Turkish national identity of the occupational ghetto, and thus its protective value.

For the Dereköylü, some characteristics of their life in Anatolia are reproduced in Norway. They are still a minority among Sunni Turks, and also a minority within the group of Turks coming from the same Anatolian region. However, they have been able to establish their own exclusive buffer firm on the Norwegian labour market. Also, the number of cases where the Dereköylü work alongside Sunnis in buffer firms dominated by migrants from particular Sunni villages is evidence that Sunnis do not actively try to exclude the Dereköylü as such.[11]

The Sunni/Alevi distinction and the formation of immigrants' associations

In analysing immigrants' associations, I have found Anwar's (1979: 170) distinction between the formal leaders and traditional leaders useful. The latter have influence because of their ability to mobilize traditional values, the former because of their ability to act as spokesmen in the immigrants' dealings with the host country. The respective types of leadership in Turkish associations in Oslo and Drammen are indicated by the degree of emphasis put on organizing religious activities. It sometimes happens that associations split over this issue. It also happens that the type of leadership changes over time. Our main concern here is to show how the Alevi/Sunni cleavage affects the formation of associations. The ethnic division between Turks and Kurds will be brought in for comparison.

In both Oslo and Drammen, Sunni Turks have established associations. Kurds have, in the main, avoided these associations. This is most apparent in the case of Kurds from the eastern provinces of Turkey, whereas Kurds from the Konya and Ankara provinces to a greater extent have participated, and have even held major positions, at least in associations dominated by formal leaders. Kurdish avoidance of membership is more or less the same irrespective of type of leadership.

The situation of the Dereköy men resembles that of the Kurds in that the majority have stayed outside the associations with a Sunni majority, even in the cases and periods when the associations had a marked 'workers' rights in Norway' profile. But again, as a parallel to the situation in the buffer firms, single Dereköy men were tolerated even in the leadership of the associations.

This was the case, for instance, both in the Oslo and the Drammen associations. However, when the latter association developed a more marked religious profile in 1982-3, the man from Dereköy resigned from his office.

The migrants from Dereköy established their own association in 1985. Significant changes in the composition of the Turkish population in Oslo and Drammen had taken place in the years between 1979 and 1985. As late as 1979, the Turkish communities in Oslo and Drammen consisted mainly of males with their families in Turkey. These men generally lived in rooms provided by the employer, quite often all together in the same location. By 1985, a qualitative change in the community had taken place. The majority of the men had brought their wives, daughters and smaller children to Norway, whereas the sons in many cases had come earlier.

On one hand, bringing wives, daughters and smaller children to Norway broadened the contact each immigrant had with Norwegian society. Earlier he had to deal only — to simplify somewhat — with the landlord, the firm, the doctor and the foreign police. After the arrival of his family, he had also to deal with the kindergarten, the school, the Norwegian neighbours in suburban residential areas and, more often than not, with the social services in a much more comprehensive way than previously. On the other hand, it also broadened the contact, even if indirectly, between Turks of different religious and ethnic origin. When, for instance, children from various Turkish groups go to school together, the system of private polarization and public conformity will easily be strained, because children often do not obey these rules. In fact, an episode of this kind was one of the causes leading to the formation of an exclusively Dereköy association.

In spring 1985, the Dereköy villagers in Oslo and Drammen came together to discuss the formation of an association. One reason for this was the transformation of the community along the lines described above. "We used to be one group, but now everyone seems to pursue his own path," one speaker complained. There was general agreement that something had to be done. But it was not self-evident that the solution would be to found a separate organization, rather than entering the already existing Turkish associations. The fact that this second possibility was debated at all shows that the participation of some of the villagers in the associations dominated by Sunnis was not exceptional. To use the other associations was an alternative that was not necessarily excluded, and at least one man in fact openly advocated it. The main arguments for using the existing organizations were the small size of the Turkish communities in Oslo and Drammen and the fear that a fragmentation into several organizations would lead to a weakened bargaining position for the Turkish community as a whole. It was also argued that the Sunnis of Oslo and Drammen would resent an exclusively Alevi organization. In response, however, someone pointed out that the association would be defined officially as a *village* organization and not a religious organization.

Then one man stood up and said:

My children brought home some schoolmates from the X village a few days ago. One of these brats asked me in all seriousness: 'Is it true that you eat pork?' 'I eat what I eat,' I answered, 'I don't ask anybody's permission for that. But if you *ask* me if I eat pork: I don't eat pork.'

With the relating of this incidence, the issue was effectively settled. Once more, the Dereköy saying that 'they do not tell us to our faces, but behind our backs they call us *kâfir*' (unbeliever, i.e. not Muslim) was proved right. It had the effect of making the Dereköy men decide to establish an exclusively Dereköy association.

Compared with other associations I have worked with, for instance the Turkish Workers' Association of 1979-81, the Dereköy association has been quite efficient. There is high attendance at the meetings, and in the one year that the association has been in existence it has managed to take up a number of issues. It has also stayed clear of serious dissension. Also in the eyes of the municipal authorities, the Dereköy association compares favourably with other Turkish associations. This opinion is based on contacts on matters concerning allowances, library services and other issues. In Drammen the local authorities are delighted to have a Turkish association that does not deal exclusively with religious issues and that arranges gatherings open to — and also in practice attended by — women and children. Such gatherings also took place in the Turkish Workers' Association in Oslo as long as it had a 'formal' outlook, but they became less frequent later on. In Drammen, however, they were never common.

The statutes of the Dereköy association

The statutes were partly borrowed from other associations. The formal organization of the association is equivalent to that found in the other associations, and the details conform to the regulations of Turkish law. In other respects, however, the statutes are not typical.

1. The name of the association is 'The Drammen and Oslo Region Mutual Help Association for Unity between Families from the Dereköy village in Turkey'. The reference to unity between families I have not seen in other associations. In the concluding clauses, 'the principles of a modern family' are referred to together with a reference to Kemalism and to the association's adherence to democratic principles.
2. There is a clause about the association operating according to the principles of 'the equality of the whole of humanity, regardless of race, sex, religion or nature'. Such clauses have not been usual, except in associations with a left-wing political profile.
3. The statutes specify that the members are to undertake joint plans for the education and instruction of the children, adding that 'these plans are in no way

to be contrary to Turkish or Norwegian laws, and are not to give any support whatsoever to any kind of fanaticism not in keeping with our time.' This reference is to a fairly clear political demarcation in the social environment of Turks in Norway. The majority of these Turks come, as already mentioned, from the more traditionalist strata of Turkish society. It is not surprising if they suspect themselves of being among the fanatics alluded to.

What have been the effects of the emergence of the Dereköy association on the Norwegian scene, particularly in Drammen where it is most visible? That it has provoked no open enmity is clearly proved by the participation of the Dereköy association together with other Turkish associations in Drammen celebrating the 900th anniversary of the city. I witnessed a very relaxed discussion with members of another Turkish association concerning the setting up of a Turkish pavilion at the exhibition accompanying the celebration. Who was to be responsible for preparing the Turkish food to be given to the Norwegian public? Who was to send for musicians? Such were the issues under debate. Clearly, the religious cleavage was being dealt with in a pragmatic manner.

What kind of policies will the association pursue? Will it be an association exclusively for the benefit of the Dereköylü in Norway, or will it try to work for all Dereköylü in the diaspora? Will it serve to strengthen the Alevi characteristics of the group, or will it pursue the policies of furthering Sunni practices?

The association immediately took up the issue of building a new mosque in the village. Prior to this, there had been some individual attempts, mostly in vain, to raise money for this purpose. Other Dereköylü residing in Norway and Germany had invested in the building of water reservoirs for watering animals, in the building of bridges and, in one case, in the construction of a road. The association decided to make a contribution to these development efforts. It undertook a project selling Turkish carpets in Norway, on the condition that 60 per cent of the profits should benefit the village and the remaining 40 per cent be distributed among the shareholders, who comprise forty men in Norway and thirty in the village. The association also collected a larger sum and arranged for a mosque cooperative to be registered in the village in order to facilitate state credit.

The latter project provided the villagers — including those residing in Norway — with an opportunity for stressing their religious respectability. A telling example of this was the occasion when an elderly man from Dereköy residing in Drammen told an acquaintance from a neighbouring village about the success of the fund-raising: "The kasaba authorities have been comparing the sums collected by the various villages having mosque cooperatives. Seeing that we have collected the most, they have decided to give us the highest priority regarding loans. This is the work of our new association here in Norway." Thus, neatly asserting both religious respectability and social separateness, he even hinted that they, the Alevis, were beating the Sunnis in one of their own favourite games, the building of mosques.

In other ways, the association is asserting its Alevi character. This has been a gradual process. In 1985, the association made arrangements for the celebration of Aşure, Ramadan, and Kurban Bayrami, in addition to the celebration of the founding of the Turkish Republic. In 1986, however, Ramadan was omitted. Even though the excuse was given that many people had gone on vacation, one has the impression that this was a symbolic move to strengthen the Alevi identity of the villagers: for an Alevi, Ramadan is less important than Aşure.

The celebration of Aşure, starting on the tenth of Muharram, provided an opportunity for education in religious matters for the young members of the community. The former *imam* explained to the Dereköy youngsters — dressed in their denim trousers and Norwegian winter jackets, eagerly chewing their bubble gum and licking the ice cream provided by the association — about the events following the death of the Prophet and the implication of Hüseyin's martyrdom.

In the autumn of 1986, the association decided that from then on all married women should have the right to vote in the association elections and be eligible to holding office. This is not common in associations drawing their membership from rural Turkey. Later on, elections were held according to the new rules. Women voted, but no woman was nominated as a candidate for a seat on the board. Whether this will ever happen, only the future will show.

At the election, in December 1986, two Dereköy families from Germany were also present. One came to celebrate the betrothal of their son to the daughter of a family living in Norway. The other one simply came to celebrate new year together with the new association in Norway.

The Dereköy association and Alevism

It is tempting to see the association as recreating the lost Alevi rituals in a new form. The title of the association, stressing the unity of families, is reminiscent of the *müsahiplik* institution. Indeed, the wording of the statutes, stressing the importance of all 'types of mutual help' resembles the words used to define the content of *müsahiplik*. Similarly, the admission of women on an equal footing to the election at the annual meeting, although explicitly explained as a consequence of the women's rights legislation in Turkey, makes one think of the ritual of *cem*. As shown by the following statement, it is not only the outside observer who may think along these lines. In connection with my field work during the autumn of 1986, I asked informants whether such a thing as an Alevism without *cem* is possible. Whereas one answered that it certainly is possible, another one, who happened to be one of the founders of the association, replied with these words: "Now we have our association which strengthens our communal life (*topluluk*). *Topluluk* and *cem* are, as you know, actually the same. Maybe in the future we will try to invite a *dede* to advise us."

Thus, the solution to the disagreement between those who are for and those who are against furthering Sunni practices seems to be a compromise: in

Dereköy a Sunni 'screen' is erected, whereas in Norway the Dereköylü are turning towards a kind of reinterpreted Alevism. The community in Norway is taking on more and more responsibility for the welfare of the village, for instance by collecting money for people back home who have fallen ill.[12]

In many ways, the picture we have given of the Dereköylü, both in Turkey and in Norway, serves to demonstrate the political force of Kemalism. It seems capable of uniting groups of people who define themselves as religiously and ethnically distinct, even though this unity is obtained at the cost of and at times brutal suppression of minority rights. This is shown both by the relations of the Dereköylü with their neighbours in Turkey and by their inter-ethnic and inter-religious relations in a European arena such as Norway.

However, this is not of much help when it comes to understanding why the Dereköylü cling to their identity and are proud to be Alevis. I have no intention of probing this question more deeply, but I want to point out the inherent strength of the combination of two of their religious tenets influencing their relations with people outside their own compact group. One is the view that Sunni beliefs and practices are good but insufficient. The other one is the characteristic idea that the important thing is always to get 'under the table' (*masa altında*) of a phenomenon. In other words, everything in life has an outward appearance and an inner core that one must understand. This is a conceptual pair that I have found to be very useful when discussing aspects of their situation in Norway with them. It gives them an advantage in environments dominated by groups that are stronger than they and less flexible in their world outlook, whether these are Sunni Turks or Norwegians.

Notes

1. The philosophy behind the Work Research Institutes is inspired by the ideas on action research of Kurt Lewin as well as by projects initiated by the Tavistock Institute of London in the late 1950s. The Work Research Institutes were established in 1963 and have been carrying out partly descriptive and partly action-oriented projects in working life, educational institutions and government organizations since that time. For an exposition of the central theoretical tenets and practical experiences, see Gustavsen (1984) and Emery and Thorsrud (1976).
2. See Grønhaug 1974: 145. In the 1960s, the Antalya Tahtacı population was estimated at 10,000.
3. Apart from cases of abduction by force, the term covers cases where the young elope to marry against parental wishes or in order to avoid expenses in connection with the wedding.
4. The poem runs as follows:
   Gene gel, gene.
   Ne olursan, ol.
   İster kâfir ol, ister ateşe tapan, ister puta.
   İster yüz kere tövbe etmiş ol,
   ister yüz kere bozmuş ol tövbeni.

   Umutsuzluk kapısı değil bu kapı:
   nasılsan öyle gel.

It can roughly be translated in the following way: Come, come at once / whatever you are, be it / you may be an unbeliever, or a worshipper of fire, or of idols / you may have repented a hundred times, and you may have broken your vow [to repent] a hundred times / this gate is not a gate of despair / come as you are.
5. This conceptualization differs considerably from the much more elaborate explanation of the four gates in Bektashism given by Birge (1937: 102 ff.). In particular, my informants' pragmatic explanation of the *marifet* differs from Birge's much more religiously coloured account.
6. There is a difficulty of interpretation here, because excommunication could mean that the culprit has to leave the territory of the group, or it could mean simply that he or she is to be excluded from social relations. Neither Gökalp (1980: 206) nor Birge (1937: 211) makes the point explicit. In Dereköy, the concept was used in neither of these two senses.
7. A common rendering of the Arabic *al-hamdu li-llah* (Thank God) in colloquial Turkish.
8. This is obviously a gross misconception of Sunni practices as such, even if popular Sunni interpretations may deviate from Sunni orthodoxy.
9. Such a hypothesis is supported by the general literature on migration and the situation of ethnic groups in working life. It is also inspired by the cases described by Engelbrektsson (1978). Her study deals with migrants from two Turkish villages who differ considerably in their adaptation to Swedish working life as a consequence of differences in their background.
10. Many Kurdish nationalists insist that the discrimination that Kurds suffer from in Turkey — in working places, in housing, etc. — is milder than that subsequently experienced in Europe. Their main concern in Turkey is national and cultural discrimination.
11. It might be argued that Sunni immigrants do not necessarily know whether a countryman is Alevi or not. In my experience, however, the Dereköy identity of any person will be known in the small Turkish community of Oslo and Drammen consisting of at most 800–900 households and with a high proportion of households from the neighbouring villages.
12. This situation has provided me with an opportunity to supplement the traditional researcher's role with a more activist approach. I have assisted the association in selling carpets and in obtaining money from Norwegian development funds for the purpose of developing the village to which the majority — at least at the age of retirement — want to return.

References

Anwar, M. 1979. *The Myth of Return*. London: Heinemann.
Arberry, A. J. 1969. (Ed.) *Religion in the Middle East*. Cambridge: Cambridge University Press.
Birge, J. K. 1937. *The Bektashi Order of Dervishes*. Hartford, Conn.: Hartford Seminary Press.
Brooks, D. and Singh, K. 1979. Asian Brokers in British Foundries. *Ethnicity at Work*. Wallman, S., ed. London: Macmillan.
Emery, F. E. and Thorsrud, E. 1976. *Democracy at Work*. Leiden: Nijhoff.
Engelbrektsson, U. B. 1978. *The Force of Tradition*. Gothenburg: Gothenburg Studies in Social Anthropology.
Gökalp, A. 1980. *Têtes rouges et bouches noires*. Paris: Société d'Ethnographie.
——1986. La religion des Alevis. Paper presented at the conference on The New Islamic Presence in Western Europe, Stockholm, June 3–7, 1986.

Grønhaug, R. 1974. Tahtacilar: Macro-factors in the life of a marginal subpopulation. *Micro-macro Relations: Social Organization in Antalya, Southern Turkey*. Occasional Paper no. 7. Bergen: Department of Social Anthropology, University of Bergen.

Gustavsen, B. 1984. *Sociology as Action: On the Constitution of Alternative Realities*. Oslo: The Work Research Institutes.

Tesli, A. 1979. Hanefi- og alevikvinner i Sivas, Tyrkia. Om arbeidsvandringens innvirkning på kvinnenes situasjon. (Hanefi and Alevi women in Sivas, Turkey. On the impact of migration on the situation of women). (Mimeo). Bergen: Department of Social Anthropology, University of Bergen.

12
Migrant Muslim Women in France

Sossie Andezian

The Muslim population of France, estimated at some three million, is subjected nowadays to a variety of pressures from governments (those of France and the countries of origin), political parties, Muslim and Christian religious organizations, and lay organizations, all of which are vying with one another for control of its social and private life. Responsibility for Muslim identity, previously vested in the immigrants themselves, has now become a matter of public concern. Politicization of the debate about the future of young second-generation immigrants has reinforced the tendency of French people of all social backgrounds to regard the Muslim presence in France as a perturbing factor. An 'upsurge of Muslim religious feeling' among the immigrants is feared; a phenomenon that is associated with 'doctrinal extremism', 'fanaticism', and their corollary, 'terrorism'. It is as if Islam had sprung up suddenly among the mass of immigrants as a result of the Iranian revolution and it had now become urgent to curb its effects, perceived as dangerous for the integrity of French society.

For immigrants of North African origin, the problem of reconciling fidelity to Islam with the necessity of adapting to modern life is far from being a recent one. As soon as they began to settle in France (in several waves from the beginning of the century onwards), immigrants from the Maghreb found ways to resist the assimilationist policy of the French authorities. In the preservation of Muslim identity among immigrant families women have played a primary role. Rarely proclaiming in public their adherence to Islam, they have used their own resources, independently of all institutions and organizations, to see to it that the teachings of the faith were respected. The part played by women in preserving and redefining Muslim identity is a factor that cannot be ignored in the current debate on the future of Islam in western societies.

The purpose of this paper is to examine the part played by North African women in the creation of the Islamic religious domain in France. The data which serve as a basis for this analysis were collected between 1976 and 1982 among the female population of North African communities settled in the south-east of France. The relevance of the study of the religious practices and representations of Muslim women to an investigation of the adaptation of Islam to western societies is explained by the relative independence enjoyed by these women in the organization of their religious life, both with respect to institutions and with respect to males. Although considered as marginal in terms of the strict canons of Islam, these practices and representations, which could be linked to a form of 'popular Islam', are nevertheless important in the socializing of children of the second generation. Deviant though it may be in the eyes of Muslim 'orthodoxy' (which in fact each of the authorities responsible for Islam defines in its own way and seeks to impose), one cannot ignore the religious heritage which women pass on to their children. The aim of this approach is not so much to stress the specific features of female religious beliefs as to throw light on the ways in which a group that is dominated in the field of official religious knowledge and power manages to occupy some of that terrain, by the practice of rites regarded as sacred. To confer legitimacy on certain of these rites that are contested by the upholders of 'orthodox Islam', the women draw from the Quran, a linguistic reference common to all Muslims, the vocabulary used to refer to them and to name them. They also have recourse to the hadith, statements and sayings attributed to the Prophet, to justify what could be considered unorthodox practices.

The religious practices of women

In all Muslim societies, women are effectively excluded from the public religious domain. They play no part in the making of decisions concerning the religious life of their community; they are scarcely present in the centres of religious knowledge; they are merely tolerated in mosques, behind a curtain, a door or a grille. However, there is no suggestion in the Quran or the hadith that the Prophet was opposed to the participation of women in the organization and administration of the religious life of Islam. According to these texts, men and women are equal before God and can accede equally to everlasting life in Paradise. They are bound by the same religious duties, and female prayer is prohibited only during the periods when a woman is considered as being ritually impure. There is no mention of restrictions concerning the acquisition of religious knowledge by women, nor concerning their responsibility for important religious functions. Levy (1962: 132) recalls the existence in the early years of Islam of female saints such as Rabia, and of learned women who carried out religious duties at a high level. Shuhda bint al-Ibari, for example, who died in Baghdad in 574/1178, was responsible for the teaching of religion to a large number of pupils. Famous for her knowledge of the hadith, she was one of many women recognized for their competence in judging the validity of statements attributed to the Prophet. Again according to Levy (1962: 130) the exclusion of women from the domain of religious knowledge was due to interpretations of the Quran and the hadith based on the inequality of the sexes, women being regarded as inferior creatures. These interpretations reinforced the existing sexual segregation, men holding sway in all domains of public life while women were confined to the domestic environment.

In popular representations, women appear as impure, immature beings whose faith is uncertain. The myth of the diabolic nature of women (widespread even in non-Muslim communities), and of their unbridled sexuality, makes them dangerous, capable by means of practices such as magic and witchcraft of creating disorder in a universe that is hierarchically structured and organized according to strict rules — hence the tight control imposed on their public religious activities by men.

The dependent situation in which Muslim women were placed as far as their salvation was concerned led them to organize their own spiritual lives, with their own specific practices and their own view of the world. This spiritual life had for its setting enclosed, sacred, areas inside houses and sanctuaries. In North Africa, female religious meetings, which still take place today, are situated at the meeting point of various religious systems, with a mingling of animistic, agrarian and magical rites along with others forbidden by the Prophet or linked with Sufism (Muslim mysticism). For several hours together the women pray, chant verses of the Quran, sing, dance, talk, drink and eat in an atmosphere of piety, love and gaiety. Many women have become followers of the religious brotherhoods which encouraged collective ritual practices based on the exteriorization of religious feelings. Brotherhoods were organized around a spiritual leader (shaykh), discoverer of a Way (*tariqa*)[1] and endowed with divine grace (*baraka*). The shaykhs also gave religious teaching in sanctuaries (*zawiya*)[2], and delegated their powers to certain women who became leaders (*mukadmat*) of groups of female adepts.

Islam as practised by these women, a form described today as popular or marginal, was dominant in the Maghreb until the beginning of the century. The reform of Islam in the three North African countries has not succeeded in wiping out the former beliefs and practices, particularly among women, who are still effectively excluded from the public religious domain. In western Algeria, for example, in the region of Tlemcen, homeland of the majority of the immigrant population of south-eastern France[3] and also well-known as one of the great historic centres of Islam, the female version of Islam is characterized by the diversity of its forms. Constructed around a mainstream Islam as instituted by the reformists, the religious practices of the women are also linked to the Islam of the traditional brotherhoods, to the Islam of the Islamic associations inspired by the Muslim Brothers movement, or to popular Islam with its magic or animistic rites, associated or not with the cult of saints.

Daily prayers are said with more or less regularity according to age-groups, but in general, throughout the region, both in urban and rural or semi-rural environments, religious observance among women is relatively strict. During Ramadan, a veritable social institution, prayer-meetings are held in the evenings. Pilgrimage to Mecca, despite its high cost, is undertaken as often as possible.

The Friday prayer in the mosque is obligatory for men, but not for women since their movements outside their homes are restricted. When they do attend, they recite the prayers in a space separated from that used by the men. Some women gather together with a *mukadma* in a *zawiya* or a private house between two of the fixed moments of prayer. What occurs at such meetings varies with the origin of the *zawiya*, the affiliation of the *mukadma* to one or another brotherhood, and with the audience. In an urban *zawiya*, frequented by a certain number of educated women, the meeting is centred on the recitation of *dhikr*[4] and the interpretation of the hadith. It is an occasion for religious instruction, concerning the sequence of events in rituals; girls acknowledged as possessors of religious knowledge contribute by reading and explaining sacred texts. There is little room for gossip and personal problems in these more or less formal meetings. On the other hand, at meetings in villages or the working-class areas of towns, activities may extend far beyond the limits of the purely religious domain. The *zawiya* becomes a collective meeting-place for a whole series of social exchanges between women. The feminine universe is there unveiled; women freely exteriorize their emotions, their experiences, their thoughts. Female identity finds full expression there in its deepest and most genuine form.

All the religious feasts of the canon give rise to particular ceremonies organized by women and for women. Many women still take part in the pilgrimages of the traditional brotherhoods.

The religious life of Algerian women in the south-east of France is just as complex in its beliefs and rituals but remains more hidden from view despite women's greater access to the outside world. The principle of sexual segregation of space is more rigidly respected in a society that favours promiscuity. Female religious activities are described as profane both by men and by many women. Immigrant women, lacking the religious instruction which is today available to those who remained in their homeland (principally through the media, in religious broadcasts, or through religious talks), tend to perpetuate traditional family and local religious practices. Occasional attempts are made by Islamic associations to educate them in the rudiments of Quranic teaching, but with little success.

"They get together for so-called prayer meetings, but they do nothing but talk, pass on gossip, bicker — they sing, they dance, they laugh. Do you call that prayer?" This comment by a young Algerian woman illustrates the impression that may be given to an outside observer by the religious meetings organized by immigrant women. But continued attendance at this type of meeting reveals the existence within the groups of an intense spirituality, which finds its expression chiefly through the emotions. I have described and analyzed elsewhere the form of these ceremonies (Andezian 1983a, 1983b, 1986), and I have likewise described the role of women in the organization of the religious activity of their families (Andezian 1985). Here I shall chiefly discuss the specificity of the expressions of female spirituality and the possibility of their integration into the religious life of Muslims living in France. I shall deal only with collective practices, since my aim is to highlight the ways in which a group identity is built up through the common performance of rituals.

The conditions in which women's religious activities are carried out have been entirely created by the women themselves, with no male mediation. This has been the task of the older women, anxious to preserve some space for things sacred in the profane environment of immigration. Gradually a group responsible for the administration of the religious life of the community has been set up, its members nominated for the most part by the community as a whole on the basis of their knowledge, piety and reputation: *mukadmat*, washers of corpses, singers of holy songs. These religious 'agents' are supposed to carry out their duties with no financial reward, but in practice they collect the donations offered as *sadaqa*[5] during the ceremonies.

The women who carry out these duties have no need to know how to read or write. The religious instruction they give involves the oral transmission of prayers, litanies and songs, and the teaching of the ritual gestures that accompany them. Access to the function of *mukadma*, which depends on the approval of the community and is ratified by a religious leader (often a shaykh who is head of a religious brotherhood) requires deep understanding of human relationships. The *mukadma's* role is not limited to the direction of prayer-meetings: she must also keep an eye open for problems, pass on requests addressed to the saints, help people in difficulty, find solutions to personal conflicts. Any *mukadma* who falls short of what is expected of her will be criticized and dismissed.

The collaboration of these religious agents is requested by families for the celebration of the various landmarks in life, of a success, safe return, recovery from illness, or simply to introduce *baraka* into a house. The *mukadmat* themselves organize ritual prayer sessions regularly (once a week) or on the occasion of the major Muslim festivals. When they are affiliated to a brotherhood they invite the shaykh to visit them, and they also accompany certain women to Algeria to take part in the annual pilgrimage of their brotherhood. Symbolic goods thus circulate between immigrant women and their family or friends who have remained at home.

Other ritual functions are carried out by women who, despite the commercial nature of their activities, are seen as rendering service to Muslim believers: butchers who sell *halal* meat,[6] women who sell clothing used in rituals, supervisors of the Moorish baths necessary for purification rituals.

The spiritual life of female immigrants in the south-east of France is structured to a greater or lesser degree in different towns and neighbourhoods. Sometimes their religious activities may be integrated with ceremonies organized for men in the family circle (they rarely attend prayers in the mosque). They are nonetheless isolated from the men and perform their own rituals, listening from time to time to the prayers recited in the men's area and relayed by loudspeaker. Ceremonies that are specifically for women take place at periods when the women are inactive, in the afternoon, between two spells of domestic activity. As far as possible, the days chosen correspond to those regarded as holy days in Islam: Friday or Monday, the latter being, according to the women, the day of the birth and death of the Prophet. Meetings take place either in a private house or in a neighbourhood social centre or in a room rented and furnished specifically for the purpose. The audience consists of women of all ages, belonging to the social networks that link North African immigrant women in the south of France: neighbourhood, family and friendship networks (Andezian and Streiff-Fenart 1981). Participation in the celebration of family events is obligatory and forms part of the relationship of exchanges between members of the same social network. As for attendance at the prayer meetings organized by a *mukadma*, though it is voluntary and theoretically open to any Muslim woman, in fact it too is based on the networks of female relationships.

Although these meetings do not take the place of the religious duties which all Muslims must fulfil (profession of the faith, the five daily prayers, the fixed rate of almsgiving, the fast of Ramadan, pilgrimage to Mecca), the women justify their existence by referring to the difficulties they have in going to the mosque. The prayers recited during these meetings, like all the other rituals performed there, remain supererogatory.

Modes of appropriation of the religious domain by women

Whatever the event that is to be celebrated, each ceremony involves the same ritual sequences: opening rite — prayers — meal — songs and dances — closing rite. There is thus an alternation of religious rites with social activities that casts doubt on the spiritual nature of these practices, and on their legitimacy. For the women, the indisputably Islamic nature of these practices is attested not only by their antiquity but also by the part they play in creating a strong community feeling.

Each session begins with the recitation, by a religious agent or a woman appointed to lead the ceremony, of the *Fatiha*, the first *sura* (chapter) of the Quran. This text, an introductory prayer that forms part of the liturgy, is spoken at the beginning of any religious service and also in other circumstances, such as celebrations of marriage. It is also used to greet any piece of joyful news and to accompany blessings and expressions of good wishes. By reciting the *Fatiha*, the women place their religious ceremonies under God's protection.

After this introductory prayer that marks the sacred nature of the meeting, the leader invites the audience to take part in the *dhikr*. This sequence, which varies in length according to the circumstances and the number of participants, consists of three series of prayers: the *hizb*, the *dua* and the *dhikr* itself, Sufic practices which have their origins in the Quran.

The *hizb* (literally, section of the Quran) is based on the chanting of verses from the Quran in the manner of psalms. In women's meetings, the text most frequently chanted is the *Shahada* or Muslim profession of faith which asserts that God is unique and Muhammed is His Prophet.

The *dua* or invocation refers in the Quran to any relationship between man and God. This practice, based on the incantatory value of the Word, is a request addressed to God by means of texts from the Quran or traditional prayers. In the women's assemblies, the *dua* or *talab*, used in the precise sense of a request, consists of the invocation of God's aid to overcome the difficulties of life. The request gains in effectiveness to the degree that it is collectively supported. It is backed up by litanies glorifying God, the Prophet and the saints.

Hizb and *dua* are preparatory phases leading up to the *dhikr*, the aim of which is to establish a direct liturgical contact with God. Sufic congregations and some North African brotherhoods derived from them have developed specific vocal and respiratory techniques for the practice of the *hizb* and *dua*. Based on the continuous repetition of liturgical formulae, the *dhikr*, an ejaculatory prayer, provokes states of ecstatic trance by these physical mechanisms and also through the loss of sensation. The *dhikr*, or memory, which evokes sacred names, is encouraged by the Quran and recommended in numerous hadith. These texts exhort believers to call God to mind on all occasions.

The Sufic practice of collective *dhikr* evolved rapidly towards forms of spiritual concerts in which stress was laid on the necessity of achieving ecstasy. In order to make the state of trance more readily attainable, other rites were linked with the *dhikr*: for example, the ritual dances which have been a subject of controversy throughout the centuries. According to Mole (1963), both those who uphold and those who condemn the dances in Islam have drawn their arguments from verses of the Quran and prophetic traditions which are open to misunderstanding.

The feminine version of the *dhikr* is characterized by the celebration of divine names and attributes, but also of the names and attributes of the Prophet and the saints. These litanies, veritable messages of love accompanied by the clapping of hands, cries, bodily gestures, and weeping, exhilarate the gathering and create an atmosphere favourable to the entry into a state of trance. Sometimes, the mere evocation of God or the Prophet is enough to arouse in certain people an irresistible urge to dance, the dancing being a sign of their spiritual fervour. This dance is referred to by the term *zuhd*, which means asceticism; its strictly codified form requires the presence of a specialist to guide, by voice and music, the movements of the dancer. A true language, inscribed in the family heritage and passed on by the elders, it is the culminating point of the expression of female religious emotion. The rite was invented by spiritual forebears who are situated among the descendants of the Prophet, but it is also recognized as having a historical basis and is verified by experience and by its physical effects. As a set of symbolic gestures performed in order to obtain divine grace, it is effective only if it has the value of a sign both for the dancer and the spectators — hence the importance of the participation of the whole assembly in the preparation and execution of these dances.

This *dhikr* sequence seems to be a re-interpretation by the women of Sufic rituals drawn from the Quran, using specifically feminine modes of expression (vocal, musical and gestual) taken from their own cultural heritage. The phenomenon involved could be described as an 'interpenetration of religious levels', with reference to the expression 'interpenetration of cultural levels' by which Bakhtin (1968) defines the relationships between popular culture and learned culture. The lawfulness of such practices is more than ever questioned today, with the various attempts to 'purge' Islam of the 'relics' of anti-Islamic beliefs. In reply to their critics, the women maintain the legitimacy of their religious practices by insisting on the importance of purity of intention (*niyya*) in all religious acts. They quote verses from the Quran which accord to the religion of the heart priority over observance of rites in this purity of intention.

The remaining sequences of the female religious ceremonies — the eating of a sacrificial meal, the exchange of words and of goods and gifts — represent the practical application of fundamental values of Islam such as mutual aid and solidarity, and help to consolidate the community of believers. The ceremony concludes with a final prayer of thanks to God for all his goodness.

The female religious practices described here form part of the religious history of the Maghreb, which is still evolving in immigrant communities. The female versions of Islam reveal strategies for the definition of identity within the immigrant population. On one hand one can observe the assertion of specific characteristics based on the possession of a common social status, the observance of the same rites and the use of the same modes of expression; on the other hand, attempts at integration into the larger Muslim community. The women define themselves as Muslims by their submission to God, expressed in their fidelity to the cultural practices and social behaviour prescribed by religious law. The many discussions which take place between the different ritual sequences of their meetings are centred on the notion of *haram* (prohibition) in order to determine what is allowed and what is forbidden within the Muslim community. The need to assert Muslim identity is nowadays all the stronger as the installation in France of North African immigrants who have progressively abandoned the idea of returning home[7] brings with it the threat of 'dissolution' in French society.

Notes

1. *Tariqa*: a spiritual way that leads to God. The term is also used to refer to a religious order.

2. *Zawiya*: formerly a monastic convent where followers of different religious orders received their training. Nowadays headquarters of any brotherhood and mausoleum (real or supposed) of the saint who founded the brotherhood.
3. This study was carried out mainly in the Bouches-du-Rhône département, in areas with a high concentration of North African immigrant families. The largest part of this population belonged to one of the early waves of immigration and came from localities in one particular area of Algeria. The continuing relations between these immigrants and their home country, and the numerous family and village community bonds that exist have led them to reproduce certain cultural models in their new situation, and ensure a certain homogeneity in cultural practices.
4. *Dhikr*: the meanings given to this term are explained further on in the text.
5. *Sadaka*: synonym for *zakat*, obligatory alms-giving, one of the five religious duties imposed on all Muslims; but can also refer to supererogatory alms as is the case here.
6. *Halal*: lawful; i.e. the flesh of animals ritually slaughtered.
7. For most of the women I met during religious meetings, the idea of long-term settlement in France is not a recent one. Whereas they themselves consider that they have made a success of their entry into French social and economic life (some of them have salaried jobs, speak perfect French, and enjoy a satisfactory financial situation) without repudiating their origins, the problem is not the same for their children, who are subjected to pressures forcing them to make a definite choice.

References

Andezian, S. 1983a. Pratiques féminines de l'islam en France. *Archives des Sciences Sociales des Religions* 55 (1): 53–66.

——1983b. Appartenance religieuse et appartenance communautaire: l'example d'un groupe d'immigrés algériens en France. *Maghrébins en France, émigrés ou immigrés*. Paris: Editions du CNRS.

——1985. Pour une approche de l'islam dans l'immigration algérienne en France. *Les Algériens en France, genèse et devenir d'une migration*. GRECO 13 CNRS. Marseille: Publisud.

——1986. Women's roles in organizing symbolic life: Algerian female immigrants in France. *International Migration: The female experience*. Simon, R. J. and Brettell, C. B., eds. Totowa, New Jersey: Rowman and Allandheld Publishers.

Andezian, S. and Streiff-Fenart, J. 1981. *Les réseaux sociaux des femmes maghrébines immigrées en Provence-Côte d'Azur*. Thèse de Doctorat de 3ème Cycle. Université de Nice.

Bakhtin, M. 1968. *Rabelais and his World*. Cambridge, Mass.: MIT Press.

Levy, R. 1962. *The Social Structure of Islam*. Cambridge: Cambridge University Press.

Mole, M. 1963. La danse extatique en islam. *Les danses sacrées: Sources Orientales*. Paris: Editions de Seuil.

Part III
Additional Themes for Future Research

13
The Urban Sociology of Religion and Islam in Birmingham

John Rex

Those who study the meaningful life of cities have long been aware that religious organizations such as Christian churches play a part in shaping the attitudes of citizens towards the urban system and towards the state and social class. Equally they have been aware that the religious meaning systems which are expressed within these organizations are inherited from an earlier age in which religion was even more important socially, economically and politically.

The obvious focus for an urban sociology of religion in countries like Britain has been the study of Christian churches, but today, in a multi-social and multi-cultural society immigrants have introduced a new variable into the equation. Along with the Christian churches one has Hindu and Sikh temples and Islamic mosques. These new places of religious worship and practice are, moreover, much closer to their role in societies in which religious issues are still lively and important. This paper, therefore, focuses on the mosques to ask what function they perform in the urban system and in urban conflict, or how far their continuing function in relation to a larger world system influences urban life.

What this paper seeks to explore is how far the traditional questions of the sociology of religion developed in order to understand the role of Christian churches in European national societies and urban communities can be extended to deal with the insertion of non-Christian religion into Christian and secular societies, and with the fact that religious groups in migration must have at least a dual function on the one hand in relation to the societies of settlement, but on the other to sending societies. To complicate matters further one has to recognize that in the British/Pakistani case the 'sending society' is not a totally discrete entity but one which is bound to the metropolis by the complex and conflictual ties of colonialism.

It is not to be supposed that all the questions involved can be resolved in this essay. Its task is essentially an exploratory one. It sets out some of the traditional questions of the sociology of religion and places alongside of these an account of the sectarian division of Islam in Birmingham and the social attitudes of the various sects. It also looks at the origins of some of these sects in Pakistan. The meaningful interconnections between the theological beliefs and organizational structure of the sects and the social position and interests of their adherents are suggested but obviously require much deeper sociological and historical analysis.

The traditional questions of the sociology of religion are posed, for the present writer at least, by Troeltsch (1931), Richard Niebuhr (1975) and Max Weber (especially in 1965a and 1965b).

Troeltsch suggested that Jesus Christ himself had no social teachings. He was concerned with something called 'the Kingdom of God' and he was able to assume that his followers knew what he was talking about. Nonetheless a problem arose for subsequent generations who had to say what the relationship was between the Kingdom of God on the one hand and the institutions of the world on the other. A basic dichotomy opened up between those who believed that the Kingdom of God was not of this world and those who argued that the Kingdom must come in the world, that is to say between conservative and revolutionary versions of Christianity. Between these two, however, almost every other possibility emerged. Paul, for instance, saw the "powers that be" as being "ordained by God"; St Augustine saw political institutions as having the task of preserving peace amongst fallen men; and, finally, St Thomas Aquinas saw these institutions in accordance with relative natural law through which men could find their way back to the Vision of God.

Richard Niebuhr neatly summarizes the options available to religion in industrial societies when he speaks of the religion of established churches, the churches of the disinherited and the churches of the middle classes. In the first case the church supports the institutions of the state; in the second, the churches demand a radical reversal of the social order; and, in the third, a doctrine of individual piety is substituted for any social doctrine.

Niebuhr obviously draws upon the work of Max Weber and his churches of the middle classes reflect Weber's notion of the Protestant Ethic (1965a). Weber, however, went much further than this. In his *Sociology of Religion* (1965b) he introduces a fourfold distinction between asceticism and mysticism of inner-worldly and other-worldly varieties. Protestantism in western Christianity is seen as representing inner-worldly asceticism in relation to economic affairs and Hinduism at the other extent as representing other-worldly mysticism. Islam is also seen as representing a type of inner-worldly asceticism. Each of these sets of attitudes, however, may be developed in relation to politics, to economics, to sexual matters and to art and science. Finally, Weber also makes an important distinction between the ideas of religious functionaries and what he calls the religiosity of the masses.

It is in fact this notion of the 'religiosity of the masses' which strikes one most strongly as one approaches the study of religion amongst Muslim immigrants. The first duty of a Muslim is to establish prayers in his place of settlement, but what is then established is not, of itself, an intellectual activity. Intellectuals and ideologues may feed off it but the essence of the focus of prayer and worship which are established is that they allow for the untutored expression of mass religiosity. In studying immigration one cannot but be struck by the fact that such mass religiosity is still a powerful force amongst poor and often rural immigrants in a way which is no longer true of workers in the modern secular society of the welfare state.

There are, of course, many divisions and sectarian tendencies within Islam. Like Christianity it is not a unitary phenomenon and embraces a wide range of orientations towards the secular world. The questions which we have to ask are:

1. What is the position taken by each sect towards the institutions of the secular world on a scale of radicalism–conservatism?
2. How far is Niebuhr's distinction between three kinds of churches applicable? Are there equivalents to Niebuhr's churches which see the 'powers-that-be' as ordained by God? Are there revolutionary sects which envisage a total overthrow of the political order by violent or peaceful political action? How far are the transformative tendencies of the sect's religion channelled into individual piety?
3. Where do the various sects stand in terms of Weber's fourfold classification of inner-worldly and other-worldly asceticism and inner-worldly and other-worldly mysticism? How far are these fundamental religious attitudes developed in relation to economics, politics, science and art and sex and the family?
4. Finally, what is the relationship between differences in intellectual positions amongst teachers and leaders and religiosity of the masses?

Each of these questions must be answered for Pakistanis in Birmingham in relation to (a) the national English society and the urban society of Birmingham; (b) in relation to Pakistani society; (c) in relation to the structures of colonialism, independence and neo-colonialism.

What follows is not a systematic set of answers to these questions, but may at a descriptive level provide material essential to answering these questions.

In the City of Birmingham there are some forty to fifty mosques or madrasas (places of prayer and study) and the sociologist accustomed to the sparsely attended Christian churches[1] cannot but be impressed by the sight of hundreds of Pakistani workers prostrating themselves in prayer. Clearly religion for these workers is a very real and vibrant part of their lives.

With this said, however, it must immediately be added that such religious expressions represent more than a simple and naive peasant consciousness. If they did not, there would be a single Islam expressed in all the mosques. In fact there is a considerable insistence on distinctiveness, and a great deal of sheer sectarianism.

Pakistani Muslims are mainly Sunnis, but 15 per cent of Muslims in that country are Shias and there are Shia as well as Sunni mosques in Birmingham. Most Sunni Muslims belong to the Hanafite Madhhab and follow the teachings of the early Persian scholar Abu Hanifa, but the movement called Markazi Jamiat Ahl-e-Hadith, which is forcefully represented by a mosque with a well-educated Maulana, claims to go back before the rise of the madhhabs for the source of its teaching to the Quran and to the early hadith which gave an account of the Prophet's actions. The Hanafites are also divided between those who follow the teachings of the Deobandi theological school on the one hand and that of Barelvi on the other. This latter difference is important in that while the Deobandis take the view that emphasis should be on the carrying out of Islamic duties, the Barelwis are led by Sufis who preach a more mystical doctrine of the withdrawal from the world and from basic animal passions. Finally, apart from all of these is the Ahmadiyya movement, considered beyond the pale of Islam by orthodox Muslims, but represented by two mosques or centres in Birmingham.

Religious and political organizations also affect one another. On the margins between the two spheres is the Pakistani movement Jamaat-e-Islami. Founded by Maulana Mawdudi before partition this movement had two characteristics: one was that it holds that the task of developing, integrating and applying Muslim doctrine to contemporary situations (*ijtihad*) can be undertaken in any generations by a great teacher such as Mawdudi himself; the other that it is committed to a programme of conversion and proselytization for non-Muslims. After partition it devoted itself to the idea of an Islamic, as distinct from a secular, state in Pakistan. Although the movement has had little electoral success in Pakistan, it is influential amongst immigrants and the works of Mawdudi are widely on sale in Islamic bookshops attached to mosques. It is suggested by some that Jamaat-e-Islami enjoys Arab financial support and the same is suggested in the case of Jamiat Ahl-e-Hadith. It is not clear however whether such a financial facility has changed the emphasis of either movement.

Jamaat-e-Islami has given support to the Zia regime in Pakistan, albeit support of a critical kind, and it is through its organization and teaching that the regime can count upon the support of many migrants. On the other hand support for the late Zulfiqar Bhutto and his daughter Benazir is also widespread and news of the elder Bhutto's execution was followed by a prayer meeting and violent demonstrations in Birmingham.

There are four Muslim councillors on the Birmingham council. These include two Pakistanis, one of whom is a Marxist and a friend of Tariq Ali, a leading British Marxist, one a Yemeni and one an East African woman married to an Englishman. All of these councillors are supportive of programmes of special rights for Muslim citizens, as are the various worker associations despite the fact that they are Marxist-inspired. Marxism and other secular political stances are apparently not seen as incompatible with Islam.

Summing up the Islamic presence in Birmingham we may say that the following organizations and tendencies are represented:

1. Hanafite Sunnis including: the ritualistic and legalistic Deobandis and the mystical Barelwis with their Sufis
2. Jamiat Ahl-e-Hadith which goes beyond the madhhabs to the Quran and the hadith
3. Shias
4. Jamaat-e-Islami
5. Ahmadiyyas
6. Secular minority politics overlapping with various secular political doctrines including Marxism

Cross-cutting these divisions is another division deriving from the source of financial support. One very important fact is that some sects and individuals enjoy Saudi-Arabian and other support. This may mean that they are influenced by divisions in these other societies as well as in Pakistan.

We must now explore the differences between these sects, first in relation to Pakistani society and colonialism and secondly in relation to the social systems of Britain and Birmingham. Hamza Alavi (1985) has attempted to show the role of some of these movements in Pakistani politics and society. His conclusions are as follows: The Deobandis had affiliated themselves to the Indian Nationalist Movement from the end of the nineteenth century because they found Islamic law and Islamic education being displaced by European institutions and because they were supported by weavers whose trade was devastated by colonialism. Before they finally came to support the separate state of Pakistan they supported Indian nationalism and justified this by arguing for the separation of the private domain of faith from the public domain of politics.

The Barelwis by contrast "prefer a more populist Islam, more infused with superstition and also syncretism that make up the religious beliefs of the peasantry". They emphasize "belief in miracles and powers of saints and pirs and worship at shrines and dispensing of amulets and chains". The pirs are divided into two classes. On the one hand there are those whose role is one of primitive magicians. On the other there are those who teach a doctrine of mystical discipline to achieve escape from animal passions and build around themselves bands of disciples. This notion of pirs also becomes absorbed into the wider notions of Sufism imported from Iraq and Iran at an early stage.[2]

Jamiat-Ahl-e-Hadith together with Jamiat Ahl-e-Quran (which recognizes only the Quran and rejects the validity of the hadith) is seen by Alavi as being an extreme sectarian movement which does not recognize the members of the other Muslim sect and regards them as Kafirs.

Jamaat-e-Islami, according to Alavi, believes that the 'existing state must be captured and brought under the control of those who are the true bearers of militant and authentic Islam'. Unfortunately this theocratic goal has not been achieved and the electoral performance of Jamaat in the controlled elections organized by Zia in 1985 was derisory.

Finally, the Shias, although forming only 15 per cent of the population have, under the inspiration of the Ayatollah Khomeini in Iran, demanded the imposition on the whole of Pakistan of the Shia code, an extraordinary demand which has only had the counter-effect of leading to demands that Pakistan be declared a Hanafite Sunni republic.

The capacity of any of these movements to operate amongst migrants is limited by lack of their own finance. The result has been either extreme poverty or seeking subventions from the oil-rich Arab states. It is difficult to estimate the effect of such financial support on, for instance, the Yemeni councillor in Birmingham, or Jamiat Ahl-e-Hadith, or on Jamaat-e-Islami, because those concerned are reticent about discussing their financial support. Interestingly, however, Jamiat Ahl-e-Hadith supporters are sometimes pejoratively called 'Wahabis' referring to the version of Islam ruling Saudi Arabia.

We must now turn to the second and more difficult question of how these various sects and tendencies develop within a British city. How far may they be seen as having equivalent tendencies towards conservatism, revolution and compromise to those found in an earlier age amongst Christian sects and churches? It is worth noting that this is a more important question in the case of Islam than it is in the case of contemporary Christianity, because the Muslim sects can rely upon the engine of mass religiosity to make their pretensions significant. A religious leader can have far more effect if he can rely upon the community of the faithful.

Amongst the Deobandis and the Barelwis, however, there is little sign of political activism or militancy. Although the Deobandis, with their emphasis on living according to the law and morality of Islam, would appear to exemplify what Weber called inner-worldly asceticism, they make a clear distinction in their own minds between the private and the public sphere. Islam is above all a way of life for families and for local communities. It requires a very strict standard of sexual morality centering around the idea of female modesty and it is concerned about education and its effect in this area. But it does not require any strong political stance on other matters. Islam is on the whole critical of capitalism and supportive of the welfare state and the injunction to be a good citizen is usually fulfilled by support for a moderate Labour Party. The main prospect of the Deobandis, like other sects, coming into conflict with the Labour Party would be if the local or national Party became too obviously engaged in 'progressive' programmes involving stances on sexual morality.

The Barelwis represent the alternative to inner-worldly mysticism. They are deeply involved with the day-to-day problems of their community and cannot be said to withdraw from the world. Yet, at the same time, Sufism advocates a systematic discipline to escape from the animal passions with which all men are born. On the whole, therefore, one may expect the Barelwis to be quietistic in political terms, except that their hostility to permissive sexual morality will be even more marked than that of the Deobandis. Possibly for this reason the Barelwis have been slightly more sympathetic to the case for Muslim political representation than have the Deobandis. It was they who supported (albeit cautiously) an attempt by a Muslim county councillor to oppose and unseat one of the sitting Labour city councillors.

Jamaat-e-Islami directs the attention of Muslims more to the politics of the Indian sub-continent than it does to those of Britain. It is particularly concerned that an Islamic state should be established in Pakistan and if it is critical of the Zia regime, it is not because it is authoritarian but because it has been insufficiently supportive of Islam. So far as life in Britain is concerned the emphasis of the teachings of Maulana Mawdudi is on family matters and even so far as the larger world is concerned the emphasis is still upon a puritanical sexual code. The one paragraph in his chapter on 'The Principles of the Shariah' which deals with political matters runs as follows:

> To safeguard the unity and solidarity of the nation and to achieve the welfare and well-being of the Muslim community, believers have been exhorted to avoid mutual hostility, social dissensions and sectarianism of all kinds. They have been exhorted to settle their differences and disputes in accordance with the principles laid down in the Quran and the Sunnah and if the parties fail to reach a settlement they should bury their differences in the name of Allah and leave the decisions to Him . . . (Mawdudi 1980).

It would seem that where there is no question of the estabishment of an Islamic state the political teaching of Jamaat-e-Islami relates only to the internal relations of groups within the minority community.

Jamiat Ahl-e-Hadith is also concerned as much with international as with national affairs and the problems of the minority in migration. Like other groups and sects it lays emphasis upon the sexual and family aspects. Its programme may be inferred from an item in its magazine *The Straight Path* (1984) which reads as follows:

When will our True Celebration be?

When Muslims stop being Muslims by name only and become sincere practising Muslims.
When the rulers of Muslim countries adopt the Islamic way of life with sincerity and conviction.
When Muslims regard their Muslim brothers as parts of their own body.
When Muslim countries and their people unite together under the banner of Islam.
When there will be one united voice of the Muslims throughout the world free from division and disunity.
When they make it their aim to live honourable lives and die honourable deaths.
When the sacred city of Jerusalem and the Muslim land of Palestine will be free from unlawful occupation.
When the Muslims of Kashmir, the Philippines and Pathani will gain self-determination and win their freedom.
When Afghanistan and Eritrea rid themselves of their oppressions and once again become Islamic.

When hypocrisy and insincerity are eradicated from the Muslims and justice and honesty will be established.

What this statement does is to place the problems of Muslims in Britain firmly within a wider context of the anti-colonial Muslim revolution. It would seem that on this level Jamiat Ahl-e-Hadith is the least quietistic of the Muslim sects in Birmingham. It will be noted that one cause which is not supported in the Jamiat's manifesto is that of the Ayatollah Khomeini in Iran. Clearly this is a Sunni rather than a Shia document.

Amongst the Shias Khomeini enjoys wide support. The desire of the Shias of Pakistan to establish the Shia code there is paralleled by the support which Khomeini receives amongst Pakistani-Shia exiles. They were less satisfied with the aid given to minority communities by the City Council than any other group and were so disillusioned with the Labour Party that some of their members were inclined to support the Conservatives. There were other reasons for this too. The Shias were opposed both to the permissive society and to the rioting of West Indian youth and saw the Conservative emphasis upon moral discipline and law and order as close to their own. On the other hand they were not supportive of the Zia regime and saw hope for Pakistan as lying in the return to power of Benazir Bhutto and the Pakistan Progressive Party.

In their attitudes to British society the representatives of the mosques of a variety of different sects held a number of positions in common. All saw the secularization of society and the universal emphasis upon sexuality and permissiveness as something to be utterly opposed. Against this they set the Muslim ideal of the family and the Muslim ideal of womanhood. They saw urban riots as being the consequence of a breakdown of discipline amongst the young and, however much sympathy they might express for West Indian unemployment, regarded the training which they gave to their own children in afternoon classes as a preventive against any such development. All too were unhappy about the effect of participation in ordinary schooling on their young people, and supported specific programmes to reform such schools.

The Muslim Liaison Committee was an organization on which all the mosques and other associations were represented. Some of those who participated went to the extreme of demanding separate Muslim schools, but, more modestly, others campaigned for *halal* meat in the school-meals service, proper religious instruction in schools, separation of the sexes and appropriate clothing for physical education and swimming classes and an increase in the number of single-sex schools. Members were divided on the approach which should be adopted by their representatives in negotiations. The present officers, however, were inclined to proceed cautiously, forming a working group with headteachers of certain schools and with educational administrators to establish guidelines, rather than publicly making 'demands' and using public political means of bringing pressure to bear on the Council. There was potential here for a split between the radicals and those who were more cautious and this indeed might become the most important political issue on which the different sectarian tendencies discussed above might show themselves.

More generally the political aspirations of the various Muslim groups may be fulfilled through participation in local politics. There are now probably a dozen municipal wards in which the Muslim vote would be decisive in a council election and, not surprisingly, there are now seven councillors drawn from the Muslim community. The questions which remain, however, are how far these councillors as well as the white councillors representing Muslim wards may be pressured to represent Muslim interests effectively and whether there is likely to be any attempt to increase the number of Muslims on the council. These are fertile areas for the future development of splits between militants and conservatives.

Generally, since more Muslims are poor or unemployed workers, the Muslim community has looked to the Labour Party to represent it, but there are real tensions in this relationship. One of the councillors mentioned above (the Marxist) has openly supported the call for so-called 'black sections' in the Labour Party and currently faces expulsion. Another member of the now defunct Metropolitan Council (a higher level of government) also faces expulsion because of his attempt to unseat and replace an existing white Labour councillor at a Labour selection conference. As a result of these tensions a new party called the Democratic Party has been formed which, if it gains support at all, will appeal largely to Muslims. The various mosque leaders identify themselves as radicals or conservatives according to whether or not they support these politicians in their conflicts with Labour. Most think it unwise to break with the Labour establishment. Some are prepared to keep their options open to see whether the Democratic or an Independent Muslim councillor attains credibility. Finally, some of the Shias and possibly other middle-class groups are actually inclined to support the Conservatives.

The reasons given for supporting or not supporting Labour are in the main concerned with the party's stand on sexual and family issues and its willingness to give money to Muslim projects. So far as the first of these issues is concerned the Labour Party is criticized for its permissiveness, the issue of support for homosexuals being often quoted. So far as the second is concerned the feeling is that the Council should give money not merely for language (mother-tongue) classes, but for moral and religious education. Combining both points, several mosque leaders have expressed the opinion that the Labour Council gives money to support homosexuals and other deviants and yet refuses to support a kind of education which promotes law and order.

The possibility of politics of a different kind is presented to anyone in Birmingham by the Handsworth riots which occurred primarily in the form of conflict between the West Indian population and the police. On the issue of the riots my informants in the Muslim community were unanimous in their condemnation of the behaviour of the rioters. The nearest to support for the rioters was an occasional agreement with the notion that West Indian youth deserved sympathy because of their severe experience of unemployment. Even when this was said, however, it was suggested that if the West Indians had any equivalent of the mosques they would both be more likely to gain employment and less likely to riot. There was indeed some interest in converting West Indians and a small number have in fact become Muslims.

Militancy and the politics of violence are not on the agenda as far as the Muslims' dealing with domestic or British issues is concerned. It should be remembered, however, that the Muslim community sees itself as involved in wider struggles in the Indian sub-continent and elsewhere. The street disturbances after the execution of Bhutto were one example of this, and protests at the harrassment of the community by the police after the assassination of the Indian Deputy High Commissioner were another. Currently, moreover, there has been a response by the Muslim communities around the world to the American bombing of Libya. Thus, while the basic posture of the community on domestic affairs may be one of quietism it is not to be assumed that there is no tension in the relation of these Birmingham Muslims to western society. What happens to the community in Birmingham may therefore depend in part on world events.

We now return to the questions posed by the sociology of religion at the beginning of this paper. How far are the questions posed by Troeltsch, Niebuhr and Weber applicable to the various Muslim sects which we have discussed? In the first place it should be noted that there is an equivalent problem to that of the Christian churches and their concept of the Kingdom of God. According to Islam the world works according to the law of God. In nature this means that there are natural laws which are universal and which can be studied by science. So far as human beings are concerned, if they are truly Muslims they will seek to know God's law and act in accordance with it. There is however the possibility of ignorance and disobedience, and those who do not follow the law of God for either reason are 'Kafirs'. The problem for Islam therefore is to show how the secular world may be made subject to the law of God.

Prima facie thus would suggest that Islam is a militant religion which should seek to conquer the world and subject it to God's law. Such indeed is the ultimate object of Islam but in the here-and-now, as with Christian millennialism, many compromises have to be entered into. As we have seen, the Deobandis in India during the struggle for independence had been prepared to ally themselves with Indian nationalism rationalizing their stand on the ground of the separateness of the private domain of faith and the public domain of politics. Again the Barelwis' mysticism was coupled with an orientation to the conquest of the flesh rather than the conquest of political institutions. There were many other examples of such pragmatic and quietistic adjustments to the world of the here-and-now and this, indeed, seemed to be the characteristic stance of the Islamic sects in the early period of immigration and minority status.

The crusading goal of Islam was almost universally directed towards overcoming the temptations and corruptions of sexuality as it was exhibited in the market-place of western society. In Weber's terms the attitude to sex was one of inner-worldly asceticism — in the world, because sex was considered to be a gift of God to be used by man, but ascetic in that it was to be used to create and sustain the family rather than bring enjoyed promiscuity. Only among the Sufis in the Barelwi groupings was a more extreme idea, that of conquering and rejecting sex, promulgated, and then only for the Sufis or pirs themselves. The attitude of inner-worldly asceticism towards sex was at the heart of the attitude to the family, the maintenance of which was the central theme of Islamic social teaching. From this followed a whole set of attitudes and policies towards education which preoccupied Muslim leaders more than anything else. Education was vital because, wrongly organized, it could destroy the family and amongst migrants at least the family was the very basis of society.

On wider social and political questions the leaders of the mosque communities held educated views, though they rarely found occasion to argue for these. Inner-worldly asceticism did not allow the disciplined forms of usury which characterized the Christian Protestant sects. Capitalism, in theory at least, could only take the form of a partnership in which the investor shared fully in the risks as well as the profits of the investment and the Pakistani banks were influenced in their dealings with businessmen by this teaching. Nonetheless doctrine on this matter was sufficiently accommodating to allow a flourishing commercial life in the form of shopkeeping to occur and Muslims were no less adept in this sphere than Sikhs or Hindus and more so than Christians.

The welfare state was fully in accordance with Muslim teaching and was seen as sustaining the family. Indeed when the matter was raised in interviews in the mosques it was frequently suggested that family allowances had first been introduced by one of the early caliphs. Thus, although their support for the family and for shopkeeping as a way of life might have drawn Muslims to support Conservatism there was a sense that Labour's support for the welfare state made it the natural party of Muslims.

On the broad ideological issue of capitalism versus socialism there was a very definite view. Islam represented a middle-way between communism which promoted collectivism at the cost of the loss of individual and family freedom, and capitalism which promoted selfishness and greed along with individual freedom. Internationally this meant that Islam was viewed as a third force in a divided world. Locally it meant that moderation was urged in political activity on the left or on the right.

The larger questions of the attitude towards the State boiled down to relatively simple ones of attitudes towards local and immediate political institutions. A Muslim was enjoined to be a good citizen and that citizenship was expressed by involvement in the political dispensation offered by the Labour establishment in the city. There were some reservations about this, Labour being criticized for encouraging the permissive society and for not recognizing in financial terms the work done by the mosques in promoting discipline amongst the young and preventing their participation in riots; but all in all for the moment Labour politics fulfilled the purposes of Muslims. So far as the attempt of some leaders to articulate an independent position went this was usually regarded as suspect and as being the result of individual ambition.

Summing up the social attitudes of Muslims in Birmingham we may say that they recognize that they are in a minority situation. They cannot change the world or create an Islamic state. What they can do is to be good citizens and to share in the normal and moderate attempts of working people to improve their lives. More immediately, however, there is the question of the family. Normal secular society is seen as undermining the family and promoting a decadent and promiscuous world of social relations. While fitting in with the institutions of the society of settlement on other matters, therefore, Islam proposes in the here-and-now to sustain an Islamic way of life at community level. This has repercussions on other institutions, more particularly on the schools. It even points to a degree of separatism of the Muslim community from the rest of society.

What this suggests therefore is that Muslim society in Britain will be characterized by a political quietism qualified by a drive to sustain and promote a distinctive type of marriage and family life. The same people however who are members of this immigrant minority community are also Pakistanis and Muslims. As such their social and political attitudes are directed not solely towards British society but towards Pakistan, the Muslim world and the place of Pakistan and Muslims in a post-imperial world.

As far as Pakistan itself is concerned the goal of many of the Muslims of Birmingham is the establishment of an Islamic state. Even the Zia regime which claims to share this goal is not sufficiently committed for them and the goal of Jamaat-e-Islami is to build such a state, transforming it from its present secular nature to a state which works to create an Islamic order on earth. It should also be noted, however, that not all practising Muslims share this goal and that as a political party Jamaat-e-Islami has not won significant support in Pakistan. All that one can say is that some Muslims (the Shias no less than the Sunnis) have clearly political goals in relation to Pakistan.

The transformation of a state and a society whose population is primarily Muslim is, however, only one aspect of the orientation of Muslims to politics. Islam is also the religion of the resurgent anti-colonialist movement which in various parts of the world seeks to reclaim the control of former colonial societies not merely from direct colonialism but from neo-colonialist rulers. Thus the cause of the Pakistanis and of the Kashmiris and of the people of Afghanistan are causes which many Muslim publications support. These are supported by all Muslims. On the other hand the regime of Khomeini in Iran enjoys only Shia support. The general theme of all these movements however is that all Muslim lands must be rid of alien control and that they should have the opportunity of establishing Islamic States.

Compared with all these goals the orientation of Pakistani Muslims to

Birmingham and Britain may seem of minor importance. But for purposes of day-to-day living the Islamic nature of this orientation is to be taken seriously. In Weber's terms it is based upon the inner-worldly asceticism and the inner-worldly mysticism of the different sects. In those of Niebuhr it involves something between the churches of the disinherited and the churches of the middle classes, a belief in the radical transformation of society on the one hand coupled with a degree of political quietism on the other.

We are still very far from a systematic sociology of the religion of the various Muslim sects even in the case of Pakistanis in one city in Britain. What has been said here may serve, however, to suggest an agenda for study involving a deeper analysis of the Birmingham and British material as well as comparative work of a similar kind amongst Muslim communities in other parts of Europe.

Notes

1. This is less true of the Roman Catholic Church, and of the Pentecostalist Churches among West Indians, but the vibrancy of religion in these classes reflects immigrant interests.
2. Alavi does not discuss Sufism as such and refers only to the recognition of pirs. The leading Barelwi figures in Birmingham, however, are explicitly called Sufis.

References

Alavi, H. 1985. Pakistan and Islam: Ethnicity and Ideology. Unpublished paper presented to the Middle East Discussion Group, Oxford, in November 1985.
Mawdudi, A. 1980. *Towards Understanding Islam*. Leicester: The Islamic Foundation.
Niebuhr, R. 1975. *The Social Sources of Denominationalism*. New York: Meridian Books.
The Straight Path. 1984. Vol. 5, No. 6 (July 1984) Birmingham.
Troeltsch, E. 1931. *The Social Teachings of the Christian Churches*. London: Allen and Unwin.
Weber, M. 1965a. *The Protestant Ethic and the Spirit of Capitalism*. London: Allen and Unwin.
——1965b. *The Sociology of Religion*. London: Methuen.

14
Ethnic Residential Patterns in Dutch Cities: *Class, Race or Culture?*

Hans van Amersfoort

In this chapter I will deal with the explanation of residential patterns of immigrant groups in Dutch cities. I have to give some descriptive information to make it possible to follow the argument. But my main purpose is to explore to what extent general theories about the social position of immigrants in western Europe are corroborated by studies of the settlement patterns in Dutch cities. The descriptive material presented in this paper is derived from other publications, especially from Van Amersfoort (1982b), Van Amersfoort and De Klerk (forthcoming) and De Klerk and Van Amersfoort (forthcoming).

Immigrants in the Netherlands

The Netherlands is a small and densely populated country. Compared with other western European countries the number of immigrants is small. Immigrants comprise 5 per cent of its population of 14,500,000. (For West Germany this figure is 7.6 per cent, for France 7.8 per cent and for Belgium 8.9 per cent.) The composition of this immigrant population is highly complex (Van Amersfoort 1985). It is impossible to pay attention to all kinds of, sometimes very small, groups as diverse as German, Japanese, Ugandan Asian and Chilean. In a discussion of the social position of immigrants and for comparison with other western European countries, however, three immigrant populations are the most relevant; the Surinamese, the Turks and the Moroccans. These three immigrant groups are the most numerous and they have increased substantially during the 1970s.

The Surinamese

The largest immigrant group, about 200,000 persons, is formed by the Surinamese. Small groups of Surinamese had lived in the Netherlands for a very long time. But these were tiny groups of intellectuals and middle class people. After World War II migration developed gradually from the small territory of Surinam (375,000 inhabitants in 1971) with its limited possibilities for social mobility, to the Netherlands. This was possible because Surinam (until 1975) had home-rule and the Surinamese were Dutch nationals. In 1967 there were 16,000 Surinamese in the Netherlands, half of them lived in Amsterdam. But their number grew constantly. In 1972 there were already 43,000.

When the migration stream gained momentum its social composition changed. It was no longer a migration of middle class people, but it had spread to the rank and file. It also became ethnically more diverse. For a long time migration to the Netherlands was limited to the Surinamese negro population (locally called Creoles) who form 40 per cent of the country's population. But after 1970 the other groups, the Hindustani (also 40 per cent, descendants of contract coolies from British India) and Javanese (15 per cent, descendants of Javanese contract coolies) began to come to the Netherlands as well. In 1974 the Surinamese government of a Creole party with just one vote majority, declared that the country would become a republic in 1975. This caused a rush to the Netherlands particularly, but by no means exclusively, among the Asian population. When the country became independent 110,000 Surinamese were residents of the Netherlands (Van Amersfoort 1982a; 137-48). After 1980 the Netherlands made it difficult for Surinamese to settle in the country. But because Surinam has in the meantime become a military dictatorship small numbers are still coming to the Netherlands, now claiming that they are international refugees.

All in all some 150,000 people born in Surinam are now living in the Netherlands. As nearly all of them have Dutch nationality, they are statistically difficult to trace. It depends on the definition of Surinamese in how far we want to include the descendants in the total number of Surinamese in the Netherlands. The rate of intermarriage is high and the boundaries of the group are obviously open. I think that a number of 200,000 is a fair estimation for 1986.

The Surinamese population in the Netherlands is very heterogeneous. The duration of stay, level of education and ethnic grouping shows a great variety. Though the older generation is under-represented and the generation under twenty years is over-represented when compared with the Dutch population, the Surinamese population has not (and never had) the striking demographic structure and unbalanced sex ratio we find among labour migrants. The Surinamese migration is not a labour migration, it has not developed in answer to the pull of the Dutch labour market (Bovenkerk 1983). It originated with people seeking social advancement for themselves or their children and acquired a definite political character after 1974.

Turks and Moroccans

The Turkish and Moroccan migration to the Netherlands is part of the more general Mediterranean migration to western Europe (Van Amersfoort et al. 1984). In the 1960s the Dutch started to recruit labour for older industries that required great numbers of unskilled workers, like textiles, ship building, and coal mining. However, the influx of foreign labour remained modest, and Turks and Moroccans appeared relatively late on the Dutch labour market. In 1965 there were only 8802 Turks and 4506 Moroccans in the Netherlands (Penninx 1979: 92–152). It was seen as only a temporary phenomenon, both by the Dutch government and by the migrants themselves. It was a typical labour migration, starting with men who had left their families behind. They intended to return after a few years of hard work and frugal living to invest their savings in the family farm or a shop. Until the mid-1970s the Moroccans maintained this traditional pattern of circular migration (Van Amersfoort 1978). But as usual in this kind of migration, the perceptions and aspirations of the migrants change. Instead of returning home after a few years, they bring their families over. For legally settled immigrants, Dutch law makes it relatively easy (as compared with Germany and Switzerland) to bring over direct dependants. This family-reunifying migration of wives and children was not influenced by demand on the labour market but by the internal dynamics of this particular migration process.

The labour migration as such practically came to a halt with the oil crisis of 1973. The Dutch government did not issue new work permits after that time. But the migration continued and even increased, due to the arrival of women and children. The migration of the 1970s changed the demographic structure of the Turkish and Moroccan population in the Netherlands dramatically. After 1980 the migration figures dropped quickly, and it looks as if the migration has more or less ended. At present, 80 per cent of the Turkish and 65 per cent of the Moroccan husbands have brought over their families. It is a matter of speculation whether these percentages would have been higher if the economic crisis had not caused such high unemployment among young Turks and Moroccans. It is possible that under favourable conditions the migration would have continued for some time, especially among Moroccans. It is clear, however, that the basic character of the migration would have remained the same. The immigration figures of the 1970s do not indicate that Dutch society is in any danger of becoming flooded with immigrants, as the popular press suggests. They show simply the completion of the labour migration process of the preceding years.

The study of residential patterns

In the 1920s the Human Ecology school in Chicago started the study of residential patterns in modern industrial societies. The segregation of cultural groups is a universal trait in pre-industrial cities. But in these societies segregation of groups has a different meaning. These societies were composed of small scale communities that enclosed the individual all his life. In industrial societies (and even more in post-industrial, if you prefer that term) the scale of interaction has changed tremendously, and related to that the nature of interaction has changed from being personal and diffuse in content to impersonal and role specific. Park, who had a sharp eye for the processes regulating participation in industrial society, saw the city as the spatial expression of these processes (Van Amersfoort 1980: 114–18; Park et al. 1925; Park 1952; Theodorson, 1961).

The ideas of Park and their application to the growth of the city by Burgess were to a certain extent simplistic, their descriptions were impressionistic and in their work explanation and description merge. But their basic ideas have been fruitful and have stimulated much research. With the coming of the computer age the description of processes in cities has changed in character as much more material can be handled systematically. These possibilities have brought all kinds of technical questions to the fore. There is a whole literature on the measurement of social segregation (Peach 1975; Taeuber and Taeuber 1965; Lieberson 1980). I will not dwell on the technical problems of measurement but just point out that the discussions about more accurate measurement and description were very important for all kinds of 'theoretical' questions. An important question in the USA is if there is (or was) a difference in the segregation between several white immigrant groups and the negro population (Lieberson 1980). An important question for the present western European cities is how ethnic patterns in these cities develop.

But even more basic is the question of what the relation really is between social position and settlement pattern. It is generally accepted that in modern cities spatial segregation is a measure of social segregation and thereby of the participation in the basic institutions of society. But is the settlement pattern only an expression of the participation in society or is the settlement a cause of this participation? Is the settlement pattern, to put it in research terms, a dependent or an independent variable? The answer to this question is not only of academic interest. It has also policy implications, especially in welfare states like the Netherlands where the government controls an important part of the housing stock and regulates its allocation. When the housing pattern reflects only the social position of an ethnic group, a policy aiming at an improvement of this position can neglect the housing situation and must take measures in other fields as in education or the labour market. But when the housing situation and the settlement pattern are a cause of the participation in society, it makes sense to try to influence the pattern.

The study of ethnic groups in American cities shows that there is indeed an independent effect of the settlement pattern. Over the generations less segregated groups show more occupational mobility than more segregated groups (Lieberson 1963).

The difficulty with a question like this is that our traditional way of posing it is false. It is not so much a matter of dependent and independent variables but of interdependent variables that work under certain conditions (e.g. an expanding labour market). The housing pattern is both a cause and a result of social participation. Which part of the truth we stress depends *inter alia* on the time perspective we have. The effects of the settlement pattern on the development of the social participation become visible only in the course of generations. In western Europe most immigrant groups comprise recent settlers. It is therefore understandable that most studies have a short time perspective or no time perspective at all and tend to describe the settlement pattern as an expression of the social position of the immigrants.

But even when we limit ourselves to the short time perspective there are different interpretations of the settlement patterns. These interpretations are part of more general ideas or theories about society, but I think they can be singled out and made specific. If the interpretations or theories about the position of immigrants in western European cities are not meant to be dogmas they can be tested by applying them to empirical cases. That is precisely the aim of this paper.

The interpretation of immigrant settlement

The sorting out of immigrants

We have stated that residential patterns are generally looked upon as an expression of the social position of groups. But we have not said why this should be so. The concept social position of a group is in itself not easy. I will not go into detail about its conceptualization. Let me just state that the social position of an immigrant group is a construct of the 'average' position of the group members in four institutional fields, the legal system, the school system, the labour market and the housing market (Van Amersfoort 1982a: 2-24, 51-74.)

Park's sociology was based on the observation that modern society is characterized by a loosening of community ties (see especially his leading article in Park et al. 1925). The individual is no longer encapsulated in solidarity groups. The only solidarity unit left, the nuclear family, encloses only part of the individual's life cycle and has increasingly diminished since Park's days. In these circumstances prestige criteria like family-belonging lose their impact. Income becomes the predominant differentiating factor in society, followed by stages in the life cycle. The individual is set free to move to where he can buy or rent a house appropriate to his income and family needs. And indeed people do move and by doing so differentiate the city socially along these basic variables.

Park and Burgess lived in a period of economic expansion and innovation in transport technology. In these circumstances the modern, more desirable housing is to be found at the outskirts of the growing city. The older houses lack amenities and become obsolete. The wealthier and/or younger people move out and we find them far away from the city centre in the suburbs. Vancancies in low-priced housing, where the immigrants can find a first foothold are to be found in the deteriorating parts of the inner city. A whole range of inquiries in western industrial cities confirms that this generally speaking, is indeed how the social differentiation is structured (Timms 1971: 144-68).

Immigrant settlement was seen by Burgess as a special case of this process of social structuring. The Chinatowns and the Little Sicily's were areas of adaptation, niches where newcomers tried to find their way in the new situation. During this adaptation they sought support of others in the same situation and colonies emerged based on language, religion or regional belonging. These primary group ties do not cut across the basic variables but are a specific form of it. As the income differentiation within the group increases and decreases vis à vis the total population, the ethnic neighbourhood vanishes. Especially when in the course of time the demographic structure becomes more heterogeneous and family status becomes more effective as a variable.

In describing the concentrations of European immigrants of his days, Burgess was remarkably correct. However, he was completely mistaken about the nature of the settlement pattern of rural blacks settling in the northern cities (Liberson 1980; Van Amersfoort 1982b). But the nature of the negro ghetto or the Jewish ghetto in medieval or Nazi times we can leave out of the consideration. No such absolute concentrations of immigrants can be found in Dutch cities, nor in other western European cities, as far as I know. In harmony with the spirit of their time Park and Burgess were in the habit of formulating 'laws' and drawing biological analogies. They compared settlement patterns with examples of plant ecology and used their descriptive terms (invasion, succession) in their explanation. No scholar would word his arguments like this anymore. So we will restate the Park and Burgess argument as follows: the settlement pattern is the result of competition over housing in a free market situation, where price and quality are closely linked. The immigrant can pay little rent and has to start from scratch. Therefore he has to start with taking lodging in the inner city, in parts where the housing is substandard.

The housing classes of Rex and Moore

Rex and Moore based their study of Sparkbrook in Birmingham on the ideas of Park and Burgess (Rex and Moore 1967). But they did not accept the theories of their predecessors completely, nor was Birmingham similar to Chicago in all respects.

Rex and Moore had a different approach to sociological theory. Park and Burgess did not bother to relate actions on an individual level with their explanation of the macro level. This will always remain a difficult problem for the social sciences where the social level of explanation is sometimes not at all translatable into the individual level. Though Rex does not retreat to psychological explanations, he is bound to a sociology that explains residential patterns in terms of the action frame of reference of typical residents (Rex 1968).

The second point of difference is a societal one. The housing market in

Chicago is different from the housing market in England or the Netherlands where, certainly in the cities, the housing situation is characterized by a large public sector. In the public sector as well as in the capitalistic sector there is competition over housing, but the rules of the game are different. Allocation of houses depends on a politically determined distribution system and individuals are related to the housing market according to their status in this system.

On the basis of these considerations Rex and Moore define six housing-classes, groups that have different and sometimes conflicting interests in the housing market: the landlords who let houses and their tenants, owner-occupiers, people in council houses, people in furnished accommodation and finally the 'poor buyers', people who can find entrance only by buying property but using it as a lodging house to meet the costs. The description of these interest groups and their interaction with one another forms the gist of the book. But it provides us only with an explanation of the first stage of settlement; how the pattern will develop in the future is difficult to say when we read Rex and Moore.

The central idea of Rex and Moore's study is that competition in a British housing market (and a Dutch one probably too) is a more complex issue than competition on a price-regulated market. An analysis of this competition can offer an explanation of the conflicts that arise out of this competition. The settlement patterns are the outcome of these conflicts.

Bringing in culture

Though the approach by means of housing-classes makes it possible to view the perspective of each interest group and to consider their particular values, Rex and Moore describe Sparkbrook as though the inhabitants shared the same sentiments on what constitutes the most desirable housing situation. This point has been criticized by Dahya. He maintained that the behaviour of the Pakistani on the housing market was not to be explained by the constraints they met on that market, but by their positive orientation to the kin and village group and the meaning that home-ownership has in that context (Dahya 1974). This is a serious point. When there is a specific Pakistani response to home-ownership where council houses are not attractive to them, they will behave differently from British and West Indian citizens and also (in the long run) differently from the way suggested by Rex and Moore.

Since Dahya several studies of the settlements of Asian groups in Britain have been made. Indeed there seems to be a stronger orientation towards home-ownership among them. A problem for the interpretation of this inclination is the difference in the stage of the migration development among the different Asian groups. In general their migration has developed out of a circular migration of peasants who sought only to augment the family income. This is a familiar pattern in peasant societies under population pressure (Van Amersfoort 1978). In a later stage the men instead of returning home bring over their families, though the idea of returning some day to the ancestral village is often kept alive, at least among the first generation. As long as the migrants perceive themselves primarily as peasant-villagers, their settlement has a different meaning for them, which leads (or can lead) to a different settlement pattern.

But as Dahya himself points out at the end of his article, the cultural orientation which leads to a specific settlement pattern may be only effective during a limited time span. Even when the myth of return persists in a population settled for generations in a country, it is not likely that this ideology has the same consequences for individual behaviour and decisions in practical matters. The frame of reference for action on the housing market will shift from the kin group and village community towards British society. If I understand the development of the various Asian populations in Britain well, this is what we will see happen (Robinson 1981; Flett 1984). There remains an interesting difference in housing situation between several Asian and the West Indian immigrant groups as a result of different cultural orientations.

It is impossible to make a choice between the culture or class interpretation, because the situation of recent immigrants is also singled out by Rex and Moore as giving the people a specific relation to their environment and leading to 'ethnic colonies'. In general social geographers would be very surprised if they could not relate the pattern of settlement to variables such as duration of stay and demographic structure. So we have the situation that explanations, based on a different frame of reference (housing-class position, development stage of migration, culture) are all fitting and not contradicting each other. However, in the long run, with the arrival of new generations, they lead to different scenarios.

Race as class?

Dahya has criticized Rex and Moore because they assume a common value orientation among their various housing-classes. It is a point Pahl also holds (Pahl 1975: 247). But Pahl's objections to the housing-classes appear very different from Dahya's. He supposes that a real class position determines the whole orientation to the world. Classes worth that name divide the population fundamentally into opposite formations with different values, interests and prospects.

The housing-classes are only relatively stable interest groups. The position of individuals may change during their life-time and certainly in the course of generations. The conflicts arising from the housing-classes may centre more on intermediaries like local authority officers than on the directly conflicting parties. This does not sound basic enough and it offers insufficient analytical clarity. Can we not find the real division in society from which the social position of individuals can be more fundamentally understood?

This is a recurrent theme in Marxist and revisionist Marxist writing and we must not exclude it from the possible interpretations of immigrant settlement. The unsolvable problem seems to be to define the dividing line between the two real classes. In classical Marxist analysis the basic division in society would be found in the labour market. But that has proven to be unworkable in modern societies, with the rise of white collar workers, states bureaucracies and the separation of management and capital. Modern writers like Dahrendorf and Pahl look at the power structure to find the fundamental dividing line. But the power structure has many dimensions (at least capital and politics), each with a whole range of positions and there is no conclusive agreement about the line between the haves and have-nots.

A theoretical discussion of this matter falls outside the scope of this chapter. But we have to consider briefly a notion derived from this Marxist class concept, suggested by the black power movement in the USA and which has spread to West Indian circles in England and the Netherlands. Do the blacks form a class opposed to the white settled population?

As I have argued before, it is not possible to apply the classical Marxist notion of class to immigrant groups in western Europe (Van Amersfoort 1982a: 63–6, 205). It is possible to apply a Marxist class concept to such societies as those in present-day South Africa or nineteenth-century plantation societies in the Caribbean. But for societies like the Dutch, we have to modify essential elements of the concept (for instance that the ruling class is dependent for its maintenance on the subjected class) beyond recognition. But fundamental lines can divide a society outside the realm of classical Marxist theory. In the seventeenth century Netherlands, small groups of wandering gypsies did not form a class in that sense, but they were exterminated in a xenophobic rage. Can it be that the immigrants in western European society are excluded from social participation in a fundamental way, that they form in this sense a class or, as I prefer to define it, a minority (Van Amersfoort 1982a: 10–30).

When we put the question this way we have to re-define immigrants. It is clear that immigrants such as the Germans, Japanese or British in a city like Amsterdam have to be excluded. We must find an operational definition for what in radical circles are called the blacks. I have no way other than defining the Turks, Moroccans and Surinamese as the 'black' immigrants. If we hypothesize a fundamental dividing line between 'white' and 'black', we must find a correlation between the settlement patterns of these three immigrant groups.

Immigrant housing in Dutch cities

Housing in Dutch cities

The shortest way to give a general idea of the differentiation of the housing stock in Dutch cities is to follow the historical development. In the older parts of Dutch cities, the construction dates from medieval times (as in Utrecht) or the seventeenth century (as in Amsterdam). In these parts we can find great diversity. Rich and poor lived in the same area. There was no separation between work and residence. The enormous houses of the wealthy Amsterdam merchants included the dwellings of their servants and also contained their offices and storage rooms. The dwellings we find at present in these areas are consequently very heterogeneous. Some of them are of low quality, but other houses have been converted to highly fashionable apartments. We find also a remarkable number of hotels and lodging houses in these older areas. The kind of residential segregation we almost take for granted nowadays did not exist when these areas were built. It developed only towards the end of the nineteenth century, when the technical innovations of the industrial revolution brought the rapid development of transport systems. The Dutch economy that had flourished in the seventeenth century suffered from a long decline in the eighteenth century; in the nineteenth century it expanded more slowly than its neighbours.

The Dutch state became modernized only after the constitution of 1848, after which time Dutch society made a new start. After 1870 the stagnant Dutch cities started to grow again. Around the old centres arose rings or belts of hastily constructed dwellings to house the new populations that were coming in. These immigrants to the cities consisted to a great extent of rural people who had lost their living in the agricultural crisis of the last quarter of the century or had become redundant following the introduction of the mechanization of agricultural production. At the same time better transport facilities made suburbanism possible for the wealthy families. They started to leave the city, to take new homes in the Dunes or along the attractive coast of the Zuiderzee.

The often appalling conditions in the newly constructed parts of the cities led to the first government intervention. The Housing Act of 1901 gave the municipalities the right to impose certain minimum standards. It also made it financially possible for the municipalities to construct their own housing according to these standards, the so-called *woningwetwoningen* (houses constructed under the Housing Act). It took some time, of course, before the effects of the Act became visible. But gradually a growing number of these publicly financed houses were constructed and there was a steady rise in quality in the newly built parts of the city. Particularly in the period between the wars, when construction costs were low, much better neighbourhoods were put up. World War II hit the Netherlands severely; the last winter of the war in particular caused great damage. After the war the country recovered only slowly and the building industry, which lacked equipment and materials, achieved only a modest output. It is only after 1955 that we see again a rapid expansion of Dutch cities and towns.

The post-war period was characterized by a serious shortage of houses and the government was compelled to intervene again. To protect the population against black-market prices, rents were frozen and all houses were subject to a distribution system. These measures were necessary in the grim post-war period, but in the long run they had two serious disadvantages. In the first place the connection between the quality and the price of a house was broken. The frozen rents reflected the building costs but not the quality or the maintenance costs. In the second place the distribution system became in course of time more and more open to political manipulation. Contrary to the accepted wisdom the system protected not so much the poor as the settled. It was the newcomers in the housing market, young families and immigrants who paid the price for the low housing costs of the older generation. With the decline of the housing shortage the system was not superseded as it was supposed to be. Though it was modified, it had become politically impossible to abolish it. It regulated competition for the most desirable housing, that is, for the houses where the relation between quality and rent was most favourable for the tenants. With the steady rise in building costs these were, roughly speaking, the *woningwetwoningen*, built in the periods 1920-40 and 1955-70 (the houses constructed after 1970 were considered to be good but expensive).

This admittedly very general picture can be easily followed in Amsterdam, because this city was not destroyed during the war. The building periods follow each other in orderly fashion, like the layers of an onion. It is only in the last decade that urban renewal projects have broken the historical sequence (see map 1).

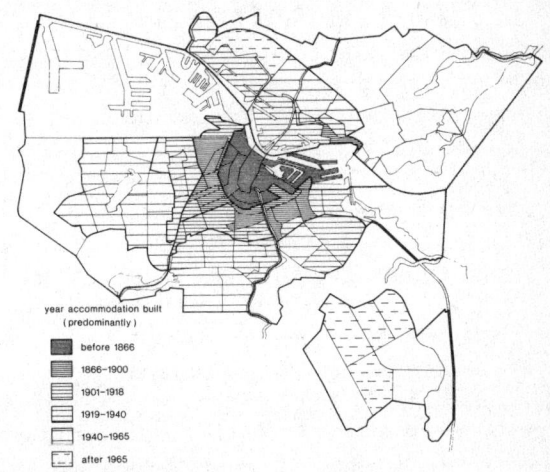

Map 1. Amsterdam: periods of urban expansion

Another remarkable aspect of post-war development, at least in the big cities, entailed the regulation of rents which discourage private investment in housing. Pension funds which had always been invested in houses as promising a modest but solid profit vanished from the housing market. The strong political preference of the Labour Party (which dominated the councils in Amsterdam and Rotterdam in particular) for public housing also drove owner-occupiers and the rising number of aspiring owner-occupiers out of the city. Suburbanization, which with the coming of the automobile era would have increased anyway, was strongly stimulated by the building policy of the big cities.

All these factors resulted in a turnover of population which on the Dutch scale can be called massive. To give one example: the population within the boundaries of the municipality of Amsterdam fell from 920,000 after the war to 685,000 at present, notwithstanding the immigration of about 80,000 Surinamese and Mediterraneans, and tens of thousands of young Dutch people. This turnover and diminishing of population meant that the competition over family dwellings in post-war garden districts diminished and the number of single people wanting to live on their own in the inner city increased.

Immigrant housing, especially in Amsterdam

Several studies have been made of the housing of immigrant groups in the Netherlands. The best general overview is given in the monograph by Van Praag (1981). But there have also been studies of separate cities as the recent one by Bovenkerk et al. (1984) on Utrecht and by Musterd (1985) on Tilburg. There are also studies of housing relevant to our discussion that concentrate not on the settlement pattern but on aspects such as the quality of houses, the use of distribution channels, and the rent the people have to pay relative to their income (Shadid, Kornalijnslijper and Maan 1984).

It appears from these studies that each city is somewhat different from the others. The number of immigrants varies from 13 per cent in Amsterdam to 9 per cent in Utrecht. Moreover, the composition of the immigrant populations differ substantially. Amsterdam has an 'over-representation' of Surinamese, Rotterdam of Turks and Utrecht of Moroccans. But in an international perspective we may say that the differences between Dutch cities are differences of degree and not of kind.

In the Netherlands the housing of immigrants has mainly been studied with reference to the Dutch population. The results of these comparisons are invariably that the immigrants and especially the Turks and Moroccans are worse off. They occupy smaller dwellings, though their families are larger and they occupy more often older dwellings lacking amenities like bathrooms and central heating. The Surinamese have found entrance more often in the public housing sector, therefore their housing conditions are generally better. But this has been in the more expensive part of the public sector and they pay high rents.

At a certain stage studies like these can be worthwile and they can be useful in the formation of public opinion. But they provide us with little insight into the dynamics of immigrant settlement. The comparison with the Dutch population at a certain point in time is not automatically a satisfying point of reference. The housing situation of the Dutch population changed enormously after 1960 and is influenced strongly by demographic developments. At the same time the settlement of Turks, Moroccans and an important part of the Surinamese is of a recent date. The increasing segregation during the 1970s that Van Praag described in 1981 was perhaps the result of the recent influx.

I will therefore examine more closely the developments in Amsterdam, a city for which we now have reliable data since 1973 (see maps 2, 3 and 4).

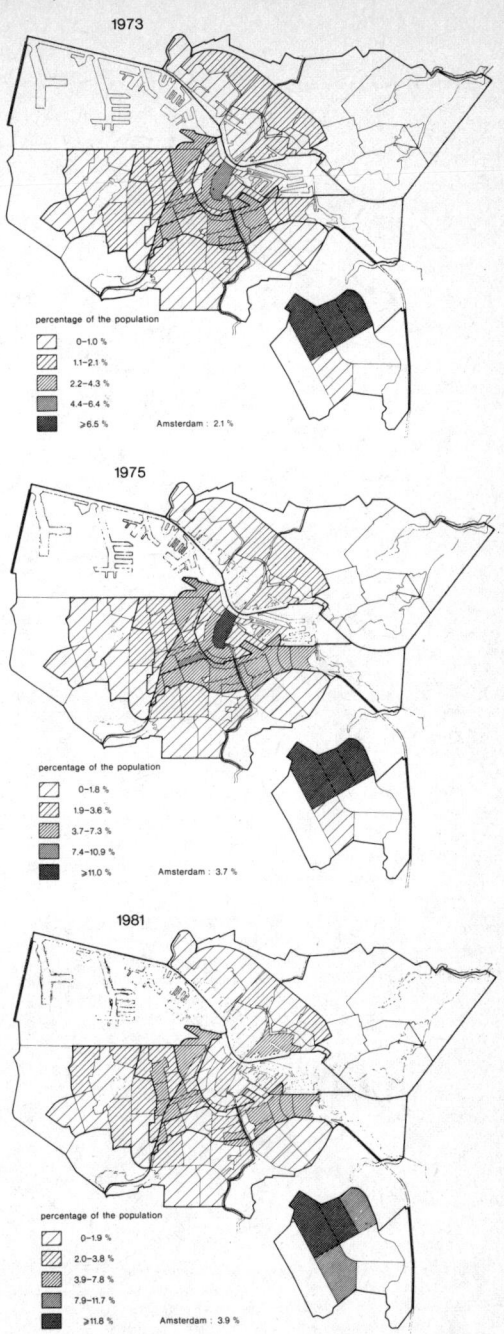

Map 2. The development of the Surinamese settlement pattern in Amsterdam, 1973-81

232 *Additional Themes for Future Research*

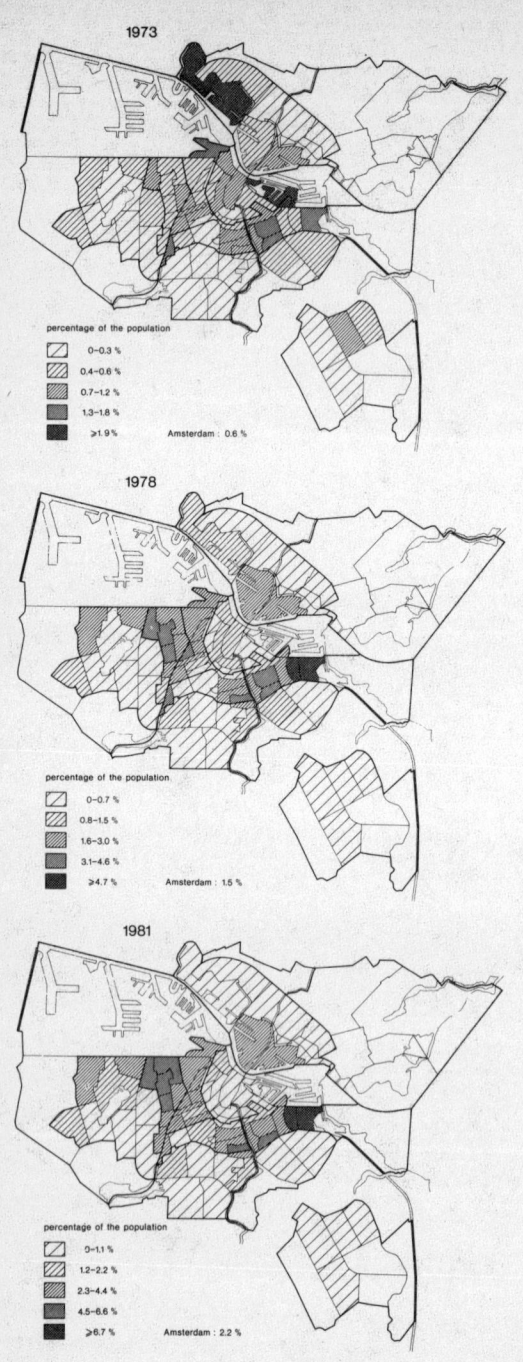

Map 3. The development of the Turkish settlement pattern in Amsterdam, 1973-81

Map 4. The development of the Moroccan settlement pattern in Amsterdam, 1973–81

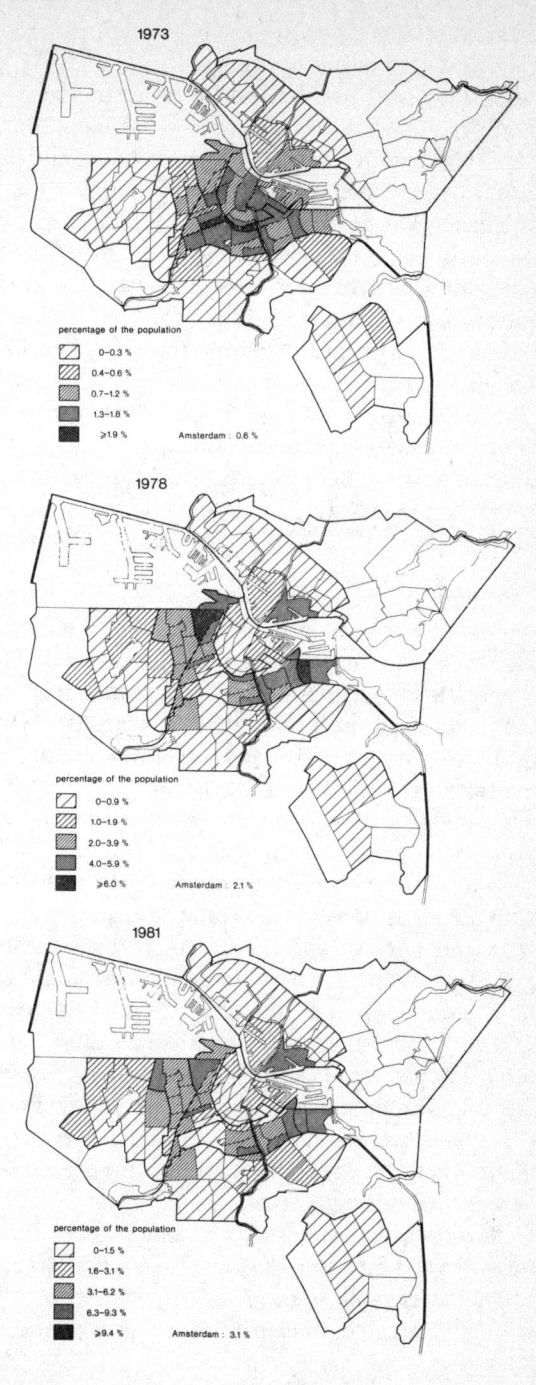

Surinamese in Amsterdam

The most conspicuous point in the Surinamese settlement pattern is their over-representation in the southeast part, Bijlmermeer, a new town constructed after 1965 and consisting wholly of public housing, considered to be good but expensive. As the area is still under construction there is a constant offer of new houses and the number of vacancies is much higher than in the districts of the city proper. The Bijlmermeer has now 60,000 inhabitants and houses 10,000 of Amsterdam's 35,000 Surinamese. Within the Bijlmermeer there was a strong concentration of Surinamese in certain high rise blocks in 1970–5. But this concentration has sharply diminished since the Surinamese families are moving from flats to single family dwelling. If we look at the city proper we see also some interesting movements. The strong immigration in 1974/1975 is reflected in the concentration in the city centre, but only six years later this concentration has dissolved again. There is some over-representation (outside the Bijlmermeer) in the nineteenth-century belt, but there is an obvious spread over the city. Studies of urban renewal projects show that the Surinamese along with the Dutch benefit from most of them, whereas the Moroccans especially seem to be driven out by the slum-clearing process to other sub-standard neighbourhoods.

Turks and Moroccans

The Turks and Moroccans have a very different pattern from the Surinamese. In 1973 the pattern was mainly the result of the presence of boarding and lodging houses 'specializing' in Turks or Moroccans. But with the further development of the migration this predominance vanished. With the immigration of women and children we see the Mediterranean populations move to the late nineteenth-century belt; that is to say to the area of privately owned, cheap, low-quality family dwellings. Gradually we see that they gain entrance into the areas of relatively cheap public housing, built in the period 1920–40 or in the period 1945–65. Contrary to the Surinamese, the Turks and Moroccans are not over-represented in the areas of expensive public housing.

The similarity of the Turkish and Moroccan pattern can be explained by similarity in social position and the development of the migration. Both populations operate at the same time on the same part of the housing market. The remarkable dynamism in the settlement patterns in a relatively short period is closely linked with the dynamics of the migration process. Now that the Turkish migration is more or less completed and the Moroccan is going on very slowly, the pattern will become more stable. The second period of change can be expected at the time when the young Turks and Moroccans start to form new households and enter the housing market.

If we compare the Amsterdam situation with that in other Dutch cities, we see the same tendencies. Everywhere the Surinamese are better off than the Turks and Moroccans. The latter immigrant groups show a strong concentration in the areas of low-quality nineteenth-century housing. But there are also some differences. The most important among them is the frequency of home-ownership among the immigrants. In Amsterdam there are few owner-occupiers. The city policy has for more than sixty years been guided by an ideology seeing public housing as the only form of housing suited for a progressive city. Only 7 per cent of the houses are inhabited by the owner (in the Netherlands 35 per cent). Therefore we find among the immigrants only 4 per cent owner-occupiers. The role played by public housing and owner-occupiers depends on the political colour of the municipality. Amsterdam and Rotterdam as *red* cities have a stronger emphasis on public housing than other cities. But in all major cities the role of public housing is important.

It is, however, not only the share that private houses have on a local market that is important. If we compare the number of Turks and Moroccans who have bought their houses in several cities, we see a remarkable variation. The municipalities can refuse Turks and Moroccans the right to bring over their families when there is no adequate housing for them. Some municipalities did this and more or less forced the migrants who wanted to bring over their wives and children to buy a house. (At a time when the prices were very high.) As Bovenkerk et al. have aptly described for Utrecht, it was mainly dependent on the local authority if buying was the only way to get a house at all (Bovenkerk et al. 1984: 49–59). Utrecht changed this policy when it became obvious that it was leading to very high concentrations in the most degraded parts of the city and did *not* stop the migration. Amsterdam was more liberal. It permitted the immigrant to bring over his family and to solve the problem of housing them afterwards. The characteristic phenomenon of the 'poor buyers' as described by Rex and Moore and from a different perspective by Dahya is in some Dutch cities clearly visible but in others it is not, depending on the municipal policy in the past decade.

Because the Surinamese were, as Dutch nationals, never in the position of having to apply for a residence permit, we do not find the phenomenon of the 'poor buyer' among them. They were much more oriented towards public housing. The owner-occupiers among them we find, just as among the Dutch population, primarily in middle class suburban areas and in the smaller towns.

Explaining residential patterns

The patterns that we have seen in Dutch cities show at first glance a striking resemblance to the description by Burgess. They first settle in the twilight zones of the heterogeneous inner city and penetrate from there into the adjacent districts of least desirable housing. However, there are also important differences from this classical situation.

In the first place, the number of immigrants in Dutch cities is small compared with the American cities in the classical immigration period. Secondly, the change in the pattern of first settlement is much faster in Dutch cities; the Burgess model fits only a short period of time. The reason for this rapid change lies in the mechanism of housing allocation in the Dutch cities where the public housing sector is predominant. In these cities a competition has developed that has a striking similarity to the competition over housing as described by Rex and Moore. The more desirable houses in the public sector were only opened up to immigrants after political scandals that forced the municipalities to formulate a very strict policy (Van Amerstoorf 1982b: 71-4). These conflicts we find in the 1970s in one form or another in all Dutch cities (Prinsen 1983). But whatever the resistance of the Dutch population, sooner or later the immigrants got into the system of public housing allocation. The Surinamese as Dutch nationals gained entrance to the allocation system almost immediately. Their entrance into the more expensive part of the public housing sector demonstrates that also in this sector penetration starts where there are vacancies for which there is little or no competition. This explains too why immigrants have been able to settle in the western post-war neighbourhoods of Amsterdam only in the last period. These districts consist almost completely of relatively cheap family dwellings. The competition for this kind of housing has declined with the declining number of Dutch families in the city population. The conflicts over housing and the nature of neighbourhoods still exist and form the basis for racist agitation. But this seems to have little influence on the allocation of housing and the developing of the settlement patterns.

The ethnic patterns in Dutch cities have been very much in the process of development over the last fifteen years. This does not give much possibility for a fundamental interpretation of race as a class. It is possible to assume that all the variations and developments are only of minor importance when compared with the basic one; but it is very difficult to say what this basic one would be. If we assume a black settlement pattern to exist we have to merge the Surinamese, Turkish and Moroccan patterns. But it is difficult to give an interpretation to the result. In fact the Surinamese settlement pattern with its predominance in the Bijmermeer resembles more the pattern of white immigrants like the Germans and Japanese.

The Turks and Moroccans have very similar patterns. But when we pursue our analysis down to the small scale of the building block, we find no evidence of an Islamic pattern emerging. The Turks have dispersed in the last few years somewhat more than the Moroccans. I expect the Turkish and Moroccan patterns to become less similar in the future, but this is no more than a hypothesis. We see this separation presently in the use of ethnic institutions. The mosques in the Netherlands are clearly divided according to nationality, both in the committees that manage them and in the believers who visit them. Though nearly all Muslims in the Netherlands are officially Sunni, in practice the force of folk-beliefs is strong and separates them into different Islamic modes. It is of course impossible to forecast how these national-local-Islamic cultures will develop in the future and if there is any chance that they will merge into one Dutch-Islamic subculture.

In the realm of settlement it has been suggested that the Turks and Moroccans from a peasant background would have a greater urge to buy a house because they are not familiar with renting a house and certainly not with a system of public housing. It is true that in some cities and towns the Mediterranean immigrants have bought their houses. But as has been indicated already, there is a direct link with the municipal policy of issuing residence permits. So if there is any cultural predisposition towards home-ownership it is only operative when the access to the public housing allocation is blocked.

Our final answer to the question of which explanation of settlement patterns holds best in Dutch cities must be that an analysis based on the concept of housing-classes fits the Dutch cities best. The interpretation along the lines of race as a class is obviously far removed from reality in Dutch cities and does not help us to give a meaningful interpretation of Dutch housing patterns. The role of culture, as far as housing patterns are concerned, seems to be very limited. It is possible that specific religious or national (most Turks and Moroccans do not differentiate between them) values have influence in other fields of social participation (education, health care, for example), but on the housing market behaviour seems to be guided by practical considerations. But all approaches seem to underestimate the influence of demographical factors (both on the immigrant side and on the side of the host population) that have played a predominant role in the recent developments in Dutch cities.

Note

I wish to acknowledge the assistance of J. ter Haar, of the Institute of Social Geography at the University of Amsterdam, who drew the maps included in this paper.

References

Amersfoort, H. van. 1978. Migrant Workers, Circular Migration and Development. *Tijdschrift voor Economische en Sociale Geografie* 69: 17-26.
—— 1980. *Woonsegregatie, gettovorming en de overheid*. Blauw, P.W. and Pastor, C., eds. Soort bij Soort, Deventer: Van Loghum Slaterus.
—— 1982a. *Immigration and the Formation of Minority Groups. The Dutch Experience 1945-1975*. Cambridge: Cambridge University Press.
—— 1982b. Immigrant Housing in a Welfare State. The Case of the Netherlands in the Nineteen Seventies. *Research in Race and Ethnic Relations* 3: 49-77. Greenwich, Conn.: J.A.I. Press.
—— 1985. Immigrants in the Netherlands. *Tijdschrift voor Sociale en Economische Geografie* 76: 144-9.
Amersfoort, H. van and Klerk, L. de. Forthcoming. The Dynamics of Immigrant Settlement. Surinamese, Turks and Moroccans in Amsterdam. *Immigrants in West European Cities*. Glebe, G. and O'Loughlin, J., eds.
Amersfoort, H. van, Muus, P. and Penninx, R. 1984. International Migration, the Economic Crisis and the State: an Analysis of Mediterranean Migration to Western Europe. *Ethnic and Racial Studies* 7: 238-68.
Bovenkerk, F. 1983. De vlucht. Migratie in de jaren zeventig. *Suriname, de schele onafhankelijkheid*. Willemse, G., ed. Amsterdam: Arbeiderspers.
Bovenkerk, F. et al. 1984. *Vreemd volk, gemengde gevoelens*. Meppel: Boom.

Dahya, B. 1974. The nature of Pakistani ethnicity in industrial cities in Britain. *Urban Ethnicity*. Cohen, A., ed. London: Tavistock.

Flett, H. 1984. Asians in Council Housing, Arguments and Evidence. *Race and Residence in Britain*. Ward, R., ed. Birmingham: Economic and Social Research Council.

Jackson, P. and Smith, S., eds. 1981. *Social Interaction and Ethnic Segregation*. London: Academic Press.

Klerk, L. de and Amersfoort, H. van. Forthcoming. Surinamese Settlement in Amsterdam. *The West Indian Experience in Britain and the Netherlands*. Cross, M. and Entzinger, H., eds. London: Tavistock.

Lieberson, S. 1963. *Ethnic Patterns in American Cities*. Glencoe, Ill.: The Free Press.

———. 1980. *A Piece of the Pie. Blacks and White Immigrants since 1880*. Los Angeles: University of California Press.

Musterd, S. 1985. *Verschillende structuren en ontwikkelingen van woongebieden in Tilburg*. Amsterdam: Vrije Universiteit.

Pahl, R. 1975. Urban Processes and Social Structure. *Whose City?* Pahl, R., ed. London: Longman.

Park, R.E. 1952. *Human Communities. The Collected Papers of R.E. Park*. Vol. II. Glencoe, Ill.: The Free Press.

Park, R.E., Burgess, E.W. and McKenzie, R.D. 1925. *The City*: Chicago: University of Chicago Press.

Peach, C. 1975. *Urban Social Segregation*. London: Longman.

Peach, C., Robinson, V. and Smith, S., eds. 1981. *Ethnic Segregation in Cities*. London: Croom Helm.

Penninx, R. 1979. Ethnic Minorities. Report of the Netherlands Scientific Council for Government Policy No. 17. The Hague: Staatsuitgeverij.

Praag, C.S. van. 1981. Allochtonen, huisvesting en spreiding. *Sociaal en Cultureel Planbureau*. Cahier 22. Rijswijk.

Prinsen, J. 1983. *Buitenlandse werknemers en de verdeling van huurwoningen*. Nijmegen: Instituut voor Toegepaste Sociologie.

Rex, J. 1968. The sociology of a zone of transition. *Readings in Urban Sociology*. Pahl, R., ed. London: Oxford University Press.

Rex, J. and Moore, R. 1967. *Race, Community and Conflict*. London: Oxford University Press.

Robinson, V. 1981. The Development of South Asian Settlement in Britain and the Myth of Return. *Ethnic Segregation in Cities*. Peach, C., Robinson, V. and Smith, S., eds. London: Croom Helm.

Shadid, W., Kornalijnslijper, N. and Maan, E. 1984. *Huisvesting etnische minderheden*. Universiteit van Leiden, Leiden: DSWO Press.

Taeuber, K.E. and Taeuber, A.F. 1965. *Negroes in Cities*. Chicago: Aldine.

Theodorson, G.A., ed. 1961. *Studies in Human Ecology*. New York: Harper and Row.

Timms, D.W.G. 1971. *The Urban Mosaic*. Cambridge: Cambridge University Press.

15
Social Relations and Cultural Continuities: *Muslim Immigrants and their Social Networks*

Yngve Georg Lithman

Every discipline develops in the interaction between data and concepts, and an implication of this is that new areas of inquiry may force reconsiderations both of data techniques and the social scientist's conceptual tool box. As a social anthropologist coming to the fields of international migration, immigration and immigrant life, the veracity of this observation is confirmed almost daily. Anthropology, and I will here refer to both social and cultural anthropology, and make no distinction between them, developed in the social contexts of what is now the third world, and a fundamental premise was that the social and the cultural were virtually but encodings of each other in what were by and large perceived as static and isolated local communities, studied through the vehicles of the prolonged participant observation field work, often spanning a year or more. This mode of inquiry, traditional anthropology, if one so chooses to designate it, produced and produces powerful analytical insights. The influence of anthropology on concepts such as culture and social organization and the elucidation of the interconnectedness between the social and the cultural are noteworthy achievements.

When anthropologists turn their attention to migration and the situation of immigrants, however, we are faced with social and cultural realities which force developments both with respect to data collection and concepts. The field work orientated towards the holistic understanding of a socio-cultural system is in some instances an inefficient mode of data collection, and the content of concepts such as culture developed largely in situations very different from those characterized by the variety and fluidity often typical of those in which migrants live their lives.

Following a short presentation of some features of the Muslim presence in Sweden, this article will elaborate on these points, primarily through a discussion of Muslim immigrant life in Sweden. It attempts to give examples of the way social interaction may be structured among immigrants with a Muslim background. The individual cases of Muslim life which will be presented are based upon a general theoretical notion about the interplay between social relations and cultural constructs which also will be briefly presented.

Concepts, Field Work and Data Collection

In discussions of the life of migrants, the concept of culture is often invoked as a major explanatory factor. Not only are actions often seen as the consequence of migrants acting in accordance with a 'culture' they have brought with them, but we may even observe the emergence of a whole mode of discourse regarding migrants with a focus on the culture concept. In this perspective, concepts such as culture conflict, being between two cultures and culture distance emerge as major ingredients in the conceptual apparatus.

For several reasons, this approach leaves much to be desired. Its starting point is a too inclusive and undifferentiated view of culture and a non-problematized view of the relationship between culture and human action.

The too inclusive view of culture is particularly manifest in constellations such as Swedish culture, Turkish culture, and, even and not infrequently, Muslim culture. The first observation to be made with respect to this use of the culture concept is that it obscures all that is to be explained, and particularly so with respect to migrants. Culture, in this line of reasoning, becomes a supreme moral order, prescribing actions, while people become robotized, seen as fulfilling cultural dictas or buckling under the pressure of conflicting imperial moral orders. Also, culture is treated as a self-contained monolithic entity, unrelated to feed-back from experiences people make in their interactions and impervious to change. Also, issues of culture change become impossible to handle if culture is seen in this self-contained manner.

It should be added, that this kind of use of the culture concept in migration studies tends to draw attention, for us, to the more spectacular — in the sense of being apart from *us* — aspects of life of the people in the receiving societies. The whole gamut of everyday life is seldom covered under labels such as Turkish culture or Muslim culture.

In the social sciences generally (including anthropology), however, the concept of culture has been the subject of much pondering, especially during the latest decade, and the developments have been many and diverse. A common ambition has been to cut the culture concept to '. . . a narrow, specialized, and . . . theoretically more powerful concept' (Geertz 1973:4). The Levi Straussian-inspired attempts to regard culture as a structuration based on binary contrasts and a set of transformational rules, the American cognitivist approach inspired by linguistics and associated with names such as Goodenough's and the semiotic approaches, such as Geertz's, where culture is seen as shared codes of meaning, are some of the major trends in this reorientation towards the theoretical distinction of the concept.

The way the subject-matter of an inquiry is conceptualized has implications also for data collection techniques, and anthropology will in this respect have to embark on a more diversified course of action in order to accommodate the variety and fluidity represented by migrant and immigrant situations. As perhaps in no other social science, anthropology has been associated with one particular data collection method, the prolonged participant observation field work. In the archetypical anthropological field site, the Pacific island or the African village, this provided an excellent vehicle through which to gain an understanding of the workings of a socio-cultural system, and thus excellently fitted to the holistic ambitions. This argument has been developed by Lithman (1983).

When examining what anthropologists actually do during their field work, however, one finds a wide variety of methods, spanning virtually everything from just 'tagging along' to surveys satisfying the minutiae of statistical sophistication. Indeed, already in the forties, the researchers at the Rhodes-Livingstone Institute in present-day Zimbabwe were well on their way to what became network analysis. Here, the impetus rested in large measure in their attempts to account for the adjustment of migrant labour to town or compound living. Thus, the study of migration and migrants already some forty years ago prompted methodological developments in anthropology.

Anthropological studies of migration and immigrants in our own societies raise demands for further developments in our data collection techniques. There is, of course, a severe danger in postulating a dichotomy between our societies and other societies. Numerous field-work situations in our own societies would in many ways not fall outside the range of variations recognized as ordinary field sites. Studies of neighbourhoods, professions, some types of studies of immigrant groups, as well as studies of specific interactional fora, be they drinking-bars or classrooms, are but some examples. There are, however, certain features in modern and complex societies, as exemplified by Sweden, which become problematic when combined with a more routine-type anthropological inquiry.

One such feature relates to the structure of the life situations of, say, an immigrant youth in a Stockholm suburb. In the course of a day, he or she might find him- or herself in any number of situations which have had different requirements for recruitment, in which the personnel might be very different, in which the values transacted might be very different, sometimes perhaps even antithetical, and the integrative forces between the different situations may be virtually absent. I am here referring to situations such as the home, peer-group (perhaps in the plural, and according to ethnic diacritica), the soccer club, the work or study situation and the mosque. Put differently, the individual may be seen as a member of several networks, and these networks may in large measure coincide only with respect to this person.

To describe these networks is of course in part an empirical question, and a highly interesting one at that, but the point here is that the circumstances which have been described will have consequences for field-work strategy. Full-blown field work could, of course, be used in each of these situations, for example, the family or the class-room. This would, however, serve to distract from what would often be a proper focus of the inquiry — how immigrants cope with the totality of their situation. If this is the aim, the field-work strategy to pursue must be a more person-centred one than is usually the case.

Two other features of our societies which also have consequences for field work should be mentioned. One is, that there is often in our societies a close correspondence between the spatial frame, recruitment of personnel to the interaction in this frame and the interaction itself. 'Family life in an apartment' may be a label for one example of this, and a guest, a stranger, transforms the situation into an event which can be labelled 'having guests'. The second feature to be mentioned is that places such as Stockholm suburbs in large measure lack an equivalent of public watering-holes, or, more succinctly, there is a lack of places where non-defined, non-instrumental activity takes place. The implication for field work is that it is more difficult to perform an informal crawl via networks of friends of friends. Instead of waiting about and meeting friends via friends, the introduction to new acquaintances takes on a considerably more formal character, and also involves diaries and communication technologies whereby people nowadays have to synchronize their actions.

The Interplay between the Cultural and the Social in Migrant-related Studies

A prominent feature of immigrant situations is that the relationship between the social (people's social relationship and anchorages), and the cultural (people's constructions about meaningfulness), is more problematic than in most other situations. In more ordinary anthropological field work, one often sees how the social and the cultural in considerable measure may be taken for mutual encodings of each other. The integration between the two spheres is evident.

In migration-related inquiries, however, one often finds that the relationship between culture (meaning) and social relations is even more complex than in studies of more homogenous socio-cultural settings (see also Lithman 1986). In the latter, one may in a more direct fashion link the cultural constructs to the social relations which are their carriers (and the concept of socio-cultural system refers exactly to the possibilities to see this bilateral integration, how the social encodes the cultural and the cultural encodes the social). In immigrant situations, on the other hand, people will in some measure become parts of new social relations, and earlier social relations will partly be reinterpreted or even, for geographical and other reasons, be impossible to maintain. The cultural constructs will also change, in part as a consequence of the fact that the immigrant loses his or her place in a meaning-creating (i.e. culture-building) context in the country of origin. Furthermore, in the immigration country, the immigrants will encounter new ranges of cultural forms and contents which in larger or smaller measure will penetrate, build and reshape their systems of meaningfulness, their culture.

These observations force some theoretical and methodological questions. A cultural construct, in the line of reasoning advanced in this paper, has to have a social grounding, and such social groundings, relations between people, have to have their culture, i.e. their meaningfulness. One consequence of this is that the research methodology will have be sensitive to the fact that many migrants, as mentioned above, in the course of a day may find themselves in a number of culture-carrying contexts. Furthermore, the integration between these contexts as far as personnel or cultural constructs is concerned has to be treated as a variable. Indeed, as far as the single actor is concerned, in some cases the ability to handle widely diverse situations while still perceiving of him- or herself as following a single life-course trajectory is a striking feature. This observation also cautions against too simple notions about people having to strive for a unity of the social situations of which he or she is a part irrespective of whether this need is argued from a psychological or sociological (role theory) perspective.

The methodological issues facing an anthropologist in migrant studies obviously directs attention to network studies. The problem here, however, is that these in large measure have a focus on social structure, and thus with the morphological and interactional properties of networks. Anchorage, reachability, density and range on the one hand and content, directedness, durability, frequency and intensity on the other have become fairly standardized concepts (cf. Mitchell 1969). The concern with social structure manifests itself also in the uses to which network studies have been put, from the elucidation of the roots of conflicts on an ocean-going research vessel (Bernard and Killworth 1973) to a search for theoretical developments in exchange theory (Kapferer 1972). The increasing facilities available for sophisticated computerized treatment of network data seem to have pushed network analysis further in the direction of concern with social structure (compare, for example, White, Boorman and Breiger 1976). Also, some of this concern in network analysis with social structure has focused on individual manipulations of the social environment.

The concern with networks in this article relates to a somewhat different ambition, to see the mutual grounding in each other of the social and the cultural in culturally and socially complex situations. Is it possible to draw provisional conclusions about the longevity of certain cultural orientations upon the basis of network inquiries? The premise for an ambition of this kind would then be that such a longevity presupposes a grounding in certain kinds and constellations of social bonds between people. Is it, likewise, possible to draw provisional conclusions about the longevity of certain kinds or constellations of social bonds as a consequence of their encoding of cultural constructs?

The premise for this would then be, that so much 'cultural capital' has been invested in these bonds, that in the absence of drastic events, these bonds are likely to last.

These are the types of question this paper attempts to raise. It certainly draws upon the experiences of network analysis, and concepts such as density and strong and weak links reflect insights which have been germane to this effort. However, as networks are here used as a vehicle to understand social and cultural continuities and change and their relationship to each other in duo- and multiethnic and culturally complex situations, the aim is different and modes of procedure will also be different.

The Islamic Presence in Sweden

There exists no official estimate of the number of Muslims in Sweden, nor is it easy to arrive at an estimate. Of the 640,000 foreign-born residing in Sweden (1983), some 515,000 came from European countries. There is no way of knowing how many Muslims have come to Sweden from European countries such as Yugoslavia and France. A general belief, but nothing more than a belief, is that these figures are negligible. In Table 1 the number of residents in Sweden from countries with a significant Muslim population are presented.

Table 1. Number of foreign-born persons in Sweden, 1983, from selected countries

African countries		Asian countries	
Algeria	696	Bangladesh	558
Egypt	1,023	Iraq	2,184
Ethiopia	2,693	Iran	4,554
Gambia	520	Jordan	479
Ghana	193	Lebanon	2,642
Kenya	353	Malaysia	469
Morocco	1,786	Pakistan	1,370
Nigeria	190	Syria	2,331
Somalia	186	Turkey	17,487
Sudan	141		
Tunisia	1,113		

Several comments can be made about these figures. From Ethiopia, a significant portion probably comes from Eritrea, and has a Muslim background. With respect to both Ghana and Kenya, the number of persons with a Muslim background may well be negligible. For Nigeria, perhaps one third has a Muslim background if the belief that most Nigerian immigrants come from southern Nigeria is correct. For several countries in the Middle East, it is virtually impossible to have a firm opinion as to the proportion who are Muslim, Christian or belong to yet other denominations. Lebanon is of course a good example of this. With respect to Turkey, we know that approximately one third are

Christians from eastern Turkey. The reason why India has not been included in Table 1 is because it is believed that the number of Muslim immigrants from this country is negligible.

The figures presented above of course also illustrate the low number of immigrants from countries in Africa and Asia settled in Sweden. In 1983 there were 12,202 and 61,229 respectively. In 1984, the African and Asian immigration to Sweden clearly reflects the tightened Swedish immigration rules. Persons who are political refugees or have similar reasons for residence as well as members of families joining the rest of the family (family reunion reasons) are virtually the only ones to be granted residence and work permits. In 1984, significant numbers of immigrants came from Ethiopia (164), Morocco (74), Iraq (713), Iran (1445), Lebanon (809) and Turkey (290).

Drawing this information together, one may suggest that among the immigrants to Sweden with a Muslim background, there are some 7000 persons from African countries, less than 20,000 from Asian countries (except Turkey) and in addition some 12,000 from Turkey.

To this should be added another two notes of caution. We have no knowledge of the extent to which these people are actually practising Muslims, and we have no systematic knowledge about the way children of these immigrants are raised. In the literature, however, one finds examples both of cases where the parents are quite anxious to maintain a cultural continuity with what are perceived as the cultural values and traditions, including religious ones, with the country of origin, but also where the parents firmly reject many of the things associated with the countries of origin.

Sunni organizations in Stockholm

Three Muslim organizations for Sunni Muslims have been approached in the study upon which this paper is based, Förenade Islamiska Församlingar i Sverige, FIFS, (Associated Islamic Parishes in Sweden), Svenska Muslimska Förbundet, SMF, (The Swedish Muslim Union) and the Islamiska Centerunionen i Sverige, ICUS, (the Islamic Centre Union in Sweden). The last mentioned of these is fairly recent, and not (yet) recognized as eligible for governmental support as an immigrant association or for grants from the Swedish council for free (i.e. non-state) churches. The other two receive appoximately 600,000 SwCr. together per annum from this source. The first two emerged when a common association was divided at the beginning of the 1970s.

All three organizations, incidentally, claim to welcome all Muslims, also Shiites. SMF appears to have the most organized activity in the Stockholm region, and our prime attention has been focused on the activities performed by the local parishes attached to this Union.

SMF, which claims 8000 members in Stockholm, has eleven local parishes in the Stockholm region, whereof three are located in central Stockholm. These are in fact small mosques, being referred to by the name of the streets on which they are located or, in the case of Rinkeby, with the suburb where it is to be found. Several of the mosques are also in some measure associated with certain countries or areas of origin. Högbergsgatan is primarily associated with north Africans, Apelbergsgatan with Saudis, Rinkeby with Turks, while Torsgatan is thought of as having visitors of varied national and linguistic affiliations. This division, however, must not be exaggerated, since, as several informants put it, 'one often has to go to the one closest to one's job or to where one lives.'

Rinkeby and Apelbergsgatan have their permanent *imams*, and the ambition is to have a permanent *imam* for each mosque. The one in Rinkeby is from Turkey, and has received his training in a state run university-affiliated programme. His salary is paid for by the Turkish state through the embassy.

One may mention that the activities in some measure are structured to satisfy demands emanating out of Swedish society. Högbergsgatan, for example, has a member register, with 1013 names, and produces an annual report, both efforts obviously influenced by requirements for Swedish governmental support.

The ICUS has four 'parishes', three in suburbs, Alby, Upplands-Väsby and Märsta, and one in central Stockholm, Saltmätargatan. They claim to have some six to seven thousand members in Sweden, and the large majority of these are Turks. They have three *imams* trained in private institutions in Turkey. These, it is claimed, have a far superior training to the ones coming from governmental institutions. They also have been in training far longer, for a minimum of fifteen years.

All these Muslim organizations describe their activities in very similar words. Quran schools for children are a universal feature. Study circles in Islamic matters are common, as are various cultural activities such as book lending and also cassette and video lending. Assistance in various conflicts, marital or generational, as well as general guidance are often mentioned as important activities. They all, of course, have a strong core of religious activities, including prayers and other religious rites.

A Friday Prayer

The entrance to the Torsgatan mosque is unmarked, except for some lettering on a discreet door: 'Islamiska församlingen i Stockholm'. Most Swedes passing the entrance on their daily rounds to subways, buses or their homes on this busy city-centre street may not have noticed either the entrance or the lettering on the door. At certain times during the day, especially on Fridays and Sundays, there is however a steady flow of people, many distinctly immigrant in their demeanour, through this door. A fairly narrow flight of stairs leads to the basement, and a number of racks of clothes-hangers line the lower part of the staircase. The staircase turns sharply, and the visitor is faced with a stainless steel wash basin with several taps and a small doorway to the left. Passing the doorway, one finds oneself in a large basement room of about 20 square meters, covered with carpets of an oriental design. Straight ahead, there is another small room, obviously an office, with a couple of chairs, a desk, and a plethora of binders, magazines and books. To the right, a larger entrance opens to a somewhat bigger room, also covered with carpets. The first room, in particular, has parts of the walls covered with sheets of cloth, and when you look closer, you see that they are arranged in order to disguise sewage and water pipes. A large clock shows the time. In the larger room, there is a niche and also a small staircase — both perhaps simple in design but representing beautiful additions to the room. The walls are lined with posters displaying sayings from the Quran.

Facing one of the walls, an older man calls to prayers in a penetrating voice a few minutes before one. The two rooms, holding perhaps a hundred persons, are now full of people, of obviously very diverse origins. Some are dressed in what most Swedes would consider as Arab clothing. Others have a distinctly African appearance. If you inquire, or if you are an astute observer of clothing and languages, you will learn that others are Pakistani or Turkish. Indeed, the Turks may well turn out to be in the majority. There are still people arriving, stopping to wash at the entrance. Some do this rapidly, an ignorant observer may even say perfunctorily, while others spend quite some time at it. There are quite a few young men present, and also some boys with their fathers, but no women.

My own presence, as a Swedish non-Muslim, creates a slight problem. It is, they explain, their ambition to have someone to interpret the presentation of the *imam* into Swedish after he has finished when there is a Swedish non-Muslim guest. However, they are not quite sure who will serve as *imam* this day, and they are therefore not sure that they can provide a service of this kind. The language used by the *imam* will decide whether there is someone able to translate into Swedish.

The prayer starts at one o'clock and lasts for slightly less than half an hour. The *imam*, the leader of the service, speaks Turkish, and I recognize a few Arabic expressions. The kneeling provokes some commotion, as the rooms are really too small for the number of people present.

Towards the end of the ceremony, when the sermon by the *imam* is over, someone arranges a placard at the exit door, announcing that there is a fund collection for the *Mujahedin* in Afganistan, and places a plastic bowl beside it. As people leave, they put their donations in the bowl, and before long a very respectable pile of 100-crown bills virtually fills the bowl.

When the ceremony ends, one of the people closely attached to the mosque comes up and relates to me some of the things the *imam* has said. If you wake up on the day of atonement, and you miss an eye or a limb, and you ask Allah why, you will find out that it is because you were not a good Muslim during your time on earth. It is, the *imam* has explained, only while on the earth that you can prepare yourself properly for the afterworld.

Most of the people leave fairly quickly, but some small groups remain. Most of the visitors, it is explained to me, have to go back to their jobs, and are therefore in a hurry. Those who can often stay a little while to talk. And, eventually, most visitors leave. A few remain, sitting on the floor, reading.

Four Muslim Immigrants

Some data about four Muslim immigrants will be presented below. As already stated, the purpose of this paper is to give an account of one attempt to relate social networks to culture, or, rather, everyday culture-building. In particular, these immigrants' relationship to Islamic matters are of interest.

The data collection consists, apart from general interview work, of elicited network data. Each interviewee was asked (1) which persons he would approach to discuss personal problems, (2) which persons he felt closest to, (3) which persons he associated most with in his leisure time, (4) which persons he associated with during his work or study, (5) which persons he could approach to get help in practical matters, (6) which persons he went to the mosque with, and (7) out of all the believing Muslims he knew which were most significant.

The interviewee was allowed to mention at the most six persons in each of the seven dimensions described above. Often, the description of the dimensions was much fuller than just a few words. Wives or children were not to be included among the persons. A significant part of the interview was also that the interviewee was to describe the degree of relationship between all the various persons he had mentioned. Each of the persons mentioned was categorized at the end of the interview period, and this information covered country of origin, sex, and relations to the Muslim faith.

The data presented here is thus cognitive, not interactional. Another limitation is that we interviewed only men, and therefore have no material relating to women's networks. The aim of this study, however, was not to produce statistically based statements about the frequency of different types of networks. Instead, it serves to demonstrate some of the variations in Muslim immigrant social networks and to reflect upon which kinds of meaningfulness, that is culture, these networks may seem to carry as far as the interviewee is concerned.

The interpreter

R is a man in his early forties, who has been in Sweden for more than ten years. His parents were engaged in farming in a Maghreb country. He is married to a woman from a Nordic country, not Sweden, and they have a couple of children. He describes himself as a believing, non-practising Muslim. After the interview he says that the information he has given would not change if he was allowed to include people in his homeland in the answers, nor does he foresee any political problems if he were to return.

In his replies, he mentions altogether twelve persons. How these were distributed over the various dimensions can be seen in Table 2. What is immediately noticeable is that there are only three persons, b, c, and e, mentioned in more than one dimension. Also, R could not mention any persons in dimensions 6 and 7 specifically addressing themselves to Muslim practices.

Table 2. People and dimensions in R's network

Dimensions: (1) talk about personal problems, (2) closeness, (3) conviviality, (4) work/study contacts, (5) practical problems, (6) going to the mosque, (7) significant believers

Persons	\multicolumn{7}{c}{Dimensions}
	1	2	3	4	5	6	7
a		x	x				
b		x	x				
c		x	x				
d		x					
e		x	x				
f			x				
g			x				
h			x				
i				x			
k				x			
l				x			
m				x			

In Figure 1, the relations between the persons mentioned by R, as perceived by R, are presented, as are some of their other characteristics. Thin lines represent acquaintances, thick lines that people know each other with a higher degree of familiarity.

It should be pointed out that R is not included in Figure 1. Instead, it depicts what may be called R's 'socially significant others'. Judging from the number of dimensions in which they were mentioned, some of these persons, in particular b but also c and e are obviously closer to R, and may be presumed to have a generally greater influence on the way that R develops a socially grounded knowledge, meaningfulness. Put differently, one may suggest that these persons have a greater significance for culture-building as witnessed by R's creation of meaningfulness.

This observation should not be confused with the notions of 'strong bonds' in network literature, but is also an attempt to discuss the quality of network links in a general manner.

In Table 3, each person's number of 'thick' and 'thin' relations with others are presented. From this information, one sees that two persons, g and h do not have very much to do with the others. They are, however, significant for R's leisure time activities. One is a Moroccan, the other an Iraqi, both born in Muslim contexts but not active Muslims in Sweden. In should be pointed out that R has not included these persons among those he feels close to, in spite of the fact that he only mentioned five such people and thus could have added another.

250 *Additional Themes for Future Research*

Figure 1. The interpreter: relations between socially significant others

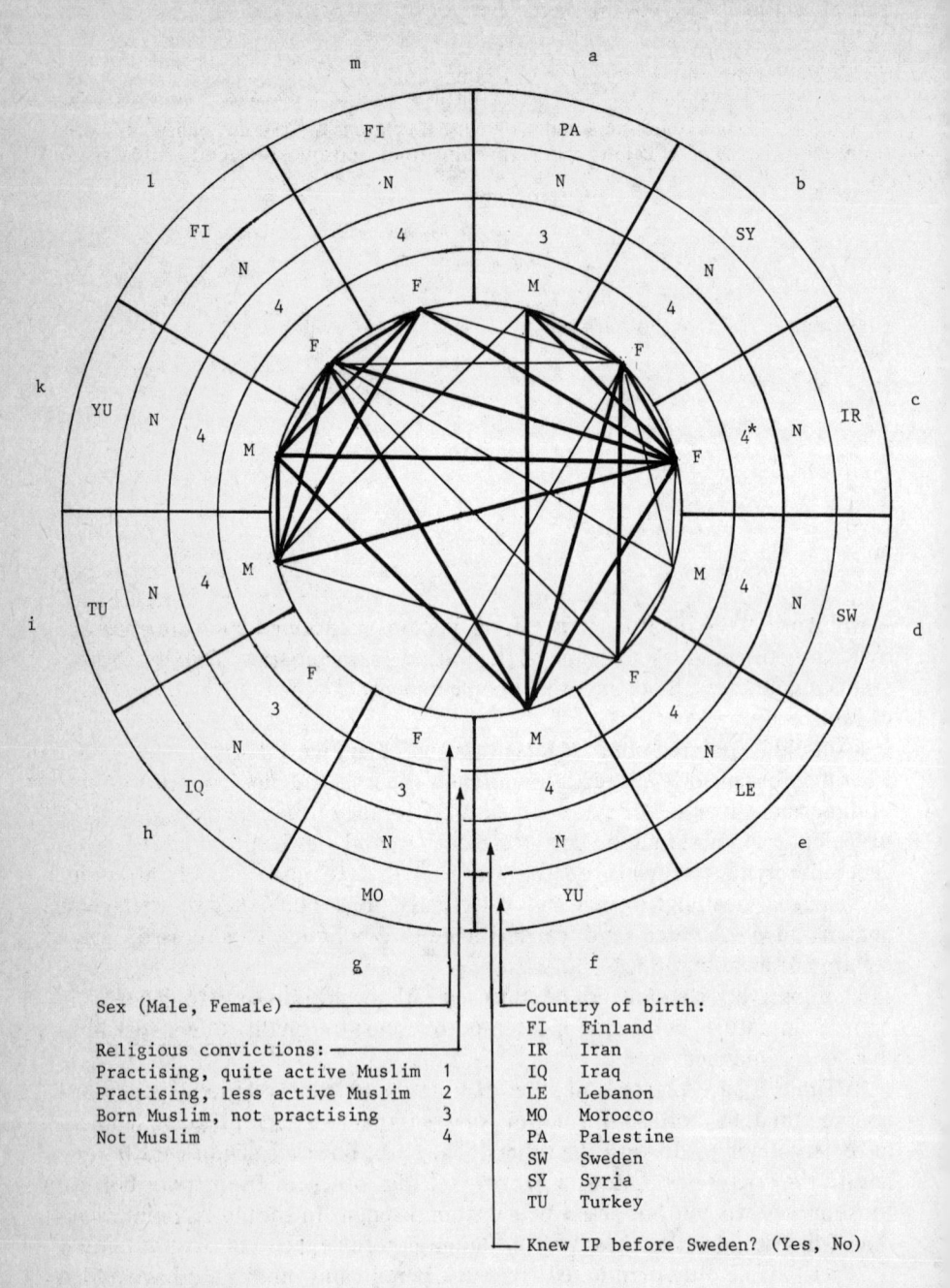

Sex (Male, Female)

Religious convictions:
Practising, quite active Muslim 1
Practising, less active Muslim   2
Born Muslim, not practising   3
Not Muslim   4

Country of birth:
FI Finland
IR Iran
IQ Iraq
LE Lebanon
MO Morocco
PA Palestine
SW Sweden
SY Syria
TU Turkey

Knew IP before Sweden? (Yes, No)

* Born Muslim, convert to Christianity

Table 3. The number of 'thick' and 'thin' relationships between persons in R's socially significant others

Persons	Thick relationships	Thin relationships
a	3	1
b	6	3
c	7	1
d	0	4
e	1	3
f	5	0
g	0	1
h	0	0
i	5	2
k	6	0
l	5	3
m	4	1

Another person, d, to whom R feels close, has very little interaction with others in the network. He is, however, aquainted with four of the others. A Swede, d, was raised as a Christian.

A Christian Lebanese-born woman, e, is a person to whom R both feels close and with whom there is considerable leisure-time interaction. She is closely (more so than is evident from the above information) related to the only person R has mentioned in three of the dimensions.

The remainder of the people in R's network all have fairly significant knowledge of each other. A prominent feature is that those R has mentioned in the dimension related to work (b, i, k, l, m) also have thick relations with others, such as c and f. The persons mentioned in the work dimensions also by and large have thick relations with each other.

The work dimension is obviously important in the attempt to account for the shape of R's network. R combines work as an interpreter, social welfare officer for immigrants, and immigrant teacher. Indeed, one may regard R's network as characteristic of an immigrant who has become involved in the professional assistance system for immigrants, and who has lodged a considerable part of his social existence in the friends and acquaintances he has made in this activity. This also helps to explain the strikingly large number of different countries of origin, the twelve persons representing nine different countries. The persons mentioned in more than one dimension, b, c, and e, despite not being those with whom R associates most during work, also belong in the same professional category as R, as witnessed also by the thick relations between these (with the exception of e, who is b's girl-friend) and those with whom R associates most during work.

One may also note, that of the twelve people mentioned, three were born in a Muslim context, but none of them is a practising Muslim.

What does R's network tell about cultural continuities? One observation is that country of origin or religion does not account for any significant features in

R's network. One may also suggest that the existence of only one Swedish-born person in R's network is a conspicuous feature, and as mentioned above is his wife from another Nordic country. But even though Swedes with one exception are not represented among R's socially significant others, R's existence in large measure reflects the social interaction which has emerged in activities which emanate in Swedish society from the professional activities directed towards immigrants.

Really strong social links may perhaps be lacking between R and other persons, which would help to account for why R does not feel that there are others he can talk to about personal problems. Likewise, his social anchorages do not give significant expression to what are often regarded as 'primordial' sentiments, for example ethnic and religious ones.

By and large, it appears that the culture-building processes in which R is involved lack a specificity related to the maintenance or development of specific cultural orientations, e.g. deriving from a specific country of origin or a specific faith. There is, perhaps, one exception: one may well suggest that R and his socially significant others devote some or considerable attention to the definition of what an immigrant existence in Sweden is all about, and thus also what Swedes really are all about.

The Student

S is a student in advanced university training, some thirty years old. He has been in Sweden for more than 10 years, and came here as a guest student. He lived together with a Swedish woman for several years, but he now lives alone.

He was born in Iran, and raised in a Shia Muslim context, but now declares himself a non-believer. When interviewed, he mentions persons a–f in the different dimensions (see Table 4).

Table 4. People and dimensions in S's network

Persons	Dimensions						
	1	2	3	4	5	6	7
a		x	x	x			
b		x		x			
c		x					
d			x				
e				x			
f				x			

One striking feature of Table 4 is that the persons mentioned are all within three dimensions. That he does not mention anyone in dimensions 6 and 7, those related to religion, may be less surprising, given his self-declared atheism. However, in spite of his advanced studies, which should have given him the time and opportunity to do so, he does not feel that he has developed any social relations with other students. Likewise, he does not think there is anyone he can approach for help in practical matters.

However, there is one person with whom he has a multi-stranded relationship, a, and b, c, and d are mentioned as people being close or providing emotional support. e and f are leisure-time friends.

In Figure 2, the relationships between S's friends are depicted. The dyadic character is striking. a and c each have relationships to other persons whereof one is the same, f, b and d have contacts with one other person each. e is not acquainted with any of the others. Otherwise, however, the relationships are of the 'thick' nature with the exception of the relationship between c and d.

There are three persons born in Iran in the network, and three persons born in Sweden. However, there is no clustering on the basis of country of origin. Indeed, one of the Iranian-born is not acquainted with the other two, but a Swedish-born person has a thin relationship with this Iranian-born and also a thick relationship with another Iranian-born.

Religious activities are also inconsequential issues in this context. Although the Iranian-born were raised in a Muslim context, they now all, according to S, are non-practising non-believers.

What may be said about this network in terms of culture-building? R is not immersed in a network of friends and mutual friends, but instead associates extensively with some specific people on an individual basis. With some of these he has a shared national origin, but these do not constitute themselves as an effective social entity. The Swedes are unacquainted with each other. The individualistic nature of S's network, in the sense that specific cultural traditions play no role in its shape, is perhaps illustrated by the fact that the individuals mentioned in more than one dimension, a and b, represent both different countries of origin and upbringing, but have a thick relationship with each other and are fairly close to R.

The Cleaner

Both R and S are religiously inactive persons. The case of T is completely different. T is a very devout person, who prays every day and who claims to participate whenever possible in organized religious activities in the mosque.

T was born in Turkey and is now a man slightly over thirty, married and with several children. He has been in Sweden approximately fifteen years and, as he himself describes it, was brought by his father to Sweden, the father having immigrated earlier. He grew up in the agricultural areas in the Konya province in Turkey, but in Sweden he has been occupied in the cleaning trade. He is presently unemployed.

A striking feature is the prominence of close relatives and an *imam* in his network of socially significant others. To simplify the following discussions, these persons have been indicated in Table 5, where the persons mentioned by T are matched by the dimensions in which they were mentioned. There are four

254 *Additional Themes for Future Research*

Figure 2.   The student: relations between socially significant others

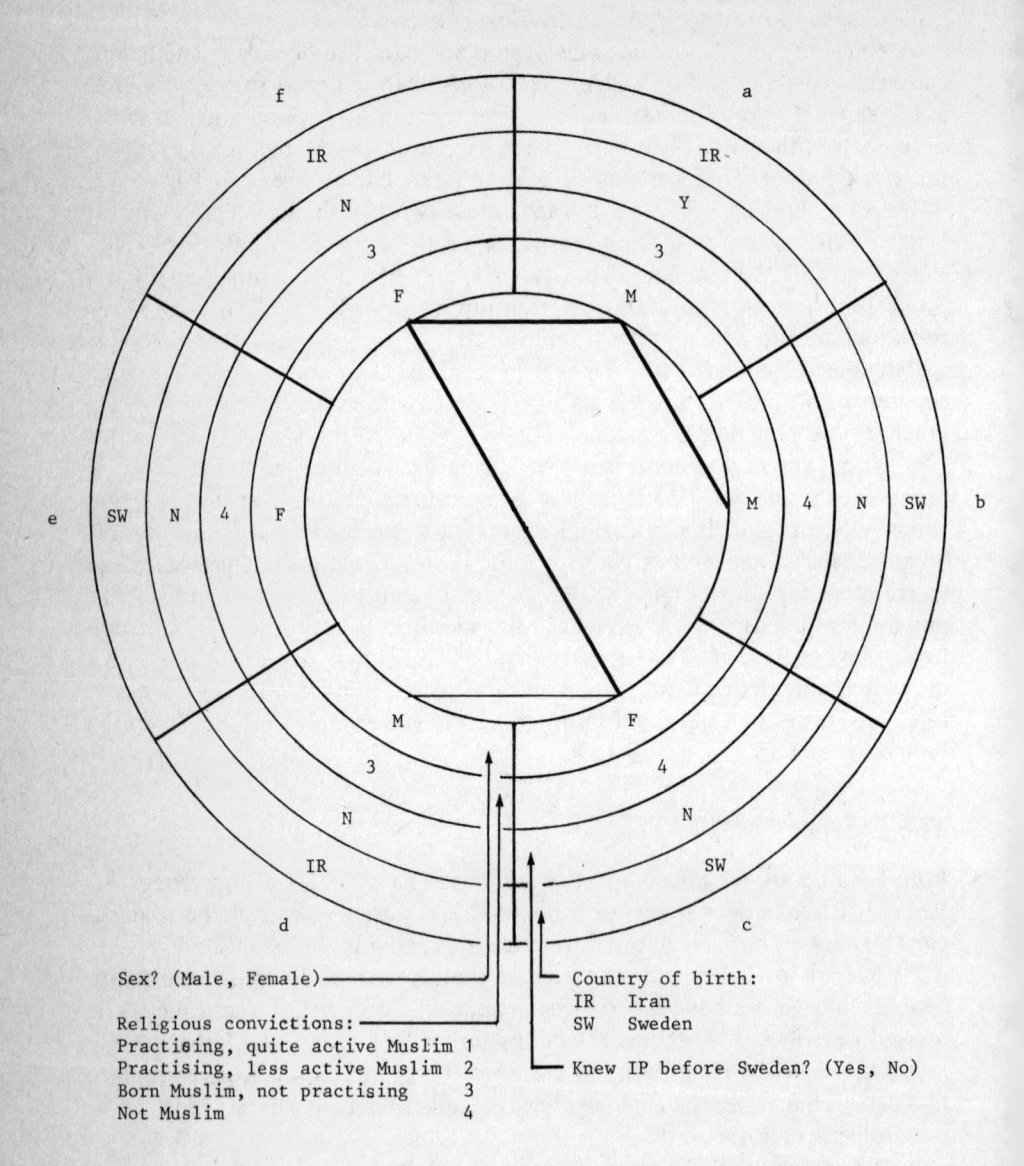

Sex? (Male, Female)

Religious convictions:
Practising, quite active Muslim   1
Practising, less active Muslim   2
Born Muslim, not practising   3
Not Muslim   4

Country of birth:
IR   Iran
SW   Sweden

Knew IP before Sweden? (Yes, No)

persons mentioned in several dimensions, one of them a, the *imam*, another d, the brother. However, b and c also belong in this category. The other relatives, g, h, i, are referred to only in the dimension concerning practical problems, and e and f only in the dimension concerning work. It may be mentioned that although T is presently unemployed, he may well — due to the structure of the job market for cleaners — have a fair relation to the job market, with sporadic jobs and also as an occasional helper to those presently employed.

Table 5. People and dimensions mentioned in T's network

Persons	Dimensions						
	1	2	3	4	5	6	7
a (*imam*)	x	x	x		x		x
b		x		x			
c		x	x				x
d (brother)		x		x	x		
e					x		
f					x		
g (father)					x		
h (sister)					x		
i (mother)					x		

The relations between the people in his network, as stated by T, is represented in Figure 3, and some of the characteristics of the individual people are also included. Several things are immediately recognizable. There are several people with ties reaching several others. In Table 6, this is computed. It should also be noted that there are no self-contained clusterings around, for example, the work interaction dimensions. Instead, the two persons mentioned only in this dimension, e and f, together have relationships with both T's brother, father, mother and sister (d, g, h, i) and also with b.

Table 6. The number of 'thick' and 'thin' relationships between persons in T's socially significant others

Persons	Thick relationships	Thin relationships
a	2	0
b	4	0
c	1	2
d	6	1
e	3	1
f	6	0
g	6	2
h	4	0
i	4	0

The only women named by T are his mother and sister. If one looks at country of origin, all persons in the network are Turks and Muslims. The degree

256 *Additional Themes for Future Research*

Figure 3. The cleaner: relations between socially significant others

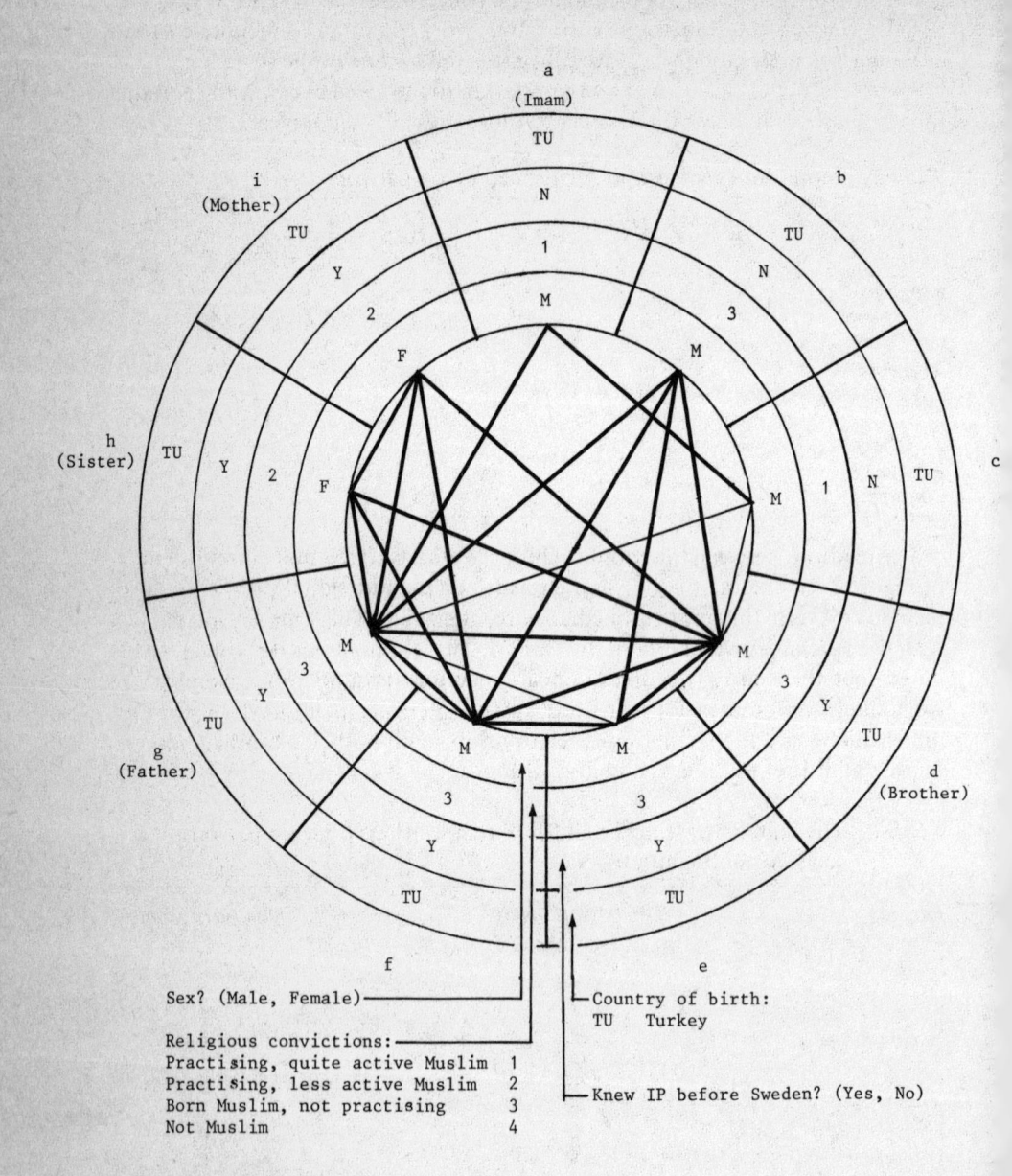

Sex? (Male, Female)

Religious convictions:
Practising, quite active Muslim   1
Practising, less active Muslim   2
Born Muslim, not practising   3
Not Muslim   4

Country of birth:
TU Turkey

Knew IP before Sweden? (Yes, No)

of attachment to Islams varies considerably however. Some, a and c, are actively religious people, the mother and sister (h and i) are practising Muslims, while b, d, e, f and g were born into a Muslim tradition but are now religiously inactive.

What may be adduced from the culture-building properties of T's socially significant others? Some suggestions are fairly obvious. It is firmly based in people from one sending country, and it has a pronounced component of relatives. There does not appear to be any significant reason to suggest that any persons in the network will introduce culture-building material from sources or experiences which are not fairly common to them all (overlooking gender divisions). T's network gives the impression of representing one derived from an ethnically organized 'community', where occupational and other roles are arranged along ethnic lines and where interactional contact with the surrounding society is limited. It may also be noted that the degree of religiousness also varies considerably between the persons in the network. However, differences in religiousness is seemingly no obstacle to thick relations between people, as witnessed by the link between a (the *imam*) and g (the father). It is thus tempting to suggest that religious observances, both with respect to the self-definition of the people concerned and the content of interaction, is not an immediate cause for reformative culture-building for people in this ethnic group. The Muslim component is an important part of its existence, and is taken for granted, although individual religiosity may perhaps vary to some extent.

The Educated Believer

U is an unmarried person from Bangladesh, who arrived in Sweden a few years ago and who is now engaged in a demanding education at university level. He is an actively religious person.

U's network of socially significant others contains quite a few persons, and is also fairly complex with respect to the relationships between these persons. In Table 7, the persons and the dimensions in which they were mentioned are presented.

The relationships between these people, as enumerated by U, are given in Figure 4. One can immediately recognize three separate clusters, one embracing persons within the arc starting with q and finishing with h, one including k–m and a third n–p. i is mentioned in two dimensions by U, but is fairly marginal in terms of the structure of the network, having a link to only one other person, albeit a strong one.

n–p represents a self-contained cluster of persons with which U interacts frequently in his studies. m is also a study friend, but with a contact (through U, as it happens), to a Chinese couple, k and l, with whom U has a convivial relationship.

The third cluster contains only actively religious people, some of them very

258 *Additional Themes for Future Research*

Table 7. People and dimensions mentioned in U's network

Persons	Dimensions						
	1	2	3	4	5	6	7
a		x	x	x	x		
b	x	x	x				x
c		x					
d		x				x	
e		x					
f					x		x
g							x
h				x			
i				x			
k		x					
l		x					
m				x			
n				x			
o				x			
p				x			
q						x	x
r						x	x
s						x	x

religious. In terms of the dimensions in which they have been mentioned by U, they divide themselves into a category of people born in Bangladesh, a–h, and one category of persons mentioned only in the context of the religious dimensions, q–s. One may note that there is a considerable linkage between all persons born in Bangladesh. There is also a considerable linkage between persons q–s and the Bangladeshis, although r, a Yugoslav-born, only has thin relationships with the others.

What may be said of the culture-building aspects of U's network? It clearly indicates the existence of four aspects of U's social being. His study mates and his convivial friends represent two of these. His relationships with Muslims are clearly of two kinds, one oriented towards persons from the same country of origin, and one more generalized. It is clearly the case that within this Muslim part of his social existence, there exists a cultural continuation directed towards a specific country of origin. In the immigrant situation, this orientation, with Islamic connotations, has to some extent merged with what other Muslim people have brought with them, or created in Sweden, but has also maintained a clear identity (as witnessed by the distribution of persons along the dimensions in U's account).

Figure 4. The educated believer: relations between socially significant others

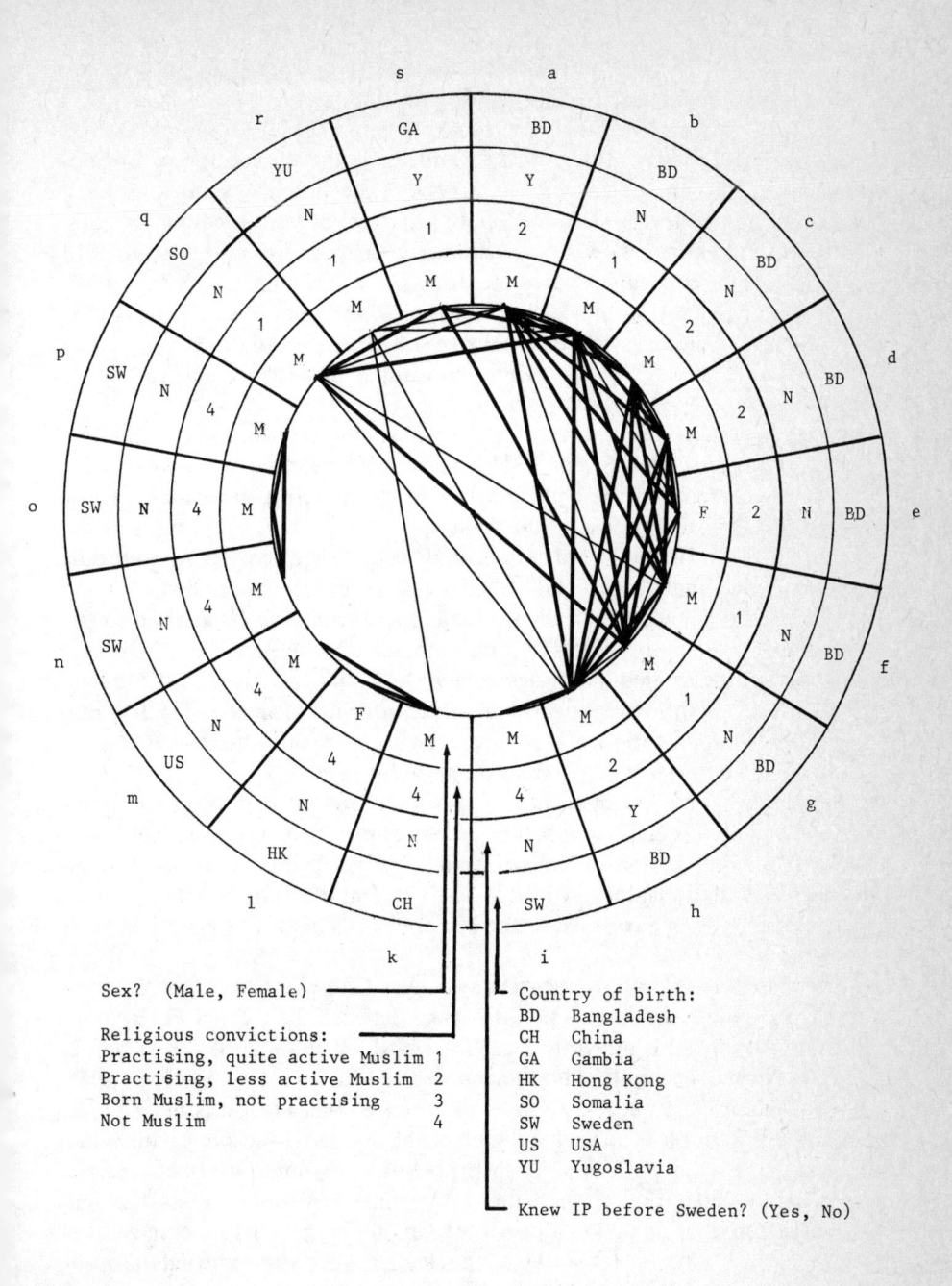

Sex? (Male, Female)

Religious convictions:
Practising, quite active Muslim 1
Practising, less active Muslim 2
Born Muslim, not practising 3
Not Muslim 4

Country of birth:
BD Bangladesh
CH China
GA Gambia
HK Hong Kong
SO Somalia
SW Sweden
US USA
YU Yugoslavia

Knew IP before Sweden? (Yes, No)

Structure and Meaning

What, if anything, do the observations which have been made about these persons' networks tell us about their relationship to the Islamic tradition? Are their networks, their social relationships, one thing; their meaning-creation with respect to Islam something altogether different? Or, is the argument which has run implicity through this article defensible: that their social relationships do indeed tell us something about the way they conceptualize Islam?

This phrasing of the issue immediately provokes at least a couple of additional questions. One is how mass media or influences from other sources of 'institutional culture' may be accounted for in a model with a heavy emphasis on inter-personal relationships. The other is to what extent the attributes of the persons in an individual's network really makes it possible to discern aspects of that individual's way of regarding life, for example, how the Islamic tradition is viewed.

Institutional culture is naturally a powerful source of meaning-creation in a country like present-day Sweden. This, however, may not present a major problem with respect to the ambitions of this article. In fact, it may well be argued that there is by now a wealth of support for the thesis that mass media and other forms of institutional culture may well expose people to a multitude of messages, but that their social effectiveness is severely limited where these messages are not mediated in inter-personal relationships. In a variety of disciplines, this is now more or less a commonplace observation. The 'two-stage theory' of how mass media messages reach the public, pointing to the crucial role of a kind of information broker in introducing them into small group discussions, as well as the work of Kurt Lewin on small group discussions as vehicles of behavioural change, are classics in this regard.

This means that institutional culture does not represent a phenomenon external to the model of social relationships and meaning-creation presented here. It may well have an important mirror function, but being mediated through inter-personal relationships, it will also, to the extent that it has reached persons effectively, be possible to trace in the social characteristics of people in their networks.

How do the networks above suggest anything with respect to the interpretation these people make of Islam? The difference between the cleaner (T) and the educated believer (U) is illustrative in this regard. When interviewed, T and U gave very different accounts of how an immigrant Muslim solved problems relating to an Islamic existence. The cleaner did not find this a major issue. To him, there was a very simple solution to all such problems, to ask the *imam* who knew, he explained, the answers to all such problems. The similarities between the persons mentioned by the cleaner in the network interview also suggests that such a limited differentiation makes it possible to maintain this fairly uncomplicated attitude. In a sense, the enclave in which the cleaner lives is so strong that the traditional authority of the *imam* is not challenged from within.

The educated believer, on the other hand, gave long, discursive answers to questions of how an immigrant Muslim solved problems relating to an Islamic existence. To him, it was very important that the right interpretation of the Quran be made since all answers are contained in the Quran. One had to be very careful to ensure that the people who interpreted the Quran knew what they were doing since misinterpretations are common. In fact, these very issues had prompted him to study Arabic at university.

The educated believer's thoughtful and elaborate answers to the issues of the Islamic tradition in the immigrant situation are readily understood in the context of the variety of Muslims with whom he associates. In his network, there are Muslims from three continents, representing even more nations and languages. For those like the educated believer who wish to create a Muslim community in Sweden, the interpretative stance becomes a necessity.

Conclusion

In this paper it has been argued that the variety and fluidity of European migration forces a resharpening of some of the instruments of the anthropologist's tool box. In particular, concepts such as culture must be given a more precise and methodologically operative definition. The argument here has also suggested that perhaps more person-centred ethnographies may be advantageous, at least in some sorts of inquiry.

The empirical material introduced, dealing with immigrants of a Muslim background, has attempted to show the viability of linking network data not so much to socio-structural as to culture-building concerns. The premise for this has been that 'the social' and 'the cultural' are in some respects to be seen as encodings of each other, or one permitting as well as reducing the likelihood of certain developments in the other.

Observations from the case material clearly indicate that a Muslim background in itself may be fairly insignificant as far as the migrant's situation in Sweden is concerned. The two cases of practising Muslims also show that Islam may impinge very differently on the social and cultural lives of believers.

The mode of inquiry demonstrated here can be put to several uses. It serves well as an exploratory device, where a limited input of resources can produce an initial understanding of the social and cultural issues of a group or category of people, and thus give a more focused direction to a subsequent investigation. This same economical approach could also be useful in longitudinal inquiries. Changes over time in the composition of the socially effective others can be systematically observed with limited research input.

Typological and theoretical concerns also raise significant issues. Is it possible to construct typologies, and hence move towards an understanding of modalities? The answer to this question relates to another — is it possible to arrive at a more systematic understanding of the relationship between culture, meaning-building, on the one hand, and social relationships, as depicted in the form above, on the other? It is anticipated that work along these lines will lead to a better understanding of migrant situations.

Note

I wish to thank Christer Norström for able assistance with the data collection for a project on Muslim immigrants in Sweden (see the section on 'The Islamic Presence in Sweden').

References

Bernhard, H.R. and Killworth, P.D. 1973. On the Social Structure of an Ocean-Going Research Vessel and Other Important Things. *Social Science Research* 1973:145–84.
Geertz, C. 1973. *The Interpretation of Cultures* . New York: Basic Books.
Hughes, E.C. 1961. *Students' Cultures and Perspectives*. Lawrence: University of Kansas Law School.
Kapferer, B. 1972. *Strategy and Transaction in an African Factory*. Manchester: Manchester University Press.
Lithman, Y.G. 1983. Pitching a Tent in Suburbia: Anthropologists' Problems on Home Turf. Paper presented at a Seminar on Qualitative Methods, Madrid University. *CEIFO document*. Stockholm: CEIFO, University of Stockholm.
────── 1986. Analyzing Variation. *Ethnos* 1986:259–84.
Mitchell, J.C. (Ed.) 1969. *Social Networks and Urban Situations*. Manchester: Manchester University Press.
White, H.C., Boorman, S.A. and Breiger, R.L. 1976. Social Structure from Multiple Networks. *American Journal of Sociology* 81:730–80.

16
Three European Intellectuals as Converts to Islam:
Cultural Mediators or Social Critics?

Tomas Gerholm

The number of Muslims in western Europe is steadily increasing. The major part of this growth can be understood as a simple consequence of international migration. For various reasons, people from the 'House of Islam' arrive here bringing their religious baggage. Numerically much less significant — but for a student of culture perhaps more interesting — are the Europeans who adopt the religion of the immigrants. In the well-known manner of converts, they often become more royalistic than the king. But it also happens that they bring an inquisitive mind to their new religion interpreting it in new ways. Thus they may contribute to the continuous evolution of Islam helping to mould it to fit the conditions of contemporary European society. Will they also help us, who are not Muslims, to understand Islam better? Will they have an impact on the development of Islam in its countries of origin? These are the questions to which I hope to suggest answers, by considering the cases of three European intellectuals who have embraced Islam. They are the Swedish painter Ivan Aguéli (1869–1917), the Polish–Jewish journalist Leopold Weiss (1900–), and the French philosopher and politician Roger Garaudy (1913–). Conversion to Islam is thus not only a recent phenomenon. I have avoided a concentration on the present because it easily deviates into sensationalism and makes such conversion look like little more than one of the transient fads and foibles of the day, thereby perhaps overshadowing the points of theoretical interest. It is, of course, debatable how representative these cases are. Still, they raise questions that might be pursued in further research.

After discussing the personal background to their conversion, as described by themselves, I move on to features of Islam that were of central importance to these men and which make their choice, in retrospect at least, seem logical. I also discuss how they understand the concept of conversion as applied to their own cases. Leaving their own motives aside, I suggest some conditions for successful conversions, that is not only having a conversion experience but being able to maintain a new religious belief. Finally, I examine their activities as Muslims and try to show that as Westerners they seem to be condemned to carry on a dialogue with their original cultural heritage, never really — except perhaps in one case — becoming integral parts of their adopted religious tradition. I begin, however, with a brief review of the social phenomenon of recent European conversion to Islam.

No one knows how many Muslim converts there are in Western Europe, but it is probably safe to say that they constitute a larger category than most people realize. Let us take France for example. France has a total Muslim population of approximately 2 or perhaps close to 3 million. Islam is thus the second biggest religion in France, even if one were to regard Protestantism as a religion on its own. The estimates of the number of converts range from approximately 50,000 (Krieger-Krynicki 1985:135, Lamand 1986:29) to at least 200,000 according to official Muslim spokesmen in Paris (Rocher and Cherqaoui 1986:7). Even the lower of these figures is a significant number, and it is steadily growing.

Both journalists and researchers are paying more and more attention to this phenomenon. *Le Nouvel Observateur*, in its edition for 7-13 February 1986, carried a dossier on Islam in France dealing mainly with the Islam of the immigrants but also devoting a couple of pages to that of the converts. Some illustrious names are mentioned: Maurice Béjart, the choreographer (who has told the story of his conversion to Shi'a Islam in his autobiography, *Un instant dans la vie d'autrui*, published in 1979); Michel Chodkiewicz, director of the publishing house Editions du Seuil, for three decades a follower of the Sufi tradition within Islam, translator of and commentator on two of its masters: Ibn al-Arabi and Abd al-Qadir; Roger Garaudy, for many years a leading figure within the French Communist Party and a prolific writer on philosophical themes. As is evident both from the material in *Le Nouvel Observateur* and, especially, from a recent book (Rocher and Cherqaoui 1986), the conversions are not at all limited to intellectual circles. Islam recruits new believers from all levels of society and for various reasons, pragmatic as well as spiritual ones, of course. Among the intellectuals, not only in France but also in Switzerland and England, the encounter with the writings of René Guénon — a major French metaphysician, savant of many religions and towards the end of his life a Muslim, living in Cairo until his death in 1951 — has often been of crucial importance.

In Great Britain there are a number of intellectuals who have embraced Islam, most frequently in its Sufi form. Names such as James Dickie, Gai Eaton, and Martin Lings could be mentioned. The first and the last of these are prominent scholars of Islam, while Gai Eaton is a writer (see, for instance, his book *Islam and the Destiny of Man* published in 1985) associated with the Islamic Cultural Centre in London. On a more popular level one finds Sufi brotherhoods attracting many young people, often with a background in left-wing politics (Rocher and Cherqaoui 1986: 147-8).

This political background is even more obvious in the case of the Muslim community in Spanish Granada. In the one-time Arab quarters of Albaicín, overlooking Alhambra, a group of 700 young Muslim converts have gathered to form an almost self-sufficient community dedicated to the 'return of Islam to Andalusia'. The majority of these converts seem to consist of former left-wing activists, and their version of Islam has quite a political ring (see Rocher and Cherqaoui 1986: 175-86).

Whereas Switzerland has been the home of a number of European Sufis — Frithjof Schuon and Titus Burckhardt, to mention only the best known — West German converts seem to favour a more orthodox type of Islam (Rocher and Cherqaoui 1986:8). In Denmark, there is an active group of followers of al-Ahmadiyya. Not much is known about the Muslim sector in the Swedish community, except that it is growing. A few authors — among them Gunnar Ekelöf, perhaps the greatest Swedish poet of this century — have taken an interest in Sufism without ever entering a *tariqa*, a Sufi brotherhood. A new phenomenon that has attracted much attention in the media is a small number of converts to orthodox Islam. Swedish women appearing in traditional Islamic garb and a Swedish man entering a Saudi competition in Quran recital: this is something quite different from a bookish interest in Sufism that may not have any public consequences. Some sources claim that Stockholm has nearly a thousand converts, but this figure is probably much too high.

From Ivan Aguéli to Abdul Hadi al-Maghrabi

Ivan Aguéli has belatedly become recognized as one of the forerunners of modernism in Swedish art, inspired by Cézanne and Gauguin. His paintings were produced mainly during two periods of his life, in 1890-95 and in 1911-17. The sixteen 'empty' years in the middle of his life were the years of his most intense activities as an anarchist, anti-vivisectionist and religious seeker.

Aguéli was born in 1869 in the small Swedish town of Sala and he died forty-eight years later in Barcelona, run over by a train. Most of his life was spent abroad, Paris being the centre to which he always returned after shorter or longer journeys to Egypt and India. When he first arrived in Paris in 1890 on a Swedish grant for painters, he was already deep into religious studies. To this was added the Anarchist sympathies of the intellectuals with whom he associated in Paris, so that he soon described himself as a 'Swedenborgian Anarchist' (Gauffin 1940:111). In 1894 he was arrested for complicity in an Anarchist conspiracy. He spent several months in prison awaiting trial, 'le procès des trente', in which he was finally acquitted but some of the others were given sentences of up to twenty years. Aguéli's letters from the Mazas prison to a Finnish friend in Paris indicate that this was the time when he began gravitating towards Islam. Upon his release he left France for a first visit to Egypt which did not last more than a few months. Back in Paris he continued his religious studies. His formal conversion did not take place until a few years later, probably in 1898. In early 1899 he departed for India in order to study "the impact of Islam on other races than the Arab one" (letter to his beloved Marie Huot, a poetess and a dedicated anti-vivisectionist, in Gauffin 1941:61). He was very impressed with what he found, summing it up (with some self-irony) in the same letter: "As you see, I have become a fanatic Muslim . . ." (Gauffin 1941:62).

Madame Huot, whose jealousy knew no bounds, forced him to come back to Europe both by cutting his financial supplies and by letting him know that the French were about to introduce bullfighting: he was needed at home to help stop it. With mixed feelings Aguéli returned to Paris to do what he could to avert the threat. On June 4 1900, he and Madame Huot waited outside the bullring at Deuil for the corrida to begin. When the bullfighters' landau approached, Aguéli pulled a gun and fired two shots, missing the matador but injuring (lightly) the bandillero. On account of his 'idealism', he escaped any serious consequences of his action.

The following year, in 1901, he met a young Italian doctor, Enrico Insabato, who shared Aguéli's interest in the Islamic part of the world but perhaps more for political than for purely religious reasons. Together they worked out a plan to settle in Egypt in order to work for a *rapprochement* between what was best in East and West. A couple of years later they were both in Cairo, and on 22 May 1904 the first issue of a weekly newspaper, *Il Convito/An-Nadi*, was published. It was bilingual, each issue having both an Italian and an Arabic section which did not completely mirror each other. Aguéli seems to have done most of the editorial work. He was also a frequent contributor to both the Italian and the Arabic parts using one or the other of his two pseudonyms, 'Abdul Hadi al-Maghrabi', his real name as a Muslim, and, less modestly, 'Dante'.

The first issue carried an editorial statement signed by Enrico Insabato but in all probability it was the work of both men. The purpose of the newspaper was to work towards an alliance of the good forces in both 'Arabia' and Europe. True progress in the East would only be possible if the Muslims were able to revert to the Islamic sources of their civilization and to refrain from slavishly aping the West.

> Thus I am determined to let Europe know the true Islam and to try with all my might to prevent a new kind of Crusade, whereof certain fanatics are dreaming. On the other hand, I wish, in the interest of all civilization, that Islam be pure and strong. I am also determined to let the Muslims know the real Europe, the great qualities of which no one would dispute. (*Il Convito*, 22 May 1904, p. 1).

By "the true Islam" Insabato probably meant Sufism, for this was a topic that his collaborator Abdul Hadi was going to devote himself to in many articles. Besides religious themes in a narrow sense, the paper was also concerned with the great political questions of the day arguing for a greater role for Italy in the Arab world. The implicit criticism of British rule in Egypt earned *Il*

Convito both friends and foes. Single issues of the paper found its way to many corners of the Arab world, including Yemen, and contributed to the goodwill which Italy enjoyed in many Arab quarters. The real ruler of Egypt at this time, Lord Cromer, was not amused, if one is to believe Aguéli's letters which make many hints at the difficulties created by the British authorities. After a few years *Il Convito* was forced to cease publication. In 1909, Ivan Aguéli returned to Paris and Marie Huot. He continued to publish articles in the French press under his Muslim name, and it was through his mediation that René Guénon, in 1912, was initiated into a Sufi order (Laurant 1985:18). Aguéli's return to Paris coincided with his return to painting. But that is another story.

From Leopold Weiss to Muhammad Asad

Leopold Weiss was born in 1900. His family lived in the Polish city of Lwów, then part of the Austrian Empire. In deference to a family line of rabbis, his parents — although not themselves religious in any deeper sense than by habit — gave Leopold a solid Jewish education that seemed to destine him for a rabbinical career. But quite early he began to turn away from Judaism:

> In spite of all this budding religious wisdom, or maybe because of it, I soon developed a supercilious feeling toward many of the premises of the Jewish faith. To be sure, I did not disagree with the teaching of moral righteousness so strongly emphasized throughout the Jewish scriptures, nor with the sublime God-consciousness of the Hebrew Prophets — but it seemed to me that the God of the Old Testament and the Talmud was unduly concerned with the ritual by means of which his worshippers were supposed to worship Him. It also occurred to me that this God was strangely preoccupied with the destinies of one particular nation, the Hebrews. The very build-up of the Old Testament as a history of the descendants of Abraham tended to make God appear not as the creator and sustainer of all mankind but, rather, as a tribal deity adjusting all creation to the requirements of a 'chosen people' . . . (Asad 1980:55–6).

Leopold drifted into a "matter-of-fact rejection of all institutional religion" (*ibid.*: 56). After World War I, he took up studies of philosophy and history of art at the university of Vienna, but without great energy. He wanted to become a writer and this wish led to his first break with his family. Lean years followed in Berlin where he tried to establish himself as a freelance writer, had some success as an assistant to the film director F.W. Murnau, and finally entered the newspaper world as a reporter.

In 1922, a close relative invited him to Jerusalem. He went by way of Alexandria, the Nile Delta, across the Suez Canal and Sinai to Palestine and Jerusalem. His very first encounter with Arabs made a deep impression on him and to this was added many experiences during his subsequent stay in Jerusalem. During this time he began writing occasional articles for the prestigious (but desperately poor) *Frankfurter Zeitung*. This was the beginning of a career as that newspaper's special Middle Eastern correspondent that was to last several years and then lead on to a similar position at the *Neue Zürcher Zeitung* and other papers.

Weiss travelled extensively in the Middle East, studied its history and its present situation, and felt both attracted by the central features of the Islamic way of life, as he understood it, and repelled by what he perceived as the continuous loss of faith and growing infatuation with the West. It was during a heated discussion of this theme with a provincial governor in Afghanistan that the latter suddenly said: "But you are a Muslim . . . only you don't know it yourself." (Asad 1980:293). Eight months later, in 1926, when Weiss was back in Berlin and newly married, he converted formally to Islam. The decisive event was an experience that he felt proved beyond doubt that the Quran was not just a book written by a wise man but really the word of God. His wife converted shortly after, and they set out on their first pilgrimage to Mecca.

Only a few days after their arrival in Mecca, Elsa Weiss died from an unusual tropical disease. Leopold stayed on in the country and gradually established close links with members of the royal family, especially Prince Feisal but also the king himself, Ibn Saud.

From then on, Leopold Weiss or Muhammad Asad, as he is now known, associated himself with several attempts to further the cause of Islam by trying to establish the social and political conditions for a truly Muslim life. High hopes were pinned on Saudi Arabia, but Asad was ultimately disillusioned. He also looked, for a time, towards the Sanusiyya in Libya. But it was the creation of Pakistan as an Islamic state that more than anything else provided him with a possibility to devote himself to this task. In 1952 he even became Pakistan's ambassador to the UN. Still, his greatest contribution to the cause of Islam may very well have been books such as the already mentioned autobiography, *The Road to Mecca* (1980, first edition 1954), and *Islam at the Crossroads* (1982, first edition 1934), to name only two of them. After a long life outside of Europe, he now lives in Portugal.

From Roger Garaudy to Raja Garoudi

In the present generation, Roger Garaudy is, no doubt, *le doyen des convertis célèbres* (Rocher and Cherqaoui 1986: 191). He was born in Marseille in 1913 and was a leading member of the French Communist Party for more than two decades. In 1945 he became a member of the Central Committee and in 1956 he entered the Polit-bureau, where he remained for twelve years. He was also a member of parliament for almost two decades. From the early 1950s onwards — until the rise of Louis Althusser in the middle of the 1960s — he was the leading ideological spokesman of the party. After criticizing the attitude of the French Communist leadership for being silently supportive of the Soviet invasion of Czechoslovakia in 1968, he was excluded, to begin with, from the Central Committee at the beginning of 1970 and, a few months later, from the party itself.

Garaudy was the main defender of Marxist orthodoxy in the debates on existentialism raging in France after the end of World War II. After Stalin's death in 1953, Garaudy began to take a more positive attitude to existentialism when he viewed it in the light of the early humanistic writings of Marx. These were beginning to be more widely known outside specialist circles at approximately the same time. In several books from the late 1950s, especially *Perspectives de l'homme* (1959), he develops a kind of Marxist humanism open to a dialogue not only with existentialism but also with phenomenology and neo-Thomist personalism. This new ecumenical attitude led, in the 1960s, to a special exchange of views with Catholic intellectuals, for example in *De l'anathème au dialogue* (1965).

After the break with the Communist Party, his intellectual home for three decades, Garaudy intensified his 'dialogues' with other ideological currents. In a series of works, *Paroles d'homme* (1975), *Le projet espérance* (1976), *Pour un dialogue des civilisations* (1977) — with the significant subtitle: *L'Occident est un accident* — and *Appel aux vivants* (1979), Garaudy develops the theme that western civilization has become a destructive machine annihilating the contributions of other civilizations to the human project and in the course of this process also losing sight of its own contribution. By using the collective experience of mankind, Garaudy hopes to launch a 'planetary' attempt to create new relations between man and nature, man and society, man and the divine.

Then, in 1981, Garaudy both presented his candidacy for the French presidency and took the step of converting to Islam. This new phase of his development was manifested in books like *Promesses de l'Islam* (1981a), *L'Islam habite notre avenir* (1981b), and *Biographie du XXe siécle* (1985) with the subtitle: *Le testament philosophique de Roger Garaudy*.

Since his conversion, Garaudy has been a celebrated guest in many Islamic countries. He was invited to give a speech on the millennial anniversary, in 1983, of the founding of al-Azhar, the foremost university in the Islamic world (although there were also indignant reactions against his unorthodox views).[1] Less grandiose, perhaps, but equally significant was the selection of him to give the main speech at the conference of European Muslims (i.e. mainly converts) in Granada in 1985.

The reasons for conversion

Looking now at the reasons given by our three converts for their conversion, one finds many common themes but also quite different accents. Let us return to the already quoted letter by Abdul Hadi to Madame Huot.

> I have been once to their mosque [that of the Tamils] and I realized that these men have much to teach me. In their presence I feel how my tenseness subsides, how my anxiety and violent impulses are soothed. These expressions of peace, serenity and openness we have never encountered in Europe. One must be a rigid 'intellectuel' not to be healed among these men. . .

> The foundation of Islam is very beautiful. It is neither a religion nor a civilization like the others. It is a state of mind that, one day, I wish to analyze. This state of mind has created a set of ceremonies, customs, manners and preferences that in the beginning seem arbitrary, childish, lacking in order, but that actually, if one studies their psychology, their causes, their origin, their hidden meaning, appear as evolutionary phases, consequences and expressions of the same mentality. (Gauffin (1941:62).

Something similar to what Aguéli experienced is also what Asad comes back to, time and again, in his *The Road to Mecca*. Islam is present in every gesture, and every gesture is a sign of something that he feels modern European man has lost. But Asad has also recourse to something else, and that is a sort of rational argument which is very characteristic of contemporary apologetics on behalf of Islam:

> It not only teaches us that all life is essentially a unity — because it proceeds from the Divine Oneness — but it shows us also the practical way how every one of us can reproduce, within the limits of his individual, earthly life, the unity of Idea and Action both in his existence and in his consciousness. To attain that supreme goal of life man is, in Islam, not compelled to renounce the world; no austerities are required to open a secret door to spiritual purification; no pressure is exerted upon the mind to believe incomprehensible dogmas in order that salvation be secured. Such demands are utterly foreign to Islam: for it is neither a mystical doctrine nor a philosophy. It is simply a programme of life in accord with the 'laws of nature' which God has decreed upon His creation; and its supreme achievement is a complete coordination of the spiritual and the material aspects of human existence. In the teachings of Islam, both these aspects are not only 'reconciled' to each other in the sense of leaving no inherent conflict between the bodily and the moral existence of man, but the fact of their coexistence and actual inseparability is *insisted* upon as the natural basis of life. (Asad 1982: 17–18).

Garaudy also touches upon this theme of the equilibrium, harmony and unity of Islam in many passages of his many books, for instance in this one: "[I]t would be contrary to Islam, the religion of 'unity' to dissociate contemplation from action, interior from exterior" (Garaudy 1981a: 47). But the main theme in Garaudy's argument is different:

> For three centuries the Occident has rejected this third heritage: the Arab-Islamic heritage which could have and still can not only reconciliate it with the other wisdoms of the Earth, but also help it to become conscious of the human and the divine dimensions from which it has severed itself by realizing onesidedly its will to power over nature and over man. For Islam . . . has not only integrated, fertilized and spread the oldest and the highest cultures — those of China and India, of Persia and Greece, of Alexandria and Bysantium — from the Chinese Sea to the Atlantic. To disintegrated empires and dying civilizations it has also brought the spirit of a new collective life. Islam has given men and their societies their truly human and divine dimensions of transcendence and community. And on the foundation of this simple and strong faith there has flourished a renewal of the sciences and the arts, of prophetic wisdom and law. The first renaissance of the Occident took place in Muslim Spain four centuries before that in Italy. It could be a universal renaissance (Garaudy 1981a: 19).

With Aguéli it is the experience of the Islamic way of life that seems to be the main motivating force. This is also very powerful in the case of Muhammad Asad, but he adds a rational and almost profane argument for Islam based on its alleged congruity with Nature. Finally, in the case of Garaudy, it is obvious that he has found in Islam a model for the kind of synthesizing dialogue that he has been engaging in for thirty years.

Garaudy's image of Islam as model for a possible synthesis of previous civilizations is very much in accordance with the Islamic image of itself as a synthesis and correction of the previously revealed religions. This claim is one of the great strengths of Islam in its encounter with both Judaism and Christianity: the latter two are in a sense contained and superseded by the former. In the case of Christianity, one might venture the hypothesis that the longstanding aversion for Islam — not to say hatred of it — has something to do with the feeling that Islam has done symbolic violence to the Christian faith by appropriating *parts* of it into its own dogma (just like Christianity itself did with Judaism). To the medieval mind the Islamic conquest of the Holy City must have been a fitting symbol of this state of affairs.

A convert's image of western civilization

A common thread running through the three men's verdict on western civilization is its allegedly one-sided materialism. Western civilization is viewed as a partial development of man's potential resources, whereas — in principle, if not in fact — Islam offers a more harmonious unfolding of the inherent possibilities of life. According to this view of the matter, Islam represents the synthesizing movement of the human spirit while Christianity and the civilization to which it has given rise stand for an aberration leading to an overdevelopment of the material side of life and a corresponding underdevelopment of the spiritual side. Many converts, not only the three I have selected here for special scrutiny, have felt the appeal of precisely this synthesizing movement of the third great 'Abrahamic' religion.

If one tries to view the matter as a detached observer (to the extent that this is at all possible), it may strike one that today western civilization is actually much more of a synthesis than present-day Islam. Returning to the golden age of Islamic civilization, when the heritage of the Greeks was salvaged and being added to, Islamic civilization played a role that in some ways reminds us of the present situation in Europe and the United States — cultures which, among many other things, also are museums of other civilizations. It is here that the various other civilizations of the planet receive some kind of hearing and where they can always expect to find an audience, even if marginal. It is here that there will always be a minority of enthusiasts ready to plead their cause. Few other civilizations have taken such an interest, and such a hermeneutic interest at that, in other civilizations as western civilization has done. Or, to bring men back in, few, if any, other civilizations have had so many individuals so inclined to try to understand a foreign system of beliefs and practices as is the case with Western civilization. This attitude has been wedded to a position of strength, no doubt about that, and a conviction of the ultimate superiority of western culture. It is this situation of an expanding centre drawing into its orbit a culturally heterogeneous periphery that has created the structural foundation for a category of intellectuals, in both centre and periphery, criticizing and opposing the dominant culture. In this way Europe and the United States have become societies where an unprecendentedly large proportion of their intellectual elites are questioning the very basis of their own societies.

The meaning of 'conversion'

So far I have spoken as if 'conversion' were an unproblematic concept. It is not. Rocher and Cherqaoui (1986: 20) quote an interview with Eva de Vitray-Meyerovitch, an intimate savant of the Sufi tradition: "One does not convert to Islam. One embraces a religion that contains all the others." On the strength of their many interviews, they observe that the majority of the European converts "question strongly the term 'conversion': this transition is experienced as a continuity, a growth, a fulfilment . . . " (*ibid*.: 21). This is also how at least two of our three converts seem to look at their own lives. For Aguéli, Swedenborg remains a constant reference and in his letters he often praises the Muslims for practising the Christian virtues more faithfully than the Christians themselves do. And Garaudy (1985: 265) goes to great lengths in defending himself against the suspicion that he has made a sharp bend on his road through life:

> The vocation of all my life was to seek the point where the act of artistic creation, the political act and the act of faith were one and the same. I have found, in Islam, a faith that is at the same time a religion of beauty and an ethics for action. I have entered into its fold without rejecting anything of what Jesus had brought into my life . . ., nor of what Marxism had taught me about analysis of society and effective action in society . . . Islam does not appear in my life as a rupture, but as a fulfilment.

Muhammad Asad's case is more ambiguous:

> Sometimes it seems to me that I can almost see the lives of two men when I look back at my life. But, come to think of it, are those two parts of my life really so different from one another — or was there perhaps, beneath all the outward differences of form and direction, always a unity of feeling and a purpose common to both? (Asad 1980: 46)

Muhammad Asad shows us in this passage what we already know, namely that each life, each autobiography as well as each biography, is a reconstructed life. With a little extra effort, Asad would probably have been able to show the logic behind the transformation of Leopold Weiss into Muhammad Asad: *plus ça change, plus ça reste la même chose*. The past exists for the sake of the present. All three authors invent a past that is compatible with their present lives. Two of them invent a continuity while the third holds the possibility open, at least, that a sharp break has occurred.

There may be a sociological reason for this difference. Aguéli and Garaudy have continued to live among people who knew them from the time before the great change. They still have a need to explain themselves, whereas Muhammad Asad alone broke radically with his past spending half a lifetime outside of Europe among the people of his adopted faith. It is, perhaps, symptomatic that Ivan Aguéli never became Abdul Hadi but for special purposes and that Roger Garaudy will never be Raja Garoudi except under very particular circumstances. Leopold Weiss, on the other hand, effectively became Muhammad Asad. These speculations lead us on to another aspect of conversion.

The social basis of conversion

It is tempting to seek sociological explanations of the conversions of Aguéli, Weiss and Garaudy. Not that the stated reasons for their conversions are not, on one level, quite enough. But even if one is not trying to explain away a sincerely felt religious conviction, the social scientist will always be interested in looking for the social conditions of a successfully maintained religious conviction. It is one thing to adopt and hold a belief privately, another one to maintain it publicly. As Berger and Luckmann (1967: 158) have said: "To have a conversion experience is nothing much. The real thing is to be able to keep on taking it seriously: to retain a sense of its plausibility."

The converts we are dealing with here have certainly faced an uncomprehending, if not openly hostile, audience. Making one's newly acquired religious conviction known to persons to whom one is bound by multiple ties requires both courage and a certain recklessness. It also exposes one to sanctions of various sorts. Rocher and Cherqaoui (1986) found a couple of examples of converts who had felt they must keep their new faith secret, in order not to hurt a close relative. Extrapolating from this evidence, one can easily imagine a situation in which the final step of conversion is never taken because of the repercussions it might have among people who are important to one. In other words, those who are most likely to move from religious convictions held in private to religious affirmations made in public are those who need not worry particularly over the impact that their conversion might have on their 'significant others'.

This argument has a respectable pedigree in the social sciences. Durkheim, in his *Le Suicide* (1897), was making a similar point: suicide rates varied between populations in such a way that groups in which the individual was less securely bound to others 'produced' higher rates than those groups in which the individual was tied to other people by many and multi-stranded ties. Durkheim made little of the personal motives of the suicide candidate and concentrated instead on the factors impinging on the likelihood that a wish to take one's life would actually be carried out. By the same token, it may be the degree of social embeddedness that decides the likelihood of a successfully maintained conversion. The similarity actually goes further, since, from the point of view of those around him, the convert is undergoing a kind of 'social death', in a sense taking his or her own life. Leopold Weiss is a case in point. His father considered him dead when he learned of his conversion.

Seen from this perspective, what do the lives of Aguéli, Weiss and Garaudy tell us? The picture is not conclusive but perhaps worth contemplating.

Ivan Aguéli had broken with his father but was close to his mother, as is witnessed by his letters and the money she continually sent him. His relations to the Swedish community of painters in Paris were often strained, but he also had several devoted friends on whom he made severe demands. He was apparently well received by influential French painters and he was also accepted into Anarchist circles. In the early 1890s he was both painting and pursuing his religious and political studies. *Le procès des trente* and his subsequent months in prison changed the situation somewhat and probably radicalized his religious search which continued during his first travel to Egypt. He became a Muslim in Paris, apparently without making a great affair of his conversion. It was in India, where he was a stranger to all, that he first faced the public and was easily accepted as a Muslim.

There are elements of a 'Durkheimian' isolation and marginality here, but altogether Aguéli seems to have been part of the Parisian Bohemia, more or less integrated into it, more or less following its rules. Although the letters from the prison indicate that the decisive step may have been taken in his cell, Aguéli is not an utterly isolated person. It may be more fruitful, in his case, to look at the figure of the artist in the public imagination of his times. This was very much the epoch of the romantic artist, the visionary, who was expected to be slightly bizarre and even an outrage to the bourgeois customers who in buying his paintings also bought the sensations and the scandals. In other words, there may have been great tolerance of Aguéli's ideas in the circles in which he moved and perhaps even a kind of incitement for him to seek the different and the new.

Leopold Weiss, on the other hand, fits very well into the frame of the convert who is maximally free of old ties and then integrates himself more and more deeply into a new network. He broke with his father at an early age, he joined a metropolitan group of would-be writers and journalists, he finally became a foreign correspondent in the Middle East who for practical reasons had very little contact with his old Central European friends but who, instead, developed his links with people from the host societies ever more. When his formal conversion finally came, he had already become part of a new network of significant others. The trajectory of Leopold Weiss becoming Muhammad Asad is an exemplary conversion — exemplary in Durkheimian terms — in that the social foundation of his old religious outlook is being undermined, partly by his own willing, partly by the force of circumstance, long before his conversion. The social base of his new religious conviction is firmly established, this also long before the conviction itself is there.

When it comes to Roger Garaudy, one enters the area of pure speculation since, as far as I know, there is very little autobiographical material available. Garaudy is a prolific author, but his writings are impersonal and rhetorical. Still, the outer ramifications of his story are telling in themselves. After many, many years as a leading member of the French Communist Party, Garaudy is expelled, first from the Central Committee and then from the party itself. Although this development had been forshadowed for some time, it was a very radical break in his life. Durkheim would have a strong case for regarding Garaudy, at this stage, as maximally vulnerable both to social death and some kind of 'resurrection'. One could possibly argue that ever since his serious problems within the Communist Party began, Garaudy has been carrying on 'dialogues' with traditions, religions and civilizations rather than with concrete persons. This must be a state of maximal liminality, to speak with Victor Turner (1969), a state of flux and indeterminacy, which is another way of understanding Garaudy's permanent personal revolution.

Cultural mediation or cultural criticism?

In a very general sense the heroes of this story are all cultural mediators. None of them is satisfied with just practising his new faith, he also wants to explain it to others, to bridge the gulf between himself and them. This is done, however, in rather different ways and with varying degrees of success.

Muhammad Asad, alias Leopold Weiss, is the best example of a convert who could be labelled a successful cultural mediator. In his first book as a Muslim, *Islam at the Crossroads* (1982, first published in 1934), he is addressing his fellow Muslims and trying to influence them both in their faith and in their attitude to western civilization. On both matters he stays very close to the line of Islamic orthodoxy, and he does not for a second pretend that he has always been a Muslim. In his second and widely read book, *The Road to Mecca* (1980, first published in 1954) he is now turning to a western audience and trying to explain not only how Leopold Weiss could become Muhammad Asad but also what Islam looks like from the inside.

Aguéli's work for *Il Convito* is also a work of mediation. The Orient is explained to the Occident and vice versa. But to the extent that this mediation is successful, it is the result of a pretended identity. In both the Arabic and the Italian text, Aguéli appears under his Muslim name, Abdul Hadi al-Maghrabi. In the Italian articles, signed by Abdul Hadi and in the editorial comments sometimes introducing them, there is never any mention of the fact that the author is a European turned Muslim. For the work he wanted to accomplish, it was necessary to appear as an enlightened 'native' in the eyes of the European readers, and not as a renegade. The name Abdul Hadi made him an authentic Muslim, and his views showed how worthy of respect these Muslims really were. For Abdul Hadi appeared as an internal critic of contemporary Islam propagating a return to what he considered to be the essence of that faith. To his Arab readers, on the other hand, the name Abdul Hadi was a sign, just as important, that he was a fellow believer and not a foreigner trying to interfere with the religion of Islam.

The complex situation of the European convert to Islam — trying to address a message both to his culture of departure and his culture of arrival — emerges perhaps most clearly in the case of Roger Garaudy. In his case nothing could be gained by his appearing under another name (although, as we know, he has such a name). For Muslims in the Islamic world, it is important that Garaudy stays Garaudy so that he can be described as 'the greatest philosopher in Europe' (as I heard him presented in Yemeni mountain villages in 1982) or as 'the greatest Occidental philosopher of the XXth century' (as he was presented at the millennial anniversary of al-Azhar (*Le Monde* 24 March 1983) while simultaneously announcing that he is a convert to Islam. There is an interesting process of legitimation going on here. Since western culture — in spite of everything that is being held against it — carries high prestige even in the Muslim world, the fact that a leading spokesman for it turns to Islam is a sign of the innate superiority of that faith. (The process is similar to all the attempts to 'prove' the Quran by showing how well it accords with the latest findings of science.) But while Garaudy can be used — and is used — for this purpose, it is not possible for him to intervene in internal Islamic matters. His cultural capital as a masterthinker of western civilization can only be used for legitimizing Islam *in general*. Were he to propagate his own version of Islam among Muslims who were born as such, it is likely that his origin — including his previous conversions — would be held against him. This is not only a hypothesis, this is actually what occurred at the celebration of al-Azhar's first millennium.

These cases have been picked at random. Obviously, no conclusion could be drawn on the basis that two of them, Aguéli and Garaudy, demonstrate the difficulties for converts trying to play the role of mediators between the two cultures they know so well, while only one of them, Asad, testifies to the possibility of such a venture. Still, the two problematic cases point to general circumstances that could be of decisive importance also for others attempting cultural mediation of the same kind. The general relations of forces between western societies and the countries of the Muslim world is such that at least eminent intellectuals of Garaudy's type are likely to end up in the same dilemma. They will be used for legitimizing Islam in the eyes of those Muslims who are at all in need of some kind of legitimation. It is also likely that the form of Islam they will thus support, perhaps in spite of themselves, will be of a mainstream, orthodox kind. This is certainly the misgiving of many reformminded Muslims living in Europe. In their eyes, European converts to Islam are serving the interests of the conservatives in the Muslim world.[2] Their fears seem to be born out by the case of Garaudy.

But if these intellectual converts threaten to be used as a support for conservatism in the 'East', they may very well become the allies of a liberal, tolerant attitude in the 'West'. It is here that their criticism of western society and their description of the essence of Islam can have a positive effect. Western culture has a special and almost revered niche reserved for its critics. Many of them — in the tradition of Montesquieu's *Lettres Persanes* — have used fictions or real (but idealized) countries, in order to make their critical points. It is perhaps in this light that we should view the efforts of both Aguéli and Garaudy. Muhammad Asad, on the other hand, has proved that it is not altogether impossible to raise a reasonable voice that is listened to on both sides. The explanation of this feat could be that Muhammad Asad, aside from his personal qualities, has always been a spokesman for Muslim orthodoxy, not a radical protagonist of Sufism like Aguéli or of an ecumenical vision like Garaudy. Cultural mediation works best in the middle of the field.

Notes

1. I am indebted to Professor Jan Bergman at the University of Uppsala, Sweden, for an eye-witness report from the celebration at al-Azhar.
2. During the conference in Stockholm Professor Mohamed Arkoun, of the Sorbonne University in Paris, made this point with characteristic vigour.

References

Asad, M. 1980/1954. *The Road to Mecca*. Gibraltar: Dar al-Andalus.
—— 1982/1934. *Islam at the Crossroads*. Gibraltar: Dar al-Andalus.
Béjart, M. 1979. *Un instant de la vie d'autrui*. Paris: Flammarion.
Berger, P. and Luckmann, T. 1967. *The Social Construction of Reality: A Treatise in the Sociology of Knowledge*. New York: Doubleday Anchor Books.
Durkheim, E. 1897. *Le Suicide: étude de sociologie*. Paris: Alcan.
Eaton, G. 1985. *Islam and the Destiny of Man*. London: Islamic Texts Society/George Allen and Unwin.
Garaudy, R. 1959. *Perspectives de l'homme: existentialisme, pensée catholique, marxisme*. Paris: Gallimard.
—— 1965. *De l'anathème au dialogue*. Paris: Pion.
—— 1975. *Paroles d'homme*. Paris: Laffont.
—— 1976. *Le projet espérance*. Paris: Laffont.
—— 1977. *Pour un dialogue des civilisations: l'Occident est un accident*. Paris: Denoël.
—— 1979. *Appel aux vivants*. Paris: Seuil.
—— 1981a. *Promesses de l'Islam*. Paris: Seuil.
—— 1981b. *L'Islam habite notre avenir*. Paris: Desclée de Brouwer.
—— 1985. *Biographie du XXe siècle: le testament philosophique de Roger Garaudy*. Paris: Tougui.
Gauffin, A. 1940-1. *Ivan Aguéli: Människan, mystikern, målaren*. Two volumes. Stockholm: Sveriges allmänna konstförening.
Krieger-Krynicki, A. 1985. *Les musulmans en France: religion et culture*. Paris: Maisonneuve Larose.
Lamand, F. 1986. *L'Islam en France: les musulmans dans la communauté nationale*. Paris: Albin Michel.
Laurant, J.-P. 1985. *René Guénon*. Paris: L'Herne.
Rocher, L. and Cherqaoui, F. 1986. *D'une foi l'autre: les conversions à l'islam en Occident*. Paris: Seuil.
Turner, V. 1969. *The Ritual Process: Structure and Anti-structure*. London: Routledge and Kegan Paul.

Glossary

Abdal   occupationally specific subgroup in Anatolia of musicians, dancers, basketmakers, etc
Ad   name
Ahl-i-Beyt   the Prophet's closest family
Alevi   follower of Ali
Alim (pl. *ulama* or *ulema*)   Muslim scholar
Aşure   feast celebrating Noah's landing on Mount Arafat
Ayinicem or *cem*   central Alevi ritual

Baba   father; religious leader in Bektashi order or in Alevi village community
Baraka   divine grace
Başlik   brideprice
Buyruk   order, command

Cem or *Ayinicem*   central Alevi ritual
Çepni   Turkoman tribe

Dar al-Islam   the realm of Islam
Dede   grandfather, religious leader in Bektashi order
Dhikr   prayer consisting of the repetition of God's name
Dua   personal prayer, prayer of supplication (as opposed to *namaz*, ritual prayer)
Düşkun   immoral, unchaste

Eftal   recommended act
Eid, also *Id*   principal Islamic holiday
Ezan   call for prayer

Farz   obligatory act
Fatiha   first *sura* (chapter) of the Quran

Gavur unbeliever, adherent to a polytheist religion; in popular usage often wrongly applied to Christians and Jews
Güah sin

Habous, also *waqf* pious foundation
Hac pilgrimage
Hadith sayings and actions attributed to the Prophet
Hajj pilgrimage
Halal lawful
Haram forbidden by Islamic law; also sacred
Hijrah emigration, exile; referring to Muhammad's flight to Medina in 622
Hizb prayer consisting of repetition of verses from the Quran
Hoca, also *khoja* religious expert

Ibadat the five main religious duties of Islam: bearing witness of one's faith, prayer, alms-giving, fasting and pilgrimage
Id, also *Eid* principal Islamic holiday
Ijtihad independent judgment in a legal or theological question
Ilim knowledge
Imam leader of the communal prayer, religious leader
Imam nikahı marriage sanctioned by *imam* only, not by civil authorities
Izzat family honour

Jami mosque, especially Friday mosque
Jellaba traditional male dress
Jihad righteous struggle
Juma prayer communal prayer at noon

Kafir unbeliever
Kameez, also *qamiz* upper part of traditional female dress
Kapı gate
Kasaba administrative unit; small town
Kaza possibility of making up for neglected religious duties, like fasting, *namaz*, etc
Khoja, also *hoca* religious expert
Khutba sermon on the occasion of the Friday noon prayer
Kız kaçırma marriage by abduction
Kurban sacrifice
Kurban Bayramı sacrificial feast commemorating the sacrifice of Abraham (Ibrahim)

Madhhab school in the sense of the (four) established interpretations of Islamic law
Madrasa school, especially for religious studies
Mahalle quarter of a village
Makruh non-recommended act
Masjid mosque
Mezhep religious sect or denomination
Minafık hypocrite, sower of disunity
Muezzin announcer of the hour of prayer
Mukadma woman in charge of a religious group in the traditional Islam of North Africa
Musahiplik companionship
Musalla area set aside for prayer

Namaz ritual prayer

Namus honour
Niyya good intention

Qamiz, also *kameez* upper part of traditional female dress
Qibla(h) direction of Mecca

Rakı brandy
Ramadan lunar month during which Muslims fast from sunrise to sunset

Sadaga voluntary alms-giving
Salat ritual prayer
Saygi respect
Şeker Bayrami feast marking the end of Ramadan
Semah dervish dance
Şeriat religious law
Sevap merit
Shahada Islamic profession of faith
Shalwar baggy trousers, part of traditional female dress
Shariah religious law
Shaykh spiritual leader
Sırrıhakikat esoteric truth
Sorgu interrogation
Sufi adherent of Islamic mysticism
Sunna life of the Prophet as a guide to right conduct
Sura chapter of the Quran

Tahtacı woodcutter; occupationally distinct group of Alevis
Talab request addressed to God
Tariqa spiritual way, doctrine of a Sufi order
Topluluk group, community

Umma the community of Muslim believers

Vasiyetname will

Waqf, also *habous* pious foundation

Zakat obligatory alms-giving
Zawiya sanctuary, religious meeting-place, establishment of a religious order
Zuhd asceticism

Subject Index

Abdals 175, 176
acculturation 25, 90
Afghanistan 212, 217, 247, 268
Africa *see also* East Africa; North Africa; West Africa 123, 128, 244-5
Ahmadiyya 12, 17, 18, 38, 76, 78, 209, 210, 265
Alawis 38
Alawiyya 138
Alevis, Alevism 88-106, 174-95
Algeria, Algerians 34, 124, 125, 126, 131, 244
   in France 107, 108, 109-10, 118-19, 123, 124, 125, 129, 130, 131, 196-204
Americans 99
anthropology 10, 239-43, 261
anti-semitism 117
anti-zionism 117
Arabic 5, 19, 44, 45, 101, 114, 117, 121, 125, 127, 131, 165, 261, 266
Arabs 8-9, 53, 81, 110, 115, 118, 140
asceticism
   inner-worldly 207-8, 211, 216, 218
   other-worldly 207-8
Asia 244-5
assimilation 24, 90, 132, 134, 196
Assyrians 94
Aşure 178, 192
Austria 81, 85

Bangladesh, Bangladeshis 37, 161, 164, 167
   in Great Britain 33, 34, 35, 39, 46, 51, 53
   in Sweden 244, 257-8
banks, Muslim 39, 216
baraka 198, 200
Barelwis 38, 209, 210, 211-12, 215-16, 218
Bektashis, Bektashism 105, 175, 179, 185, 194
Belgium 3, 81, 85, 120, 133-43, 159-73
Bengali 44, 45
Berber 126
beur, Beur 117, 118-19, 123-32
burial (according to Islamic law) 9, 29, 43, 55, 64-6, 76, 114, 183
butchers (of *halal* meat) 39

Campbellpuris 37
Canada 161
Capitalism 40, 211, 216
Catholicism, Catholics 43, 113, 164, 172, 218
cem, Cem (*Ayinicem*) 93, 103, 179-80
Çepnis 176, 180, 181, 182, 183
Christianity, Christians, Christian society 3, 5, 8, 28, 41, 43, 50, 69, 75, 101, 150, 153, 161
   and Islam compared 5
   as a minority religion 79

as the foundation of secularism 110
conservative versus
  revolutionary 207
Great Britain as a 32
relation to Islam 271-2
sociology of 171, 207
churches of the disinherited, concept of 207
churches of the middle classes, concept of 207
churches, Christian
  social teachings of 206-7
  study of 206
  support of Islamic activities 14, 21, 22, 85, 121, 164
Circassians 95, 96
circumcision 9, 114
Čistiyya 160
citizenship 54, 90, 112, 116, 117, 119, 124, 216
colonialism 206, 208, 210, 217
Communism, Communists 40, 101, 108, 183, 216, 268-9
Conservative Party (Great Britain) 213, 214, 216
conversion to Christianity 28, 75
conversion to Islam 115, 176, 209, 215, 263-77
  converts' interpretation of 272-3
  social explanation of 273-5
converts to Islam
  British 53, 264-5
  Danish 265
  Dutch 16-17
  French 110, 115, 263, 264
  German 78, 81, 265
  Spanish 265
  Swedish 265
  Swiss 264, 265
  West Indian 215
corporal punishment 29, 101
culture 25, 32, 46
  Alevi 180
  and settlement patterns 225-6, 236, 237
  Arab 130, 131
  concept of 239-40, 242-4, 261
  French 132
  institutional 260
  Islamic *see also* culture, Muslim. 3, 110, 133, 165, 236
  Kabylian 117
  Muslim *see also* culture, Islamic.

19-20, 23, 32, 113, 126, 240
of immigration 127
popular and learned 203
transfer of 25-6
transformation of 19-20
Cyprus 53

Dar al-Islam (House of Islam) 41, 51, 263
Denmark 81, 265
Deobandis 38, 160, 171, 209, 210, 211-12, 215
Dervish 180, 183
dhikr 199, 200-4
diaspora 36, 80, 90, 102, 152, 157
dietary rules, Muslim 55, 107, 112, 113, 116, 128, 151-2
discrimination 2, 24, 92, 97, 98, 127, 151, 194
dress, women's *see also* school dress; school uniforms. 35, 40, 88-9, 95, 100, 102, 103, 126

East Africa, East Africans *see also* Africa. 33, 35, 36, 37, 38, 53, 171, 209
education 139, 140
  British, and Islam 48-50, 216
  British, and Muslim children 66-73
  Christian 69
  Jewish 267
  multi-cultural 55
  of girls 46-7
  physical 49, 67-8, 213
  religious *see also* Islamic education; religious instruction. 19, 42, 48-9, 66-7, 69-70, 81, 82, 84-5, 99, 113, 151
  sexual 40, 49, 55, 70, 73, 76
Egypt, Egyptians 28, 34, 110, 131, 244, 265, 266-7, 274
Eid *see also* Id al-Kabir. 35, 39, 41-2, 48-9, 50, 62-4, 67, 76, 109
emigration *see* migration
endogamy 96-7, 99, 176
Eritrea 212, 244
Ethiopia 244-5
ethnicity, ethnic groups *see also* minorities. 16, 17, 20, 23, 24, 28, 29, 30, 38, 134-5, 141, 188, 193, 194, 220, 222, 224, 236, 257
  among Alevis in Berlin 88-106
  and mosque attendance 13, 37

family, the 19, 21, 39
  and Islamic law 46
  and secular society 217
  as the basis of Islamic society 46
  Muslim concern for 211-17
  Muslim ideal of 213, 216
fasting see also Ramadan. 107, 115, 128, 147, 148, 149, 150, 178
France 3, 81, 107-32, 244, 264
fundamentalism see also intégrisme; Islamism. 28, 38, 81, 82, 93, 141-3, 153, 183

Gambia 244
Ghana 244
ghetto 24, 130, 137, 244
  educational 127
  occupational 186-8
Great Britain 3, 32-77, 120, 161, 171, 206-18, 227, 264
Greeks 12
Gujerat 37
Gulf states 131
Guyana 53
Gypsies 227

hadith 75-6, 169, 197, 198, 199, 202, 209, 210
halal food, provision of 67-9, 74, 92, 200, 204, 213
Hanafi, Hanafite, Hanafitic 38, 79, 209, 210
harkis 109, 126
heterodoxy 136, 174
Hinduism, Hindus 22, 63, 206, 207, 216
hocas see also khojas. 97, 99, 101, 148, 155

ibadat 20, 29
Id al-Kabir see also Eid. 109
identity 103-4
  Alevi 193, 194
  ethnic 28, 31
  female 199, 203
  Muslim 10, 24, 27-9, 31, 80, 89, 107-8, 109, 112, 114, 120-1, 134, 137-8, 141-2, 196, 203; and education 113; and Quran lessons 84; and the mosque 13; role of women for maintaining 196-204
  Turkish 188
ijtihad 209

imams 9, 11, 14, 15, 17, 21, 23, 25, 36, 39, 42, 43, 45, 50, 109, 136, 165, 172, 246, 253, 260
  and integration 27
  and the interpretation of Islam 27
  as leaders 18
  economic support of 140
  educational level of 26-7
  functions of 18-19
immigration see also migration. 1, 90, 121, 131, 136, 141, 161, 230, 235
  to Belgium 133-4
  to France 108-10, 196, 204
  to Great Britain 32-3, 53
  to Norway 185-6
  to Sweden 244-5
  to the Netherlands 8-9, 234
  to West Germany 78
  transformation of 109, 120, 170
India, Indians 33, 35, 36, 51, 53, 159-61, 171, 186, 245, 265, 266, 276
Indonesians 8-9
integration of Muslims 9, 10, 26, 27, 30-1, 82, 86, 90, 97, 110, 114, 123, 126, 127, 128, 130, 140, 141, 142
  and Quran lessons 83-4
  and the imams 27
  definition of 24
  Islam as a means of negotiating 120
  symbol of 76
  viewed as blocked by the Jewish community 116, 117-18
intégrisme see also fundamentalism. 142
intellectuals, Muslim 3, 105, 112, 116, 129, 138, 167, 170
Iran, Iranians 8-9, 34, 53, 81, 108, 121, 210, 211, 213, 217, 244-5, 252-3
Iranian revolution 196
Iraq, Iraqis 37, 210, 244-5, 249
Islam
  as a means of negotiating integration 120
  as a minority religion 79, 111, 217
  as a provisional identity 120
  as lived by Turkish workers' families 79
  as viewed by Muslim intellectuals 116
  Barelwi version of 210
  characteristics of 39
  converts' image of 270

cultural expression of 23
fear of 2, 93, 108, 120, 121, 128, 141, 196
feminine 136, 196–204
'folk', in Berlin 83
'imaginary' 120
integral nature of 115, 128;
   Deobandi position on 210–11, 215
in the Netherlands 30–1
lack of representatives of 83, 85, 118
legal status of, in West Germany 80, 83
Maghrebi 111
masculine 136
popular 197, 198
practical nature of, in the Tablighs 162
public nature of 80, 148
secularization of 117, 142
self-image of 40, 271
women's practice of 196–204
Islamic calendar 62, 146, 178
Islamic education see also education, religious; religious instruction. 13, 27, 33, 36, 37, 40, 44–5, 55, 66, 80, 81, 82, 83–6, 113, 140, 155, 165, 210
and women 199
'mobile madrasas' 165
of British *ulema* 45
of girls 46–7
teaching methods of 44–5
Islamic institutions 3, 9, 10, 18–19, 103
Islamic law see also Shariah. 9, 45, 46, 54, 178, 210
Islamic resurgence, Islamic revitalization, Islamic revival 2, 6, 37, 39–40, 42, 93, 128, 136
Islamism see also fundamentalism; *intégrisme*. 141, 143
Islamiyya Primary School 73
Ismailis (Ismaelis) 38, 128
Israel 107, 117, 118
Italy, Italians 3, 12, 89, 108, 133, 134

Japan 161
Jews 12, 21, 32, 43, 50, 63, 65, 107, 108, 111, 112, 113, 116, 117, 120
Jordan 244
Judaism 30, 107, 120, 172, 267
   relation to Islam 271

Kabylia, Kabyles 117, 129, 130
Kashmir, Kahmiris 212, 217
Kemalism 75, 175, 190, 193
Kenya 244
khojas 9
Kurdish 187
Kurds 91, 94, 95, 96, 97, 99, 103, 104, 183, 187, 188, 194,
Kuwait 14, 23

Labour Party (Great Britain) 211, 213, 214, 216–17
language classes see also mother-tongue teaching. 36, 45, 51, 127, 214
Laz 95, 96
leadership, Muslim 45, 46, 47–8
   imams as 18
   in France 118
   in Great Britain 54
   in India 160
   in Norway 188
   in West Germany 54
Lebanon, Lebanese 108, 110, 121, 244–5, 251
Libya 14, 23, 34, 37, 166, 268
lobby, Muslim 51, 54

Maghreb, Maghrebis 108, 109, 111, 117, 119, 125, 126, 127, 130, 131, 133, 161, 198, 203, 248
Malaysia 34, 244
Mali 110
marriage 9
   among Alevis 176–7, 193
   arranged 46–7, 96, 105, 125
   ceremonies 43
   Muslim concern with 46, 211, 212, 213, 217
Marxism, Marxists 69, 93, 209, 210, 226–7, 269, 272
mass media 4, 5, 24, 27, 118, 120, 121, 130, 166, 199, 260
   and the *beur* 127
   effect of, on Muslim children 45
Mecca 11, 23, 44, 64, 114, 160, 167, 171, 178, 199, 201, 268
Medina 11
Mevleves 175
Middle East 34, 121, 268, 274
migration see also immigration. 1, 53, 103, 111, 156, 157, 174, 175, 176, 182, 185, 187, 194, 206, 212, 215, 221, 225–6, 235, 239, 240, 261, 263

and secularization   89
chain   33, 37, 91, 94–6, 100, 105, 157,
circular   221, 225
from peasant societies   225–6
of Alevis to Norway   185–6
of Moroccans to the Netherlands   221
of Surinamese to the Netherlands   220
of Turks to the Netherlands   221
specificity of Turkish labour migration to West Germany   90
minorities   *see also* ethnicity, ethnic groups.   25, 88, 94, 96, 97, 104, 109, 111, 120, 141, 151, 161, 174, 175, 184, 187, 188, 193, 210, 212, 215, 217, 227
economic and social situation of, in the Netherlands   23–4
in Turkey   91
place of, in democratic societies   134–5, 142
missionary activities   *see also* proselytizing; re-islamization
among Muslims   128, 160, 161
among non-Muslims   161, 163, 167, 168, 169, 170
modernization theory   89
Moluccans   12, 14
Morocco, Moroccans   18, 23, 25, 34, 121, 135, 139, 171, 172, 186
in Belgium   164
in France   110, 115–16, 121, 124, 129
in Sweden   244–5, 249
in the Netherlands   8, 9, 18, 23, 25, 219–38
mosques   *see also* prayer-halls.   11, 12–13, 17, 22, 33, 39–40, 165, 170, 171, 172
Alevi attitude to   178
and youth activities   47
as a symbol of the Umma   109, 114
'devotional'   162
distribution and number of, in West Germany   79
founding of   11, 12, 135–8, 164
'free'   28
Friday   56
'front-room'   12
function of, in urban life   206
functions of, in Birmingham   41–5, 56

funding of   36–7, 39, 51, 80, 112, 191
in Birmingham   35–8, 58
in Stockholm   245–6
'mosque committees'   139–40
national organization of   136, 236
number of, in Belgium   134
number of, in France   128
number of, in Great Britain   57
planning permission for   36, 51, 55, 56–61
Tablighi mosques in Belgium   164, 167, 168
mother-tongue teaching   *see also* language classes.   49, 51, 55, 85–6, 127, 214
provided by the Turkish consulate in Berlin   82, 85,
Muharram   178, 192
Mujahedin   247
mukadma   198, 199, 200, 201
Muslim institutions   3, 9, 10
Muslim organizations   *see* Index of Muslim Organizations *for specific organizations*.   4, 5, 26, 49, 51,54, 56
in Belgium   138–41
in France   196
in Sweden   245–6
in the Netherlands   13, 14, 15–18, 21, 22–3, 25
in West Berlin   80–3, 93, 102–3
mysticism
inner-worldly   207–8, 211, 218
other-worldly   207–8

Naqshbandis   38
nationalism   82, 86, 93
Indian   210, 215
Kurdish   194
nationality   *see also* citizenship.   13, 16, 17, 90, 99, 116, 118, 119, 124, 135, 220, 236
identified with religion   110, 112, 119, 237
Netherlands, the   3, 8–31, 81, 120, 157, 219–38
network analysis   241, 243–4, 248–62
networks, social   *see also* network analysis.   93, 95, 96, 98, 103, 114, 118, 137, 138, 241, 274
Nigeria   244
North Africa, North Africans   196–204
Norway   3, 174–95

orthodoxy, Muslim   80, 95, 161, 194, 197
  and European converts   275-6
  and political extremism   89
  lack of among the Alevis   184
orthopraxis, Muslim   80

Pakistan, Pakistanis   8-9, 17, 34, 37, 38, 51, 53, 161, 167, 171, 206, 207, 208, 209, 210-13, 217, 268
  in France   110, 123
  in Great Britain   33, 34, 35, 36, 37, 39, 51, 53, 208-18
  in Norway   186
  in Sweden   244, 247
  in the Netherlands   8-9, 225
Palestine, Palestinians   110, 118, 121, 212
Palestinian cause   116, 117-18, 121
Pathans   37
Pentecostalism   218
personal autonomy   99
Philippines   186
pilgrimage   109, 114, 171, 199, 200, 201
pirs   210, 216, 218
plural society   24-5, 29, 30
Poles   108, 134
polygamy   21, 29
population, Muslim
  in Belgium   133
  in France   109-11, 123, 196, 264
  in Great Britain   33, 53-4
  in Norway   186
  in Sweden   244-5
  in the Netherlands   9
  in West Berlin   79
  in West Germany   78-9
Portuguese   99
prayer   107, 115, 147-56, 162, 169, 208
  call to   56-7, 76, 114
  female   197, 199
  Friday   25, 33, 35, 39, 41, 42, 55, 56, 62-3, 67, 76, 156-7; and women   43, 199; in school   48-9; in Stockholm   246-7
prayer-halls   *see also* mosques.   9, 10, 12-15, 18, 19, 21, 22, 25, 26, 27, 31, 35, 114, 128
prayer-meetings   199-201
prayer times   42, 56, 61-4
press, Muslim   17, 43, 54
Primat des Gaules   121

proselytizing   *see also* missionary activities.   128
  among Muslims   136, 138, 160
  among non-Muslims   114, 161, 209
protector countries   112, 115, 116
Protestantism, Protestants   32, 85, 111, 172, 207, 216
Punjabi   44
Punjabis   37, 38

quietism   211, 213, 215, 217, 218
Quran   26, 27, 36, 40, 44, 45, 99, 112, 126, 128, 169, 177, 197, 198, 201-3, 209, 210, 212, 247, 261, 268, 276
  teaching of   11, 13, 18-19, 26, 27, 99, 114, 137, 154, 165
Quran lessons   *see also* Quran schools.   80, 83-4, 88-9, 99-103, 127, 151, 154
  and the Turkish state   89
Quran schools   *see also* Quran lessons.   18-19, 37, 91, 93, 99-103, 246
  control of   80
  pedagogy of   137

racism   5, 32, 36, 55, 71, 109, 111, 117, 123, 236
  struggle against   118, 119, 121
Ramadan   13, 18, 41, 92, 109, 114, 115-16, 119, 128, 148, 178, 199
  and the Alevis   192
re-islamization   24, 161, 168, 169
religion of established churches, concept of   207
religiosity of the masses, concept of   207-8, 211
religious instruction   *see also* education, religious; Islamic education.   13, 18-19, 36, 47, 51, 55, 66, 69, 71, 85-6, 139, 199, 200
remittances   5, 90, 104-5, 139, 175
rituals, Islamic   9, 79, 105, 146, 147-9, 151-2, 156-7
  Alevi   91-2, 179-83, 192
  female   197-203

sadaqa   see also *zakat*.   200, 204
Saudi Arabia, Saudis   12, 14, 23, 37, 38, 112, 137, 139, 172, 210, 211, 268
school curriculum   69-71
school dress, Muslim concern with   *see also* school uniforms.   66-7, 169

school meals, Muslim concern
    with 67-9
school uniforms   *see also* school dress.
    48, 55, 68, 74, 76
schools
    Catholic 50, 72
    Church of England 50, 72
    girls' 50, 213
    Jewish 50, 72
    mixed 29, 47, 113
    Muslim 50, 55, 67, 71-3, 165, 213
second generation 6, 29, 89, 90, 97-9,
    100-4, 117, 118-21, 142, 196
    in France 123-32
    socialization of 197
sects, Islamic 38, 80, 81, 83, 207-18
    and migration 215
    compared to Christian sects and
        churches 211
    conversionist 171
    revolutionary 208
secularization, secularity, secular
        society 4, 40, 75, 89, 91, 93, 95,
        107-8, 110, 115, 127, 128, 134,
        150, 162, 163, 206, 213
    and Islam 79
    and the family 217
    and workers 208
    Kemalist 175
    of British society 32
    of Islam 117, 142
    Turkish 88
segregation
    residential 219-38
    sexual 198, 199
    social 221, 222, 228
Senegal 110
Şeriat   *see* Shariah
sermon, Friday noon 42
sexual morality 211-14, 216
Shabiriyya 160
Shariah, Şeriat   *see also* Islamic law. 18,
    20, 146, 149, 152, 157, 180, 183
Shaykh of al-Azhar 121
Shia, Shi'as, Shiites, Shiism 38, 129,
    211, 213, 214, 217, 245, 252, 264
    in Birmingham 209, 210
    relation to Alevis 91, 175
Sikhs 35, 206, 216
slaughter, ritual 9, 29, 55, 73-4,
    112-13, 141
socialization 150, 151, 197
    into the Tabligh 168-9

sociology 4, 10, 16, 159, 171, 175, 206,
    207, 215, 218, 223, 224, 243, 273
Somalia 244
South Africa 171
Spain, Spaniards 3, 12, 99, 133, 134,
    265
state
    Islamic 209, 212, 217
    welfare 208, 211, 216
stigma 89, 90, 174, 187
Sudan 244
Sufism, Sufis 38, 93, 138, 157, 159-60,
    198, 202-3, 209, 210, 211, 216,
    218, 264, 265, 266, 272, 277
Sulaymancilar   *see also* Süleymanli
    movement. 138
Süleymanli movement   *see also*
    Sulaymancilar *and in* Index of
    Muslim Organizations: Islamic
    Cultural Centres. 17, 28, 81-3,
    154
Sunna 26, 27, 212
Sunnis, Sunnites 38, 79, 175, 176, 194,
    210, 211, 213, 217, 236, 245
    in Birmingham 209
    relation of, to Ahmadiyya 17
    relation of, to Alevis 91-2, 177-9,
        183, 184-5, 186-9, 191, 192-3
Surinam, Surinamese 15, 23
    in the Netherlands 8-9, 15-16, 17,
        18, 22, 23, 219-38
Sweden 3, 81, 239-62, 265
Switzerland 81, 265
syncretism, cultural 129
Syria, Syrians 110, 244

Tabligh, tebliğ, tebligh   *see also in* Index
    of Muslim Organizations: Jama' at
    at-Tabligh. 138, 154, 159-73
Tahtacis 175, 176, 193
tariqa 198, 203, 265
Third World 131, 174, 185, 186, 187,
    239
Tunisia, Tunisians 121, 131
    in France 110, 112
    in Great Britain 34
Turkey, Turks 17, 18, 23, 25, 34, 75,
    78-106, 111, 113, 139, 149, 150,
    153, 161, 244-5, 247, 253, 255
    and religious activities in West
        Germany 80-3
    and secularization 91
    in Belgium 133, 135, 139, 140

in France   108, 110, 111, 112, 113, 114, 123
in Great Britain   34
in Norway   174-95
in Sweden   244-5, 246, 247, 253-7
in the Netherlands   8-9, 10, 12, 13, 14, 15, 16, 17, 18, 21, 22, 23, 25, 28, 31, 219-38
in West Germany   78-106, 146-58; enclave of, in West Berlin   92-5, 104
Turkish   19, 81, 95, 101

ulema   45
unemployment   23, 24, 41, 47, 123, 125, 138, 167, 169, 214, 215, 221
United Arab Emirates   131
United States   161
Urdu   43, 44, 45
Urufis   175

violence   2, 31, 121, 127, 128, 208, 209, 215, 271
voting   25-6, 116, 124, 214

Wahabis   211
West Africa, West Africans   53, 108, 110
western society, Muslim image of   40, 45, 271
West Germany   3, 76, 78-106, 120, 146-58, 182, 192
West Indies, West Indians   53, 74, 213, 214, 215, 218, 225, 227

Yemen, Yemenis   37, 38, 44, 53, 209, 211, 267, 276
Yezidis, Yezids, Yezidler   94, 178
Yugoslavia, Yugoslavs   110, 244, 258

zakat   see also sadaqa.   42, 204
zawiya   38, 198, 199, 204

Name Index

Abbès, Sheik 128
Abd al-Qadir 264
Abdul Hamid I 78
Abdulla, M.S. 78, 79, 81
ad-Din al-Hilali, T. 171
Agha Khan II 128
Aguéli, Ivan 263-77
Ahmed, I. 62
Ahsan, M.M. 56, 62
Alavi, H. 210
Ali Aziz Effendi 78
Ali (ibn Abi Talib) 91, 129, 175, 177, 179, 180
Ali, T. 209
Althusser, L. 268
Amersfoort, H. van 219, 220, 221, 222, 223, 224, 225, 227, 236
Andezian, S. 200, 201
Aristotle 129
Arkoun, M. 3, 277
Asad, M. (L. Weiss) 263-77
Atatürk, M. K. 88-9

Bakhtin, M. 203
Bastenier, A. 120, 142, 143, 171, 172
Bath, H. 104
Bayart, J.-F. 108
Béjart, M. 264
Bendjedid, C. 131
Berger, P. 273

Bergman, J. 277
Bernard, H.R. 243
Bhutto, B. 131, 213
Bhutto, Z. 209, 215
Birge, J.K. 175, 180, 181, 183, 185, 194
Blaschke, J. 157
Boorman, S.A. 243
Bouchared, R. 130
Bovenkerk, F. 220, 230, 235
Breiger, R.L. 243
Brooks, D. 186
Burckhardt, T. 265
Burgess, E.W. 222, 223, 224, 235

Caemmerer, H. 79, 83
Cafer Sadik 178-9
Celaleddin, Mevlana 179
Cézanne, P. 265
Charif, M. 130
Cherqaoui, F. 264, 265, 268, 272, 273
Chodkiewicz, M. 264
Chopel, F. 129, 130
Costa-Lascoux, J. 111
Cromer, Lord 267
Crozier, M. 171

Dahrendorf, R. 227
Dahya, B. 225-6, 235
Darsh, S.M. 64
Dassetto, F. 120, 142, 171, 172
Deferre, G. 124

Name Index

Dekmejian, R.H. 142–3
Dhaouadi, Z. 171
Dickie, J. 264
Dubetsky, A. 92
Durkheim, E. 273, 274, 275

Eaton, G. 264
Ekelöf, G. 265
Elsas, C. 20, 93
Emery, F.E. 193
Engelbrektsson, U.-B. 91, 157, 194
Etienne, B. 103, 171
Etzioni, A. 171

Feisal, Prince 268
Flett, H. 226
Friedberg, E. 171
Fullerton, M. 68

Gaboriau, M. 171
Garaudy, R. 263–77
Gauffin, A. 265, 266, 270
Gauguin, P. 265
Geertz, C. 240
Gellner, E. 146
Ghazi, A. 118
Gieringer, F. 79
Gitmez, A.S. 92, 93, 104
Goffman, E. 168
Gökalp, A. 105, 174, 175, 176, 180, 181, 182, 194
Goodenough, W. 240
Grønhaug, R. 175, 193
Guénon, R. 264, 267
Gustavsen, B. 193

Haar, J. ter 237
Haci Bektaş Veli 179, 180
Hanafi, H. 157
Haq, M.A. 167, 171
ul-Haq, Z. 209, 211, 212, 213, 217
Harun al-Rashid 178
Hassan II 25, 110
Hodgins, H. 35, 36, 59
Howarth, R.B. 69
Huot, M. 266, 267, 269
Hüseyin (Hussein) 178, 192

Ibn al-Arabi 264
Ibn Saud 268
Ilyas, M. 159–60, 171
Ilyas, Y. 159, 161
Insabato, E. 266

Jesus Christ 69, 207
John, B. 79, 83
Joly, D. 76

Kacel, K. 130
Kapferer, B. 243
Kaplan, C. 154
Kappert, P. 80
Karpat, K. 91, 92
Khimone, R. 130, 132
Khomeini, Ayatollah 183, 211, 213, 217
Killworth, P.D. 243
Klerk, L. de 219
Kornalijnslijper, N. 230
Krieger-Krynicki, A. 264
Kudat, A. 94, 104

Lamand, F. 264
Laurant, J.-P. 267
Lévi-Strauss, C. 240
Levy, R. 197, 198
Lewin, K. 193, 260
Lieberson, S. 222, 224
Lings, M. 264
Lithman, Y. 241, 242
Lounès, L. 130
Luckmann, T. 273

Maan, E. 230
McDermott, M.Y. 56, 62
McKenzie, R.D. 222, 223
Mandel, R. 105
Marx, K. 269
Mawdudi, A. 38, 171, 209, 212
Merad, A. 171
Merton, R. 171
Mirpuri, M.A. 49
Mitchell, C. 243
Mole, M. 202
Molière 129
Montesquieu 277
Moore, R. 224–6, 235, 236
Muaviye (Muawiya) 178
Muhammad, Prophet 11, 41, 45, 56, 170, 175, 177–8, 180, 192, 197, 198, 201, 202, 203, 209
  emulating 160, 162, 168, 169
Murnau, F.W. 267
Musterd, S. 230
Muus, P. 221

Nagel, T. 155, 156, 157
Napoleon 113

Niebuhr, R. 207-8, 215, 218
Nielsen, J. 33, 76
Noah 178
Noor, M. 36
Norström, C. 262

Olsen, E.A. 89, 95, 105
Omar 177
Osman (Othman) 177

Pahl, R. 226-7
Park, R.E. 222-4
Peach, C. 222
Penninx, R. 221
Philippe le Bel 128
Poliakov, L. 107
Poulter, S.M. 76
Praag, C.S. van 230
Prinsen, J. 236

Rabelais 129
Rabia 197
Resmi Ahmed Effendi 78
Rex, J. 224-6, 235-6
Robinson, V. 226
Rocher, L. 264, 265, 268, 272, 273

Saddiki, T. 129
St Augustine 207
St Paul 207
St Thomas 207
Sayad, A. 157
Schiffauer, W. 157
Schmiede, H.A. 157
Schnapper, D. 107, 111, 120
Schuon, F. 265
Sebbar, L. 130
Ségur, Comtesse de 130
Shadid, W. 230

Shuhda bint al-Ibari 197
Singh, K. 186
Soymen, H. 157
Stevens, C. 73
Streiff-Fenart, J. 201
Sulami 157
Swedenborg, E. 265, 272

Taeuber, A.F. 222
Taeuber, K.E. 222
Tesli, A. 176
Theodorson, G.A. 222
Thomä-Venske, H. 84, 104
Thorsrud, E. 193
Timms, D.W.G. 224
Toprak, B. 105
Touraine, A. 171
Townsend, H.E.R. 66
Tozy, M. 167, 171, 172
Troeltsch, E. 207, 215
Troll, C.W. 171
Turner, V. 275

Vitray-Meyerovitch, Eva de 272

Waardenburg, J. 3, 152, 157
Wach, J. 171
Weber, M. 157, 207-8, 211, 215, 216, 218
Weiss, E. 268
Weiss, L. 263-77
White, H.C. 243
Wihtol de Wenden-Didier, C. 108
Wilpert, C. 92, 93, 94, 100, 104
Wilson, B. 171

Yacine, A. 171
Yalman, N. 91
Yezid (Yazid) 178

Index of Muslim Organizations

Ahmadiyya Mission to the
    Netherlands *see* Rabwah
    Ahmadiyya Mission to the
    Netherlands
Amicales 25, 121, 172
Association d'Etudiants
    Musulmans 138

Centre Islamique et Culturelle de
    Belgique 136, 139–41, 165–7, 172
Conseil Supérieur des Musulmans de
    Belgique 141
Council of Mosques 43

Darul Uloom Islamia 36
Dereköy Association *see* Drammen and
    Oslo Region Mutual Help
    Association for Unity between
    Families from the Dereköy village
    in Turkey
Directorate of Religious Affairs 14, 17,
    23, 25, 136, 139
Drammen and Oslo Region Mutual Help
    Association for Unity between
    Families from the Dereköy village
    in Turkey 189–92

Fédération des Mosquées et des
    Associations Culturelles et
    Islamiques de Belgique 165–6
Federation of Islamic Associations and
    Communities in Berlin 81–3, 85, 105
Federation of Muslim Organizations in
    the Netherlands 16–17
Federation of Turkish Islamic and
    Cultural Associations 17
Förenade Islamiska Församlingar i
    Sverige (FIFS, Associated Islamic
    Parishes in Sweden) 245
Foundation for the Welfare of Muslims
    in the Netherlands 17

High Islamic Institute 85

Islamic Centre Foundation 17
Islamic Council of Europe 23, 76
Islamic Cultural Centre 73, 264
Islamic Cultural Centres 81–3
Islamic Federation *see* Federation of
    Islamic Associations and
    Communities in Berlin
Islamic Mission *see* United Kingdom
    Islamic Mission
Islamic Resource Centre 50
Islamiska Centerunionen i Sverige
    (ICUS, Islamic Centre Union in
    Sweden) 245

Jama' at at-Tabligh 138, 154, 159–73
Jamaat-i-Islami (also Jamaat-e-
    Islami) *see also* United Kingdom

Index of Muslim Organizations

Islamic Mission. 38, 209, 210, 211, 212, 217
Jamiat Ahl-e-Hadith *see* Markazi Jamiat Ahl-e-Hadith
Jamiat Ahl-e-Quran 210

Lahore Ahmadiyya Anjuman Isha' at Islam 17

Markazi Jamiat Ahl-e-Hadith 38, 47, 50, 209–13
Milli Görüşcü 154
Muslim Brotherhood *see also* Muslim Brothers. 138, 161
Muslim Brothers *see also* Muslim Brotherhood. 28, 157, 198
Muslim Educational Trust (MET) 72
Muslim Information Centre 17
Muslim Liaison Committee (MLC) 49, 72, 213
Muslim Organizations in the Netherlands Foundation (MON) 17
Muslim World League *see also* Rabitat al-Alam al-Islami. 137, 139, 141, 166, 172

Netherlands Islamic Parliament 17
Netherlands Islamic Society (NIS) 17
Nurcu 154, 157

Rabitat al-Alam al-Islami *see also* Muslim World League. 14, 23
Rabwah Ahmadiyya Mission to the Netherlands 12, 17

South London Islamic Centre 67
Sparkbrook Islamic Association 38
Svenska Muslimska Förbundet (SMF, Swedish Muslim Union) 245

Turkish Community in Berlin 82–3
Turkish Islamic Cultural Federation *see* Federation of Turkish Islamic and Cultural Associations
Turkish-Islamic Union for Religion (DITIB) 82–3, 85, 89, 104
Turkish Workers' Association 190

Union of Moroccan Muslim Organizations in the Netherlands (UMMON) 17
United Kingdom Islamic Mission 36, 38